RECENT
THEORIES OF
HUMAN
DEVELOPMENT

R. MURRAY THOMAS

RECENT
THEORIES OF
HUMAN
DEVELOPMENT

Sage Publications, Inc.
International Educational and Professional Publisher
Thousand Oaks ■ London ■ New Delhi

For information:

Sage Publications, Inc.
2455 Teller Road
Thousand Oaks, California 91320
E-mail: order@sagepub.com

Sage Publications Ltd.
6 Bonhill Street
London EC2A 4PU
United Kingdom

Sage Publications India Pvt. Ltd.
M-32 Market
Greater Kailash I
New Delhi 110 048 India

Printed in the United States of America

Library of Congress Cataloging-in-Publication Data

Thomas, R. Murray (Robert Murray), 1921-
    Recent theories of human development / by R. Murray
Thomas.
        p. cm.
    Includes bibliographical references and index.
      ISBN 0-7619-2247-4 (pbk.)
      1. Developmental psychology—History—20th century. I. Title.
    BF713 .T485 2000
    155—dc21   00-010059

This book is printed on acid-free paper.

01   02   03   04   05   06   7   6   5   4   3   2   1

Acquisition Editor:	Jim Brace-Thompson
Editorial Assistant:	Anna Howland
Production Editor:	Sanford Robinson
Editorial Assistant:	Victoria Cheng
Cover Designer:	Michelle Lee

Contents

List of Figures

Preface

The task of explaining how and why people grow up as they do is a never-ending puzzle which, over the centuries, has invited the attention of philosophers, theologians, scientists, essayists, poets, and novelists who have filled books, journals, lecture halls, and the Internet with their proposals. The purpose of *Recent Theories of Human Development* is to describe a sampling of more than three dozen of those proposals that appeared during the final two decades of the 20th century.

The purpose of the book is not only to illustrate trends in the form and content of theories that rose to prominence over the period 1980-2000, but also to inspect a number of ways that the concept *theory* itself was interpreted within that period.

Brief versions of several of the book's models were published in Chapter 18 of *Comparing Theories of Child Development* (Wadsworth, 2000). I wish to express my appreciation to Thomson Learning for permission to include segments of those versions among this volume's descriptions.

1

Theory Trends

To help readers understand the historical roots from which the recent theories in Chapters 2 through 12 have grown, this introductory chapter offers a brief sketch of nine influential models of human development that appeared during the 1880-1980 era. The sketch begins with an explanation of what is intended throughout the book by the terms *theories, human development,* and *recent.*

For the purpose of this opening chapter, a simple, bare-bones definition of *theories* should suffice. Subsequently, in the introductions to Parts I and II, I'll describe a number of more complex definitions from recent times. So for now, *theory* is defined as "a proposal about (a) which components or variables are important for understanding such a phenomenon as human development and (b) how those components interact to account for why the phenomenon turns out as it does." Other terms I'll use as synonyms for *theory* are *model, explanatory scheme,* and *paradigm,* although it's apparent that some authors assign separate meanings to each of those terms.

The expression *human development* refers to the way people change with the passing of time.* Critics might complain that the word *change* should be qualified to show that the change is in a desired direction. Thus, a child's growing taller and mentally more adept would properly be considered *development,* whereas an elderly person's shrinking a bit in stature and having trouble remembering names would be *change* but not *development.* However, because there can be considerable disagreement among theorists about what sort of change is *desirable, proper,* or even *inevitable,* I believe defining development simply as "change" is still appropriate because it accommodates a greater variety of theories

---

* I recognize that adding the phrase "with the passing of time" is redundant, since change can occur only as time advances. My including "passing of time" is merely a nod to conventional daily speech.

than would be the case if some qualifying adjective were attached to *change.*

Defining *recent* is a bit tricky, because new theories typically do not appear of a sudden and full grown in a manner that establishes precisely the date of their origin. Most theories evolve gradually and depend heavily on forebears, so they usually represent variations on past themes rather than entirely new explanations of human development. The following, then, is how *recent* is defined for the purpose of selecting the book's contents: Recent theories are ones that rose to prominence during the two-decade period 1980-2000.

The phrase *rose to prominence* refers to schemes that prior to 1980 were found less frequently in books, journals, and the popular press than they were over the years 1980-2000. Therefore, neither B. F. Skinner's radical behaviorism nor Jean Piaget's theory of mental development would qualify as *recent* because both were widely known before 1980.

The task of choosing recent theories is further complicated by the fact that far more proposals about human development achieved prominence over the two decades 1980-2000 than could be included in one rather brief book. Thus, selection standards were needed for reducing the total number to a manageable few. To guide the selection process, I decided to feature three characteristics of the theories that appeared during the 20-year period: (a) *key themes* that were reflected in certain groups of theories, (b) the influence of *social movements* in stimulating the creation of theories, and (c) the great *diversity* of topics and issues that theorists addressed.

The chosen themes were: psychobiological perspectives, dynamic systems (including connectionism), ecological models, modes of interaction, and embellishments of Piaget's and Vygotsky's works. Theories illustrating these themes form the major portion of the book's Part I: *Extensions of Tradition.*

Noteworthy social movements that began principally in the 1960s, expanded in the 1970s, and produced theories of development during the 1980s and 1990s included movements focusing on the condition of people living in poverty, on disadvantaged ethnic groups, on females, and on individuals with unconventional sexual preferences (homosexuals/bisexuals). Those theories form the book's Part II: *Products of Social Movements.*

Finally, instead of analyzing a few theories in great detail, I chose to describe several dozen in brief form in order to suggest the great diversity of interests theorists displayed in their proposals over the 1980-2000 era. As a consequence, no chapter focuses on a single theory. Instead, each offers a variety of models intended to reflect the breadth of creativity and divergent viewpoints that theorists displayed. There is nothing sacrosanct about the particular examples I chose to illustrate diversity. Others from the professional literature would have served equally well.

The last chapter, which forms the book's Part III: *Final Observations,* summarizes the preceding chapters and estimates the future of human development theories.

ANCESTRAL TRAILS

It may help readers place recent theories in their historical contexts if we first identify the backgrounds of several major types from the past and then suggest what connections those types appear to have with the ones described in Chapters 2 through 12. The nine overlapping types or *isms* whose pathways are traced include spiritism, mentalism, dynamism, functionalism, behaviorism, holism, constructionism, a derivative of Marxism, and cognitivism. The discussion closes with a suggestion about why theorists continue to create new models or variations of existing explanations of development.

Of particular interest for the purpose of this book, the following nine varieties differ from each other in the answers they offered for these questions:

- What are the components of human thought and action?
- When we speak of human development, what is it that develops, how, and why?

Spiritism

Studies of people's beliefs about development in widely diverse cultures support the conclusion that everyone holds convictions about how and why humans grow up and act as they do. Within any culture there is usually substantial agreement about such matters. This consensus within a culture is typically called *folk psychology* or *naive psychology* or *cultural psychology*—a collection of notions not usually organized as a formally stated theory; nevertheless, they guide the way most members of a culture interpret their own and others' growth and actions. I use the word *spiritism* to label these belief systems because folk psychologies are so often in the form of religious convictions in which supernatural forces—gods and other spirits—are assigned crucial roles in affecting people's development and behavior.

With the passing of time, a society's folk psychology is often cast in a structured oral or written form that helps ensure its stability from one generation to the next. It is also the case that especially creative and articulate individuals can influence a belief system by proposing new features that become incorporated into the views of development widely held within the culture. Lao-tzu is credited with so influencing Taoism, Kung Fu-tzu with affecting Confucianism, Mahavira with Jainism, Gautama Siddhartha with Buddhism, Moses with Judaism, Jesus with Christianity, Mohammed with Islam, Joseph Smith with Mormonism, and Mary Baker Eddy with Christian Science.

Components of human thought and action

Two typical distinguishing features of spiritism are (a) the type of development on which such belief systems focus and (b) the inclusion of a key personality component called the *soul* (Thomas, 1997).

In regard to focus, spiritist schemes are chiefly concerned with moral development—with people's values and the goodness of their behavior—rather than with physical, intellectual, vocational, recreational, or emotional development. It isn't that people who subscribe to folk psychologies are not interested in physical, intellectual, or vocational matters. Rather, it's because such theories generally propose that people's physical, intellectual, and vocational fates are affected by how well individuals abide by the moral precepts laid down by the supernatural forces that control the world. Violating religious dicta can incur the displeasure of the gods or spirits who then may vent their wrath by punishing the transgressor with illness, accident, loss of employment, mental illness, loss of friends, loss of property, crop failure, fire, flood, earthquake, and more.

In most folk conceptions, a human being is composed of a physical part (the visible body) and a nonphysical part (an invisible aspect that engages in thought, feeling, and self-awareness). The nonphysical portion is often divided between a mundane, conscious thinking mechanism (in Western parlance, the *mind*) and a more ethereal component or set of components (in Western parlance, the *soul*). The soul is thought to be in closer touch with supernatural forces than is the mind, is thought to represent the true essence of the person, and is believed to continue existing in some mystical form after the demise of the body and mind.

In parallel with the folk beliefs to which the general populace has subscribed, philosophers over the centuries have speculated in a more formal manner about the composition of the mind and how it develops. One version that gained widespread attention in Western cultures was known as *faculty psychology,* built on the proposition that the mind is divided into separate capacities, powers, or functions called *faculties.* Typical faculties bore such labels as *reason, memory, common sense, imagination, will, courage,* and *reverence.* Such an architecture of the mind was much in vogue among scholars from the time of medieval theologians Albertus Magnus (1193-1280) and Thomas Aquinas (1225-1274), through the philosophers of the Renaissance, and up to the end of the 19th century. In colonial America, Puritan sermons abounded in allusions to this model of the mind, thus attesting to the general understanding of it on the part of both the preachers and their parishioners (Miller, 1963, pp. 242-244). However, authors frequently disagreed about the labels and functions of the different faculties and about where in the human body each capacity was located.

Practitioners of the pseudo-science of phrenology drew maps showing the places in the brain where they imagined the various faculties resided. These phrenologists then sought to measure the strength of different faculties by inspecting the contours of the skull, on the assumption that a cranial bump identified a strong faculty residing in the brain below and that a valley on the skull reflected a weak faculty in the brain beneath.

By the early 20th century faculty psychology had fallen into disrepute among academicians, set aside in favor of new theories, even though the word *faculty* in relation to mental capacities is still found in general use today, as in "She has a well-tuned faculty for humor" or "He 's completely lost his faculties."

It's apparent that folk theories of human development and behavior are not simply relics of the past but, instead, are alive and thriving today. The overwhelming majority of the world's peoples base their understanding and treatment of others on the basis of folk beliefs. Furthermore, folk psychologies are significant in their function as the intellectual soil from which formal theories grow, because it's theorists' dissatisfaction with aspects of folk beliefs that motivates them to devise what they hope are more accurate explanations of development than folk traditions have provided. As for faculty psychology, it would be an error to think it was permanently killed off nearly a century ago, because on the brink of the 21st century—as we shall see in Part I—something much akin to faculties would surface, thinly disguised in modern nomenclature.

What develops, how, and why

There is no agreement among the world's multitude of naive psychologies about what it is that changes during development nor how and why such change occurs. Folk theories often fail to discuss these issues directly, so conclusions about people's beliefs regarding the development process frequently must be inferred from how people treat others, and particularly from their childrearing practices. Variations across cultures in such matters can be illustrated with the following four examples.

According to one version of Christian theory, children are born with a propensity to misbehave. It is their nature to act in evil ways because they are under the influence of an immoral spirit, Satan, who is bent on destruction. This proclivity of children to behave in evil ways is the result of their inheriting the original sin of Adam and Eve who disobeyed God's commandment in the Garden of Eden. Ever since that incident, Satan has served as each newborn child's master and guide. Therefore, to help children develop into obedient and constructive members of society, parents and other caregivers are obligated to counteract youngsters' inborn evil natures by teaching them proper Christian behavior. Such teaching may include punishment—perhaps even "beating the Devil out of them." Proper development, then, consists of the growing child learning to abide by Christian moral values through instructional techniques ranging from gentle persuasion to harsh discipline (Thomas, 1979, Chapter 10).

A different explanation of development is found in Hindu lore, which proposes that death brings an end to the human body and that the body disintegrates into the four elements that compose all tangible matter—earth, fire, air, and water. But the person's soul continues on, to be encased in a new body which carries the soul until that new body also departs. The most important content of a transmigrating soul is the *karma* it carries into a newly created body. Karma is like a moral bank account that bears the consequences of all the good and bad deeds performed by the person during his or her sojourn on earth. One's karma—the algebraic sum of prior good and bad behavior—determines most of the fate that the new body will experience during its lifetime. In other words, most of how a person develops during the present lifespan has been predetermined by the behavior of the body that bore that same soul during a previous lifespan. Although people can do very little to affect the course of their present existence, they do have the power to influence the fate of the body that their soul will inhabit during the soul's next lifespan. They exert this influence through how well they abide by the doctrine of the Hindu holy scriptures. Consequently, the primary aim of one's life is to live in a fashion that portends a better existence for the next body in which the soul will be encased. Hindu theory is therefore founded on a concept of inherent justice—the kind of development people experience during their present lifetime is exactly what they deserve, for they themselves determined their current fate by their actions during a prior existence (Thomas, 1988).

Differences between folk psychologies are also illustrated in Levy's comparison of parents' notions of learning and teaching in a Tahitian village and in a Nepalese town. The Tahitians whom he studied assumed that children learn to perform tasks chiefly by themselves, in keeping with the gradual maturational unfolding of their abilities. Thus, differences among children in their development were attributed to differences in children's inborn natures. From a Tahitian perspective, no one teaches children very much.

> [Children] learn by watching and by playful trial and error that the adults often find amusing but sometimes annoying. . . . In a learning situation—as opposed to a simple direct command—to tell a child what to do (as opposed to the occasional what *not* to do) . . . is intrusive and taken as a sign of unjustified adult mood-driven irritability and impatience. (Levy, 1996, pp. 128-129)

In contrast to Tahitians, the Nepalese adults whom Levy interviewed saw verbal instruction as a necessary vehicle for learning even the most basic behaviors, such as walking, eating, speaking, and bladder control. The ability to use and understand talk was thought to be an essential part of all training, a necessary condition of task mastery.

> In [Nepal] the untaught child would be incompetent not only in his or her physical skills but in his or her moral nature. As one man puts it, "Unless parents control and educate children, children will have bad characters." [So] the "natural man" is not only inadequate in his skills but morally problematic. In Tahiti, the child who learns by itself "naturally" achieves both task and moral competence. (Levy, 1996, p. 132)

In summary, what develops in our illustrative form of Christian theory is the person's knowledge of, and adherence to, Christian moral principles. Such development is effected by adults teaching and enforcing those principles. What develops in Hindu theory is an individual's destiny in a future existence by virtue of how well the person abides by Hindu doctrine during her or his present time on earth. In contrast, Tahitian folk psychology attributes development to innate growth processes that determine how and when different forms of skill and knowledge will appear. However, in the commonsense psychology of the Nepalese, all skills, knowledge, and moral values depend on children's continually being instructed from the earliest months of their lives.

Finally, it seems apparent that most people throughout the world base their understanding and treatment of others on some variety of folk psychology. However, in addition to shared folk beliefs, there are theories that individuals have created in an effort to produce more accurate explanations and predictions of development than naive psychologies offer. These intentionally devised, formal proposals are the ones inspected throughout this book. The theories discussed in the remainder of this chapter are limited to types devised during the past century-and-a-quarter, starting with the time that psychology as a discipline first disengaged itself from the fields of philosophy and religion.

Mentalism: Structuralist Versions

From earliest recorded time, philosophers have speculated about the nature of the noncorporeal human—the mind and/or soul—and how it develops. In the waning years of the 19th century, the traditional philosophical mode of conjecture about such matters assumed a new form of systematic introspection and controlled laboratory experiments in which trained observers sought to chart the components of their own minds and of the minds of people they formally studied. The proponents of this departure abandoned concern with such matters as the soul and supernatural spirits, concentrating instead on the development and operation of *mind*. The movement, which began in Germany and subsequently extended to other parts of Europe and to North America, marked the birth of psychology as a recognized, separate science. Two of the men most intimately associated with the movement were Wilhelm Wundt (1832-1920) and Edward Bradford Tichener (1867-1927).

Wundt was a German with degrees in medicine and physiology who established the first recognized psychological laboratory at the University of Leipzig over the years 1875-1879. Tichener, an Englishman, was among the scores of students who studied under Wundt. Tichener subsequently established his own psychological laboratory in the United States at Cornell University. Although historians have sometimes pictured Wundt's and Tichener's theories as identical, there actually were significant differences between the two.

Components of human thought

Wundt conceived of mind as not a single, homogenous whole but, instead, as divided into such differentiated psychical processes as willing, attending, sensing, feeling, thinking, using language, and more. His interest was in discovering the contents of people's immediate consciousness and in explaining how consciousness operates. A principal method of investigation was introspection, which consisted of trained psychologists delving into their own minds as they intentionally (by the exertion of will) grasped sensations from the environment and then consciously thought, felt, and spoke about that experience.

Tichener, on the other hand, disagreed with Wundt's conception of mind as composed of mental processes. He asserted, instead, that *mind*, in its most basic condition, consisted entirely of images. In people's daily lives, they experience events that are recorded in mind as sensations or images. For Tichener, *mind* was the totality of those sensations. Consequently, the most fundamental task for psychology was to reveal the basic sensation-elements to which all complex mental processes could be reduced. Highly trained, precise introspection was the method by which such components of mind could be detected.

> Wrote Tichener (1909): "Be as attentive as possible to the object or process which gives rise to the sensation, and, when the object is removed or the process completed, recall the sensation by an action of memory as vividly and completely as you can." Persistent application of this method would in Tichener's view eventually produce a complete description of the elements of human experience. . . . As early as 1897 he drew up a catalog of elements found in the different sense-departments. There were, for instance, 30,500 visual elements, four taste elements, and three sensations in the alimentary canal. (Leahey, 1987, p. 190)

Thus, in Tichener's scheme, various combinations of selected sensation elements in the mind produce the patterns of thought people display.

What develops, how, and why

Wundt did not believe that children were born with the components of consciousness (attending, sensing, feeling, and the like) in those components' distinctive, differentiated, mature condition. Instead, he assumed that "mental processes differentiated from an inchoate mass to an interrelated organization of different cognitive processes" (Kendler, 1987, p. 44). He recognized that he could not test this hypothesis directly, since children's immaturity prevented them from engaging in the sophisticated sort of introspection that trained psychologists could perform. In effect, children could not accurately analyze and report their own thinking processes. But Wundt also believed that over the course of history such cultural products as language, myth, and custom grow—like the human mind—through a system of developmental differentiation. Therefore, by imagining that the pattern of development of individual minds parallels the pattern of cultural evolution, he was able to estimate how children's minds develop by means of his analyzing how cultures emerge. He suggested that "the range of existing human cultures represents the various stages in cultural and mental evolution, from primitive, tribal to civilized, rational man" (Leahey, 1987, p. 187). Wundt called this method of historical analysis *Völkerpsychologie* in contrast to the sort of introspection he used in his laboratory. He proposed that experimental psychology which employs introspection exposes the "outworks" of the mind, whereas *Völkerpsychologie* probes deeply into the development process.

In Tichener's system, people's minds develop as a result of their experiences which enable them to accumulate a storehouse of sensations. By the time he died at age 60, Tichener had become a complete devotee of *positivism*—that philosophical position which insists that valid knowledge about the world must be founded exclusively on the methods of natural science. In the opinion of positivists, any convictions or speculations that go beyond observable, objective facts cannot be valid. Consequently, Tichener abandoned the aim of explaining the causes of events and limited himself to describing "the facts." In doing so, "he departed even farther from Wundt's attempt to penetrate the hidden mental processes underneath the outer, sensory phenomena" (Leahey, 1987, p. 191).

To summarize, Wundt's version of mentalism portrayed *mind* as a collection of processes which, with the passing years, become increasingly differentiated out of the rudimentary, amorphous whole that characterizes the newborn's mentality. Tichener, on the other hand, envisioned the mind as an accumulation of thousands of sensations derived from experiences—sensations that serve as building blocks of the thought processes people exhibit. Tichener applied the term *structuralism* to such theories, since the theories' creators were concerned with the structure of consciousness. Within the academic-psychology community, these two pioneering models would hardly outlast the two men's lives, as most psychologists would find other models more convincing.

Dynamism

At the time that Wundt and Tichener were studying mind by means of introspection, Sigmund Freud (1856-1939) was fabricating a psychoanalytic theory of development out of the dreams and recollections of childhood experiences described to him by patients in his Viennese psychiatric practice.

Components of human thought and action

A central assumption undergirding Freud's theory is that human thought and action are driven by a pair of internal forces—a life instinct (*eros*) and a death instinct (*thanatos*). The life instinct is imbued with a strong measure of sexual drive (*libido*), with the term *sexual* broadly interpreted to mean a sensual, pleasure-seeking power. The life instinct energizes people's creative, development-oriented, procreative, affection-seeking acts. The death instinct is a destructive counter force that competes against the life instinct in directing human behavior (Freud, 1973, pp. 5-6).

Thus, psychoanalytic theory, with instinctual drives at its core, proposes that humans are dynamic organisms constantly impelled to satisfy their needs by transactions with their environments. I use the term *dynamism* to classify such theories as Freud's that feature needs or drives as central factors in development. Other theories that could also qualify as dynamic schemes are those proposed by Freud's one-time European colleagues Carl Jung (1959) and Alfred Adler (1927a), and by such Americans as Henry Murray (1938) and neo-Freudians Erik

H. Erikson (1964), Erich Fromm (1994), Karen Horney (1937), Karl A. Menninger (1960), and Harry Stack Sullivan (1965).

The chief functionaries in Freud's personality theory are three hypothetical interacting operatives dubbed *id, ego,* and *superego.* In contrast to Wundt's and Tichener's exclusive focus on consciousness, Freud assigned an important role to the unconscious mind so that a person's id, ego, and superego might operate at different levels of consciousness, extending from the unfathomable dark depths of the unconscious to the bright clarity of immediate consciousness.

The id, which resides solely in the unconscious, is the psychic agent representing the instinctual drives. The id operates on the *pleasure principle*, demanding immediate satisfaction of needs without regard for any limitations that the environment places on need fulfillment. The ego serves as an umpire or arbiter between the id's demands and the environment. The ego operates on the *reality principle*, negotiating methods of need fulfillment that are acceptable within the person's present physical and social setting. The methods the ego devises for simultaneously satisfying the id's drives and the environment's restrictions are called *ego defense mechanisms* or *ego adjustment mechanisms.* Then, with the passing of time, the rules of need fulfillment that the environment imposes are gradually incorporated into the developing individual's personality in the form of a *superego*, which consists of both a conscience (society's "don'ts") and ego ideal (society's "do's"). The superego is a kind of internalized parent that psychically punishes individuals for their unacceptable acts and rewards them for admirable behavior.

What develops, how, and why

Over the first decade of life, the personality's three operatives develop in the following order. The id is present at birth, containing "everything that is inherited . . . that is laid down in the constitution—above all, the instincts" (Freud, 1973, p. 2). Because the instinctual drives must find expression in the environment (seeking sources of nourishment, protection, affection), the ego begins to develop as the arbitrator with the environment. The ego evolves through recognizing the nature of the world, particularly the environment's opportunities and restrictions, then inventing techniques for negotiating solutions. These adjustment mechanisms gradually accumulate, becoming increasingly refined as the result of a person's improved physical/intellectual abilities and a broadening range of experiences, thereby furnishing the individual a growing understanding of the physical and social universe.

Freud proposed that children progress through a series of psychosexual stages between the time of birth and mid-adolescence. He contended that as the young grow up, they are intensely concerned with a sequence of body regions— *erogenous zones*—and with gaining sensual satisfaction in those regions. The first zone (year 1, oral period) is the mouth, used for ingesting food and drink and for investigating things (mouthing objects). The second (year 2, anal period) is the anal/urethral zone, where satisfaction is gained from retaining and expelling feces and urine. The third (years 3-5 or so, infantile-genital period) is the genital zone, which is distinguished by a psychic conflict as the child begins to view his or her opposite-sex parent as a desirable source of sexual satisfaction. But the thought of such a socially forbidden incestuous relationship generates guilt imposed on the child by the newly evolving superego, causing what Freud called the Oedipus conflict for males and the Electra conflict for females. To resolve this conflict, the child's distressed mind automatically represses into the unconscious any thoughts of the tabooed sexual encounter, and the child rejects sexual interests for the next few years (ages 4-5 to 11-13, latency period). The final area of attention is the genital zone (ages 14-16 to 18-20, mature-genital period). Upon the arrival of this final period, the youth normally seeks an opposite-sex partner with whom to establish a lasting love relationship.

In proposing his psychosexual explanation of development, Freud was not as interested in people who advanced through the growth stages with little or no difficulty as he was interested in those whose development had gone awry. Consequently, his theory was mainly a device for explaining the sort of unsatisfactory development observed in the lives of the neurotic patients he treated. In Freud's opinion, whether children's development is trouble-free depends on how well they fulfill their instinctual needs as they advance through the psycho-sexual stages. If children's caregivers—and particularly their parents—understand proper psychosexual growth and treat the young in keeping with that understand-ing, then development goes well. But if caregivers and others with whom children intimately interact fail to understand what constitutes healthy psychosexual growth, children will be mistreated and their development distorted.

Functionalism

During the years that mentalist and dynamic theories were being created in Europe, a functionalist explanation of development emerged in America. Functionalism was guided by an aim quite different from the aims of the models we've inspected so far. You may recall that the purpose of spiritist theories was—and continues to be—that of clarifying (a) the nature of supernatural forces that control the universe and influence human development and (b) the proper relationship that should obtain between people and those forces to ensure that development progresses properly. The aim of such mentalist theories as Wundt's and Tichener's was to describe the processes and structures of the conscious mind, while the aim of Freudian theory was—and still is—to explain and correct development that's gone wrong.

In contrast, the aim of functionalism was to show how development equips humans to adapt to their physical and social environment so they might better endure and prosper. In effect, functional theory was based on Charles Darwin's proposal in *On the Origin of Species* (1859) that the innate motive behind the behavior of all organisms is to enhance those organisms' chances of survival.

From this perspective, the function of development is to outfit people with increasingly better skills and knowledge for sustaining life and thriving.

Functionalism was the product of such turn-of-the-century American philosopher-psychologists as William James (1890), John Dewey (1891), and James Rowland Angell (1903, 1904). Another functionalist pioneer, James Mark Baldwin, drew heavily on Darwin's theory by tracing a parallel between the phylogentic development of the human species and the ontogenetic development of the individual child in his books on *Mental Development in the Child and the Race* (1895) and *Social and Ethical Interpretations in Mental Development* (1897).

Components of human thought and action

Angell distinguished between Wundt's and Tichener's structuralism and this new American proposal by asserting that structural psychology was concerned with mental contents, while functionalism focused on mental operations. Angell wrote that functionalism's

modern investigations . . . dispense with the usual direct form of introspection and concern themselves . . . with a determination of what work is accomplished and what the conditions are under which it is achieved. (Angell in Leahey, 1987, p. 277).

Whereas functionalists rejected Tichener's variety of introspection, which was designed to discover a multitude of elements of consciousness, they accepted introspection as well as observations of other people's behavior as suitable grist for psychology's theoretical mill.

Leahey (1987, p. 277) notes that the functionalists asserted, "What endures over time [and is the result of development] are mental functions: Contents come and go, but attention, memory, judgment—the mental faculties of the old psychology rehabilitated—'persist.'"

What develops, how, and why

As already suggested, *what* develops in functional theory are the traits and skills that enable the growing child and youth to cope ever more adequately with the environments they inhabit. *How* development progresses is determined by the evolving physical and mental skills of children as they interact with their physical and social contexts. The superior capacity of humans to learn—to profit from experience—is critically important to their surviving and prospering under highly diverse and ofttimes shifting environmental conditions. *Why* such development takes place is explained by Darwin's premise—that living beings are innately programmed to act in ways that optimize their chances of survival. In Angell's words,

An organism represents, among other things, a device for executing movements in response to the stimulations and demands of the environment. In the main these movements are of an organically beneficial character, otherwise the creature would perish. (Angell, 1904, p. 8)

In assessing the long-term significance of functional theory, Howard Kendler writes:

Functionalism can be called the most reasonable orientation in the history of psychology or the most trivial one. The first judgment can be justified by the functionalists' decision to study both consciousness and behavior within a framework that emphasizes an organism's adjustment. The second point of view can be defended by arguing that functionalism is merely a transition position between structuralism and behaviorism and consequently has no importance in its own right. (Kendler, 1987, p. 111)

Behaviorism

In 1913, John B. Watson (1878-1959) jolted the psychological community with an article entitled *Psychology as a Behaviorist Views It* (1913). He dismissed the study of consciousness as being of no significance and substituted instead the study of people's observable actions—their behavior.

Psychology as the behaviorist views it is a purely objective experimental branch of natural science. Its theoretical goal is the prediction and control of behavior. Introspection forms no essential part of its methods, nor is the scientific value of its data dependent upon the readiness with which they lend themselves to interpretation in terms of consciousness. (Watson, 1913)

Whereas functionalists studied behavior as a key to people's mental activity, Watson insisted that behavior and the environmental conditions that influenced it were, in their own right, the proper objects of interest. In his early writings, Watson accepted the existence of conscious thought, but regarded consciousness as the psychologist's tool rather than a suitable object of investigation. In later years he rejected the notion of consciousness entirely, asserting that thinking is no more than silent speech, and therefore is a behavior and not a state of mind. He declared that *mind* or *consciousness* have "never been seen, touched, smelled, tasted, or moved. It is a plain assumption just as unprovable as the old concept of the soul" (Watson & McDougall, 1929, p. 14).

In the decades following Watson's formulation of behaviorism, a variety of other theorists created their own versions of the model, with the result that behaviorism and its derivatives dominated American psychology over the next half century. By the 1950s and thereafter, the most famous behaviorist in America would be a Harvard University professor, Burrhus Frederic Skinner, whose rendition can serve as our example of a behaviorist conception of development.

The central premise on which Skinnerian behaviorism was built is that the habitual ways people learn to act are determined by the consequences that have followed people's actions in the past. As children grow up, they accumulate an increasing array of ways to behave in different life situations. In other words, for any situation, the young acquire a variety of ways they can respond. These ways form their repertoire of behavior potentials or options. Which option they will choose to adopt on any given occasion is determined by the consequences that have followed the use of that option on earlier occasions. Rewarding consequences (*reinforcers*) that have accompanied an action strengthen the likelihood that such an action will be used in the future in similar circumstances. Nonrewarding and aversive consequences (*nonreinforcers* and *punishments*) that have followed a behavior serve to weaken the probability that such a behavior will be adopted on comparable future occasions (Skinner, 1974).

Components of human action

Skinner, unlike Watson, did not deny the existence of mind or consciousness, but he considered the unobservable mind to be an obscure, untrustworthy site in which to find the causes of people's actions. Since there is no agreement among psychologists about the structure, content, or operating principles of *mind*, dwelling on such matters merely distracts people from the publicly observable controllers of behavior—the rewarding and punishing consequences. He therefore rejected introspection as a source of accurate information and—in his role as a scientist seeking objective truth—depended on observing behavior and its consequences as the proper method for understanding and predicting people's actions. Because there are no components of thought in Skinner's scheme, his theory features only components of action—behaviors and subsequent consequences.

What develops, how, and why

As a child grows up, two things develop: (a) the variety of behavior options (potential ways of acting) that the child acquires and (b) the child's preferences among those options. As children interact with their environments, they learn to prefer rewarding over nonrewarding actions. Thus, the way to alter an individual's conduct is to manipulate the consequences that accompany such conduct—arranging for approved behavior to be followed by reward and disapproved behavior to be followed by nonreward or punishment. Hence, in order to modify people's ways of acting it is unnecessary to understand what they "have in mind"—their beliefs, theories, desires, intentions—because all behavior is controlled by consequences, not by intangible thoughts.

Holism

During the years of behaviorism's dominance in America, a competing conception of development appeared from Germany under the title Gestalt theory (Koffka, 1935; Köhler, 1929; Lewin, 1936; Werner, 1961). (In German, the word *Gestalt* means *configuration, shape,* or *form.*) The Gestalt or holistic view emphasizes the development of the child as a unitary, integrated organism. Such a holistic view, typical of continental European theorists in many scientific disciplines, contrasts with the British associationism from which behaviorism partially derived. Associationism represents a tradition that conceives of development as proceeding by small, additive increments that gradually accumulate to form the personality and the child's repertoire of acts. But to the holistic or field theorist of European background, a new stimulus or experience does not simply add a new element to a child's store of actions or knowledge, leaving the previous elements undisturbed. Instead, each new experience alters the relationship of many or all of the existing elements that have made up the personality to the present time, so the patterning of the entire personality is influenced. Kurt Lewin (1890-1947), who immigrated to the United States from Germany in 1939, was the Gestalt psychologist who exerted the most lasting influence on development theory, so his theory can serve as our example of Gestalt models.

Components of human thought and action

A key concept introduced by Lewin is that of *life space*. In his scheme, a person's life space consists of all the facts that influence the individual's behavior at a given time. For Lewin, a *fact* is not solely an objectively verifiable observation from the "real world." Instead, a fact is any element within the person's psychological environment that affects the individual's thought or behavior. Life space, therefore, includes forces of which the person is unaware as well as things the person accepts as real or true, whether those things are publicly verifiable or are mere fantasies.

What develops, how, and why

In Lewinian theory, *what* develops is the configuration of components of a person's life space as a consequence of a maturing individual interacting with physical and social environments.

The *how* of development was summarized by Lewin as a set of growth principles that represented five sorts of changes in the regions that compose a person's life space.

- The growing child's life space becomes increasingly *differentiated*. For example, in the realm of language, the very young child uses the word "go" to include a wide variety of activities, without distinguishing times, places, persons, modes of transport, and the like. The older child can differentiate these activities into an array of related concepts, such as "let's go," "he went," "she'll always go," "if we go by car," "they'll go, while we stay," and more.
- Boundaries between regions become increasingly *rigid*, so that in using language the young child will more often mix terms (using *borrow, lend, keep,* and *take* interchangeably) that an adolescent will assign separate meanings.

- During the process of development, life space *expands* in terms of time, space, and the number of regions or components. So an adolescent's life space is more likely to include concepts of *China, the 19th century, the Great Depression*, and *religious conviction* than is the young child's life space.
- The regions within life space become increasingly *organized* and *interdependent*. Organizational interdependence consists of different regions becoming arranged in hierarchical systems or sequences of action designed to achieve more complex or distant goals. Whereas the young child is mystified by a diagram of how to build a model airplane, an adolescent can comprehend how the parts of the diagram are coordinated, can plan the steps necessary to construct the model, and can visualize the final product.
- Development increases *realism*. Achieving a more realistic conception of life involves distinguishing between (a) what might be or what we wish or imagine things are and (b) what things really are.

Lewin's holistic perspective was a forerunner of the environmental psychology of the 1980-2000 era that focused on how people's physical/social contexts influence the development of their personalities and behavior (Chapter 4).

Constructionism

From the 1920s through the 1970s, a Swiss named Jean Piaget (1896-1980) became the 20th century's most famous developmental psychologist by conducting a great host of child-development studies from which he built a theory of mental development that traced the stages through which children construct the components of their minds.

Components of human thought and action

In Piaget's theory, the purpose of all thought and overt behavior is to enable the child to survive and flourish by adapting to the environment in ever more satisfactory ways. Piaget called the techniques of adaptation *schemes* or *schemas*. Each scheme is a technique of adjustment that can be biological or mental or both. In Piaget's words: "A scheme is the structure or organization of actions as they are transferred or generalized by repetition in similar or analogous circumstances" (Piaget & Inhelder, 1969, p. 4). Thus, schemes are habits of thought or action. A scheme can be very simple, such as the action pattern involved in a child's sucking a thumb. Or it can be complex and include mental subschemes, as in the chain of acts required for starting a car and maneuvering it down the street or in the mental chain needed for solving quadratic equations.

Schemes are the components of thought and action. They make up the individual's psychophysical self, a self that is an integration of the mind and the neuromuscular system that the person uses for acting on the environment.

What develops, how, and why

According to Piaget, development consists of the child constructing an expanding collection of schemes (mental-physical structures) by means of transactions with changing environments. Hence, schemes are what develop.

The child's construction process results from an interdependent pair of *functional invariants* (habitual acts that continue throughout life) called *assimilation* and *accommodation*.

Each time a person encounters the environment, the sensations received from that encounter (the sights, sounds, touches, scents, tastes) are compared with schemes that are already in the child's repertoire of understandings and actions. If that comparison reveals an existing scheme which seems to match—or nearly match—the sensation, then the sensation is interpreted to be a case of that scheme and is *assimilated* into the child's personality as that scheme.

However, sometimes the sensation does not appear to match an existing scheme. If, even with bending or altering the sensation somewhat, nothing resembling it is found among the child's schemes, then the encounter makes no impression on the child. The incident simply passes as if it had never occurred. But frequently the child can comprehend an episode by altering an existing scheme or two so as to produce a new scheme—a variant of the originals—that does indeed match the sensation. This process of creating new schemes by altering, dividing, or combining existing ones is termed *accommodation.* As children's transactions with their environments advance, the schemes comprising a child's arsenal of understandings and actions multiply at a rapid rate by dint of accommodation, resulting in the ever-expanding collection of skills and knowledge that characterizes the child at successive stages of development. In brief,

> The filtering or modification of the input is called *assimilation*; the modification of internal schemas to fit reality is called *accommodation*. (Piaget & Inhelder, 1969, p. 6)

To account for why young children construct fewer and simpler schemes than do older children and adolescents, Piaget proposed four causal factors that affect the development process—(a) heredity, (b) physical experience, (c) social transmission, and (d) equilibration (Piaget, 1973).

Heredity sets the pace of the internal maturation of the child's neuromuscular system. The particular level of maturation that children reach at a given time determines how well they can profit from various engagements with environments. In other words, children must be maturationally ready in order to perform particular assimilations and accommodations. Next, physical experience with the world of objects and people is required to actualize the potentials that internal maturation provides at successive stages of development. A child isolated from the world will not develop adequately. Then, after unguided physical experience has actualized maturation's potentials, social transmission in the form of instruction can further expand the child's schemes. Finally, a process of equilibration operates throughout the process of development to keep the foregoing factors in balance.

The continuing influence of Piaget was reflected in the 1980s and 1990s in the work of other theorists—neo-Piagetians—who proposed refinements in Piaget's model to accommodate features of his proposal that critics contended were either in error or warranted more precise analysis. We will meet three such revisions in Chapter 5.

A Derivative of Marxism

The German social reformer Karl Marx (1818-1883) in the mid-19th century proposed a theory of societal development that would form the conceptual foundation of communistic societies in the Soviet Union and in a variety of other nations during most of the 20th century.   He postulated that a society's style of producing and consuming goods and services determines the contents and functioning of people's minds.   In other words, thinking does not initiate actions; instead, actions create thoughts. Thus, children's mental development is a process of their internalizing the results of their transactions with their environment.

> The mode of production of material life [whether in a feudal, capitalistic, or socialistic political-economic system] conditions the social, political, and intellectual life process in general.   It is not the consciousness of men that determines their existence, but, on the contrary, their social existence that determines their consciousness. (Marx, 1977b, p. 389)

After Marxists took control of Russia in 1918, the communist leadership determined that it was important to formulate a psychology of development consistent with Marxist political theory.   The best known designer of such a psychology was Lev Semenovich Vygotsky (1896-1934).

Components of human thought and action

Soviet theory proposes two sets of components—(a) activities and (b) thoughts that represent how people envision their world.

What develops, how, and why

As children advance in age and experience, they engage in an increasing variety of activities that generate the contents of their minds.   In effect, a person's higher mental functions are social before they are internalized by the individual, and they become internalized by means of social interactions. Thus, what people do—their activities—are not just a result of what they think.   Rather, what and how they think are a result of what they do.   However, the pathway from activity to mental contents is not exclusively a one-way street;   instead, the process operates in a cyclical fashion.   Activities lead to thoughts; then thinking about the activities can lead to revising the conduct of future activities.   In this way, contemplation and evaluation influence activity, with the resulting activity affecting further thought contents and processes.

Central to the Soviet model is the concept of a hierarchy of types of activities, with a dominant or *leading activity* at the top of the hierarchy at each stage of development. That is, each period of children's development is motivated by a particular leading activity. The change from one leading activity to another brings about a change in the person's perception of life and signifies the transition from one mental stage to the next. A leading activity is marked by three features: (a) it is the chief factor establishing a given period in the child's psychological growth, (b) it is within the field of this activity that particular psychic functions emerge, and (c) the climax of the activity forms the foundation for the next leading activity. The Soviets divided the first two decades of life into six stages of development, with each stage focusing on a different leading activity (Davidov, 1985).

Stage 1 activity (birth to age 1): Intuitive and emotional contact with children and adults

Stage 2 activity (ages 1 to 3): Object manipulation

Stage 3 activity (ages 3 to 7): Game playing

Stage 4 activity (ages 7 to 11): Learning, including learning in school

Stage 5 activity (ages 11-15): Social communication for solving life's problems

Stage 6 activity (ages 15 to 20): Vocational preparation

Recent theories that incorporate elements of Vygotsky's model are described in Chapter 6.

Cognitivism

What is sometimes referred to as "The Cognitive Revolution" surfaced in the 1960s and 1970s in North America as a reaction against behaviorism's eliminating *thinking* from accounts of development. Whereas the dominant behaviorists had removed *mind* from consideration, cognitivist-oriented psychologists reinstated *mind* and assigned it a crucial role in accounts of development. The word *cognitivism* does not designate a specific theory. Rather, *cognitivism* is an umbrella term sheltering a variety of theories that propose mental structures and functions as key explanatory concepts. Since the time of mentalism, some theories that included the mind still persisted but were largely obscured by behaviorism within the American psychological community. Piaget's and Vygotsky's proposals could both qualify as cognitive theories. As a result of The Cognitive Revolution, the dominant explanations of development over the final four decades of the 20th century would be cognitivist proposals. Two of the most popular types were *social-learning models* (sometimes called *social-cognition theories*) and *information-processing* models.

Social-learning models

The best known proponent of social-learning or social-cognition theory has been Albert Bandura, a psychology professor at Stanford University (Bandura, 1986).

What develops, how, and why. In Bandura's opinion, most of children's learning results from their actively imitating what they see or hear other people say and do. Consequently, the term *modeling (observational learning* or *vicarious learning)* means that children add to their repertoire of actions by observing someone else perform an action rather than by overtly carrying out the behavior themselves (Bandura, 1969, pp. 118-120). Children can copy other people directly by witnessing their behavior or indirectly by adopting actions depicted in books, television programs, stage dramas, and the like.

The process of learning from models consists of five main functions: (1) paying attention to the model, (2) coding the model's actions so as to place the results in memory, (3) retaining the results in memory, and (4) carrying out the remembered material in actions. All four of these steps require (5) motivation, which is influenced by the consequences experienced by the observed model and by the child himself or herself when attempting the action.

Important features of modeling include (a) *goals* the person hopes to achieve, (b) the *availability* of models who are apparently attempting to reach such goals, (c) the *methods* that models employ, (d) the degree of *success* models appear to enjoy in terms of the consequences that result from their actions, (e) the ability of the child to *copy* the model's behavior, and (f) the *consequences* the child experiences when applying the modeled actions in her or his own life.

In the mid-1970s, Hilgard and Bower (1975, p. 605) wrote that "Social learning theory provides the best integrative summary of what modern learning theory has to contribute to solutions of practical problems." In the mid-1990s, Grusec concluded that Bandura's theory

> continues to be a strong force in current thinking and provides, among other things, a critical skepticism that guards against too-ready acceptance of stage-theoretical, constructivist, or evolutionary theses. It should also be noted that social cognition theory no longer holds center stage simply because its basic concepts, those of observation learning and learning through direct consequences, have become an accepted part of our knowledge base. (1994, p. 474)

Information-processing models

Classical information-processing theories have been founded on the assumption that the basic processes of human thought and action are analogous to the basic processes of computers. Both processes involve inputs, throughputs, and outputs. For example, (a) a person receives impressions (*input*) from the environment via the senses (eyes, ears, pain receptors, etc.), (b) those impressions are interpreted within the person and decisions are reached about actions that could be taken (*throughput*), and (c) on the basis of those interpretations, the individual acts (*output*) on the environment (speaks, grabs, retreats, cries, laughs, etc.). In a similar way, (a) data are entered into a computer via a keyboard, disks, or other devices (*input*), (b) within the computer the data are manipulated according to instructions provided by silicon chips and software (*throughput*), and (c) the results of the computations are expressed on the computer's screen, on printed sheets, in simulated speech, or in some other form (*output*). In the cases of both the person and the computer, the first and last of this trio of stages can be observed directly, but the middle stage is hidden from view. Therefore, to explain human development, information-processing theorists have hoped that their analysis of the inner workings of computers will cast light on human thought and action. In effect, they have sought to create computer hardware and software that can do the same things the human neuromuscular system accomplishes. In pursuing this goal, they have created the field of investigation called *artificial intelligence*. Figure 1-1 displays a simplified graphic rendition of the sort of "classical" information-processing model popular in the 1960s and 1970s.

Components of human thought and action. In classical versions of information processing, the main elements of the system were available at birth: (a) *sense organs*, (b) a means of translating sensory stimuli into *electrochemical codes*, (c) a means of combining codes from different senses (sight, hearing, touch, taste) into a *unified sensation* that can be assigned a meaning (*semantic memory*), (d) a *short-term, working-memory* function that produces a quick comparison of the unified sensation code with contents of long-term memory to determine what the code "means" in relation to past experiences, (e) *long-term memory,* which holds the coded results of past experiences for an extended— perhaps infinite—length of time, (f) a means of arriving at a decision in *working memory* about what action, if any, should be taken on the basis of the interpretation of the received stimuli, and (g) *muscle systems* that act on the world.

What develops, how, and why. Although the components of the information-processing system exist at birth, they are extremely simple and immature, far too immature to equip the neonate to survive without a great deal of help from adults. So the process of growing up consists of the components becoming more effective in their operation—sight and hearing more acute, working memory more efficient in decision making, long-term memory filled with a great quantity of records of past experiences, and muscle systems quicker and more accurate in carrying out orders.

Beginning in the late 1970s, criticisms of the inadequacies of classical models led to subsequent revisions of information-processing schemes. Those revisions can be found in certain of the psychobiological (Chapter 2) and connectionist (Chapter 3) theories of the 1980s and 1990s.

As for cognitivism in general, all of the theories described in Chapters 2 through 12 qualify in some way as cognitivist models, because all include mental processes as important features of human development.

Figure 1-1

A Simplified Classical Information-Processing Model

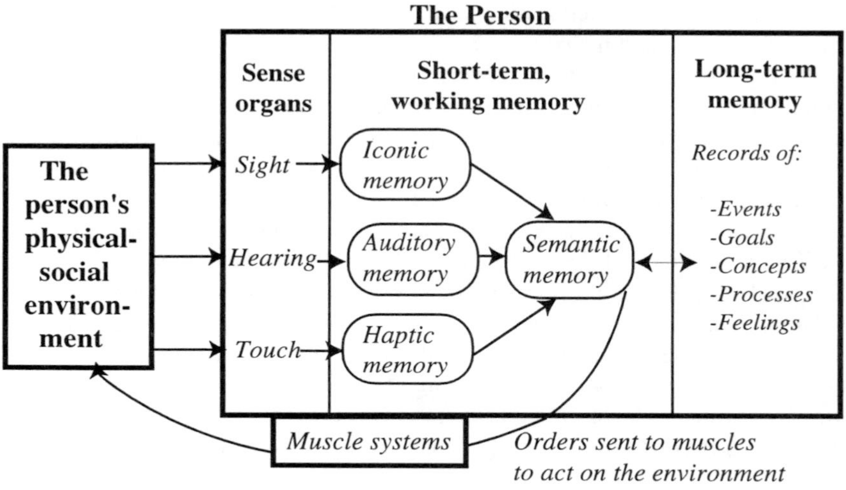

The Person

The person's physical-social environment	Sense organs	Short-term, working memory	Long-term memory
	Sight → Iconic memory		Records of:
	Hearing → Auditory memory → Semantic memory		-Events -Goals -Concepts -Processes -Feelings
	Touch → Haptic memory		

Muscle systems   Orders sent to muscles
to act on the environment

Conclusion

The foregoing condensed description of nine types of theories is admittedly simplistic, since the detailed characteristics and variations of each type are far more complex than this version has suggested. Furthermore, such a brief survey has necessarily failed to recognize many other models that appeared from 1880 to 1980. Consequently, the survey has performed a very limited function—that of (a) identifying key features of several theories that were among the most popular in Europe and the Americas during the 100 years prior to 1980 and (b) providing a historical background for understanding the recent theories depicted later in this volume's Part I.

Our next step toward understanding recent theories entails speculating about forces that account for why new explanations of development emerge and attract adherents.

FORCES OF CHANGE

New theories, or variations of established ones, are the creations of inventive persons who become dissatisfied with the explanations furnished by existing theories. And since life does not stand still but constantly changes like an ever-shifting kaleidoscope, new events are continually emerging to stimulate dissatisfaction with present theories and to offer opportunities for devising better explanations of development. The following sampling of influential events illustrates how such forces of change can operate.

Unexplained Outcomes

When development turns out in ways not readily explained by some familiar line of logic, an alternative logic is called for; and the search for such a logic may produce a new theory. In Sigmund Freud's Viennese psychiatric practice, he was baffled by patients who suffered such symptoms as blurred vision, severe headaches, impaired mobility, or numbness of a limb, despite the fact that such patients' neuromuscular systems were intact. To account for these odd phenomena, Freud surmised that physical symptoms could be produced by psychological disorders generated out of unsatisfactory childhood experiences—a conjecture that led him to his psychoanalytic theory of development.

Unusual Vantage Points

Viewing an event from a novel perspective may stimulate the creation of a new theory. Early in his adult life, Jean Piaget spent time in Paris analyzing children's answers to Alfred Binet's recently devised intelligence tests. What interested Piaget more than children's correct answers were their mistaken responses. His curiosity about the sorts of thought processes that would lead children to produce curious patterns of answers launched him on the research program from which he built his model of children's cognitive development.

Societal Upheavals

Among terms used to identify a theoretical vantage point are *worldview, paradigm,* and *perspective.* Societal upheavals often become the source of innovative vantage points that lead to new theories.

As noted earlier, the Russian revolution of 1918 ended the reign of Czar Nicholas and brought to power a Soviet government founded on Marxist social-political doctrine. What the new government then needed for Soviet psychology was a conception of human development that would be compatible with a Marxist worldview. To fill that need, Vygotsky and his colleagues provided the theory that would dominate beliefs about human development from the 1920s through the 1980s in societies under Soviet influence.

A different set of major disturbances would arise in the 1950s and expand dramatically in the 1960s. Following World War II, the populations of most of the world's territories that had been colonies of European nations, the United States, and Japan won their political freedom and strove to rule themselves as sovereign nations. Among the people who, during the latter 1950s, were still engaged in armed struggle to achieve independence were the indigenous members of the former French Indochina colony of Vietnam. The United States became involved in the conflict by actively supporting the French attempt to regain control of the colony after Japanese military forces had ruled the region during World War II. But in the United States, university students led mass demonstrations against U.S. participation in the Vietnam War, with their protests producing a period of great strife that pitted prowar against antiwar factions. The antiwar movement accompanied an even broader rebellion by an influential portion of the youth population—a rebellion against traditional social values, particularly ones relating to respect for authority, forms of sexual behavior, and the use of psychedelic drugs to achieve altered states of consciousness. At the same time, unconventional perspectives in the arts, literature, philosophy, and the sciences were emerging in Europe under the label *postmodernism,* a movement that quickly attracted disciples in other parts of the world. Throughout the rest of the 20th century, postmodernism would significantly influence theory and research in the social and behavioral sciences. The nature of postmodernism as found in those disciplines, and the things that postmodernists have rebelled against, are described in some detail in the introductions to Part I and Part II. Most of the theories of development described in Part II are, either directly or incidentally, products of postmodern worldviews.

Advocates for Neglected Social Groups

Further sources of new theories are people who contend that the development of members of particular social groups has received insufficient or distorted attention in the past. To remedy this neglect, the groups' advocates compose theories which they hope will set matters right. During the 1960s and thereafter, advocates were emboldened by the rebellious spirit of the times to try redressing the disregard and misinformation they felt had traditionally been suffered by the poor, ethnic minorities, females, and homosexuals/bisexuals. The theoretical results of these efforts are illustrated by the models of development described in Part II: *Products of Social Movements.*

Technological Innovations

The most remarkable recent demonstration of how new technologies influence theory development appeared with the invention and widespread dissemination of electronic computers. Artificial-intelligence schemes that were associated with information-processing theories during the 1970s and 1980s owed most of their form and content to progress in computer technology. And the advances in connectionist theories described in Chapter 3 would not have been possible without the expeditious introduction of ever-more-sophisticated cybernetic devices.

Among the computer-related technological advances that have promoted the creation and refinement of theories are:

- The Internet and its World Wide Web which equip researchers, seated at a computer in their home or office, to access information instantly from thousands of sources around the world, thereby providing theorists with far more empirical studies and models of human development than ever before.

- Methods of analyzing brain activity that aid theorists in their task of estimating the relationship between brain activity and people's thought and action during the process of development. Three such techniques are:
  —Computerized tomography (CT) or computerized axial tomography (CAT) scanning, which involves passing X-rays through the brain at different angles to reveal cross-section images (slices) of the tissues, providing data to be processed by a computer and displayed as images on a television screen.
  —Magnetic resonance imaging (MRI), which does not use X-rays but, instead, depends on the behavior of protons (nuclei) of hydrogen atoms that are exposed to powerful magnetic fields and radio waves. When so exposed, the protons emit radio signals that are detected and then transformed by a computer into images on a screen.
  —Positron emission tomography (PET) scanning, which uses a radioactive substance introduced into the body to produce an image that reflects the activity of the tissues being studied. The image created by the computer on a television screen is similar to a CT scan.

Not only did these tools become available to researchers during the 1980s and 1990s, but also other advanced technological aids were being introduced at an accelerating pace on the advent of the 21st century.

In summary, a variety of social and scientific events during the closing decades of the 20th century stimulated the creation of new and revised theories of human development.

THE BOOK'S STRUCTURE AND CONTENTS

As explained earlier, chapters 2 through 12 are located within three parts. Part I: *Extensions of Tradition*, consists of seven chapters which introduce theories that are either variations of earlier models or new departures whose foundations can be traced to schemes popular before the 1980s and 1990s. Part II: *Products of Social Movements*, contains four chapters describing theories created by proponents of social-reform efforts that began mainly in the 1960s, advanced through the 1970s, and resulted in conceptions of human development that appeared over the period 1980-2000. Part III: *Final Observations*, is composed of a single chapter—Chapter 13—offering (a) a retrospective summary of the theories presented in the preceding 11 chapters and (b) a prospective estimate of what might be expected of development models in the future.

Creating a human development theory is never a finished venture. The process always leaves a residue of inadequately answered questions, ones that suggest issues yet to be resolved. As a way of directing attention to such unfinished business, each of the following chapters, 2 through 12, ends with a brief section titled *Remaining Challenges.*

Part I

Extensions of Tradition

As suggested in the historical review of development models in Chapter 1, rarely is a theory an entirely new invention. In most instances, theories trace their origins to one or more earlier schemes. In this way, recent theories become extensions of existing traditions.

The dual purpose of this introduction to Part I is (a) to describe five alternative conceptions of the term *theory* that have emerged over past decades and (b) to identify the types of theories included in Chapters 2 through 8.

EVOLVING CONCEPTS OF THEORY

As time passes, not only are new versions of theory introduced, but new conceptions of the term *theory* also emerge, with those conceptions influencing the portrayals of human development that subsequently appear. The aim of the following discussion is (a) to describe several meanings of *theory* and (b) to suggest how each meaning can affect explanations of development.

In the mid-1980s, Irwin Altman and Barbara Rogoff of the University of Utah (1987) followed the lead of Pepper (1942, 1967) and of Dewey and Bentley (1949) in distinguishing among four versions of the concept *theory*, versions that Altman and Rogoff labeled *trait, interactional, organismic,* and *transactional.* Over the years, the four have evolved within the scholarly community somewhat in that listed order, with trait perspectives the earliest and transactional perspectives the latest. Although in the context of this book the four versions concern human development, it should be recognized that the four are not limited to explaining development. Instead, each is a *general paradigm* (*worldview, world hypothesis,* or *perspective*) useful for analyzing any sort of physical or social event, large or small—earthquakes, meteorite showers, wars, religious practices, political elections, marital relations, childrearing practices, classsroom activities, and an endless variety of other happenings.

One convenient way to explain the distinctions among the four is to begin with the definition of theory offered in Chapter 1.

> The term *theory* refers to a proposal about (a) which components or variables are important for understanding a selected phenomenon—such as human development—and (b) how those components interact to account for why the phenomenon turns out as it does.

That generic definition can now guide our analysis of Altman and Rogoff's varieties of theory, because the key distinctions among the four viewpoints are found in the nature of components and in the relationships among components. Therefore, the analysis of each version begins with (a) that paradigm's definition of psychology and (b) the paradigm's basic unit of analysis. Components are then described in relation to (c) their labels, (d) their locations, (e) their sources, (f) their degree of stability, and (g) how they are identified and evaluated. Finally, the version's component relationships are described in terms of (h) components' comparative powers and (i) how components affect each other. The aim of all four perspectives, when applied to human development, is to explain how, with the passing of time, events in which people participate turn out as they do.

In adapting Altman and Rogoff's descriptions to the purposes of this book, I have taken the liberty of elaborating on their presentation, adding illustrative examples, and inserting a *consequences perspective* between Altman and Rogoff's *trait* and *interactional* worldviews.

Trait Perspective

Developmental psychology defined: Developmental psychology involves studying the emergence of the individual person's psychophysical processes as the days and years advance and, in particular, identifying the components of mind or personality and describing how those components affect life's events.

Unit of analysis: The *person,* in terms of the psychophysical qualities that determine how events turn out.

Components' labels: A trait perspective's significant components are traits or dispositions that comprise the mind or personality, identified by such labels as *intelligence, emotional control, persistence, submissiveness, initiative, creativity, compassion, sensitivity,* and more. The idea of personality traits is reminiscent of faculty psychology of past centuries, with the notion of traits found today in both commonsense and scientific explanations of behavior.

Locations of components: Traits reside within the person, serving as the principal determinants of how the person thinks and acts during encounters with environments. The traits comprising one individual's personality can differ from those comprising another's personality.

Sources of components: The mind's or personality's elements derive from a combination of genetic inheritance and experiences with the environment. Some theorists (hereditarians) credit genetic causes with more influence, while others (environmentalists) attribute greater effect to an individual's environmental encounters. For instance, an extreme hereditarian will cite genetically determined intelligence as the cause of a child's excellent academic success, whereas an extreme environmentalist will cite wise childrearing practices and an enriched physical-social environment as the causes.

Component stability: Traits are considered to be quite stable, particularly over shorter periods of time, such as over a few months or a few years. Across longer periods of time—such as a decade or more—traits can change as the result of internal, genetically timed neuromuscular development and/or the accumulation of environmental experiences. Such changes are often interpreted as forming a sequence of growth stages, each consisting of a plateau (period of no significant change) followed by a transition (rapid change to a new plateau).

Means of identifying and evaluating components: Traits are usually identified and evaluated through introspection, observation, or tests and inventories that are analyzed statistically.

Introspection involves a person focusing attention on his or her own mental contents and processes—"I'm short tempered but I have a forgiving nature" or "I feel that I'm quick-witted and honest, and rather superstitious."

Observations consist of an outsider noting a person's actions on one or more occasions and estimating what combination of personality traits could account for such behavior. Hence, observations can result in such appraisals as "He acted out of jealousy" or "She's always optimistic" or "His obstinacy continues to destroy his social relationships."

Aptitude and personality tests and inventories either pose questions for respondents to answer or offer alternative choices from among which respondents select the ones they think best describe their own personality or preferences. Psychologists, counselors, and psychiatrists analyze the patterns of a respondent's answers in order to identify the mental traits they believe underlie such patterns. The task of discerning traits may be pursued with the aid of such statistical procedures as factor analysis.

Components' comparative powers: Traits are assumed to exert different degrees of power in determining how events turn out. The strength of various traits will vary from one person to another because of differences in those persons' genetic composition and social/physical environments. Furthermore, within a particular individual's personality, the power of traits can change from one stage of life to another, resulting in people suggesting that "She's different than she used to be—more confident and assertive, and surprisingly abrasive."

Components' effects on each other: Our generic definition of *theory* proposed that components "interact." But from a traditional trait viewpoint, the term *interact* does not mean that one trait alters the nature of another trait. At most, *interaction* means that various components operate in parallel and with different levels of power to affect a given episode. A teenage girl's popularity may be accounted for by her combination of very strong *social sensitivity*, moderately powerful *self-confidence,* and weak *enviousness.* Therefore, the expression *parallel action* is probably a more accurate term than *interaction* for describing how traits combine to determine the outcome of an event.

The reason two people act differently under the same circumstances is that the two apply different traits to the problems that the situation presents and/or the strengths of the traits within the two individuals' personalities are not identical.

Consequences Perspective

Developmental psychology defined: Developmental psychology is the study of the influence that an environmental event exerts on the future behavior of people who have participated either directly or vicariously in the event. That influence is referred to as the *consequence* of the event. Two theories reflecting a consequence perspective are Watson's and Skinner's versions of behaviorism. Another theory that draws heavily on the effect of consequences is Bandura's social-cognition model.

Unit of analysis: Analysis focuses on the relationship between (a) the environmental conditions that obtain during an event and (b) how a person who participated in that event will act under similar circumstances in the future.

Components' labels: Five components are *behavior potentials, behaviors, reinforcers* (rewards), *nonreinforcers* (environmental conditions that fail to encourage the future repetition of a behavior), and *punishments* (environmental conditions that the person interprets as adversive and are therefore conditions the person does not wish to experience again).

Locations of components: Behavior potentials are latent, covert actions an individual can perform, whereas *behaviors* are observed performed actions. Both the potential and overt behaviors reside in the person. Conditions that serve as reinforcers, nonreinforcers, and punishments reside chiefly in the environment outside the person.

Sources of components: Behavior potentials are genetically determined characteristics of the human organism that can arise at progressive stages of life in keeping with a genetically timed maturation process. Reinforcers, nonreinforcers, and punishments emerge from the environments the person encounters. The more varied the environments that the person inhabits, the greater the diversity of reinforcers and punishments affecting that individual's behaviors. Which behaviors a person will habitually exhibit is determined by the patterning of reinforcers, nonreinforcers, and punishments experienced.

Component stability: The stability of behaviors depends on the consistency of the consequences resulting from the person's engagements with the environment's reinforcing, nonreinforcing, and punishing conditions. Frequent changes in how environments treat—or respond to—a person contribute to instability and variability of behaviors.

Means of identifying and evaluating components: Behaviors and environmental influences are discovered and assessed by means of observation, usually by observation from the vantage points of people other than the person whose behavior is being evaluated.

Components' comparative powers: Behaviors that are frequently followed by reinforcing environmental conditions acquire greater strength (resistance to change or elimination) than do behaviors that are (a) rarely followed by reinforcing environmental conditions or (b) frequently followed by punishing conditions. The power of a specific environmental condition—such as a parent's particular treatment of a child—increases with each increase in that condition's frequency, consistency, and potency. The expression *potency*—when cast in nonbehaviorist, commonsense terms—means the degree of pleasure, need-fulfillment, or tension-reduction the recipient experiences.

Components' effects on each other: Whereas a trait perspective credits people's internal dispositions with determining people's actions in events, a consequence perspective credits events' environmental conditions (reinforcing, nonreinforcing, punishing) with establishing the behaviors people will exhibit on future occasions. Thus, environments ordain which potential behaviors will be activated as overt behaviors in subsequent similar circumstances.

Interactional Perspective

Interactional worldviews, which have been the dominant approaches in contemporary psychology, treat [people's internal] psychological processes [and] environmental settings . . . as independently defined and operating entitites. . . . Thus, behavior and psychological processes are usually treated as dependent variables, whereas environmental factors (and sometimes person qualities or other psychological processes) are treated as independent variables or causal influences on psychological functioning. (Altman & Rogoff, 1987, p. 15)

Developmental psychology defined: Developmental psychology is the study of the growth, prediction, and control of behavior and psychological processes by means of analyzing people's interactions with their environments. Thus, in contrast to trait and consequence worldviews, the person and the environment are credited with jointly causing events.

Unit of analysis: The person's psychophysical qualities and the environment's social/physical qualities are treated as two separate domains whose components interact to determine the characteristics of events.

Components' labels and locations: The important qualities of the person and of the environment vary from one theory to another. Consider, for example, the difference between the labeled qualities in Fritz Heider's commonsense-attribution theory (1958) and those in Anne-Marie Ambert's peer-abuse model (1995).

Heider's theory is designed to explain the nature of the folk psychology that appears to underlie ordinary people's explanations of human behavior. The qualities that Heider's model attributes to the person include *ability* (what the person *can* do), *intention* (what the person plans to do), *motivation* (the amount of effort the person will exert), *conscience* (what the person *should* and *should not* do), *emotional dispositions* (feelings that influence the direction and effort of the person's attempts), and *empathic attitude* (how well the person perceives life from other people's perspectives). Four significant qualities of environments in Heider's model are *opportunities and restrictions, task difficulty* (which is judged by how readily other persons of similar age and gender can perform a given task), *environmental coercion* (the pressures or *ought forces* exerted by the social/physical environment to impel people to act in approved ways), and *situation and role prescriptions* (the sorts of behavior expected of people when they are in particular settings and are assuming particular roles).

Ambert's model represents an attempt to explain the conditions under which children and youths abuse agemates. Qualities of a person that affect whether she or he will abuse peers include *moral values* (convictions about what are right and wrong ways to treat other people), *motives* (aims the person pursues), *authority and power* (the person's perception of her or his ability to abuse a peer), *aggressivity* (the person's propensity to attack others), and *empathy attitude* (how well the person perceives life from others' perspectives). Significant qualities of environments that affect whether peer abuse takes place include *supervision* (whether authorities are present), *type of activity* (whether the activity pursued in the setting is conducive to aggressive behavior), and *peer culture* (group expectations about acceptable and unacceptable behavior in such a setting) (Ambert, 1995; Thomas, 2000, pp. 564-568).

Sources of components: From a typical interactionist perspective, a person's qualities result from a combination of (a) *genetic endowment*, including a genetically timed maturation schedule that determines when different ability potentials arise during childhood and adolescence and (b) *learning* that results from experiences in the succession of environments the individual inhabits during the process of growing up. The environment's qualities derive from the physical character of settings and from the social history of the people found in those settings; the social history has fashioned each setting's current *culture* that dictates the expectations the group holds about acceptable ways for people to think and act.

Component stability: A traditional interactionist worldview considers the qualities of people and of environments to be relatively stable, at least over a period of a few months or a few years.

Means of identifying and evaluating components: Qualities of the person are assessed by means of external observation and self-report. The term *external observation* refers to other people's estimates of a person's qualities, as inferred from what the person has said and done. *Self-report* is the subject's own description of his or her qualities derived from introspection. Sometimes self-report is elicited by means of an interview (as in psychoanalysis) or by a printed personality inventory that the individual fills out, such as the *Minnesota Mul-*

tiphasic Personality Inventory (Dahlstrom, Welsh, & Dahlstrom, 1972) or *Holland's Self-Directed Search* (Holland & Rayman, 1986).

Qualities of the environment are usually based on observations, which may be supplemented with the results of tests and inventories. For example, an ability or achievement test administered to a classroom of pupils can tell something about the intellectual climate of a class in which a particular pupil is enrolled. An ethnic-attitude inventory filled out by the personnel of a business office can be useful for estimating the social environment that affects the life of an employee from a minority ethnic group.

Carefully trained and disciplined observers can be expected to produce accurate, objective descriptions of personal and environmental components.

Components' comparative powers: The components of both the person and the environment are considered stable both in composition and strength. Thus, in Heider's attribution theory, a person with a strong conscience in one environmental context will exhibit a strong conscience in another context as well. Likewise, an environment that places role restrictions on one person—such as requiring an employee to report to work on time—will impose those restrictions in equal measure on other persons as well.

Components' effects on each other: Although components combine in their various strengths to produce events, they do not alter each other in the process. In Ambert's theory, a teenage girl's moral values and motives remain the same whether the girl is tempted to ridicule a schoolmate on the school bus or to ridicule the schoolmate in history class. Although the girl's qualities remain the same in the two settings, her overt behavior differs because peer-culture expectations accept behavior on the bus that would not be approved in the classroom, and because a more imposing authority figure is present in the classroom (teacher) than on the bus (bus driver).

Organismic Perspective

An organismic worldview proposes that the person and the environment should not be viewed as separate entities that interact. Instead, persons within their environment comprise a *system,* with change in any person-component or environment-component affecting the patterning of component relationships and consequently influencing the events that take place.

> People and situations are not logically independent of one another in the real world. . . . Person and context co-exist and jointly define one another and contribute to the meaning and nature of a holistic event. . . . [So] the role of a particular aspect of individual functioning cannot be understood and explained in isolation from the totality in which it operates. (Walsh, Craik, & Price, 1992, pp. 244-245)

Developmental psychology defined: Developmental psychology is the study of how and why holistic person-environment systems change.

Unit of analysis: "Holistic entities composed of separate person and environment components, elements, or parts whose relations and interactions yield qualities of the whole that are 'more than the sum of the parts'" (Altman & Rogoff, 1987, p. 13).

Components' labels and locations: Similar to the interactionist perspective, an organismic paradigm proposes that both the person and the environment are characterized by qualities that participate in producing events, with the nature of those qualities differing from one theory to another.

Sources of components: Kurt Lewin's concept of *life space*, described in Chapter 1 (page 31) illustrates one organismic conception of component sources.

> A person's life space consists of all the facts that influence the individual's behavior at a given time. For Lewin, a *fact* is not solely an objectively verifiable observation from the "real world." Instead, a fact is any element within the person's psychological environment that affects the individual's thought or behavior. Life space, therefore, includes forces of which the person is unaware as well as things that the person accepts as real or true, whether those things are publicly verifiable or are mere fantasies.

Thus, components can derive from diverse sources. For instance, an 18-year-old college fraternity intitiate finds himself with two fellow initiates in a dark woods in the middle of the night, assigned to find a cupid statue hidden there and to return the statue to the fraternity house. We can speculate that the sources of components in the life space affecting his behavior at the moment will include

- past experiences in dark places at night that remain as memory traces (accurate or inaccurate) or as unconsciously motivated emotional reactions not in the form of conscious memories,
- the assigned goal—to retrieve the cupid statue,
- the youth's sense of direction as a result of his genetically inherited space-relation aptitude as combined with past experiences in the wilderness while on camping trips,
- thoughts and feelings about the veteran members of the fraternity who sent him and his companions on this mission,
- what the youth's two companions say and do,
- the physical setting and facilities—a dark woods on a cloudy night, cold temperature, wind and rain, warm clothing, a single flashlight shared by the three searchers,
- the youth's envisioned consequences of this adventure—catching a cold, injuring himself from stumbling over a log, failing to return to the fraternity house with the statue, losing his eye-glasses in the woods,
- and more.

Component stability: Whereas in a typical interactionist perspective, both the person-components and the environment-components are considered to be stable over months or years, in an organismic perspective the notion of stability has little meaning. Over short periods of time—minutes or hours—different combinations of components make up the person's life space. And the nature of a given component is altered by the relationship obtaining between it and the other components active at that time. Such a component as the fraternity initiate's attitude toward veteran members of the fraternity will not be the same under all circumstances—different when he is in the woods than when his brothers are toasting his health for his stellar performance on the college swim team. Likewise, his two fellow initiates' displays of confidence or despair will not likely be the same in the woods as they are at the homecoming dance or during the Greek associations' spring songfest. In short, the stability of a component depends on the extent to which the configuration of components in the life space is the same from one time to another.

Components' comparative powers: The strength of an individual's personal qualities can vary from one environmental setting to another, as a function of the strength of the different environmental qualities in different settings. In Anne-Marie Ambert's peer-abuse model, the power of a 10-year-old's *aggressive disposition* that affects whether he will abuse a peer on the playground will be greater if no teacher (authority) is supervising the playground than if a teacher is there. Likewise, the strength of a component of the environment will vary in relation to the nature of the other influential environmental components present at the time. Thus, the amount of influence that a teacher will exert on the behavior of the 10-year-old's attacker will likely vary according to whether the attacker's 25-year-old hoodlum brother is present, urging the attacker to "waste that kid."

From an organismic vantage point, perhaps the "components," because of their labile nature, should not be called anything so substantial as *components*. Instead, it may be more appropriate to designate them by a more flexible term, such as *action tendencies,* thereby implying propensities that tend to influence events. But such influence is always a function of one tendency's strength and direction in relation to the strengths and directions of other tendencies.

Transactional Perspective

Developmental psychology defined: As proposed by Altman and Rogoff (1987, p. 24), developmental psychology from a transactional worldview is "the study of the changing relations among psychological and environmental aspects of holistic unities."

Unit of analysis: The entity that is analyzed is an entire event, episode, or incident involving persons, psychological processes, and environments.

Components' labels and locations: The term *components,* in any of its traditional meanings, is really not applicable in a transactional paradigm because the focus of a transactional perspective is on the relationships among *aspects* of an event in which each *aspect* (such as a person or feature of the environment) is defined by how it contributes to the progressive changes in the event as a whole.

> Organismic orientations view the system as made up of separate elements whose patterns of relationships comprise the whole. The relations between elements are constituents of the whole; in fact, they constitute a form of element that contributes to the nature of the whole system. In the transactional view there are no separate elements or sets of discrete relationships into which the system is ultimately divisible. Instead, the whole is composed of inseparable aspects that simultaneously and conjointly define the whole. (Altman & Rogoff, 1987, p. 24)

Thus, within a given event, *aspects* which would be identified as particular persons or features of the environment (components) in an organismic or interactionist paradigm, would be seen in a transactional worldview as *action relationships.* One person in the event cannot be adequately described as separate from another. Persons are defined in terms of their relationship to each other—in terms of how they affect and are affected by other persons' action within the particular time period and physical/social environment of the event. A transactional approach assumes that the *aspects* of a system, consisting of persons in a context "that contribute to the meaning and nature of a holistic event" (Altman & Rogoff, 1987, p. 24).

Sources of components: The notion of *sources of components* is hardly applicable in a transactional paradigm. What is applicable is the notion of *aspects,* whose sources are the very event being analyzed (Altman & Rogoff, 1987, p. 24).

In contrast to the other perspectives we've inspected, transactional paradigms do not propose components that operate according to a few key principles that produce all psychological phenomena and move toward synthesizing all knowledge within a unified system. Instead, transactional worldviews use all necessary aspects and principles, including ones from earlier times as well as others that emerge in the event under study, that are necessary to explain the event.

> The focus is, therefore, on the event, with acceptance of the possibility that different configurations of principles may be necessary to understand different events. Transactionalism adopts, therefore, a pragmatic, eclectic, and relativistic approach to studying psychological phenomena. (Altman & Rogoff, 1987, p. 24)

Because the nature of each *aspect* (person or environmental feature) is defined by that aspect's relationships to the other aspects and by the nature of the event as a whole, the source of each aspect is the event. In effect, each aspect, in the form it assumes in a given event, is apparently born within the event. For instance, we might assume that the particular relationships that obtained among persons, environments, and processes in the fraternity hazing incident are unique to that incident. Those relationships never existed before in quite that form. So the confluence of the particular persons and environments that comprised the cupid-statue espisode would determine the changing relationships among the aspects and consequently the shifting, moment-by-moment character of the event.

Component stability: From a transactional viewpoint, there is no such thing as component or aspect stability. *Aspects* (defined by their relationships to other aspects of an incident and to the event as a whole) not only differ from one event to another, but they change with the temporal flow of activities within a particular incident. We thus might assume that the relationships among persons and environments in the cupid-statue episode changed from the time the initiates left the fraternity house, to the time they entered the woods, to the time they hunted unsuccessfully for the statue, to the time they found the statue, to the time they carried it to their car, to the time they returned to the fraternity house with their prize.

Components' comparative powers: Trying to identify the comparative powers of components—or more correctly, of *aspects*—opens a far larger issue that must be faced if a transactional perspective is to guide the creation of theories and research procedures that put a transactional paradigm to practical use in explaining human development. Creating an abstract vision of the characteristics of a transactional viewpoint—as in the above sketch of the Altman and Rogoff proposal—is a simple matter compared to the task of specifying the features of a theory that directs the gathering and interpretation of evidence. This means that theorists who hope to design practical models that satisfy the requirements of Altman and Rogoff's abstract version of transactionism face a very daunting challenge. The nature of that challenge may be revealed by our raising questions that must be answered by transactional theories if they are to guide the collection and interpretation of data in research studies. We can generate the questions by reviewing several key characteristics of a transactional worldview, displaying those characteristics in *italic* type, and following them with questions for which a transactional theory needs to provide answers.

- *The unit of analysis is an entire event, episode, or incident involving persons, psychological processes, and environments.*

     How is an event defined in terms of: (a) when it starts and ends, (b) its spatial composition (its context), and (c) the time period it covers?

- *A holistic event derives its nature from aspects whose transactions produce the event.*

     How should we identify and label the *aspects* of an event? What constitutes a *transaction*? How many aspects will be involved in a transaction? How should the outcomes of transactions be identified and assessed?

- *Aspects, such as persons and features of the environment, are not defined as separate identities but, instead, are defined in terms of their relationship to one another.*

     What principles or rules guide the process of defining aspects as *relationships* rather than as separate components that interact? What examples illustrate this defining process for different events?

- *The whole is composed of inseparable aspects that simultaneously and conjointly define the whole.*

What principles govern the process of aspects conjointly defining the whole? What examples illustrate this conjoint defining process for different events?

- *Events are not static but, rather, are in a continual process of change.*

    How should an event be investigated—and the results recorded and communicated—so that the flow of changes is accurately portrayed? Are periodic "snapshots" of the event to be taken, showing the event from different vantage points, then the snapshots assembled in sequence? If so, how is the transition from one snapshot to the next to be explained? Are principles governing change extracted from the observations? If so, how is that process conducted?

- *Transactional worldviews use all necessary aspects and principles required for explaining an event, including ones from existing theories as well as others that emerge in the event under study.*

    How does a researcher identify which aspects and principles are required for explaining an event? What criteria should be used in deciding which aspects and principles can profitably be derived from existing theories? How should an investigator go about extracting aspects and principles from the event itself? Is it possible to obtain an "objective" or "true" portrayal of the aspects and principles involved in an event, a portrayal free from the subjective judgments of different individuals who investigate the event? If so, how is this managed?

I must confess that I've not yet found a theory that comes close to answering all of the above questions satisfactorily. Certainly none of the models described in this book reflect the transactional worldview outlined by Altman and Rogoff. Quite the contrary. The great majority of the book's theories are examples of interaction paradigms. A few—such as the behaviorist models in Chapter 1—are examples of a consequences perspective. A few others—such as Lewin's "life-space" proposal in Chapter 1 and systems theories in Chapter 3—may qualify as organismic models. However, none completely fulfills the requirements of the Altman-Rogoff transactional perspective. Thus, it seems that transactional theories which can be put to practical use in guiding empirical research are not yet available. As desirable as the transactional perspective appears in its abstract version, the task of casting it in a form that can be applied in research studies apparently must remain an item on developmentalists' agenda for the future.

THE THEORIES IN PART I

The seven chapters that comprise Part I begin with a pair that emphasize genetic and biological facets of development (Chapter 2: Psychobiology, Sociobiology; Chapter 3: Connectionism and Dynamic Systems), continue with one featuring environmental forces (Chapter 4: Environmental/Ecological Theories), advance to a pair that illustrate derivatives of two major mid-20th-century theories (Chapter 5: Beyond Piaget; Chapter 6: Beyond Vygotsky), continue with one that describes four contrasting patterns of theory components' interrelationships (Chapter 7: Models of Interaction), and close with a mixed bag of ways to explain development (Chapter 8: A Potpourri of Theories).

2

Psychobiology, Sociobiology

Since the time that the term *psychobiology* was coined nearly a century ago, it has been assigned diverse meanings by different writers. By the 1990s, these meanings seem to have settled into two clusters that Donald Dewsbury labeled *broad sense* and *narrow sense.*

Broad-sense definitions conceive of psychobiology as the study of humans or other species as whole, unified organisms acting in environments, a mode of study that reveals "the relationship between behavioral and biological aspects of the developing organism at all levels of organization" (Crank in Dewsbury, 1991, p. 201). This view of psychobiology "takes into account not only the individual responses and functions but also considers them a part of the total and mentally integrated person's behavior" (Billings in Dewsbury, 1991, p. 199). Therefore, in the broad sense, psychobiology is not the study of a segment or component of a person, such as neural paths in the brain or the chemical composition of the body. Furthermore, psychobiology of this sort addresses questions about both the individual's development (*ontogeny*) and the evolution of the species (*phylogeny*).

In contrast, narrow-sense definitions, which have become increasingly common in recent times, portray psychobiology as

> roughly equivalent to "physiological psychology" or "behavioral neuroscience." It is as if, to some, the term "biology" meant only physiological, "wet," reductionistic science and whole-animal biology were not a part of the discipline. [In H. C. Warren's dictionary] "*psychobiology* = the field of biology which deals with the nervous system, receptors, effectors, and other topics germane to psychology. (Dewsbury, 1991, p. 202)

Dewsbury's own preference is to view psychobiology as the study of the genesis (phylogenetic and ontogenetic), control (external and internal), and consequences (for the individual and for reproductive success) of behavior. The "compleat psychobiologist" should use whatever explanatory power can be found with modern physiological techniques, but never lose sight of the problems that got us going in the first place: the integrated behavior of whole, functioning, adapted organisms. (Dewsbury, 1991, p. 203)

Sociobiology can be considered a subcategory of psychobiology. The word *sociobiology* has a much shorter history than *psychobiology*, since it drew widespread attention only in the 1970s, primarily as the result of Edward O. Wilson's book *Sociobiology: The New Synthesis* (1975). Wilson defined sociobiology as "the systematic study of the biological basis of all social behavior." Wilson's new-synthesis volume focused attention on animal societies as well as on early humans and "the adaptive features of organization in the more primitive contemporary human societies" (Wilson, 1975, p. 4). A second book, *On Human Nature* (1978), was concerned solely with the biological underpinnings of humans' interactions with each other as individuals and as groups. Then, in 1981, Wilson was joined by Charles J. Lumsden in publishing a gene-culture coevolution theory, which is the last of the four theories we inspect in this chapter.

A BACKGROUND OF NEO-DARWINISM

All models described in both Chapter 2 and Chapter 3 qualify as concerns of *psychobiology*, because each focuses primary attention on the biological substrates and correlates of thought and behavior. The principal difference between the two chapters lies in the perspectives they adopt toward psychobiology. Theories in Chapter 2 are examples of *evolutionary psychology,* a subdiscipline of psychobiology that interprets human thought and action in terms of principles of natural selection as described in Charles Darwin's *On the Origin of Species* (1859) and as updated in present-day neo-Darwinism. In contrast, the chief concern of connectionist theories in Chapter 3 is the relationship between *brain* and *mind.*

Because the illustrative models in this chapter are so dependent on core concepts of Darwinian thought and later allied discoveries, it should prove useful at the outset to recall the following concepts that are helpful in understanding the models.

- Life on earth originated around 3.5 billion years ago in the form of extremely small, simple organisms. All living things evolved from these early beginnings to produce the 2 million species of life that exist today.
- The most basic purpose or motive driving the behavior of living things is for them to survive. This is not simply the survival of an individual organism (a particular amoeba, goldfish, prairie dog, or person) but, rather, it's the survival and perpetuation of the species, or more precisely, of the genetic strain carried by that species.

- No living thing can survive on its own, separate from its environment. Every living thing must draw sustenance from its surroundings in the form of food for energy and cell construction. Every living thing must also acquire protection from destructive environmental forces—intolerable temperatures, diseases, predators, inclement weather, and the like. Organisms whose characteristics suit them well to thrive in the environment they inhabit are able to survive and produce offspring that also survive. Organisms whose characteristics fail to fit them for surviving in their environment tend to expire early and fail produce offspring, thereby ending their ancestral (genetic) line. This process, which Darwin labeled *natural selection*, was called *the survival of the fittest* by 19th-century British philosopher Herbert Spencer.

- As time passes, environments change. Climates become hotter or colder, water sources dry up, fire and flood destroy food sources and shelters, predators invade a territory, diseases spread, volcanoes erupt, continents are altered by shifts in the earth's crustal plates, and settlers fell forests and denude grasslands. In addition, the multiplying of a species within a given territory places increased demands on that territory's ability to sustain the species. Such overcrowding heightens the competition among individuals as well as species for the limited resources. Species whose genetic composition fits them to adjust and survive in that setting or enables them to migrate to a less crowded environment will sustain their genetic line and prosper. Species that cannot adequately adjust will die out.

- At the time that Darwin proposed his theory, he didn't understand the exact process of biological inheritance. But since his day, the rapidly expanding field of genetics has furnished a host of information about the roles of chromosomes, genes, and DNA (deoxyribonucleic acid) in heredity. The following are elements of that process useful for understanding the theories described later in the chapter.

- The term *species* refers to a collection of individual organisms capable of interbreeding under natural conditions. The phrase *natural conditions* requires that we create separate species categories for two organisms that can be induced to mate under experimental conditions but do not interbreed in their natural setting. Such is the case with lions and tigers, which have been interbred in captivity but do not mate in their natural state and therefore qualify as separate species.

- The process of *species reproduction* among humans and within many other species requires two parents, each of whom furnishes half of the biological material necessary to produce a new individual. The construction of this new life begins when a father's sperm cell combines with a mother's ovum to produce a new cell that immediately divides into two identical cells. The dividing process continues rapidly, with certain cell groups assuming different structures and functions which, after about nine months, have coalesced into the form of a newborn child. The architectural design for this neonate has been determined by the chemical pattern of the *genes* (each of which is a linear sequence of nucleotides along a segment of DNA) that are carried in humans (a) on the 23 chromosomes provided in the mother's ovum and (b) on the 23 chromosomes provided in the father's sperm at the time of conception. Genes, which are found in every cell of the human body (except red blood cells) furnish the coded instructions for constructing the new human's biological characteristics. This newly conceived person's 46 chromosomes contain the potential characteristics (*genotype*) from which his or her actual appearance and behavior (*phenotype*) will derive while growing up.

- A *population* is a set of individuals of the same species occupying a clearly delimited geographical area at the same time. For example, a group of people well established in a region and intermarrying within their own group would comprise a population. The term *gene pool* refers to the total genetic material available within a species population, such as all of the genes carried on the chromosomes of the people in our imagined ethnic group. Some genes—such as ones contributing to black hair—can be far more common than others—such as ones contributing to red hair. Furthermore, some genes are more dominant and others more recessive, with the dominant types more effective in determining people's realized (phenotypical) characteristics.

- There are two principal methods of increasing the variety of genes available in a population's gene pool—importation and mutation. *Importation* consists of immigrants from outside the population mating with members of the population, thereby adding foreign genes to the population's pool. Some imported genes may enrich the pool by contributing significantly to individuals' ability to survive changes in environmental conditions. *Mutation* consists of a gene being mysteriously altered when conveyed to an offspring. These *mutants* serve as different determinants in the child than did the original, unaltered genes in the parents. Most mutants are undesirable, in that they don't enhance the fitness of the species. Unfavorable mutants are often dominated by more constructive genes already in the population's pool. Thus, most mutants drop out of a population, because people carrying them tend not to survive or they fail to thrive sufficiently to pass their genetic material on to future generations. Other mutants, however, promote the ability of the species to adapt to environmental pressures. When these new creations are viable in terms of heredity—that is, they don't die out in the first generation but, instead, they move along in their mutated form to subsequent generations—they make a long-term contribution to the survival of the genetic strain.

Now, with this quick review of neo-Darwinian concepts in mind, we turn to the chapter's four recent theories that include a significant measure of Darwinism among their basic assumptions. Those theories focus on (a) the significance of birth order for personality development, (b) the evolutionary origins of pride and shame, (c) the ancient roots of inhibition, and (d) the coevolution of humans' genetic composition and their culture. The description of each theory opens with the focal question—or questions—that the theory is designed to answer. The four theories are at least remotely related to early 20th-century functionalism, which included Darwinian theory among its foundational beliefs.

AN EVOLUTIONARY-PSYCHOLOGY VIEW OF BIRTH ORDER

The focal question: How can Darwinian theory be used for explaining the relationship between siblings' birth order and the sorts of personalities siblings develop?

An evolutionary-psychology theory that addresses this question appears in the book *Born to Rebel—Birth Order, Family Dynamics, and Creative Lives* (1996) by Frank J. Sulloway, a science historian at the Massachusetts Institute of Technology. A key assumption underlying Sulloway's scheme is that the biological phenomenon of birth order inadvertently produces a competitive social relationship between siblings that systematically affects siblings' personalities.

Sulloway's model is founded on four tenets rooted in neo-Darwinism.

- Individuals compete with each other to command the resources in their environment that promote their own welfare.
- Those individuals most adept at competing for resources are the ones most likely to survive.
- Species in the animal kingdom vary in the degree to which specific behavior patterns are dictated by their genetic structure. For example, the actions of such social insects as bees and ants are determined chiefly by a genetic code, so that individual bees and ants need not learn their social roles since their role behavior is "hard-wired" into their genetic nature; they perform their roles automatically without having to decide what to do. In contrast, humans inherit relatively few automatic actions. Instead, what they inherit is great flexibility of behavior-potential that is combined with a great capacity to learn from experience. Thus, humans—by their ability to learn and create new versions of behavior that suit changing contexts—can adjust their actions to survive and thrive in very diverse environments.
- Each environment contains a limited pool of resources for inhabitants to use in their effort to survive and prosper. When the numbers of inhabitants become so great that they strain the available resources, two things can happen—(a) some inhabitants must leave (die off, be killed, emigrate) or (b) all of them can remain if some of them can change so they no longer need the traditional resources and thereby can survive on other resources available in that setting. In other words, some of the inhabitants find a new environmental "niche" into which they can fit.

Instances of species evolving to fit alternative environmental niches were observed by Darwin in the Galápagos Islands off the coast of Ecuador during his

5-year scientific expedition on the sailing vessel HMS Beagle in the 1830s. Among the islands' birds, Darwin noted 13 varieties of finches that were distinguished from each other by the size and form of their beaks, suiting each variety to feast on a different form of foodstuff. Some finches ate ground seeds, others ate cactus, 1 variety ate leaves, and 6 types ate various insects. In effect, as the generations of finches advanced, different individuals inherited characteristics that enabled them to utilize particular kinds of resources, so the environment could accommodate more finches than might survive if all had been equipped to utilize only a single food source. Darwin's observations of finches, along with his noting a similar diversity in tortoises and iguanas, led to his principle of divergence—"the modified offspring of all dominant and increasing forms tend to become adapted to many and highly diversified places in the economy of nature" (Darwin in Sulloway, 1996, p. 85).

Sulloway adopted Darwin's notions about the survival motive, natural selection, divergence, and environmental niche to interpret the influence of birth order on the personalities of siblings in human families. He depicted the family as an environment inhabited by parents and children. Parents provide nurturing resources in the form of attention, affection, praise, instruction, and such commodities as food, clothing, shelter, transportation facilities, recreational opportunities, and the like. The firstborn child is the exclusive, unchallenged recipient of these parental resources. When laterborn children appear on the scene, they are viewed as rivals for the parental affection and largesse that firstborns are not willing to share. Therefore, analogous to the situation of Darwin's finches and tortoises, the strain on family resources (parental attention) occasioned by the arrival of new siblings calls for the laterborns to find their own niches that win for them a share of parental affection and approval. In other words, laterborns are prone to become distinctively different from their firstborn siblings. However, within the family, this divergence (what Sulloway calls "niche picking") is not the automatic evolutionary function that it is in the case of finches and tortoises. Instead, divergence is heavily affected by children's observational and trial-and-error learning. While firstborn children are intentionally guarding their privileged position, laterborns are intentionally carving out their own attention-getting niches. These contrasting sibling attempts foster the development of personality differences between firstborn and laterborn offspring.

It is natural for firstborns to identify more strongly with power and authority. They arrive first in the family and employ their superior size and strength to defend their special status. Relative to their younger siblings, firstborns are more assertive, socially dominant, ambitious, jealous of their status, and defensive. As underdogs within the family system, younger siblings are inclined to question the status quo and in some cases to develop a "revolutionary personality." In the name of revolution, laterborns have repeatedly challenged the time-honored assumptions of their day. From their ranks have come the bold explorers, the iconoclasts, and the heretics of history. . . . As sibship [the number of children in the family] increases, lastborns continue to be the most radical family members. Siblings having intermediate birth ranks tend to adopt intermediate degrees of radicalism. (Sulloway, 1996, pp. xiv, 98)

Although Sulloway assigned a dominant influence to birth order, it is not birth order alone that forms personality tendencies. Rather, it is birth order in combination with such factors as gender, age, temperament, time spacing between siblings, parent-offspring conflict, and parental loss (death, separation, divorce) that "add to our ability to predict revolutionary personality," (Sulloway, 1996, p. xv). Sulloway described each of the above factors and showed how they can occur in different combinations that account for individualized personality patterns. He also contended that his linkage of birthorder and personality are found "within each of the more than twenty countries represented in my historical survey," with such differences true for both women and men (Sulloway, 1996, p. 53).

Finally, it is instructive to recognize that the idea that firstborns are conservative and laterborns are inventive did not originate with Sulloway. The notion had already been proposed by other theorists, such as the Austrian psychiatrist Alfred Adler (1927b, 1928, 1958), who suggested that

firstborns, having been "spoilt," are suddenly dethroned by the birth of a second child. This dethronement is particularly harmful when occurring before the age of 3 years. If it is successfully overcome, firstborns develop a striving to imitate their parents, to feel responsible for their sibs, and to protect others. They may develop a talent for organization. Firstborns' loss of status gives them a particular understanding of power and authority, and an admiration for the past. They may exaggerate the importance of law and order and become power-hungry conservatives. . . .

From birth, second children share parental attention with another child. . . . They are rivals par excellence. Second children often prove more talented and successful than firstborns because they exert themselves more. (Ernst & Angst, 1983, pp. 85-86)

Even though Sulloway was not the first to suggest personality differences between firstborns and laterborns, he is the one who apparently conducted the most thorough search of the literature on the subject. Whereas his conclusions may be criticized by others in this field, he can hardly be accused of failing to exercise methodological care. He reports that his model was generated and tested (a) by a meta-analysis of 196 other investigators' studies of the relationship between birth order and personality traits (emotional stability, agreeableness, conscientiousness, openness to experience) and (b) by a computerized statistical analysis of a half million items of data culled from tens of thousands of biographies across the centuries.

INNATE EMOTIONS: PRIDE AND SHAME

The focal questions: Are such emotions as pride and shame inborn, or are they learned by means of children's and adolescents' social experiences as they grow up? And if inborn, how and why did those emotions evolve to become embedded in humans' genetic endowment?

Glenn E. Weisfeld of Wayne State University adduced a line of reasoning to support the argument that certain emotions are not acquired through learning. Instead, they are basic, universal feelings built into people's genetic nature through the process of evolution. He formulated his argument as a series of "ethological principles that may be useful in identifying and analyzing emotions" (1997, p. 419).

Weisfeld's overall goal was to describe the basic behaviors of a species— particularly humans—that reflect the motives or emotions of the species' members. The collection of such descriptions is the species' *ethnogram*—an inventory of the behaviors that members of the species display in their natural habitat. To illustrate how one might go about the task of compiling such an ethnogram, he illustrated the process with the example of pride and shame. He proposed that those two types of affect are not distinctly different emotions but, rather, are the opposite ends of a pride/shame scale that permits gradations between the two extremes. He also noted that some authors conceive of guilt and shame as separate emotions. However, Weisfeld himself viewed the two as variants of the same feeling, with the pair differentiated by whether the emotion is expressed privately or publicly—guilt being the private form and shame the public variety.

In accounting for the evolutionary origins of pride and shame, Weisfeld speculated that the two were generated eons ago out of the dominant/submissive behavior in which animal species engaged—pride apparently derived from a dominant animal's exerting authority over other members of the pack, and guilt derived from the submissive behavior of members who were obliged to yield to the dominant animal's will. Pride might also reflect individuals' pleasure in faithfully fulfilling their assigned roles in the social order, with shame reflecting their chagrin at failing to execute their roles satisfactorily. In keeping with Darwinian theory, Weisfeld further suggested that emotions contribute to survival fitness. The pack or society is better suited to perpetuating itself when its members are constrained to perform complementary roles, dividing among themselves the society's labor, as in the roles of leader and follower. Pride and shame contribute to this acceptance of role differentiation.

Another principle in Weisfeld's theory is that, in order for an emotion to be considered *basic,* it must be specieswide. He concluded that pride and shame meet this standard, since there is evidence of such emotions in all societies. "In every culture, children compete for social standing from about age 2 or 3 years onward, at which time the expressions of pride and shame also emerge" (Weisfeld, 1997, p. 422).

Additional evidence of the evolutionary source of pride and shame derives from another principle: If a human emotion appears homologous with at least rudiments of that emotion in a nonhuman animal species, that human emotion probably "evolved from the animal emotion and therefore is basic" (Weisfeld, 1997, p. 429). Weisfeld cited dominant/submissive behavior observed in numerous animal species as support for his theory. Finally, because pride and shame, as basic feelings, are specieswide, they cannot be acquired through learning, that is, through modeling, practice, or instruction.

However, if pride and shame are indeed innate products of evolution, exactly what is it that develops as the child grows from infancy to adulthood? The answer is that the exact events eliciting pride and shame are determined by the values held within a culture regarding proper and improper behavior. What people acquire as they grow up are convictions about which sorts of action should elicit pride and which should elicit shame. These convictions are learnings gained from a family's childrearing practices, school instruction, a religious order's doctrines, the society's laws, and the culture's social customs. In effect, according to Weisfeld, all members of the human species—as a result of their biological inheritance—have the capacity to feel a high level of self-regard or even conceit (pride) and to feel self-deprecation and regret (shame); but the exact occasions evoking these emotions can differ across cultures, families, and even individuals as a result of people's learning experiences.

EVOLUTIONARY ROOTS OF INHIBITION

The focal questions: Do people inherit the habit of blocking out extraneous stimuli when they are trying to solve a problem, or is that something they learn from experience? Do people inherit a propensity to suppress the expression of their beliefs and feelings when such expression would seem to be unwise, or is that learned through experience? And if such tendencies are inherited, how and why did they evolve to become elements of genetic endowment?

A theory proposed by David F. Bjorklund of Florida Atlantic University and Katherine Kipp Harnishfeger of the University of Georgia is intended to explain the evolutionary origins of cognitive and behavioral inhibition. Two important functions of inhibition are those of (a) keeping a person's attention focused on the task at hand (a contribution to personal efficiency) and (b) maintaining constructive relationships among members of a group (a contribution to social efficiency).

The attention-focus function of inhibition involves

the suppression of previously activated cognitive contents or processes, the clearing of irrelevant actions or attention from consciousness, and resistance to interference from potentially attention-capturing processes or contents. . . . At a basic level, inhibitory processes control the contents of consciousness as well

as the operation of processing activities, restricting attention to only the relevant aspects of the environment and limiting processing to only those necessary for the task. (Bjorklund & Harnishfeger, 1995, p. 143)

In other words, people cannot properly perform tasks when distracted by irrelevant environmental stimuli. Inhibition is thus an essential component of attention. Among members of a species, those that can intently concentrate on
performing an activity by blocking out sources of interference (sights, sounds,
thoughts, feelings) survive more successfully—and produce more offspring to
carry their genetic line—than do members whose attention is continually diverted
by extraneous stimuli. An exception to this rule is creative behavior, which
profits from an individual's investing attention in out-of-the-ordinary stimuli and
thoughts.

The social-amity function of inhibition involves people purposely refraining
from behavior they might employ in interpersonal relations. Within such a
group as an extended family or clan or business organization, members are encouraged to suppress actions that could disrupt the smooth operation of group
ventures that promote the welfare of the group members and their genetic lines.
For example, the unbridled venting of aggressive and sexual urges within a
group can destroy the bonds of cooperation and sacrifice among members that
make their survival possible. The capacity to avoid openly expressing immediate feelings and opinions equips people to acquire the psychological strategies
that make up social intelligence. Bjorklund and Harnishfeger postulate that the
development of this capacity for social inhibition is a hominid acquisition that
evolved over the past few million years to become an important feature of the
neural structure of the modern human brain.

Basically, social intelligence is political intelligence, . . . [a sort of] Machiavellian intelligence. In hominid evolution, as social complexity increased, the
pressures to cooperate and compete with other members of the group can be seen
as the driving force of intelligence. Machiavellian intelligence requires controlling sexual, aggressive, and other "emotional" impulses, planning
(covertly) one's "moves" and anticipating the "moves" of others, and often de-
ceiving other group members in order to protect or garner important resources.
Such intelligence is obviously complex, but one necessary component of keen
social intellect is the ability to inhibit prepotent responses. (Bjorklund & Harnishfeger, 1995, p. 159)

The neural mechanisms required for intentionally suppressing stimuli and cur-
tailing urges are apparently located in the prefrontal lobe, an area of the brain
that fossil skulls suggest increased markedly from (a) the time of humans' small-
brained, bipedal australopithecine ancestors 3.5 or 4 million years ago to (b) the
first evidence of *Homo sapiens* around one million years ago. Over this period,
average skull capacity, reflecting the size of the brain beneath, advanced from
about 400 cubic centimeters to over 1,300 cubic centimeters. A significant
amount of the increase apparently occurred in the prefrontal lobe (Bjorklund &

Harnishfeger, 1995, p. 154). The notion that the control of inhibition is located in the front of the brain is supported by present-day studies of behavior changes in people who have suffered injury to the prefrontal lobe. Such individuals experience impairment of their ability to suppress impulses and intrusive stimuli.

Although the neural capacity for inhibition is already in place at birth, inhibitory skill develops during the years of childhood and adolescence as the combined result of (a) the neural system's maturing process and (b) a person's learning the how and when of inhibitory control by means of experiences with the environment. The belief that the health of neural networks is an important factor in inhibition is supported by studies of decisionmaking among people of different ages. Young children whose neural networks are in early formative stages and aged people whose networks are deteriorating have greater difficulty suppressing irrelevant stimuli during problem solving than do adolescents and younger adults whose networks are in more efficient operating shape (Bjorklund & Harnishfeger, 1995, pp. 145-146).

In conclusion, by adopting an evolutionary interpretation of inhibition, Bjorklund and Harnishfeger have been able to offer an explanation of why humans, more than any other species, (a) maintain great control over emotionally driven behavior (especially sexual behavior), (b) delay gratification for months or years in pursuit of a goal, and (c) deceive others or hide true feelings in order to gain personal advantage (1995, p. 169).

GENE-CULTURE COEVOLUTION

The focus questions: Does *human nature*, in the form of people's genetic inheritance, permit people to detect all stimuli in their environment and to interpret (assign meaning to) those stimuli in whatever way they choose? Or does inherited *human nature* restrict the stimuli people can detect and channel the ways people will interpret those stimuli? And if humans' genetic structures do constrain what people can sense and how they assign meanings to their sensations, what rules—in the form of biological and cultural conditions—govern those behaviors? Finally, can culture be passed genetically from generation to generation? If so, how does such a process operate?

Sociobiology enthusiasts Charles J. Lumsden and Edward O. Wilson of Harvard University devised a model of development they called a *gene-culture coevolution theory*. The title was intended to convey their conviction that an intrinsic link exists between biological evolution of a Darwinian form and the evolution of human culture—"a complicated, fascinating interaction in which culture is generated and shaped by biological imperatives while biological traits are simultaneously altered by genetic evolution in response to cultural innovation" (1981, p. 1). In the following brief version of the theory, I attempt to convey some principal features of the model without (a) analyzing the entire array of steps in the coevolution process or (b) including the authors' detailed mathematics that are an intimate component of their presentation. Thus, the following description is admittedly a bare-bones impression of the Lumsden-Wilson scheme, intended to convey only the authors' main concepts and line of argument. In summarizing the theory, I have taken the liberty of adding some life-like examples, analogies, and extensions that I believe are true to the model and clarify matters that Lumsden and Wilson presented in more abstract terms.

The position espoused by Lumsden and Wilson differs from the position of theorists' who assert that newborn infants are intellectually and culturally blank slates—John Locke's *tabula rasa*—onto which any sort of mental and cultural development can be etched by the environmental forces that neonates will encounter over their growing years. Instead, Lumsden and Wilson propose that what children will pay attention to and will be able to learn as they grow up has, to a considerable extent, been preselected by the biological propensities they inherited from their ancestors. The nature of those developmental predispositions can be expressed in the form of *epigenetic rules*. The "rules" are not regulations someone devised as prescriptions for how people *should* grow up. Rather, the rules are principles inherent in humans' biological composition that constrain the way people *can* and *do* develop. The expression *epigenesis* refers to the expected biologically determined growth pattern that an organism displays as it develops. The rules (a) define the biological channels or border limits within which human cultural development can occur and (b) establish the sequence and general periods of life when variants of the rules will manifest themselves. Examples of social phenomena that are thought to be particularly affected by epigenetic rules are altruism, aggressivity, emotional bonding, incest taboos, color naming, certain phobias (such as fear of snakes), territorial defense, and facial expressions.

The Lumsden-Wilson version of sociobiology appears to be founded on two core tenets:

- Social behaviors are shaped by evolution's natural-selection process. Within that process, certain characteristics (physical, mental, emotional, social) increase the survival potential of the offspring of individuals who carry genes that support behaviors which enhance survival in a given environment.
- Or, stated differently, culture consists of objects, behaviors, and beliefs shared by a group's members, but not everyone in the group will display precisely same pattern of those cultural characteristics. As environmental conditions change, individuals whose cultural pattern best fits them to prosper under the changed circumstances will survive in greater numbers than will other individuals; and those survivors' genetic tendency (genotype) will be reproduced in their offspring. Hence, the favorable cultural features of the survivors, as now reflected in their genetic potential,

will be carried into future generations. In this way, culture influences people's biological makeup and their social behavior over the ages.

With these tenets in hand, we next consider the way Lumsden and Wilson talk about culture.

Culturgens

In gene-culture theory, the components of culture are called *culturgens*.

> A culturgen [pronounced <u>cul</u>-*tur-jen*] is a relatively homogeneous set of artifacts, behaviors, or mentifacts (mental constructions having little or no direct correspondence with reality) that either share without exception one or more attribute states selected for their functional importance or at least share a consistently recurrent range of such attribute states within a polythetic set. (Lumsden & Wilson, 1981, p. 27)

As implied in this definition, the authors propose that any particular group's culture consists of physical objects (artifacts), of ways of acting (behaviors), and of concepts, beliefs, and emotions (mentifacts) held in common by members of the group. Typical *artifacts* that distinguish one culture from another are types of housing, dress, food, furniture, modes of transportation, communication media, tools, weaponry, work sites, and recreation sites. *Behaviors* typical of a culture include language patterns, rituals, and modes of social interaction deemed suitable for sustaining family members' relationships, settling disputes, selecting leaders, satisfying sexual urges, and more. *Mentifacts* can include beliefs (religious convictions, values, notions of cause and effect, historical events) and expressed emotions (grief, joy, shame).

Within a given group of people, culturgens are assigned labels that enable members of the group to understand which specific artifacts, behaviors, or mentifacts comprise a given culturgen. In effect, each culturgen is a concept created by abstracting selected characteristics shared by individual artifacts, behaviors, or mentifacts, with an identification label applied to the group. Hence, in the realm of artifacts, the labels *auto, ax, cup, computer, farm implement,* and *sword* identify six sets of material objects, with the objects included in each set sharing a particular array of characteristics with the other members of that set. Most attributes that exemplify *ax* are obviously different from those that exemplify *auto* and *computer*. And features that typify *ax* are not the same as those that typify *sword*, although these two culturgens do share certain characteristics, such as construction material (sharp metal blade) and function (cutting instrument). The labels *god, fairness, mind, cause, human rights,* and *governing power* are applied to collections of mentifacts that are linked together by particular attributes, with those attributes often differing from one culture to another.

To qualify as a culturgen in the Lumsden-Wilson scheme, one or more functions served by members of a set—as in sets labeled *horse, speak,* and *justice*—must be included among the attributes used in defining those culturgens. *Horse* includes a transportation function, *speak* serves a communication function, and *justice* fulfills a societal-stabilizing role.

Keeping in mind the authors' notion of culturgens as the components of culture, we turn to the theorists' epigenetic rules.

Epigenetic Rules

The key element in the theory of gene-culture coevolution is the role of the epigenetic rules in culturgen choice. . . . Epigenesis is the total process of interaction between genes and the environment during the course of development, with the genes being expressed through epigenetic rules. Each epigenetic rule affecting behavior comprises one or more elements of a complex sequence of events occurring at various sites throughout the nervous system. It is useful to divide these elements into two classes: primary epigenetic rules, which range from sensory filtering to perception; and secondary epigenetic rules, which include the procedures of feature evaluation and decision making through which individuals are predisposed to transmit certain culturgens in preference to others. Many, perhaps most, categories of cognition and overt behavior are channeled by a combination of the two classes of rules. (Lumsden & Wilson, 1981, pp. 35, 52)

To explain the relationship that gene-culture theory posits between the rules and the human information-processing system, I find it convenient to liken Lumsden and Wilson's version of information processing to a communication route that advances through a sequence of stations, beginning with the person detecting stimuli in the environment and ending with the person acting on the environment (Figure 2-1). The rules identify how biological conditions determine (a) which kinds of messages each station can accept, (b) how a station modifies a message, and (c) how long a station can retain a message before either losing it or sending it on to the next station.

Although the information-processing route in Figure 2-1 appears to be a one-way street, in actual operation it's a two-way thoroughfare, with messages from later stations along the route often sent back to earlier stations. How this happens can be illustrated by our identifying key functions that each station is assumed to perform.

1. At the beginning of the route, the senses (sight, hearing, touch, taste, smell, and more) detect features of the environment. However, the senses do not operate unselectively. Whereas all light waves and all sound waves within the detectable environment strike the eyes and ears, only a segment of those received features are sent on to the next station. In effect, the received impressions are modified somewhat at the sensory station. Often— perhaps always—this modification is determined at least partially by instructions derived from long-term memory, instructions evoked by some psychological or biological need or drive. Thus, a famished adolescent selects from the scan of environmental sights and sounds those objects that past experi-

Figure 2-1

A Simplified Information-Processing Model

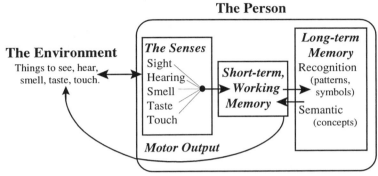

ence suggests will satisfy hunger. The scanned impression on the sense organ is held only momentarily—decaying in 250 to 500 milliseconds for sight (iconic memory) and in 3 to 4 seconds for hearing (echoic memory) (Lumsden & Wilson, 1981, p. 59). This process of selectively receiving environmental input is typically referred to as *sensation.*

2. The modified stimulus (now in the form of an electrochemical code) that derives from one sense modality—the eyes—combines with the codes from other modalities (ears, olfactory bulbs, pressure sensors in the skin) to form a multifaceted message that is sent to the short-term, working-memory station.

3. The expression *short-term* signifies that information is held at this point quite briefly and in small amounts. For most adults, the amount of information, in the form of *chunks* of data that can be "kept in mind" at one time, is no more than seven—such as a seven-digit telephone number—before the information decays. *Working* signifies that the process of manipulating information from the senses and from long-term memory occurs at this juncture. This is where *thinking* and *decisionmaking* are believed to take place. Here the combined code from the senses is compared to codes already held in long-term memory to provide an interpretation of what the received message means in relation to past experiences that are stored as memories. This interpretive act is usually labeled *perception.* Apparently, the contents of short-term memory are scanned within a single second.

4. Unless the ephemeral contents of short-term memory are promptly transferred into long-term memory, they are lost. Long-term memory can retain very large amounts of information for perhaps an unlimited period of time.

In Lumsden and Wilson's scheme, long-term memories are of two types—recognition and semantic. Recognition memory is concerned with identifying patterns (a particular person's facial features, the configuration of a house or car) and interpreting symbols (words on a page, traffic signs). Semantic memory involves analyzing the associations among symbols to produce concepts, with the term *concept* referring to a selection of qualities shared by a set of symbols (illustrative concepts can be *computer, printing, square, child, tallest, marriage, alive, speed*). In the process of working memory's comparing coded environmental stimuli with contents of long-term memory in order to assign meaning to the stimuli, a decision may be reached that the relevant contents of long-term memory should be altered. In other words, new stimuli may cause people to "learn something" and thereby "change their minds." Lumsden and Wilson propose that the process of modifying a chunk of recognition memory can require from 5 to 10 seconds, whereas altering a concept in semantic memory takes a single second (1981, p. 59).

In summary, environmental stimuli are detected by a person's sensory system, electrochemically coded, sent along the communication route, and altered on the way. How that process is carried out is determined by both (a) the biological constraints of the sensory system and the biologically fashioned treatment applied at the stations along the neural communication route and (b) the existing contents of long-term memory, which are the results of past experiences. To a great extent, those experiences are products of the particular culture (its opportunities, behavior patterns, rewards, punishments) in which the person has been reared. Such biological constraints on human cognition involve both *mode* and *time*. I use *mode* to mean the sort of treatment applied to an incoming message at each station along the communication route (the form of the received message, how it is altered, and how it is sent along) and *time* to mean how long it takes to process the message at each station.

With this cursory sketch of an envisioned information-processing system in hand, we next consider in greater detail how the epigenetic rules constrain the operation of the system at the stations along the route. As noted earlier, the epigenetic rules form two groups: primary and secondary. The primary rules concern the segment of the communication route from (a) sensory detection of environmental stimuli (the senses) through (b) short-term, working memory. The secondary rules concern the stations from (a) short-term memory through (b) motor output—that is, through a person's taking action based on decisions that were made during the interaction of short-term memory with the contents of long-term memory.

Primary rules

It's not possible to specify all of the primary rules that affect people's social behavior, because the discovery of rules (in the sense of biological conditions that influence social development) is yet in an early stage of investigation. Hence, the best that Lumsden and Wilson could do has been to illustrate the nature of several rules which enjoy the support of empirical evidence.

The analysis of typical primary rules involves the first series of stations in the information-processing route—from the senses to short-term memory. Two methods of estimating the influence of combined biological/cultural constraints on people's perceptions of their environments are those of (a) examining the similarities across cultures in the ways people sense and interpret stimuli and (b) recording how individuals change in their perceptions from the time of birth through subsequent years.

The epigenetic constraints on how humans process stimuli differ from one sense modality to another. Such differences can be demonstrated with sight and hearing.

One frequently studied visual phenomenon is people's perception of colors. Berlin and Kay (1969) had native speakers of 20 of the world's languages classify by name the items in arrays of color chips. The results showed that the names people applied fell largely into discrete clusters that approximated the same principal hues distinguished by infants—yellows, greens, blues, and reds—thereby suggesting a common evolutionary foundation among humans for color recognition. Furthermore, a given culture tended to fall into one of five sets of hue classifications that ranged from a very rudimentary set (distinguishing only black and white) to a far more complex set (distinguishing black, white, red, green, yellow, blue). Three other sets of intermediate complexity lay between those two extremes. This sequence of five sets, representing steps of increasing complexity, matched the order in which young children acquire color terms as they grow up. Such results could be interpreted as support for a gene-culture coevolution theory which proposes that social behaviors—such as color naming—are fashioned by people's biological characteristics in combination with cultural learnings passed down the generations to equip a population of individuals to survive in the particular environment they inhabit.

Included in the auditory equipment that infants bring to their world are innate rules of speech perception "that are adult-like and facilitate the development of language" (Lumsden & Wilson, 1981, p. 49). Although variations in pitch, like variations in hue, are perceived as a continuum, distinctions of human voicing— in a fashion similar to distinctions among hues—are automatically classified into categories that represent the phonemes of speech. For instance, sounds that range between /ba/ and /ga/ or between /s/ and /v/ are not heard as gradations along a continuum but, instead, are heard as one or the other of the particular pair (Lumsden & Wilson, 1981, p. 50). Thus, over the ages, humans' biological aural equipment has apparently been influenced by the cultural development of spoken language to produce a gene-culture coevolved propensity for people to categorize voice sounds into phonemes that typify a culture's speech sounds.

Secondary rules

As noted earlier, the secondary rules concern that portion of the information-processing route that involves transactions between short-term and long-term memory, transactions conducted by means of thinking processes or mental habits that promote survival. Lumsden and Wilson (1981, p. 56) suggest that cultural anthropologists usually believe people's thought strategies (schemes for drawing inferences and making decisions) are ones devised in a particular culture in the past and conveyed from one generation to the next by teaching and modeling. But Lumsden and Wilson disagree. Citing evidence from cognitive and developmental psychology, they propose that individuals do not acquire strategies of thought through cultural instruction and modeling, that is, through filling an open mind with thought strategies taught them by their elders.   Rather, the authors believe that innate epigenetic rules channel the acquisition of inference and decisionmaking methods to a substantial degree.   In other words, people are constrained by their gene-culture inheritance to think in particular ways that have proven over thousands of past generations to promote survival in encounters with typical varieties of environments.

From studies of behavior in various cultures, Lumsden and Wilson have abstracted principles that guide the evolution of epigenetic rules. Two such principles are those of *transparency* and *parsimony*.

The transparency principle. "The more the effect of genetic fitness of a category of behavior depends on environmental circumstances, the more clearly the conscious mind perceives that relation and the more flexible the response" (Lumsden & Wilson, 1981, p. 70). Over the ages, some sorts of behavior have proven so crucial to perpetuating a person's genetic line—no matter what the environmental circumstances—that engaging in such behaviors requires no elaborate conscious decisionmaking. Through the process of evolution, those actions have become genetically based elements of "human nature." Examples of automatic, unconscious human acts include the generation of deep grammar (consistent, rapid sentence production), incest avoidance (to reduce the chance of producing flawed offspring through inbreeding), and the consumption of sugar (very high caloric intake). In contrast, other sorts of behavior—if they are to promote genetic fitness—cannot be inborn and automatic, because their suitability is so strongly affected by environmental circumstances. This means that the choice of which action among a variety of options will be the wisest for the survival of the individual and the genetic line is not automatic.   Instead, the choice requires the conscious analysis of environmental conditions if a wise decision is to be reached. An example is economic behavior, which calls for choices among culturgens, such as occupations in complex societies, and for decisions about investing time, energy, and resources in the production and consumption of various kinds of goods and services. Whereas the economic activities of honey bees and ants are determined by their genetic structures, the economic activities of humans are not. Genetically, human economic-behavior potential is highly flexible. For people, the best economic option in one environment will not be the best in another. Deciding how to invest one's efforts in providing food and shelter in an Amazon jungle or on a small South Seas coral island requires different considerations and conscious analysis than doing so in New York City or in a village on the edge of the Arctic Circle. In sum, Lumsden-Wilson contend that, over thousands of past generations, epigenetic rules governing people's selection among different culturgens have been generated in keeping with the transparency principle. That is, context-free behaviors have become unconscious, automatic acts dictated by people's genetic endowment, while behaviors whose contribution to survival depends heavily on features of the environment are selected according to epigenetic rules that equip individuals to consciously estimate the likely influence of those features on survival and thus arrive at a decision about how to act.

The parsimony principle. "Epigenetic rules evolve until they achieve the least sufficient degree of selectivity" (Lumsden & Wilson, 1981, p. 71). In other words, the evolutionary process generates rules in a manner intended to get the most service out of the least expenditure of energy and the least complexity needed to get the job done. For instance, decision-making energy is conserved when behaviors that are essentially context free (such as the process of generating sentence structures) are embedded in people's genetic constitution as automatic, nonconscious actions. Likewise, energy is conserved when context-dependent behaviors that require conscious analysis of culturgens can be guided by a frugal, efficient decision-making process. Frugality and efficiency are fostered by the evolution of efficient thought processes over the ages.

One such process is *chunking.* In the human information-processing system, two conditions mentioned earlier seriously curtail the efficiency of transactions between short-term memory and long-term memory: (a) short-term memory is able to handle no more than seven (plus or minus two) chunks of information at a time while (b) no less than 5 to 10 seconds of neuronal processing time are needed for entering into long-term memory the symbols necessary to interpret a new item composed of familiar elements of information (Lumsden & Wilson, 1981, p. 62). In effect, it takes a relatively long time for short-term memory to place a small amount of information in long-term memory. However, the evolutionary process has developed chunking as a device to help cope with these biologically limiting features. A *chunk* is one of those seven pieces of information that short-term memory can simultaneously accommodate. But fortunately, a single chunk can represent more than a single fragment of information about the environment—more than such single items as *Dad's gold watch* or *our cat.* Instead, a chunk can be in the form of a concept or a process that encompasses a host of specific information. For an expert auto mechanic, the concept (as a single chunk) called *V-8 engine* is packed full of complex meanings—everything the mechanic knows about such engines. Likewise, for a well-informed statistician, the expression *factor analysis* can be a single chunk representing all steps needed for computing and interpreting factor analyses. Therefore, people whose arsenal of knowledge includes complex concepts and processes (each concept or process combined into a single chunk) are able to engage in efficient, sophisticated negotiations between short-term memory and long-term memory, even under the *7-chunk-and-5-to-10-second* restriction. Therefore, one reason that individuals become equipped to think more efficiently as they progress through childhood and adolescence into adulthood is that, by means of the learning process, they have compiled an ever-expanding collection of complexly chunked concepts and processes.

Chunking represents only one of the mental strategies that Lumsden and Wilson believe have been generated during gene-culture coevolution to enhance people's survival fitness. A further strategy is a form of *fuzzy logic* that contributes to the ease of making judgments. Another is a type of *cognitive algebra* people automatically employ in weighing advantages and disadvantages of options during decisionmaking.

Summary

As illustrated in our cursory description of the Lumsden-Wilson model, gene-culture-coevolution theory is founded on the following propositions:

- The principal features of each person's biological being are dictated by genes inherited from the person's parents.
- Humans inhabit very diverse environments, with one environment placing different demands on individuals' ability to survive than do other environments. A group's culture consists of the kinds of human survival equipment (artifacts, behaviors, mentifacts) suited to the physical and social requirements of a particular environment and shared among the environment's inhabitants. The label *culturgen* designates any specific cultural artifact, behavior, or mentifact.
- Some people's genetic potential (genotype) equips them more adequately than other people's for creating or adopting particular culturgens. People whose genetic potential prepares them to acquire culturgens that are well suited for survival in a particular environment will produce more viable offspring than do people whose genetic nature does not prepare them as well. Thus, the genetic propensity of the better survivors will be reproduced in greater amounts in later generations than will the poorer survivors' genetic composition. In this way, genetic material supporting the adoption of certain culturgens will be perpetuated into the future. Through such a process, culture affects biological transmission and behavior across the ages.

- The term *epigenetic rules* refers to the patterning of conditions in the human information-processing system that influence kinds of social behavior affected by the gene-culture coevolution process. The rules help explain the evolutionary origins of—and genetic involvement in—such social acts as incest avoidance, altruism, aggression, fear of strangers, and more.

REMAINING CHALLENGES

From the descriptions of this chapter's four theories, we can infer yet-unanswered questions that warrant attention in the future.

As explained earlier, the dominant theme of Sulloway's analysis was that the order in which children are born into a family is a significant indicator of whether those children will become (a) conservative, assertive, socially dominant, ambitious, jealous of their status, and defensive rather than (b) rebellious, inventive, and iconoclastic. In Sulloway's view, firstborns become conservative, assertive, and defensive, whereas laterborns become rebellious and inventive. The later an individual appears in a given family's succession of offspring, the more rebellious and creative that person will be. Because Sulloway focused so much attention on birth order as an influence in personality development, it is easy to overlook the fact that he believed people's personalities resulted, not simply from birth order, but rather from the confluence of a variety of factors that interact with birth order, such as gender, age, temperament, time spacing between siblings, parent-offspring conflict, and parental loss (death, separation, divorce) that "add to our ability to predict revolutionary personality" (Sulloway, 1996, p. xv). But his treatment of the interrelationships of the multiple factors was no more than sketchy. What now appears needed is a more sophisticated form of the theory that clarifies the postulated interactions by assigning degrees of power to different factors in their determining personality traits under various environmental conditions and during various stages of life.

In Weisfeld's theory of the evolution of human emotions, he illustrated his proposal with the emotions of pride, shame, and guilt. A further advance beyond Weisfeld's formulation would be to extend his general model to encompass other emotions—joy, hate, contentment, anger, frustration, euphoria, despondency, and more. The extension would be designed to show how and why each type of emotion could evolve from individuals' attempts to foster the survival of the species' genetic line.

Bjorklund and Harnishfeger proposed an evolutionary theory of inhibition, a scheme intended to explain inhibitory behavior's contribution to individuals' and species' survival and well-being. Observations in everyday life show that people can vary markedly in their ability to inhibit their actions. In social situations some people are prone to "hold their tongue," whereas others seem compelled to "shoot off their mouth." Some children are adept at shutting out irrelevant stimuli while performing a task, while others are continually distracted by intrusive events and become diagnosed as suffering from *attention deficit disorder*.

Most people in a society are able to inhibit their sex impulses enough to express those impulses in only a socially acceptable fashion, whereas others—child molesters, rapists, sexual harassers—seem unable to do so. Therefore, a question can be asked about what combination of inherited inhibitory skill and of environmental experience produces the pattern of a particular person's inhibitory behavior. Stated differently, at successive stages of the lifespan, how do genetic and other biological factors (hormone secretions, brain circuitry, nutrition) interact with the person's experiential history to determine (a) how well the person shuts out extraneous stimuli during problem solving and (b) how well the person withholds potential comments and actions in social situations? Furthermore, what criteria are appropriate to use in judging whether inhibition in a social situation has contributed to an individual's welfare in such social situations as (a) a witness being interrogated by an attorney in a murder trial, (b) a junior-high school student being pressed to reveal who tossed the cherry bomb into the lavatory toilet, and (c) a mother asking her 17-year-old daughter why she was not home from a date until after 3:00 a.m.?

A key feature of Lumsden and Wilson's gene-culture coevolution theory is their set of epigenetic rules, which are survival-enhancing functions built into the human information-processing system by past interactions between (a) the species' genetically determined biological nature and (b) environmental changes that threatened the species' survival. So far, Lumsden and Wilson have been able to identify only a few of the rules. More are apparently yet to be discovered. Finding those additional rules is thus a challenge for the future. Furthermore, the development of epigenetic rules appears to be affected by particular principles. Three principles posited by Lumsden-Wilson are those of transparency, parsimony, and chunking. Discovering more such principles is a further item for the sociobiologist's agenda.

The Lumsden-Wilson scheme also includes the notion of culturgens (artifacts, behaviors, mentifacts), which are the methods and materials a group of people have adopted to cope with their physical and social settings. The fact that the world's cultures differ from each other in so many ways suggests that the highly diverse environmental settings which peoples have inhabited over eons of time have encouraged the adoption of very different culturgens by groups living in significantly different settings. So, an additional challenge for theorists is that of explaining how genetic endowment interacting with environmental change has produced the particular culturgens that typify a particular culture.

3

Connectionism and Dynamic Systems

Neither *connectionism* nor *dynamic systems* identifies a single theory but, rather, each term refers to a cluster of theories. Dynamic-systems theories are attempts to describe the flow of relationships among the components of some *whole phenomenon,* such as the solar system, the actions of a steel spring, or the behavior of a child. Connectionism could be considered a subvariety of dynamic systems that is aimed at solving the age-old mind/brain mystery. That mystery is reflected in the questions: When people have thoughts, feelings, memories, plans, hopes, and dreams going on in their minds, what exactly is happening in their brains? In other words, what sorts of electrochemical activities among the neurons of the brain accompany different sorts of thinking? How and why do changes develop in the mind/brain throughout the lifespan?

What dynamic-systems advocates and connectionists are trying to do about those questions can perhaps most easily be explained by (a) noting what people usually mean when they speak of *mind,* (b) reviewing some characteristics of the brain, (c) comparing the *classical cognitive science* theories, launched in the 1950s, with the connectionism of the 1980s and 1990s, (d) illustrating a few of the proposals that typical advocates of dynamic systems and connectionism have offered in their attempts to clarify human development, (e) sketching key developments in brain neurology during the first two decades of life, and (f) suggesting further questions that call for answers in the years ahead.

CHARACTERISTICS OF MIND

Mind is obviously an unseeable psychological construct, not a palpable biological entity like *brain.* Even though *mind* cannot be seen, heard, or touched, people know what it is by dint of introspection. They not only recognize that activities "go in their heads," but they can identify many, if not all, of mind's assumed functions that bear such labels as *perceiving, identifying, judging, analyzing, interpreting, remembering, forgetting, knowing, believing, doubting, listing, suggesting, expecting, hoping, fearing, creating, planning,* and far more. Although behaviorist John B. Watson in the early decades of the 20th century denied mind's existence, his claim was so at odds with people's experience that very few took him seriously. Hence, our question is not whether there is such an invisible thing as *mind* but, rather, what is mind's relationship to that very tangible object, *brain.*

BRAIN STRUCTURE AND OPERATION

The human brain is composed of a great many cells—Kelso (1995, p. 44) suggests 100 trillion or 10^{14}—that are divided between two main types: *neurons* and *glia,* with far more glia (after the Greek word for *glue*) than neurons. From the standpoint of cognition, neurons are much the more important, for they are the ones that do our mental work. Glia serve connective and protective roles, keeping neurons in place and safe. The exact number of neurons in the brain is a matter of much dispute, with different authors proposing radically different quantities. Estimates range from 10 billon (Erulkar, 1994, p. 786), to 50 billion (Kolb & Whishaw, 1990), to "about 100 billion, give or take a few hundred million" (Baer, Connors, & Paradiso, 1996, p. 23), to "one trillion neurons present in the adult brain" (Noback, 1994, p. 803). The neurons that most actively participate in thinking are located in the cerebral cortex, which is the outer layer of the brain that looks rather like a large, soft, gray walnut kernel, with convoluted folds composed of infinitesimally tiny neuron cells.

It is generally accepted that the neuron is the key operating unit of mental activity. Although neurons can vary markedly in size and in the complexity of certain of their components, all share the same basic structure—(a) a central body or headquarters (*soma*) that contains a nucleus, (b) an *axon* that extends like a long arm to conduct signals from the soma out to other neurons, and (c) numerous (from a few to many dozens) shorter arms (*dendrites*) that receive signals from other neurons and conduct those signals to the headquarters (Figure 3-1). Most neurons send signals to each other across extremely short gaps called *synapses*—or *synaptic clefts*—by means of chemical *neurotransmitters* that induce an electrical charge in the receiving neuron. In fewer instances, signals are sent as electrical impulses over a diminutive *gap junction*, a protein channel that serves as a synaptic bridge (three-billionths of a meter long) connecting adjacent neurons.

> [However,] increasing evidence suggests that neurons can communicate without making intimate contact at synapses. Rather than information flowing along structured pathways like electricity flowing along wires in a circuit, such communication, called *volume transmission,* is more like a radio broadcast where signals traveling through the air can be detected by suitably attuned receivers. (Kelso, 1995, p. 231)

Figure 3-1

Simplified Schematic Version of Neuron Structure

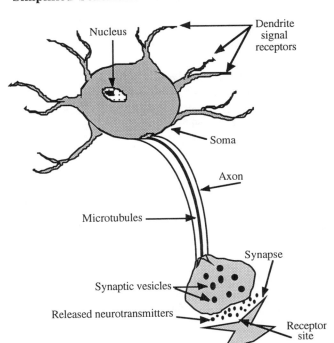

Although only one axon terminal is pictured in the generic version of neuron structure in Figure 3-1, axons typically have multiple terminals which can form synaptic connections with target neurons. Hence, a single neuron in the brain may have many synapses with many other neurons. Kelso (1995, p. 5) estimates that each neuron can have up to 10,000 (10^4) connections with other neurons and "50 plus neurotransmitters (chemicals that are necessary for the neurons to work)." A signal passing from one neuron to another is called *firing*. Neural impulses fire at prodigious speeds, sometimes several hundred signals per second. Whether a neuron will fire (induce an electrical charge in another neuron) is governed by the interaction of two sorts of chemical conditions in the initial neuron; one sort promotes firing and the other sort inhibits firing.

The traditional view of dendritic function presumes that only axons conduct nerve impulses and only dendrites receive them, but it has been shown that dendrites can form synapses with dendrites and that axons and even somata can receive impulses. Indeed, some neurons have no axon; in these cases nervous transmission is carried out by the dendrites. (Erulkar, 1994, p. 787)

From a neurobiological perspective, it is generally assumed that cognitive behavior involves the firing of different complexes of neurons that have become associated with each other as a result of the patterns of excitation and inhibition that developed among them. Thus, a cognitive act—a thought, an emotion, an intended movement—consists of the firing of the neurons that form a particular neuron network. It is also assumed that the determination of which neurons come to participate in a given network can be influenced by people's experiences with the environments they inhabit. In effect, *learning* consists of neuron networks being formed and strengthened as a consequence of experience. *Forgetting* can result from networks being weakened, broken, or their patterns distorted, either through physical or electrochemical disturbances of the neurons or through experiences that disrupt established network patterns, such experiences as a newly introduced belief or skill that conflicts with an established one or as a person receiving punishment for a behavior.

Although this gross view of mind/brain relationships seems widely adopted, the specific nature of networks and how they are formed continues to be a matter of much controversy. As a consequence, the game of mind/brain theorizing continues in a state of great ferment, with dynamic-systems proponents and connectionists currently among the most active players. Because dynamic-systems models and connectionism are partially a reaction to—and an attempted correction of—information-processing theories of the 1950s and beyond, it's useful to begin the presentation of dynamic systems and connectionism with a review of some key features of those earlier theories.

CLASSICAL COGNITIVE SCIENCE

The terms *classical cognitive science, artificial intelligence,* and *computational models* are applied to schemes invented since the 1950s that view the operation of powerful electronic computers as an accurate analogue of human thought processes. If computers can be programmed to make the same sorts of decisions that people make, then it seems reasonable to conclude that understanding how computers function can contribute to understanding how people think. Of course, it's possible that a person's brain and a computer could produce an identical solution to a problem, yet arrive at the solution by different means. Thus, understanding the computer's operations would not necessarily mean understanding the brain's operations. But then again, maybe the computer and brain do work the same way, so using the computer comparison could, indeed, help explain the mind/brain connection.

As noted in Chapters 1 and 2, the classical analogy drawn between computers and people involves assuming three stages in the way information is processed—(a) input, (b) throughput, and (c) output. In the case of the computer, the *input* stage consists of someone putting data into the computer by means of a keyboard, microphone, magnetic tape, or the like. *Throughput* concerns the computer's inner workings as determined by the machine's hardware (permanent wires and programmed silicon chips) and software (temporary directions telling the hardware how to manipulate data). *Output* consists of displaying the results of the data-manipulation on a screen, printing the results on paper, expressing the outcome in the form of sounds (simulated voices, music), or sending the results to someone else's computer via telephone lines. This process of progressing from input to throughput to output has been referred to as a *linear causation process*, with prior causal factors producing later effects.

In the case of the person, the *input* stage involves the person acquiring stimuli from the environment via such sense organs as the eyes, ears, taste buds, olfactory nerves, and pressure receptors in the skin. The *throughput* function takes place within the person's body, primarily in the nervous system, with the brain playing a particularly important role. Throughput involves the person interpreting the environmental stimuli and determining what response, if any, should be made. *Output* consists of overt responses—talking, running, ducking, laughing, typing on a keyboard, lying down, eating, or an almost infinite variety of other behaviors.

Advocates of classical cognitive science typically subscribe to some or all of the following assumptions about human thinking (van Gelder, 1995, pp. 232-233).

- *Representations.* People have in mind *representations* in the form of symbols that serve as images, signs, and mappings of the realm the people are thinking about. The representations include a person's current perceptions of the environment as well as that individual's long-term knowledge (memories).
- *Computation.* Cognitive processes involve mentally maneuvering representations according to rules and procedures. Hence, thinking is "rule-governed symbol manipulation" (Horgan & Tienson, 1996, pp. 3-4). For example, one important class of rules is that of conditional assertions. These are *if-then* statements. The *if* (or *when*) part describes the conditions of a situation. The *then* part tells the consequences—what to expect or what to do— when particular conditions obtain. Both the *if* and *then* segments can be quite simple or quite complex. Consider three conditional statements that might be in the mind of a police officer who is directing traffic at the intersection of Main Street and Cross Road:

    1. "If no cars are approaching on Cross Road (*A*), then don't stop cars that are coming along Main Street—let them pass (*X*)."
        The rule: If A is absent, then do X.
    2. "If cars on Cross Road have been stopped for as long as a minute (*M*), but there are still cars approaching along Main Street (*C*), then stop those on Main Street (*Y*) and let the ones on Cross Road pass (*Z*)."

The rule: If M and C, then do Y and Z.

3. "Whenever you hear an emergency vehicle's siren (*S*) approaching (*A*), direct cars on both Main Street and Cross Road to stop (*D*) until the emergency vehicle has passed (*P*). Then direct the cars that are in the longer row—whether on Main Street or on Cross Road—to pass (*G*) while those in the shorter row are directed to remain stopped (*N*). But whenever an emergency vehicle's siren (*S*) is receding (*R*) into the distance, do not stop all cars that are approaching your intersection (*K*). Instead, continue to direct traffic in a routine manner (*M*)."

The rule: When S + A, do D + P; then do G + N. But when S + R, do K + M.

- *Serial processing.* Rules and procedures are applied in a serial fashion. As an example of a serial procedure, the arithmetical process for doing long division consists of a sequence of steps—an algorithm—that a person applies to arrive at an answer.
- *Central processing unit.* A central headquarters directs the operation of the entire input-throughput-output system.
- *Self containment.* The throughput segment of cognition forms a world of its own. That is, after stimuli from the environment have been transformed into symbols in the mind, the manipulation of those symbolic representations proceeds entirely within the cognitive system, independent of the environment.

There is little doubt that classical cognitive science, with its computational version of artificial intelligence, has achieved remarkable success in creating machines that perform many of people's thinking feats with great efficiency. Modern-day computers calculate extremely complex sets of symbols at great speed and without error. For example, the first two mental operations of our hypothetical traffic officer are now routinely performed by computers attached to traffic lights. Sensors embedded in the roadway inform the computer of oncoming autos, and a set of rules programmed into the computer produce decisions that govern when a traffic light will turn red, yellow, or green. In addition, it would be possible to computerize the third of the officer's decisions, the one involving an emergency vehicle's siren. However, the complexity of such a system would be so great (requiring audio sensors that distinguished [a] siren sounds from other sounds and [b] approaching sirens from receding ones) that the cost would not be worth the benefit. It's more practical to expect auto drivers to have enough sense to stop when they hear an approaching siren.

Since the 1960s, applications of artificial intelligence have obviously changed many aspects of daily life, particularly in advanced industrialized societies. Computers now make decisions formerly made by clerks at the checkout counter of supermarkets, by mechanics diagnosing the malfunctions of automobiles, by welders in auto assembly plants, by bank employees, by airline ticket sellers, and by scores of other workers. Computers programmed to play chess are able to defeat all human opponents except, perhaps, the occasional grand master. In effect, by the latter 1970s it had become quite clear that machines could be programmed to imitate many of the routine thought processes in which people engage. But did this mean that all human thinking consists of manipulating symbols according to rules, so that people's brains are, indeed, high-powered computational devices? Apparently not. Theorists' early euphoria over the likelihood that they had found the key to the mind/brain problem was dampened in the 1980s by some intractable problems. Some ways that people think could not be duplicated by a computer governed by programmed rules, and there were discrepancies between the structure and functioning of computers and the structure and functioning of brains.

> Digital computers are programmed from outside; are structurally programmable; have low adaptability; and work by discrete dynamics. . . . Brains are self-organizing devices; they are structurally nonprogrammable; they work by both discrete and continuous dynamics; their functions depend strongly on the physical (i.e., biological) substrate; the processing is parallel; and processing occurs for both network and intraneuronal information. (Arbib, Érdi, & Szentágothai, 1998, p. 340)

Consider, for example, the difficulty of trying to generate and apply computational rules that account for the pattern of cognitive activity involved in a person's shopping for a new car.

> A young woman enters an automobile dealer's showroom with an idea in mind about features she desires in a new car and about the conditions of purchase she prefers. She wants a light blue, two-door, sporty-looking convertible with enough leg room in the back seat for an average-size adult. She also wants an AM-FM radio with tape and compact-disc players. As for the purchase conditions, she has in mind an upper limit on price, and she would like to pay for the car over a 24-month period at a low rate of interest. When she explains her desires to a salesman, he says he has no new light blue convertible available but shows her a dark blue one—"It's last year's model and was used as a demonstrator so it has some mileage on it, but it's in great shape and we can give you a good deal on it." However, the interest rate he quotes for financing the car is higher than the woman had hoped, there doesn't seem to be much leg room in the back seat, and there's no compact-disc player. The price he quotes is well below her upper-limit cost, so she could save money if she bought that car. While she ponders the salesman's offer, her boyfriend arrives and suggests that she visit other auto dealers before she makes a decision, because she might find a car elsewhere that better meets her expectations. But the salesman says he can lower the price on this car if she decides to take it today. Otherwise, if she returns in a few days or few weeks and wants the car, it might have been sold to someone else.

As this scene suggests, the woman's cognitive activity consists of a flow of shifting thoughts as she views the available cars, interacts with the salesman and her boyfriend, and simultaneously weighs the diverse considerations that she originally had in mind. The challenge faced by a computer programmer is that of writing a program which models such a pattern of thinking (providing rules governing the interaction of unpredictable, fortuitous considerations) and that calculates the flowing status of thought as each new factor is introduced. That challenge is apparently beyond the capabilities of programmers. Hence, such a computer analogy does not seem to represent the kind of cognitive activity illustrated in the scene at the auto dealership.

Tim van Gelder has proposed that four factors combined in the 1980s and 1990s to direct some scientists' attention away from classical theories to the promise of a *dynamic-systems* paradigm and its *dynamical modeling* for explaining the brain/mind relationship.

> First, there was increasing dissatisfaction with the computational framework as it applied to certain aspects of cognition. Second, there was suddenly available a vast range of new concepts and tools from the rapidly developing mathematical field of nonlinear dynamics. Third, computer technology had become so widely available that detailed simulation of complex dynamical systems was a realistic possibility for many researchers. Fourth, neuroscientists' knowledge of neurons and neural networks had increased to the point where it was increasingly feasible to produce dynamical models of neural process, in more or less idealized forms, and neuroscience constituted an increasingly rich source of ideas for producing dynamical models. The result of these and perhaps other factors was the well-known emergence of dynamical modeling of cognition in the form of connectionism. (van Gelder, 1995, p. 231)

DYNAMIC SYSTEMS AND CONNECTIONISM

The term *dynamic-systems perspective* refers to a class of theories that share the following postulates.

- *Systems.* The expression *system,* as used throughout the following discussion, refers to an explanation of how some outcome—such as human development—is the result of (1) components, (2) a pattern of relationships among components, and (3) processes by which the components' interactions produce (4) the outcome. Every system has boundaries that define (a) which things are components of the system and (b) which are not, either by specific exclusion or simply by omission. Frequently, a component within a system is, itself, a subsystem with its own components and their interactions. For example, the human circulatory system (with such components as the heart, blood vessels, lungs, and kidneys) is a subsystem within the overall biological system that composes the unitary person. How and why people develop as they do is explained by changes in the integrated system's components, their patterning, and the processes of their interaction.
- *Component change.* A change in the condition of one component does not leave the other components untouched. Instead, change in any component affects other components and their interrelationships in either large or small ways. Thus, present-day systems theories fit either the *organismic* para-

digm or the *transactional* paradigm described in the introduction to Part I. Systems theories are also compatible with Kurt Lewin's "life space" proposal within the Gestalt model illustrated in Chapter 1, a proposal which held that the meaning conveyed by an integrated configuration (the unified "whole child") is greater than the meaning derived from simply adding up the configuration's individual parts.

- *Closed or open.* Systems can be either closed or open. A closed system is rather like an isolated village in which no existing component (residents, goods, or facilities) ever leaves and no new components ever enter. An open system, on the other hand, is one in which components can change from time to time. So, in an open village, new residents, goods, and facilities may arrive and old ones may leave. And since the entrance or exit of components in a person's life alters the patterning of that person's biopsychological self, human development involves an open system. A person's growth and behavior are not simply the result of changes within the person's body but, rather, require transactions with selected features of the environments the person encounters.

- *Dynamic movement.* Systems are not static. Instead, they are in constant motion, with the motion sometimes more rapid and more extreme than at other times. Periods of apparent stability are interspersed with periods of perturbation and change. This constant motion is what gives systems the dynamic quality that renders them particularly difficult to study. Systems are like artists' models who will never hold still long enough to be sketched. The best analysts can do is to gather data at periodic intervals (take "snap shots" of the system in action), then seek to identify principles explaining the motion involved in the transition from one snapshot to another. Those principles are frequently expressed as mathematical formulas intended to capture the patterning of the system's movement and development (Beltrami, 1987). Furthermore, dynamic systems do not simply await orders from the environment before they act. Rather, they are naturally energized by internal forces. It is dynamic systems' nature to spontaneously form the self-organizing patterns that constitute a phenomenon—such as a growing child—at any moment in time.

The dynamic-systems viewpoint is not limited to theories of human development. It already had an extensive history in such fields as mathematics, physics, and astronomy before being adopted in its modern form by physiological and cognitive psychologists during the 1980s and 1990s. Thus, dynamic models of development are specific applications of the dynamic-systems viewpoint for explaining how and why people grow up as they do.

A Dynamic-Systems Version of the Brain

Scott Kelso of Florida Atlantic University depicts the brain as an ever-shifting wonderland of neuron networks. In other words, brains are generators of a continuous flow of dynamic neuron patterns, with the neurons that participate in a given pattern distributed in various sectors of the brain (1995). The decision about which patterns will be formed and which neurons will participate is not guided from a central headquarters. Instead, neuron networks are self-organizing. They spontaneously form their own patterns when energized by stimuli from the environment. Kelso contends that this self-organization trait is a basic principle of life. Thus, if we are to understand how the universe operates—including the human brain—we need to understand nature's organizational concepts

> because [those concepts] pertain to how complex structures or patterns can emerge and sustain themselves without any detailed instructions whatsoever. Such [self-organizing] behavior is essential to the nature of things, and is not imposed from the outside. . . . The system organizes itself, but there is no "self," no agent inside the system doing the organizing. . . . Self-organizing systems have no deus ex machina, no ghost in the machine ordering the parts. (Kelso, 1995, pp. 8, 9, 15)

Nor does the generation of brain patterns result from a sequence of causal steps (*linear causality*). Instead, patterns are produced by *nonlinear, circular* events, with many things happening at once and with some events circling back to influence characteristics of preceding events.

Dynamic systems, including the brain, can vary in their degree of stability (remaining the same) and instability (changing their composition), but they never settle into a static, balanced condition—a condition of static equilibrium. They are always in a state of nonequilibrium, poised to move into a new pattern at the instance of stimulation from inside the person or from the surround.

In summary, the task that dynamic-systems aficionados pose for themselves is that of discovering the principles governing the constantly changing patterns that compose human development, with particular attention to (a) the self-generating patterns of brain activity and (b) how that activity fits into the open system of person/environment interactions.

Dynamic-Systems Applications

Dynamic-systems theory has been used principally for explaining people's motor development, especially in such activities as crawling, walking, and running. However, attempts are also being made to apply the paradigm to other more obviously cognitive aspects of the growing child, such as perceptual, social, and emotional development (Bütz, 1997; Smith & Thelen, 1993; Thelen & Smith, 1994). The following two examples illustrate the application of dynamic-systems theory to children's movements and to infants' engagement in a simple game.

Walking and running

The aim and methods of a Thelen-Smith version of dynamic systems can be illustrated with the development of a young child's upright locomotion. Such development, which begins with prenatal and postnatal movements of the limbs, advances through the infant's crawling, to the toddler's first steps, and eventually to the adept walking, running, and hopping of the school-age child. The goal of the theory is to express each of these stages as a mathematical formula that represents the essential characteristics of a given stage. The method of generating the formula consists of measuring children's locomotive movements by means of cycles of *data points.* In the case of children's upright progression, the data points are *light points.* Imagine that we see a child walking past with tiny lights attached to several points on the body—head, shoulder, elbow, hand, hip, knee, and foot. If we take a motion picture of the passing child, we will have a series of film frames in which each light point changes a certain amount from one frame to the next. Furthermore, the frames portray a series of repeated cycles. A cycle begins when the child's right foot touches the ground and ends when, with the completion of that step, it nearly touches the ground again. The aim now is to develop mathematical formulas that represent both (a) a given light's cycle of movement and (b) the coordination of one light's cycle with others' cycles. A child developing from one stage of locomotion to another—crawling to toddling or walking to running—will be reflected in the change in the formulas from one stage to another.

An important motive behind proponents' interest in this approach has been their dissatisfaction with structuralist interpretations of development, interpretations that postulate such internal structures as Freud's ego and superego or Piaget's schemes.

> We can parody structural explanations in both motor behavior and cognitive development by saying that these theories describe behavior, give it a fancy name, and then put [the name] in the head as an explanation. Sucking is explained by an innate sucking reflex, walking by an innate central pattern generator, the syntax of language by an innate grammar. In each case an abstract and sometimes truly elegant description of behavior itself is claimed as the cause of the behavior. In brief, according to structural theories, behaviors are caused by icons of themselves. (Smith & Thelen, 1993, p. 159)

In contrast to models that posit internal structures and their relationships as causes of behavior, the Thelen-Smith model—as its advocates emphasize—directly describes behavior by tracing the pathways of its data points and by representing the outcome in formulas that serve as mathematically defined developmental principles. Roberton (1993) has praised the potential contribution of dynamic-systems theory by suggesting that

> The approach proposes a unity in nature that would allow discernment of general rules by which complex systems [in meteorology, fluid dynamics, astronomy, anthropology] are organized and take on new forms. Using the tools of theoreti-

cal mathematics and physics, the complexity of systems is described at the macroscopic level, i.e., as a "whole system" rather than at the microscopic level. Yet, it is understood that changing elements at the mircrolevel may be responsible for the changes at the macrolevel. (pp. 97-98)

Applications of this variety of dynamic-systems theory to such phenomena as cognitive, emotional, and social development are yet in their early infancy, with their likely success still in question.

At present, only the most speculative dynamic-systems accounts of cognitive development are possible. Dynamics are formal treatments of systems that change over time. Currently, the mathematics requires time series of many hundreds of thousands of data points. Because researchers in cognitive development have pursued underlying constant cognitive structures, they have not collected these kinds of data. . . . Thus, at this point in time, we can only talk in metaphors about how development might be like a dynamic system. (Smith & Thelen, 1993, p. 166)

From Thelen and Smith's vantage point, development does not consist of a child progressing toward a known conception of mature adulthood. Thus, dynamic-systems theories aren't teleological; they don't assume that development is constrained to move toward a predictable ultimate condition (as implied in Lumsden and Wilson's *epigenetic rules* in Chapter 2). So "development does not 'know' where it is going from the start. . . . There is no set end-state other than the end of life itself. We propose instead that development is the outcome of the self-organizing processes of continually active *living* systems" (Thelen & Smith, 1994, p. 44).

Intelligence, from a dynamic-systems viewpoint, is not a mental pool of knowledge that guides people's thought but, rather, it is "the ability to adapt, to fit behavior and cognition to the changing context. A smart system seems unlikely to do exactly the same thing twice. Rather, a smart system would shift its behavior slightly to fit the nuances of the particular context or would shift radically—jump to an all-new state—if the situation demanded it" (Thelen & Smith, 1994, p. 244). The development of the young child's motor skills— looking, reaching, touching, turning, walking—leads to cognitive development "through repeated cycles of perception-action-perception . . . [so that] knowing develops from doing . . . [and] the same processes that build stable, adaptive movements are the same that build stable, adaptive cognition" (Thelen & Smith, 1994, pp. 129, 311).

The Peekaboo Game

A further application of dynamic-systems theory to developmental psychology illustrates how dynamic-systems terminology adopted from mathematics and physics can be used for describing human behavior. The example is Holt, Fogel, and Wood's (1998) analysis of the peekaboo game—a simple form of play observed in numerous cultures. The game involves two participants, an infant and an older person (adult or older child). The game consists of three phases: (a) the infant observes an object momentarily being hidden from view (covered), (b) either the older person or the infant suddenly removes the barrier to reveal the object (uncovered), and (c) the adult exclaims "peekaboo" or something similar to acknowledge the infant's success in rediscovering the object. The adult's uttering "peekaboo" ends the game; or at least it ends that particular cycle of the activity. The game usually continues with further cycles. Here, then, is one dynamic-systems conception of peekaboo.

First, the major components in the system are the infant and the older person, each of whom is an *open system* consisting of internal characteristics that are subject to outside influences. Each participant brings to this social game a variety of *potential action patterns,* and applies one of those patterns in the game. The particular pattern that each person displays influences the other person's response. As in tennis, neither player acts alone but always in response to what the other has done. Therefore, the analysis does not focus separately on each participant's characteristics—intelligence, agility, mood—but, rather, on the continuing flow of the players' interactions.

> Although the participants are both active, self-organizing, open systems, the actions with respect to the other often form observable, repeated patterns. From a dynamic-systems perspective, these interaction patterns are thus cocreated by the participants and constitute an active, dynamic, self-organizing system. (Holt, Fogel, & Wood, 1998, p. 36)

Consider one popular version of peekaboo in which Mother—as the *agent* initiating the game—begins by holding an infant's blanket up in front of her own face (cover), then lowers the blanket so that Infant Daughter once again sees Mother's face (uncover), and Mother exclaims, "Peekaboo." Daughter laughs, thereby encouraging Mother to repeat the game; and the game continues over and over in such a fashion—a repetition of the same pattern of actions. In dynamic-systems parlance, such a simple, repetitive pattern is an *attractor state*, meaning that such a pattern of action is stable enough to hold itself together for multiple repetitions.

> Games are repeated, patterned, interactive action sequences. As with any behavior on repetition, the action is never precisely the same as it was on a previous occasion, yet discernible elements of similarity are observable across episodes. During subsequent repetitions, games become smoother in both action and temporal sequence after the first, tentative action interplay. (Holt, Fogel, & Wood, 1998, p. 36)

As time advances, a habitual pattern (attractor state) can be replaced by a significant variation. Infant Daughter may, herself, reach out and jerk away the blanket. She has thus become the agent controlling the uncover phase of the game, and the game's new version continues with Daughter as the active agent. Such a change is dubbed a developmental *phase shift*. When roles within the game thus change systematically, the novel pattern that emerges constitutes an *agency innovation.* In such a manner, the game, as a dynamic system, "may change over time, as the range of activities infants may perform in the first year inceases due to their emergent capacities for cognition and action" (Holt, Fogel, & Wood, 1998, p. 36).

In summary, then, human development, from a dynamic-systems viewpoint, can be defined in terms of a sequence of attractor states which undergo phase shifts that result in agency innovations.

(Dynamic-systems perspectives, as they relate to issues of *determinism* and *chaos*, are pursued further in Chapter 8.)

Although the above applications of dynamic systems suggest how cognition—the contents and operation of mind—develops out of people's actions (reminiscent of both Vygotsky's and Piaget's proposals), it does not directly address the mind/brain issue. For ways that special types of dynamic systems deal with that issue, we turn to connectionism.

The Connectionist Perspective

Connectionism is generally regarded as a subterritory within the broad domain of dynamic-systems theories, with some writers seeing certain varieties of connectionism as hybrid versions that combine aspects of both computational and dynamical viewpoints (van Gelder, 1995, p. 234). Connectionist theories are explanations of cognitive activity based on the view of brain structure and function that we sketched early in this chapter. Thus, the term *neural net models* serves as an alternative label for connectionist schemes. The hope of connectionists is that they can formulate psychological theories of mind that match the neural networks of the brain. High-powered computers are used as tools assisting connectionists with certain aspects of their task. (Computer simulations by the mid-1990s would involve 129 networks composed of 220,000 cells with 8.5 million connections among them; and computers of far greater capacity were in the offing [Kelso, 1995, p. 228]). However, connectionists don't harbor the expectation that a computer is a sufficient analogue of mind.

Connectionists typically accept the postulates about dynamic systems listed earlier, plus such additional convictions as the following (Ashcraft, 1994, pp. 116-122, 510-514).

- *Units, connections, weights.* A *unit* in connectionism is analogous to a single neuron. Whereas some theories of cognition (*modular models*) conceive of an item, such as the letter **d** or the word **dog**, being encoded in the mind as a unit at a particular location, connectionist models propose that such letters and words are actually fabricated out of far simpler elements that are located in different places in the brain. For instance, the **d** is composed of a straight vertical line, curve elements, the placement of those elements in relation to each other, line thickness, a given size, and the like. These simple units must be linked together by means of connections among the pertinent neural locations in order to form **d** in the person's mind. Even more complex elements must be connected to form the configuration **dog** and the meanings attached to that configuration. Hence, the sentence "Open the door so the dog can get out" is a highly complex composition of connections among a great host of simple units.

The strength of connections between units can be represented as weights, which can be either positive or negative. A positive weight signifies an attraction between two units or nodes in the network. A negative weight signifies resistance or opposition between units. The patterning of positive and negative weights determines which units in the entire network contribute to a concept, such as **dog**, and how much they contribute.

- *Levels of units.* In keeping with an information-processing viewpoint, there are three levels of units in cognition—input, throughput (referred to as a "hidden layer" invisible to the outside observer), and output. The three levels are interconnected so that input units encode or interpret stimulation from the environment (such as the stimulation you receive in reading this sentence), the interpretations are transmitted to the hidden-layer units which process them to yield meanings, and the result is sent to the output units that determine what action the person will take.

- *Parallel processing.* Unlike classical cognitive science theories, the process by which units combine to produce meanings and actions in connectionist models is not a serial operation in which one unit is first assessed, then a second is assessed, and so on. Instead, in producing the person's perception of **d** or **dog**, the units are assessed and combined simultaneously, that is, in parallel. Hence, the terms *parallel distributed processing* and *massive parallel processing* are used to identify the operation of connectionist models.

- *Training regimens.* In using sophisticated computers to simulate the operation of neural network activities,

One typically does not program a connectionist system; instead, one gives it a training regimen, from which it learns to solve problems. As a result . . . connectionism suggests quite different ways of thinking [than in classical artificial intelligence] about particular cognitive processes and abilities, such as perceptual recognition or language learning. (Horgan & Tienson, 1996, p. 4)

Although connectionists often use the term *computation,* they intend it to mean "discern" or "figure out" rather than "calculating cognitive activity by the application of a rule or algorithm." It is assumed that the process by which the human cognitive system operates first involves (a) the person's receiving stimuli from the environment—see, hear, touch, sniff, taste—(the input stage) and (b) the brain attempting to match the sensed features of the stimuli to combinations of units (neural network patterns) in the nervous system (the throughput stage). This initial attempt will not likely yield a completely satisfactory match, but only an approximation which then must be revised on the basis of feedback. So, by use of formulas which check the approximation against the stimuli, alterations are effected in the units of neural networks to provide a closer match. It is assumed that this process of approximation and correction proceeds in extremely rapid cycles that ultimately alter the neural networks enough to achieve an acceptable match between the stimuli and the network patterns. Such a process, referred to as *back propagation*, can be simulated with extremely high-speed computers in which units (nodes) represent brain neurons. Thus, by means of feedback cycles that involve massive numbers of rapid computations, a computer can "learn" to recognize stimuli—such as printed words—which it has not "known" before (McClelland & Rumelhart, 1986; Rumelhart & McClelland, 1986).

- *No central processing center.* Most connectionist theories, like other dynamic-systems models, do not assume a central processing unit that directs all cognitive operations. Instead, neural networks fire in response to those stimuli—either from the environment or from within the person—to which the networks have become sensitized.

As implied throughout our discussion, not only are there diverse versions of connectionism, but no version yet provides a complete explanation of cognition. Consequently, the field of connectionist theories is best viewed as a collection of theories-in-progress—proposals that sketch possible solutions to facets of the mind/brain mystery. Three typical issues that engage connectionists' attention are illustrated in the following examples.

Issue 1: Multiple simultaneous soft constraint satisfaction. Constraints are conditions a person has in mind that influence decisions. Constraints can vary in the degree to which they are malleable. In other words, constraints can extend from the very hard (unyielding) to the very soft (readily changed). To demonstrate this distinction, we can reinspect the earlier example of a woman shopping for a new car. Let's assume that she would not accept an auto unless it was a two-door convertible that included a back seat. Those two requirements were hard constraints. In contrast, she apparently would not insist that the car be the newest year's model, since she was considering last year's model; so recency-of-model was a softer constraint than was two-door convertible, which itself was a constraint influenced by the offer of a lower price. And apparently her desire for a compact-disc player was an even softer constraint, for she didn't complain about its absence. Horgan and Tiensen (1996) have observed that

> most of the constraints [that you are looking for in an automobile] are *soft*— they can be violated when your decision-making system is doing its job properly. If there is a strict bound on how much you can pay—that is, if price is a hard constraint—then you will not be able to get all that you desire in safety *and* style *and* performance, and so on. You get the best combination of desired fea-

tures that you can, but some you must do without. . . . Human cognition seems to be naturally good at accommodating not only the multiplicity of constraints but also their softness. This suggests that human intelligence is different in kind from computer "intelligence." (p. 5)

Issue 2: Innate versus acquired knowledge. An eternal debate about human development concerns a question intimately related to the focus of Chapter 2: How much—and what kind—of human knowledge and skill is embedded in a person's nervous system by genetic endowment compared to how much—and what kind—must be acquired from experience? In other words, how much do people depend on genetic inheritance for their knowledge and problem-solving skills and how much do they depend on their environment? Connectionists investigate this issue by creating software simulation programs that equip powerful computers to solve problems of interpreting unfamiliar phenomena, such as new words or phrases. The connectionist's technique involves first confronting a computer with unaccustomed words (input). Then the computer, by means of built-in instructions, manipulates the words through a "training program" (such as back propagation), so thereafter the computer will be able to "recognize" such formerly unfamiliar stimuli. Hence, connectionists, in pursuing their task, are obliged to answer the question: How much information or preparation must the computer already have before it confronts new stimuli and satisfactorily interprets them? Or, when the question is reversed, it becomes: How slight can the information in the computer be (in terms of the pattern of weights assigned to units and of the links among units) for the machine still to "learn" to solve a problem by virtue of the training routine in which it engages? Connectionists' attempts to answer these queries have produced a variety of computer instantiations intended to test the effectiveness of different combinations of embedded information (analogous to innate knowledge) and training programs (analogous to postnatal experience) (Clark, 1993).

Issue 3: Modeling theories of therapy. Lloyd (1994) describes a neural-network model of psychoanalytic interpretation of one of Sigmund Freud's and Josef Breuer's early cases of conversion hysteria, the case of Lucy R. The computer program offers analogs of the defense mechanisms of repression and hallucination corresponding to Lucy's symptoms. Significant elements of Lucy's conscious experience are represented in the model by activations of neuronlike processors in the computer's interconnected neural network. The model "learns" to associate elements of experience that were associated in Lucy's case history. Trauma is modeled in the network by learning that is accomplished at a high rate. According to Lloyd, the model suggests that changing associations among conscious elements are sufficient to generate the symptoms that Freud and Breuer reported—apparent repression, hallucination, and recovery through therapy.

MIND/BRAIN DEVELOPMENT

So far in this chapter we have focused on ways that the mind/brain relationship can be conceived. Now we consider how the mind/brain relationship seems to develop with the passing years.

Contributions to mind/brain development appear to derive from three sources: (a) an increase and differentiation of brain neurons that determine the number and form of neurons available for cognitive activity, (b) the internal maturation of neurons and their networks, and (c) the nature of people's experiences that affect the pattern and strength of associations among neurons and thereby help determine the character of neural networks.

First, consider the increase of brain neurons. Until the 1990s, conventional wisdom held that virtually all neurons available throughout a person's lifespan were laid down prenatally, meaning that nearly the entire lifetime stock of neurons would be present at birth. For instance, Noback (1994) wrote that

> Almost all neurons are generated during prenatal life, and they are not replaced by new neurons during postnatal life. . . . In order to produce the estimated one trillion neurons present in the mature brain, an average of 2.5 million neurons must be generated per minute during the entire prenatal life. This includes the formation of neuronal circuits comprising 100 trillion synapses, as each potential neuron is ultimately connected with either a selected set of neurons or specific targets such as sensory endings. (pp. 803-804)

However, recent discoveries suggest that conventional wisdom has been somewhat in error. Biologists at Princeton University reported that monkey brains constantly produce thousands of new neurons (*neurogenesis*) that travel to the cerebral cortex, where higher cognitive functions take place. And studies of other animal species have shown that neurons increase when individuals are placed in stimulating environments and learn new skills. These same processes appear to operate in humans as well (Hales & Hales, 1999, p. 10). But it still seems true that the majority of neurons are created before the infant is born, and a great quantity of synapses—representing potential neural network connections—are established during the prenatal months. Then, throughout childhood and into early adolescence, certain of the synapses mature into ones that subsequently represent well established associations in the brain. At the same time, other synapses become redundant and atrophy. Thus, the number of synapses in the young child's brain is far greater than the number in the older adolescent's or adult's brain. Baer, Connors, and Paradiso (1996, p. 499) note that "The loss of synapses in the primary visual cortex during adolescence occurs at an average rate of *5000 per second*. (No wonder adolescence is such a trying time!)"

Therefore, throughout childhood a great host of neurons and immature synapses provide the potential for developing the neural networks which are the biological structures of the maturing mind. During these postnatal years, the child's experiences play a crucial role in determining which synaptic connections are strengthened and which fall into disuse. For example, in the development of an individual's visual acuity, the rearrangement of synapses in the brain is much influenced by the sorts of visual activity in which the infant and young child engages.

> We will find that the ultimate performance of the adult visual system is determined to a significant extent by the quality of the visual environment during the early postnatal period. In a very real sense, *we learn to see during a critical period of postnatal development.* . . . [Whereas] most of the "wires" [as associations among neurons] find their proper place before birth, the final refinement of synaptic connections occurs [for vision] during infancy and is influenced by the sensory environment. [Furthermore,] other sensory and motor systems are also readily modified by the environment during critical periods of early childhood. In this way, our brain is a product not only of our genes, but also of the world we grow up in. (Baer, Connors, & Paradiso, 1996, pp. 500, 511)

Such, then, is the general pattern of neural development over the first two decades of life. During these years, the mind—in the sense of *intelligence* or the complexity and sophistication of thought—obviously matures as well. Consequently, the challenge for theorists who hope to explain cognitive development from a connectionist perspective becomes one of describing (a) the relationship between the brain's neural networks and (b) the simulated neural networks that theorists propose and seek to represent in high-speed computers. Theorists then need to (c) identify the principles and conditions that determine how and why a given state of a network changes into a subsequent state.

REMAINING CHALLENGES

In view of our brief sketch of classical cognitive science (artificial intelligence), of dynamic systems, and of connectionism, what questions call for more adequate answers in the years ahead?

First, does classical cognitive science have a future? If so, what may it be? In response, a number of supporters of dynamical modeling and connectionism would not deny the value of classical cognitive science for revealing important features of human cognition.

> A great deal can be and has been learned about cognitive problems by writing [computer] programs aimed at solving [those problems], and a great deal is revealed about theories (and their defects) by implementing [programs] classically. It is quite likely that these things cannot be accomplished in other ways. (Horgan & Tienson, 1996, p. 10)

And Stich (1994) has noted that certain sorts of "thinking," such as pattern recognition, have been modeled with comparable accuracy by both classical systems and connectionist systems, but the classical systems do it much faster. Therefore, it may well be that classical cognitive science will continue to remain alive and productive into the foreseeable future, even though it has not provided an ultimate answer to the mind/brain conundrum.

Next, what about dynamic-systems theories of the sort applied by Thelen and Smith to the development of children's upright progression? Is it likely that such approaches will be widely adopted for explaining cognitive development? In speculating about that possibility, Roberton (1993) suggests that

> The greatest drawback in stimulating others [in the field of human development] to enter this research area is probably the esoteric language in which dynamic-systems theory is packaged. It takes considerable study for those not well-versed in engineering and physics to extract some of the basic concepts. (p. 114)

Roberton was referring to the fact that newcomers who hope to employ the theory must first master such concepts as *attractor, phase space trajectory, limit cycle, saddle node, phase portrait, perturbation, damped pendulum, control parameter*, and more. Furthermore, researchers who have sought to apply the theory beyond physical actions to such areas as social cognition and emotional development have met with little success. Hence, there is a question of how much new knowledge the model can generate.

> The real test is not whether dynamic-systems theory can account for the phenomena we study, but whether it yields any new insights, integrates previously unrelated empirical facts, or in some other way leads to a deeper understanding of those phenomena. (Robertson, Cohen, & Mayer-Kress, 1993, p. 148)

Now consider the state of connectionism. We have noted that researchers' recent success in testing connectionist models by means of high-powered computer simulations has created a rapidly growing interest in the potential of connectionism for explaining cognition. But because such demonstrations are yet in an early stage of development and have been limited to a very few kinds of thought and action, it is unclear how adequately connectionist models can represent all sorts of cognition and behavior. Baev (1998) writes that

> In the contemporary discipline of artificial neural networks neurocomputing . . . only the simplest of networks . . . have been developed for analysis of the nervous system. Much more work must be done to develop more powerful methods that utilize mathematical descriptions of more complex neural networks. Modern analytical mathematical descriptions are effective only in cases of simple neural networks. (p. 221)

Clearly, not everyone has embraced connectionist theory. Proponents of other conceptions of mind remain unconvinced that connectionism offers the solution to the puzzle of how humans think and act. For example, van Geert (1993) complains that

> Recently, cognitive psychology's concept of mind as a rule system has been criticized by connectionism. Neural networks are self-organizing structures based on simple local interactions. It may be questioned, however, whether a neural network model alone, that is, a model of the underlying substratum, may solve the enigma of psychological development. Neural networks are models of

brains, and brains are parts of bodies acting in environments. Just as a theory of the physiology and anatomy of animal bodies cannot explain evolution without taking the ecological system into account, a psychological theory of development cannot be reduced to a theory of the brain. (p. 266)

Eiser (1994) harbors other reservations. He comments that some—if not all—versions of connectionism

> rest on an article of faith that research in the neurosciences will lead us, sooner or later, to the point where we will be able to translate statements about a person's thoughts precisely into statements about his or her brain activity, and vice versa. . . . A one-to-one correspondence is assumed to exist, and be in principle discoverable, between every electrically recorded piece of brain activity and every subjectively reported thought or feeling. . . . It is like being able to look at a brain-scan and determine the *contents* of someone's thoughts, to be able to put electrodes onto your head and get an interpretable read-out of your visual images or inner speech. To anyone who seriously thinks this is possible, there is only one answer: try it and see! (p. 48)

Thus, providing satisfactory responses to van Geert's and Eiser's observations is a further challenge faced by devotees of dynamic-systems and connectionism.

4

Environmental/Ecological Theories

In the somewhat distant past, such theories as Skinner's behaviorism focused so much attention on environmental factors in human development that the influence of a person's own qualities in affecting events seemed much neglected. But present-day theories labeled *environmental* or *ecological* usually paint a more balanced picture of persons' and environments' contributions to events.

To begin understanding recent proposals, we can ask: How have theorists characterized environmental and ecological models?

In response, the term *environmental psychology,* according to one popular definition. is "the study of human behavior and well-being in relation to the sociophysical environment" (Stokols & Altman, 1987, p. 1). Slightly different is Robert Cohen's description of environmental psychology as

a multidisciplinary approach to understanding person-environment transactions. Environmental psychologists are interested primarily in field research, viewing people in context, to understand the dynamic interchange between people and settings. (1985, p. 2)

Ecological psychology, in its human development form, has been portrayed by Urie Bronfenbrenner as

the scientific study of the progressive, mutual accommodation, throughout the life course, between an active, growing, highly complex biopsychological organism—characterized by a distinctive complex of evolving, interrelated, dynamic capacities for thought, feeling, and action—and the changing properties of the immediate settings in which the developing person lives, as this process is affected by the relations between these settings, and by the larger contexts in which the settings are embedded. (1993, p. 7)

A second question to ask is: What theories have been the progenitors of recent models?

Today's environmental/ecological theories include in their ancestral line the contributions of such pioneers as Kurt Lewin (1890-1947) and Henry Murray (1893-1988) who, during the 1930s and 1940s, introduced such concepts as *life space* and *needs-press*.

As noted in Chapter 1, Lewin's (1936) topological theory of development defined *life space* as all of the facts that influence a person's behavior at a given time. A *fact* in Lewin's theory is not an objectively verifiable observation from the "real world." Instead, it's any element within the person's psychological environment that affects the person's thought or actions, including elements of which the individual is unaware—such as air pollution or a flu virus—and ones the person recognizes and accepts as real—such as fatigue, a friend's affection, or a law against forgery. Some facts are from the past, currently held in conscious or unconscious memory. Some are from the present. Others are in the future, such as hopes or plans for the years ahead. Thus, by conceiving the determinants of thought and behavior in terms of *life space,* Lewin's model could accommodate persons' and environments' qualities in somewhat equal measure.

Murray's (1938) needs-press theory proposed that people's behavior is motivated by needs they attempt to satisfy through their engagements with environments. The success of such attempts is always affected by environmental pressures, that is, by limitations and demands imposed by environments. Hence, the person's needs continually vie with the environment's press to determine the outcome of events.

The link between the Lewin-Murray era and present-day versions of environmental psychology was provided chiefly by Roger Barker and his colleagues at the University of Kansas, who described person-environment encounters through the use of such neologisms as *behavior setting* (the environment in which an event occurs), *standing patterns of behavior* (typical ways people act), and *the milieu* (a behavior setting's physical objects and the time frame of an event within that setting) (Barker, 1968, 1978).

Although interest in environmental psychology flagged after the 1940s, serious attention to the specialization emerged in the 1960s, began to grow in the 1970s, and expanded markedly throughout the 1980s and into the 1990s (Stokols & Altman, 1987, p. 1). As a result, a host of environmental theories have been published in recent times, far more than could be described or even mentioned in a single chapter. I've chosen to depict only four models, selected because they illustrate four very different conceptions of the focus and structure of environmental/ecological theory. The four are (a) a theory inferred from Cohen and Cohen's summary of studies of how people's activity affects their understanding spatial relations, (b) Wicker's sense-making model, (c) Elder's life-course proposal, and (d) Holland's scheme for linking personality types to work settings.

ACTIVITY AND SPATIAL COGNITION

Psychological processes that qualify as *spatial cognition* form a specialization within environmental psychology that concerns (a) how people think about environments' physical relationships, (b) how such thought affects people's behavior, and (c) how and why their spatial cognition develops as time passes. The spatial cognition literature features a variety of perspectives toward relationships between persons and their physical surroundings. As a result, there are empirical studies and theories about how and why people

- Perceive the connection between models or maps of territories and the actual territories that those miniature copies are intended to represent.
- Come to understand navigable, small-scale environments (a school building, a neighborhood, a town) and large-scale environments (a region of a country, a nation, a region of the world, continents, the solar system).
- Think and behave differently in settings experienced as (a) crowded versus empty, (b) quiet versus noisy, (c) constricted versus expansive, and (d) public versus personal.
- Use information about objects as seen from different vantage points and distances to generate their conceptions of those objects.
- Store spatial information in memory.
- Design products that involve spatial relationships.
- Judge the aesthetic quality of spatial relationships.
- Use their activities within environments to form their conceptions of spatial arrangements.

The following model focuses on the last of these alternatives—the role of activity in spatial cognition. Although Sheila L. Cohen and Robert Cohen did not cast their analysis of activity's influence on cognition as a formal theory, their proposal contains the elements of a theory (components and their relationships) and thus for our purpose can qualify as a "theory in process." What the Cohens did was review empirical studies of spatial cognition, then summarize their findings as factors which likely affect how activity influences people's spatial knowledge.

The word *activity* in the present context refers to how people behave in an environment. The behavior can be either overt or covert. Overt activity includes such acts as walking around a neighborhood, manually manipulating parts of a bicycle while repairing the vehicle, throwing a football to a friend, and arranging flowers in a vase. Covert actions can involve such thought processes as searching for hidden faces in a picture puzzle, estimating the places in which a lost toy might be found, and contemplating alternative chess moves before shifting a chess piece.

The expression *spatial knowledge* refers to a person's beliefs about how objects are arranged in space and how territories are related to each other—beliefs that derive at least partially from activities the person has pursued within an environment.

Generalizations that the Cohens drew from the studies they summarized enable us to identify (a) variables (components) that apparently influence the spatial knowledge people acquire and (b) relationships among those variables.

Components and Their Relationships

Because of the Cohens' interest in how spatial knowledge is influenced by people's behavior, the central variable in their scheme is *activity* as reflected in the question: What sort of action takes place in an environment and how does that action affect the development of spatial knowledge? Other associated variables that alter the influence of activity on knowledge include (a) personal variables (characteristics of the individual), (b) social-status variables (characteristics of individuals' social position), and (c) environmental variables (characteristics of settings through which the individual moves).

First are *personal variables,* including:

- Mental maturity, which results from a combination of (a) genetic endowment, (b) the rate at which different cognitive skills evolve, and (c) the amount and quality of a person's past experience in different spaces.

  How a typical 12-year-old will behave in a setting and how that behavior will contribute to the child's spatial knowledge will differ from the behavior and acquired knowledge of a typical 4-year-old because of differences in the two children's mental maturity. The 12-year-old will (a) attend to more facets of the environment, (b) engage in covert as well as overt actions (while the 4-year-old depends chiefly on overt behavior), and (c) will derive more complex understandings from the setting.
- The patterning of cognitive skills. A variety of separate mental abilities is conceived to comprise *intelligence* or *mental maturity* in the Cohens' scheme. Two of these abilities are *visualization aptitude* and *directional skill.* People with greater visualization aptitude are better at understanding maps and other spatial arrangements than those with less visualization aptitude. People with a more refined directional sense are better equipped to recognize where they are situated in relation to objects of the environment.
- The amount of experience in an environment.

  As a general index of activity-in-space, defined as length of residency in naturalistic settings and amount of exposure to novel spaces, the research tends to confirm the expectation that the greater one's experiences in a space, the greater one's spatial knowledge of the space. [But] this is at best a very crude measure of activity-in-space. Although a certain amount of exposure is of course necessary to glean spatial information, it seems to be far more critical to determine the nature of the individual's activity when assessing the influence of space. (Cohen & Cohen, 1985, p. 217)

- The person's purpose or aim while in a space. The goal an individual pursues in an environment affects what that person considers important about the environment and, consequently, which aspects of the space are given attention and recalled. A youth assigned to draw a map from his home to school can be expected, on the way to school today, to attend more closely to routes, landmarks, and distances than if he were interested in recalling the types of flowers growing in the gardens he passed.
- State of health. Spatial knowledge is partially a product of a person's mobility, visual and auditory acuity, and freedom from pain.

  People who frequently walk or drive a car develop a more accurate, sophisticated knowledge of a neighborhood or region than ones who stay at home or are only passengers in cars, buses, and trains. "It is probable that an individual's mobility affects the type of his or her experiences by modifying the frequency, expansiveness, pleasure, and purpose of the activity" (Cohen & Cohen, 1985, p. 203). People with sharp eyesight are better prepared to identify spatial clues than ones with faulty sight. Those in pain can be so concerned with their discomfort that they are distracted from attending to details of their environment.
- Habit patterns. The activities in which people habitually engage affect their spatial knowledge by influencing the amount of experience they acquire with different spaces and what they note in those spaces. A study in Italy revealed that younger adults in Rome and Milan tended to draw more paths on maps of their environments, whereas older adults drew more landmarks. The difference suggested that

  the older subjects may have been less likely to have learned the city by car than the younger individuals. This interpretation rests on the assumption that landmarks are more salient features to walkers and paths are more salient to drivers/riders. (Cohen & Cohen, 1985, p. 202)

Second are *social-status variables*—factors embedded in people's assigned or earned position in the society. A person's social position affects opportunities to encounter different environments and the person's ability to extract spatial knowledge from those encounters. Social-status variables include:

- Socioeconomic level. People on higher social-class levels tend to have more elaborate and accurate spatial knowledge, partly because they enjoy more opportunities for travel and for participating in a variety of settings. "Orleans reported that middle class residents of Los Angeles, relative to lower class residents, had friends in a broader range of locations and drew maps depicting a greater part of the city" (Cohen & Cohen, 1985, p. 203).
- Educational level. The higher the level of a person's education, the more complex and accurate the individual's spatial knowledge tends to be, since education usually acquaints people with a wide array of environments.

- Sociocultural position. People's religion, occupation, and recreational pursuits influence the kinds of environments they visit and the sorts of activities in which they engage. Consequently, the spatial knowledge derived from those experiences will vary from one person to another. "Karan et al. noted that Hindu subjects emphasized temples in their maps, while Moslem subjects emphasized mosques" (Cohen & Cohen, 1985, p. 203).
- Home range. The term *home range* refers to how far people rove from their homes. For children, home range typically expands with increasing age from a small, continuous territory to a relatively diffuse, discontinuous set of activity settings that cover large areas. A person's home range—as decreed by age, socioeconomic condition, and travel—establishes the variety of environments with which the person interacts.

Third are *environmental variables* that facilitate or inhibit activities in settings, and thereby affect the spatial knowledge acquired in such places.

- Weather. In wintertime, the behavior settings people explore and the activities in which they engage will differ between Northern Canada, Florida, Mexico City, and Hawaii.
- Mode of transportation. People's attention is directed to different landmarks and routes in a city if they travel on foot, by bicycle, by bus, or by subway, thereby resulting in different versions of spatial knowledge.
- Distance between locations. The shorter the distances between locations, the more accurate people's knowledge about the sites' relationships (size, distance, direction).
- Complexity of the environment's components. The fewer the components and the simpler the relationships among them, the more complete and accurate people's spatial knowledge of that setting tends to be.
- Type of activity for which the environment is suited. The spatial knowledge people acquire in a setting is influenced by how suitable the environment is for activities in which people engage. An ice-skating rink, a roller coaster, a cafeteria, a college lecture amphitheater, and the back seat of a sports car are not conducive to the same kinds of activity and therefore do not promote the same kinds of spatial knowledge.

Posited relationships among the foregoing variables are charted in Figure 4-1. The chart is not one offered by the Cohens but, rather, is my inference about the patterning of variables as based on the Cohens' summary of empirical studies. As the arrows suggest, I have assumed that environmental factors influence both the person variables (health, amount of experience in different spaces, and habit patterns) and the activities pursued (as affected by weather, available transportation, and the rest). Person variables and social-status factors influence each other (such as, the amount and type of education affects mental maturity and vice versa), and both the person and social-status factors influence the kind and amount of activity in which an individual engages. Both overt and covert activity

Figure 4-1

Variables Affecting Activity's Contribution to Spatial Cognition

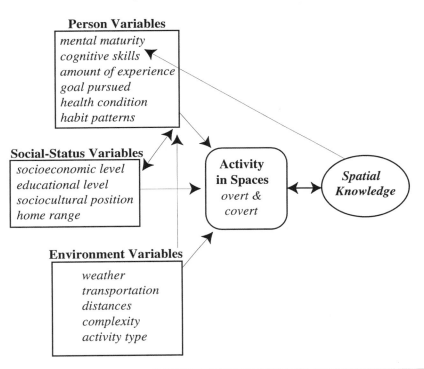

contribute to spatial knowledge which, in turn, affects mental maturity and cognitive skills. Activity in spaces and spatial knowledge influence each other, since activity contributes to knowledge and knowledge affects future activity.

Developmental Sequence

Finally, we can consider the question of how spatial knowledge develops in childhood. The Cohens concluded that "It is difficult to make sweeping statements concerning developmental progressions of [spatial cognition, because different] age groups were assessed for different forms of spatial knowledge using very different tasks" (Cohen & Cohen, 1985, p. 218). Nevertheless, the researchers were able to propose a developmental sequence for the years of early childhood based on the experimental findings they inspected.

The task of infants is to comprehend the stability of objects in the world and to coordinate, at least in terms of motor responses, the perspectives of self and others in relation to those stable objects. The toddler and preschooler are learning to deal with the world on the conceptual plane. While motor movements are still quite salient, the child is learning to establish spatial plans and goals and to coordinate actions for those plans and goals. The older child comes to demonstrate a great flexibility both in the acquisition and the use of spatial information. This child can reflect on the necessity for certain search patterns, can display spatial knowledge derived from passive as well as active experience, and can do so across a variety of spatial tasks. Though it is presumably the case that orientation abilities of infants, search behaviors of toddlers, and the memory of spatial layouts of older children are theoretically linked, the empirical sequences of these behaviors remain open to study. (Cohen & Cohen, 1985, p. 218)

MAKING SENSE OF IMMEDIATE ENVIRONMENTS

Allen W. Wicker of Claremont Graduate School has espoused a model of human development based on his convictions about the appropriateness of a *positivist* perspective versus a *naturalist* worldview. He contends that a traditional positivist paradigm cannot accurately portray how people think and act in particular environments, so a different perceptual lens must be adopted. In his critique of positivism, Wicker writes:

According to the traditional paradigm, the social/physical world is a tangible reality . . . [that] can be understood and even controlled by decomposing it into variables that are linked by describable causal relationships . . . [which] can be meaningfully examined in isolation from one another. . . . Statements of causal relations typically take the form of hypotheses—assertions of enduring relationships between variables. Hypotheses typically are presumed to be universal, . . . often stated as if the relationships are independent of temporal, social, cultural, and historical contexts. The variables incorporated in hypotheses are often presumed to be stable over time. (Wicker, 1992, p. 160)

In Wicker's opinion, a proper replacement for the traditional paradigm is what he refers to as a *naturalist alternative,* a belief system in which

what we regard as reality is a social product based on shared meanings among interacting persons. That is, reality is socially constructed. It follows that multiple realities may be derived from multiple communities. The realities that the adherents of the naturalistic paradigm explore are constantly changing processes or relationships that can be understood only when viewed in natural dynamic contexts: ". . . the aspects of a system, that is, person and context, coexist and jointly define one another and contribute to the meaning and nature of a holistic event" [Altman & Rogoff, 1987, p. 24]. . . . A primary aim of [naturalistic] inquiry is to gain an in-depth understanding—to generate an idiographic or closely comparative body of knowledge—and convincingly to communicate that understanding. Prediction and control are viewed as unlikely and secondary outcomes of research. (Wicker, 1992, p. 163)

Such beliefs led Wicker to propose a model for explaining the processes by which people make sense of environmental events. His theory is not supposed to reveal causal factors (independent variables) that permit predictions about how future events (dependent variables) will turn out. Instead, it is intended to (a) explain how and why people behave as they do in the daily environments they occupy and (b) identify significant characteristics of those environments.

A key assumption underlying Wicker's theory is that people are continually attempting to make sense out of their environmental engagements, with that attempt motivated by a tacit conviction that understanding the settings they occupy will help them satisfy their innate need to survive and prosper.

Terms identifying key concepts in Wicker's model include *behavior settings, behavior-setting programs, shared meanings, reality, mental maps, cause maps, sense-making cycles, time,* and *the social/physical world.*

The expression *behavior settings* carries Barker's original meaning of

> small-scale social systems whose components include people and inanimate objects. Within the temporal and spatial boundaries of the system, the various components interact in an orderly, established fashion to carry out the setting's essential functions. (Wicker, 1987, p. 614)

Examples of behavior settings are a classroom, an athletic club, a drugstore, a wedding, a war veterans' reunion party, a house-painting project, a family's evening at home, and an 18-hole game of golf.

Each behavior setting contains animate and inanimate components that interact in established ways to foster the setting's intended functions. For instance, a fourth-grade classroom is occupied by 23 children, 1 teacher, 1 part-time teacher's aide, 23 pupils' desks, 2 teachers' desks, a wall map of the world, 5 personal computers, 2 hamsters in a cage, flowering plants in window boxes, and a host of other items.

Behavior-setting programs are the patterns of action routinely performed within an environment. The pattern defines the setting's structure and operation and is the reason for the setting's existence.

> The *program* of a behavior setting is a time-ordered sequence of person-environment interactions that leads to the orderly enactment of essential setting functions. (Wicker, 1987, p. 614)

The program of the fourth-grade classroom includes learning goals (in reading, writing, speaking, calculating, physical science, social studies, the arts, social behavior) that are pursued by means of teaching/learning methods (teacher explanations, teacher-led discussions, students' written assignments) which utilize materials and equipment (books, motion pictures, computers). Learning outcomes are assessed by means of question-answer sessions, tests, student projects, and teacher observations of pupils' behavior.

Shared meanings are the beliefs held in common by the setting's occupants regarding the characteristics of the setting and the kinds of behavior appropriate within it. For the occupants, *reality* is not an objective description of the setting and of the relationships among its components. Rather, *reality* consists of a combination of the participants' shared beliefs and their individual conceptions of the setting. Thus, their behavior is not founded on an objective portrayal of their shared setting but, instead, on their sociophysical mental maps of the setting. The efficiency with which activities of a setting are carried out will, to a great extent, be a function of how well each participant's cognitive map matches other participants' maps.

One important type of mental map is the *cause map,* which reflects occupants' shared beliefs about how the setting's program should operate. A cause map typically includes both a vision of how things should turn out (goal, aim) and the steps necessary for producing that outcome. The elements that go into such a map derive from the person's past experiences with environments and is thus "the retained wisdom that orients individuals to particular features" of ecological settings. People usually attend to familiar features of environments that they can interpret on the basis of past experiences (Wicker, 1992, p. 175).

Individuals' encounters with environments consist of a series of five-phase *sense-making cycles.* First, life within every behavior setting involves a constant flow of events, so that every sense-making cycle begins with the person attending to aspects of one of those events, such as a change in a familiar routine. In the fourth-grade classroom, such a change might be the teacher's giving the class instructions about how to use a computer to find information on the World Wide Web. The aspects of the lesson that command attention are ones represented in the person's existing cause map—such as *booting up the computer* and *pointing to the server icon.* Features not found in that map—*web page* and *browser*— are typically overlooked. Second, the person uses the map for determining what the noticed aspects mean. Third, even though the initial comparison between the event and the map will yield an interpretation, it is likely some ambiguity will remain that requires further mental processing. Fourth, the individual will search through the cause map for other possible interpretations and, in addition, will likely search the setting for other clues—such as asking the teacher or other classmates for meanings that their cause maps produce. Fifth, this sense-making process, which can involve numerous repetitions, modifies and elaborates individuals' cause maps. As a result, events that previously were highly ambiguous and that required many cycles to clarify can, on future occasions, be processed more expeditiously (Wicker, 1992, p. 178).

Wicker's proposal about cognitive maps now equips us to infer his conception of human development. In his sense-making theory, development consists of the continual addition to, and revision of, a person's mental maps and of the behaviors based on those maps. Development is a consequence of participation in behavior settings—either direct participation or vicarious participation via parents' childrearing practices, school lessons, books, and television programs.

Time as a dimension of behavior settings can be viewed in terms of either an *event* or a *life course.* *Event time* is defined by when an activity within a setting begins and when it ends. An event in a classroom will typically continue

Figure 4-2

**The Person in a Behavior Setting Within
the Broader Social/Physical World**

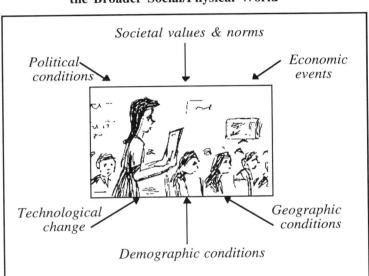

Societal values & norms

*Political
conditions*

*Economic
events*

*Technological
change*

*Geographic
conditions*

Demographic conditions

from the beginning of the class period until the closing bell. Or, if a series of separate activities is pursued during the class period—such as a lecture followed by laboratory work—the number of minutes devoted to each activity could define event length. As for *life-course time*, "I take a more expanded temporal perspective that considers the creation, growth, differentiation, decline, and termination of settings, as well as conditions that existed before they were created" (Wicker, 1987, p. 615). Thus, understanding the life course of a high school geology class requires gathering information about how the class originated, then tracing the changes it went through before its demise.

Finally, a behavior setting (classroom, brokerage office, dinner party, soccer game) does not operate in isolation but is a component of a larger *social/physical world* that consists of communities, regions, institutions, organizations, and populations that influence what transpires in a behavior setting.

"Among the kinds of forces that directly influence behavior settings are societal values and norms; political, legal, and economic events and conditions; technological developments; and demographic and geographic conditions and changes" (Wicker, 1992, p. 172). Conditions in the broader social/physical world do not affect persons directly but, rather, influence them through features of behavior settings (Figure 4-2). In other words, behavior settings and their components are mediators that communicate to individuals the messages and constraints of the broad social/physical world. For instance, societal values and cause maps are transmitted to children in the primary-school classroom by the teacher, the children's peers, school regulations, books, the Internet, and television programs.

A more elaborate version of environments than Wicker's two-level model (behavior settings within the social/physical world) is Bronfenbrenner's four-level scheme (microsystem, mesosystem, exosystem, macrosystem) (1979, 1993). Figure 4-3 illustrates the relationships that Bronfenbrenner envisioned among the four systems, with the diagram picturing significant environments in the life of a 13-year-old boy.

In Bronfenbrenner's model, the shifting environments with which a person interacts are referred to as *behavior systems.* Bronfenbrenner identified four levels of such systems, each defined in terms of how directly it impinges on the child. The settings that affect the individual most intimately are called *microsystems*, analogous to Wicker's behavior settings.

> A microsystem is a pattern of activities, roles, and interpersonal relations experienced by the developing person in a given face-to-face setting with particular physical, social, and symbolic features that invite, permit, or inhibit engagement in sustained, progressively more complex interaction with, and activity in, the immediate environment. (Bronfenbrenner, 1993, p. 15)

Figure 4-3 charts four microsystems in the life of our 13-year-old subject—his family, his junior-high school, the agemates with whom he spends time, and the Internet which he accesses by means of the personal computer in his bedroom.

At the next environmental level, the four microsystems are encompassed by a *mesosystem* which constitutes the "linkages and processes" that operate between two or more of the developing person's behavior settings. In our example, the boy's actions in the classroom and on the playfield on any given day are influenced by his impression of how his parents and peers would regard those actions. Thus, his temptation to copy answers from a classmate's mathematics test is blocked by his assumption that his parents and peers would disapprove. As the double-headed arrows suggest, not only do the behavior settings influence the boy's behavior, but also he himself influences those settings to some degree by the way he acts.

The environmental unit beyond the mesosystem is the *exosystem,* consisting of the processes operating between two or more environmental settings, "in which events occur that indirectly influence the processes within the immediate setting in which the developing person lives" (Bronfenbrenner, 1993, p. 22). The four illustrative exosystems in Figure 4-3 are the workplaces of the boy's parents, the neighborhood in which the family's home is located, the school's governing board that passes regulations affecting the pupils, and the browser in his computer that constrains the sites he can visit on the World Wide Web.

Figure 4-3

Bronfenbrenner's Bioecological Model

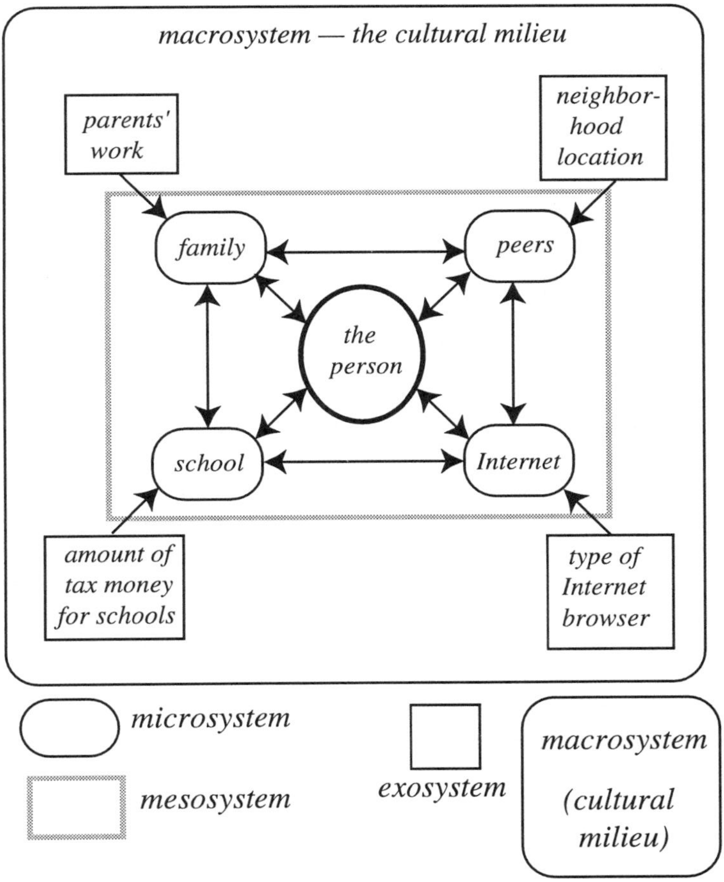

Finally, the source of influence most remote from the boy's immediate experiences is the array of physical conditions, attitudes, practices, and convictions shared throughout the society. The *macrosystem* is the *cultural milieu,* represented in Figure 4-3 as the large box encompassing the microsystems and mesosystems. The *macrosystem* is the equivalent of Wicker's *social/physical world.* Like the behavior settings of Wicker's theory, Bronfenbrenner's microsystems serve as the immediate transmitters of culture. In other words, the family, school, and companions—along with such mass communication media as books, television, and the Internet—are the functionaries that carry cultural messages directly to the child.

THE INFLUENCE OF MACRO-ENVIRONMENTS

Whereas Wicker's model focuses attention on the person acting within immediate behavior settings (micro-environments) that directly affect development, the theory proposed by Glen H. Elder, Jr., of the University of North Carolina concerns ways development is affected by events in the broader society (macro-environment), that is, in Wicker's *social/physical world* and Bronfenbrenner's *cultural milieu.* Thus, *lifespan* or *life-course* models are designed to answer the question: How is a person's development influenced by the condition of the surrounding society at each juncture of the individual's lifespan? Consequently, the theory described in the following paragraphs concerns the way development is configured for a biologically changing individual who interacts with social contexts that are sometimes stable and other times transitory.

Two propositions on which Elder's theory is based involve (a) societal stability and change and (b) the time and place in which an individual is located when social conditions are stable and when they are in flux. The first proposition holds that each child is born into, and raised within, a society that moves through phases of stability and change that can significantly influence the child's development (Elder, 1996; Elder, Modell, & Parke, 1993). The second proposition asserts that each person is located in a particular time and place in relation to the society's phases. *Time* refers to what is occurring in the society at different junctures in the person's development. Hence, *time* assumes the form of a life-stage principle which states that "the influence of a historical event on the life course depends on the stage at which individuals experience the event" (Elder, 1996, p. 52).

Important factors that affect development are: (a) the biological and psychological condition of the person at a given period in her or his development, (b) macro-societal features that affect the individual within that period, and (c) the extent to which those factors are stable or are in transition.

Among the important macro-societal features that can vary with the passing of time are ones related to:

- *public order and safety* (peace vs. war, riots, civil disobedience, strikes, crime)
- *politics* (system of governance—democratic, autocratic, socialistic)
- *economics* (prosperity vs. depression, capitalism vs. state socialism, job market, credit availability, workforce productivity, income levels)
- *social-class structure* (stability of classes, types and degrees of differences among classes, ease of mobility from one class to another)
- *ethnic composition* (numbers and sizes of recognized ethnic divisions, extent of amicable vs. antagonistic relations among divisions, likenesses and

differences among divisions [physical appearance, customs, usual roles in the society])

- *occupational structure* (types and proportions of agricultural, industrial, and service occupations)
- *transportation media* (horse and wagon, train, automobile, bus, airplane)
- *communication, information media* (word of mouth, letters, books, news-papers, telephones, television, computer networks)
- *childrearing functionaries* (nuclear biological-parents family, extended fam-ily, single-parent family, one biological parent plus one stepparent, foster family, social-service organization, school)
- *religious affiliation* (numbers and sizes of religious denominations, simi-lari-ties and differences of belief among denominations, extent of conflict among denominations)
- *health conditions and medical practices* (prevalence of different diseases, availability of drugs and medical treatment)

The relationship between when children arrive in the world and the timing of societal eras is depicted in Figure 4-4 with five age cohorts—children born in 1920, 1940, 1960, 1980, and 1995.

Consider, first, American children born in 1920 (Cohort One). World War I ended just two years before members of the 1920 cohort were born. Later that year, American women were accorded the right to vote in all public elections. In the economic sphere, the U.S. government adopted probusiness policies, issued injunctions against striking workers, raised tariffs on imported goods, and lim-ited immigrants to 164,000 annually, with immigration quotas favoring Euro-pean nations. The stock market flourished under conditions of financial prosperity, of few controls on investment practices, and of easy credit. The popularity of automobiles, radios, and movies grew rapidly, thereby offering children of Cohort One mobility and access to entertainment that children from no previous cohort had enjoyed. As the decade advanced, the Ku Klux Klan (with its anti-Negro, anti-Jewish, anti-Catholic program) grew in membership and power. Racial discrimination was widespread. Then, in 1929, the stock market crashed, helping launch the Great Depression—a disaster from which the nation would not entirely recover until industrial production rose with the advent of World War II at the end of the 1930s. To cope with the depression through-out the 1930s, President Franklin Roosevelt introduced a variety of social recon-struction measures under the label *New Deal.* Controls were placed on banks and on the stock market. A federal social-security program was inaugurated to ensure that people would have an income in their old age. During the 1930s, membership in labor unions grew rapidly, accompanied by a new level of politi-cal activity on the part of workers. The decade closed with Europe at war and the U.S. populace divided in their opinions about whether the U.S. should actively support Britain and France in the fight against Germany and Italy.

Now to Cohort Two. The question of the U.S. entering the war was settled in December 1941, when Japanese planes attacked military installations in Hawaii. Thus, many children born in 1940 would be raised during early childhood by their mothers and grandparents, because their fathers were away in the armed forces during World War II. For a substantial number of children, this early separation from their fathers would contribute to a difficult child-father relationship after the father returned home (Stolz, 1968). During the 1960s, members of Cohort Two were between ages 20 and 30, participating in the changed youth culture of that decade. For some youths—but certainly not all, and probably not the majority—this would mean rebelling against authorities, joining civil rights and antiwar demonstrations, using illicit drugs, and frequently changing sex partners. In the 1960s, Cohort Two members would become the parents of Cohort Three children and often provide a different family context than they themselves had experienced as children during and after World War II. Unlike the Cohort Two child, some Cohort Three children could more often see their family's and neighborhood's "normal way of life" as featuring marijuana and cocaine, casual sex, and rebellion against traditional authorities. Twenty years later, in the 1980s, members of Cohort Two would be middle-aged, some of them now grandparents. But with the growing incidence of divorce, many would not be with their original conjugal partners. Members of Cohort Three—now the parents of Cohort Four—would bring the attitudes acquired during their childhood to the task of childrearing, including viewpoints from the growing feminist movement that asserted women's rights to pursue their own careers, either inside or outside of marriage. Cohort Four children would grow up at a time of easy financial credit, with many parents taking advantage of credit cards to indulge their own and their offsprings' desire for material goods in a spirit of, "We deserve to live well." During the middle and latter 1990s, financial interest rates were lower, credit not so easy, inflation low, and employment rates high. The United States labor market now differed significantly from that of the 1940s when manufacturing had been a dominant source of jobs in the United States. By the 1990s, many low-skill factory jobs had moved overseas to countries with low labor costs, so that jobs in the United States were increasingly in service and sales activities, with the better-paying jobs requiring specialized skills, such as those involving computers. In the realm of sexual behavior, children in Cohort Four would newly face choices posed by the popularizing of casual sexual intercourse in the mass-communication media (television, computer networks), the advance of the gay-rights movement, and the growing incidence of AIDS (acquired immune deficiency syndrome). Finally, children born in 1995 would be affected in their late childhood and adolescence by the changes in societal conditions that would appear during the early years of the new millennium.

In summary, not only are societal trends reflected in the lives of children who constitute a given birth cohort, but the lives of individuals from different cohorts are linked in ways that also influence development, particularly when the values

Figure 4-4

Relationship of Societal Conditions and Birth Cohorts

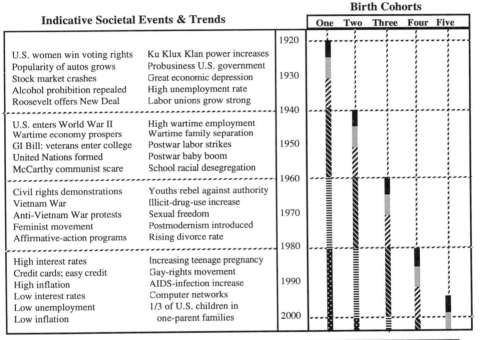

Indicative Societal Events & Trends			Birth Cohorts				
			One	Two	Three	Four	Five
		1920					
U.S. women win voting rights	Ku Klux Klan power increases						
Popularity of autos grows	Probusiness U.S. government						
Stock market crashes	Great economic depression	1930					
Alcohol prohibition repealed	High unemployment rate						
Roosevelt offers New Deal	Labor unions grow strong						
		1940					
U.S. enters World War II	High wartime employment						
Wartime economy prospers	Wartime family separation						
GI Bill: veterans enter college	Postwar labor strikes	1950					
United Nations formed	Postwar baby boom						
McCarthy communist scare	School racial desegregation						
		1960					
Civil rights demonstrations	Youths rebel against authority						
Vietnam War	Illicit-drug-use increase						
Anti-Vietnam War protests	Sexual freedom	1970					
Feminist movement	Postmodernism introduced						
Affirmative-action programs	Rising divorce rate						
		1980					
High interest rates	Increasing teenage pregnancy						
Credit cards; easy credit	Gay-rights movement						
High inflation	AIDS-infection increase	1990					
Low interest rates	Computer networks						
Low unemployment	1/3 of U.S. children in						
Low inflation	one-parent families	2000					

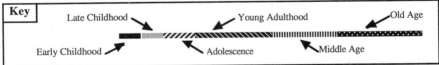

Key

Late Childhood — Young Adulthood — Old Age

Early Childhood — Adolescence — Middle Age

and lifestyles of one cohort conflict with those of another, thereby resulting in disagreements between parents and their children as well as among grandparents, parents, and the young.

Next, consider *place*, which in the present context refers to the child's combined geographical and social location at a given point in his or her life course. For example, one 5-year-old girl shares a two-room apartment with six other family members in a large city's ghetto neighborhood. The head of the household is an unwed mother—currently pregnant and on welfare—who had quit school in tenth grade to run away from home. In contrast, another 5-year-old lives in a nine-room house in the suburbs with her biological mother and father and a younger brother. Her father is employed as an accountant and her mother as a part-time real estate agent.

In summary, Elder's life-course theory focuses on the direction taken by a person's life at any stage of development as a result of events within the broader society that surrounds the behavior settings with which the person is engaged.

MATCHING PERSONS AND ENVIRONMENTS

The seeds of John L. Holland's theory of vocational choice (1985a) were sown in the 1960s and 1970s, resulting in the theory's full fruition in the 1980s.

Four tenets on which the model is founded are that (a) each individual's personality tends to represent one of six personality types, (b) psychological environments that are associated with vocations can be divided into six basic varieties, (c) each personality type is best suited to a particular one of those psychological environments, and (d) the better the match between people's personalities and their vocational environments, the happier and more successful they are in their occupations (Holland, 1985a). On the basis of these tenets, Holland reasoned that

> individuals entered specific occupational environments because of their interests and personalities, and [they] remained in those occupations because of the reinforcements and satisfactions obtained through the interactions in that environment. . . . On the other hand, incongruent person-environment links were not viewed as reinforcing and stimulated the need for change. (Walsh & Holland, 1992, p. 36)

The following list identifies traits and abilities that exemplify the six personality types and offers examples of occupations preferred by people with such personalities (Holland, 1985a; Walsh & Holland, 1992).

1. Artistic type:

Personality traits: emotional, expressive, imaginative, impractical, impulsive, intuitive, original

Abilities: artistic, creative, dance, graphic, musical, writing

Typical preferred occupations: author, actor/actress, composer, designer, playwright, sculptor

2. Conventional type:

Personality traits: conforming, conscientious, orderly, persistent, calm, efficient

Abilities: clerical, mathematical, organizational

Typical preferred occupations: accountant, auditor, bank teller, financial planner, tax analyst

3. Enterprising type:

Personality traits: adventuresome, ambitious, bold, enterprising, optimistic, pleasure-seeking, popular, resourceful, self-confident

Abilities: leadership, persuasive, rhetorical

Typical preferred occupations: business executive, buyer, professional entertainers' representative, publicity agent, sales person

4. Investigative type:

Personality traits: analytical, critical, curious, independent, inquisitive, intellectual, precise, rational

Abilities: logical-reasoning, mathematical, scientific

Typical preferred occupations: anthropologist, biologist, chemist, geologist, physicist, research psychologist, sociologist

5. Realistic type:

Personality traits: conforming, forthright, honest, materialistic, persistent, practical, modest, stable

Abilities: manipulative, mechanical, spatial-relations

Typical preferred occupations: auto mechanic, carpenter, computer technician, electrician, farmer, plumber

6. Social type:

Personality traits: compassionate, companionable, convincing, friendly, helpful, kind, responsible, understanding

Abilities: communicative, empathic

Typical preferred occupations: clinical psychologist, counselor, social worker, teacher

Holland conducted a substantial amount of empirical research to test his theory and to investigate the likely causes of—or at least the variables associated with—personality types and occupational preferences. He concluded that an individual's personality type is the result of that person's life history, a history combining (a) genetic endowment, (b) past and current cultural and personal forces, and (c) past and current physical environments. Personality "is in many ways learned," especially from social pressures in early adolescence and from childhood experiences with parents (Walsh & Holland, 1992, p. 48).

The suggestion that offspring learn personality traits from their parents' types has been supported by several studies. However, the patterns of parent-child similarity have varied somewhat from one investigation to another. In a study of National Merit Scholars and their parents, Holland (1961, 1962) found that male students with a particular personality type tended to have fathers whose current occupations were consistent with that type. But for female students, no findings were significant. Grandy and Stahmann (1974), in a study of 487 university freshmen, found a positive relationship between personality types of fathers-sons, fathers-daughters, and mothers-daughters, but not between mothers-sons. The most consistent findings in research by DeWinne, Overton, and Schneider (1978) revealed similar personality types in father-son and father-daughter combinations. Grotevant, Scarr, & Weinberg (1977), in comparing parent-child personality matches within both biological and adoptive families, found that biologically related family members modestly resembled each other in their answers on Holland's Vocational Preference Inventory (Holland, 1985b); adoptive family members were usually less similar.

REMAINING CHALLENGES

From each of the theories sketched in this chapter, inferences can be drawn about issues that call for further clarification.

Cohen and Cohen (1985) suggest that remaining questions about spatial cognition implied by their model include: What cognitive demands are necessitated by various motor activities? How are processes such as attention and integration of multiple views affected by activities? How do children evaluate the spaces in which they participate? What forms of social interactions are influenced by what types of environmental activity? How do the goals and purposes of activities vary with spaces and with development?

Wicker's theory proposes a variety of variables that interact to determine how individuals assign meanings to the behavior settings they encounter and how such meaning-making affects development. His variables includes such concepts as *behavior-setting programs, shared meanings, reality, mental maps, cause maps, sense-making cycles, time,* and *the social/physical world.* Wicker's presentation of the theory explains what each of these factors is intended to mean, but it does not explain exactly how the factors interact in a particular behavior setting and how such interaction influences the cognitive development of individuals inhabiting that setting. For example, during a given event, by what mode of analysis can we estimate how the likenesses and differences between the cause maps of participants in the event influence the outcome of the event, and how do we determine the event's influence on the mental development of each participant? Furthermore, by what process do significant conditions of the broad social/physical environment (the cultural milieu) influence the mental maps of the members of a behavior setting? In the midst of Wicker's hypothesized sense-making cycle, how may one person's method of searching for alternative interpretations differ from another's and why? Such questions and a variety of similar ones appear worth the attention of theorists interested in following Wicker's sense-making lead.

The central proposition of Elder's macro-environment theory (the notion that changes in the broader society influence people's development) hardly need be questioned. Everyone can likely describe how happenings in the general social-physical environment have affected their own lives. However, what still seems called for is a series of principles identifying the way interactions among variables in individuals' lives produce different developmental outcomes for some people than for others who live within the same cultural milieu. For example, how did the stock market crash in 1929 exert a different influence on (a) the 10-year-old son in the family of a New Yorker who had heavily invested in stocks on a margin basis and (b) the 10-year-old son in the family of a corn farmer in Nebraska who owned a few stocks? In the New York family, how did the crash affect the development of the 10-year-old son as compared to the development of the 18-year-old daughter who was currently attending an expensive private college? What principles of interpretation would equip a person to determine the role played by the Vietnam War protests and the "flower children" culture of the late 1960s in the lives of two 16-year-old Seattle high school girls, one of whom ran away to join a drugs-and-open-sex commune in San Francisco while the other completed high school and entered a convent to become a nun? Such puzzles as these invite theorists to refine macro-environment theory by identifying patterns of interaction that account for how the same societal event can exert a different influence on one individual's development than on another's.

When Holland's scheme of six personality types and six categories of vocations is applied to individuals, it becomes apparent that the six personality types do not always fit neatly into the six vocational classes. The matching is often only approximate at best, representing a tendency toward a match rather than a true fit. For instance, there are people who appear to fill their occupational roles quite satisfactorily, even though their personality type, as judged by Holland's measuring device, does not seem appropriate. And other people whose personality profile would appear suited to a given occupation do not perform well or do not feel comfortable in what is deemed their proper occupational class. In short, there are exceptions to Holland's rule, and when such exceptions appear, they require an explantion. One explanation is that the method of measuring personality types is faulty. Another is that the rule needs revision, perhaps in the form of refinements that will account for the ostensible exceptions. This, I believe, is what confronts Holland's system—the need to refine the model so it furnishes a reasonable explanation for cases that appear at first glance to be exceptions to his proposed matchings.

5

Beyond Piaget

It's quite apparent that no one has ever provided final, definitive answers to questions about human development. The proposed answers are never good enough. They always leave issues unresolved. This fact is nicely illustrated in the case of Jean Piaget (1896-1980), the Swiss psychologist who became the 20th century's most prolific and inventive child-development theorist. The magnitude of his productivity is reflected in the quantity of his publications, which extended into the many hundreds. By the year 2000, the *PsychINFO* database listed more than 4,600 publications founded on, or alluding to, Piaget's contributions. But such an impressive body of work still failed to produce ultimate answers to human development questions. Consequently, a host of puzzles have awaited the attention of later scholars, including theorists who style themselves as neo-Piagetians—followers of the trails blazed by the master. Robbie Case (1992b) has summarized neo-Piagetians' diverse innovations under three headings: (a) proposals that retain most of Piaget's postulates, (b) proposals that retain, but also refine and extend, Piaget's postulates, and (c) proposals that alter the classic Piagetian system. Thus, recent variants of the Piagetian tradition have assumed three principal forms: (a) proposed corrections of matters that critics claim Piaget got wrong, (b) elaborations of original Piagetian concepts, and (c) innovations launched from a foundation of Piagetian thought.

From among the dozens of theoretical schemes that have been inspired—entirely or partially—by Piaget's proposals, I've selected three to describe in this chapter: (a) Case's elaborated rendition of Piaget's cognitive-development stages, (b) Dupont's extension of Piaget's understanding of emotional development, and (c) Wellman's notions about children's theories of mind.

AN ELABORATED SET OF COGNITIVE-DEVELOPMENT STAGES

Perhaps the most familiar feature of Piaget's theory is his series of mental-development stages. Of the several versions of Piaget's stage structure that appeared over the decades, the best known consists of four major growth periods labeled: sensorimotor (birth to about age 2), preoperational thought (about age 2 to 7), concrete operations (about 7 to 11), and formal operations (about 11 to 15). The following are chief characteristics of the stages:

Sensorimotor Period (Birth–2). The infant advances from performing only reflex actions to finally representing objects mentally and thereby cognitively combining and manipulating them.

Preoperational-Thought Period (2–7). This stage is divided into two levels. The first (ages 2–4) is characterized by egocentric speech and primary dependence on perception, rather than on logic, in problem solving. The second (5–7) is marked by an intuitive approach to life, a transition phase between the child's depending on perception and depending on logical thought to solve problems.

Concrete-Operations Period (7–11). In this stage, children can perform logical mental operations on concrete objects that either are directly observed or are imagined. An important feature of this period is the child's developing greater ability to recognize which aspects of an object remain unchanged (are *conserved*) when the object changes from one form to another. For example, when a large ball of clay is divided into a series of small balls of clay, the typical preoperational child will not recognize that in this transformation the weight and mass of clay remain the same. The concrete-operations child, in contrast, will understand that weight and mass have been conserved.

Formal-Operations Period (11–15). During adolescence, the typical child is no longer limited by what he or she directly sees or hears, nor is he or she restricted to the problem at hand. The adolescent can now imagine various conditions that bear on a problem—past, present, and future—and devise hypotheses about what might logically occur under different combinations of such conditions. By the end of this final stage of mental development, the youth is capable of all the forms of logic that the adult commands. Subsequently, further experience over the years of later youth and adulthood fill in the outline with additional, more complex concepts so that the adult's thought is more mature and freer of lingering vestiges of egocentrism than is the thought of the adolescent. (Summarized from Piaget & Inhelder, 1969)

Neo-Piagetians on occasion have found fault with details of the master's stage structure and have sought to correct its putative weaknesses with their own schemes. One of those revisionists has been Robbie Case, a developmental psychologist who spent the 1990s dividing his professional activities between Stanford University and the University of Toronto.

The basic framework of Case's scheme is similar to, and generally supportive of, Piaget's plan of sensorimotor, preoperational, concrete operational, and formal operational periods. However, for the upper three periods, Case invented labels he felt more accurately described the sorts of mental processes children applied from early childhood through adolescence. As shown in Figure 5-1, he substituted the term *relational* for Piaget's *preoperational*, the word *dimensional* for *concrete operational,* and *vectorial* for *formal operational.*

Case was in essential agreement with Piaget's depiction of the first stage— *sensorimotor development*—but disagreed about the link between the second and third periods. Whereas in Piaget's design the preoperational phase was mainly a preparation for the operational stage, Case contended that "The period from 2 to 5 years is not just a precursor of concrete operational development. It is a distinct stage of its own, with its own sequence of operative structures and its own final operational system" (1985, p. 116). In applying the label *relational* to this period, Case indicated that from around age 2 until children enter kindergarten, they develop skills of comprehending relations between two observed phenomena, as in recognizing ways that different animals are similar to each other.

In Case's opinion, the next period (ages 5 to 11) is distinguished by the school-age child's ability to mentally manipulate perceptions that can be aligned along a dimension—including such polar dimensions as hot-cold, far-near, more-less, high-low, frequent-seldom, and the like. Hence, the term *dimensional* replaced Piaget's *concrete operations.*

Finally, Case judged that a more accurate descriptive word, *vectorial,* should replace *formal operations* to signify that children beyond age 11 or so could explain or predict what result could be expected from the interactions of two or more dimensions. For example, vectorial thought processes are required for predicting how a balance beam—such as a playground teeter-totter or seesaw—will respond to the interaction of *varied weights* at *varied distances* along the beam arms. At this fourth stage of intellectual growth "children are no longer focusing on either of . . . two dimensions separately. Rather, they are focusing on a more abstract dimension: the vector that results from [the dimensions'] opposition" (1985, p. 108).

Another of Case's innovations was his identifying within each stage a sequence of subphases (*substages*) that advance the child's thought processes from simpler to more complex and sophisticated levels. The substages, common to all four major periods, are entitled (0) *operational consolidation,* (1) *unifocal coordination*, (2) *bifocal coordination,* and (3) *elaborated coordination.* As suggested in Figure 5-1, in the operational-consolidation phase, the child is actually integrating in a secure fashion the accomplishments of the previous major period rather than adopting a significantly new mode of thought. For this reason, Case numbered the first phase 0. The subsequent three phases involve the addition of more advanced mental skills and thus are assigned numbers 1, 2, and 3. At the unifocal-coordination substage, the child is able to center attention on a variety of different factors, but can only focus on one factor at a time to solve a problem, such as one sensorimotor movement at ages 4 to 8 months, one relationship at ages 1.5 to 2 years, one dimension at 5 to 7, and one interaction of

Figure 5-1

Piaget's and Case's Stage Structures

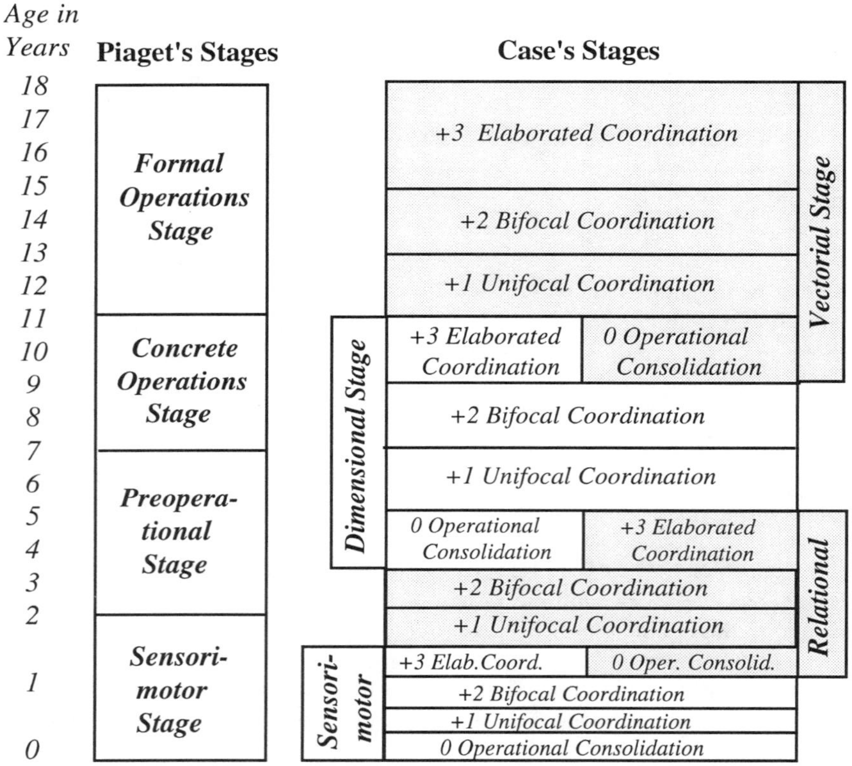

Age in Years	Piaget's Stages	Case's Stages

contrasting dimensions (vectorial) at ages 11 to 13 years. However, with greater neural maturation and with more experience, children advance to a bifocal-coordination substage where they can direct attention at two different factors to solve a problem, such as:

- two sensorimotor movements at ages 8 to 12 months, as in bracing oneself with one arm while reaching with the other arm to grasp an object.
- two relationships at ages 2 to 3.5 years, as in recognizing that a round, red block can be paired with either a square, red block or a round, blue block.
- two interacting dimensions at ages 7 to 9 years, as in recognizing that the greater width of a short, wide bowl allows it to hold the same quantity of water as does the greater height of a tall, thin glass.

- two interactions of contrasting dimensions at ages 13 to 15 years, as in recognizing that (a) the boiling point of water is affected by the interaction of temperature and atmosphere density and (b) water changes from a liquid to a vapor when that point is reached.

In like manner, at the final elaborated-coordination level of a major stage, children can coordinate two or more factors in a complex way to solve problems.

Case has used his model not only for charting children's reasoning about inanimate objects but also for interpreting children's language development and the way they think about social relations. The model is thus conceived to be a general theory of intelligence, applicable to a variety of aspects of mental development.

In a number of ways Case's scheme has advanced development theory by accounting for phenomena that were not adequately explained by earlier models. For instance, Piaget proposed that once a child's mode of thought advances to a new stage—such as from preoperational to concrete-operational thinking—the child's reasoning in all facets of life advance to that new stage. However, a host of research has shown that children's mode of thought can be very uneven. For instance, in mathematics it is typical for children to conceive the conservation of number and length before they understand the conservation of area and volume.[*] And the extent of unevenness in the stages of children's thinking can be even greater in one domain, such as physical events, than in another, such as moral reasoning. Piaget adopted the term *horizontal décalage* (meaning *displacement*) as a label for this apparent lag in a child's applying in all aspects of life a mode of thinking that Piaget proposed was characteristic of a single stage. The damage that the phenomenon of horizontal décalage does to the notion of distinct stages of growth is suggested in Thelen and Smith's (1994, p. 22) claim that "All of cognition does not move forward in lockstep. Cognitive development does not look like a marching band; it looks more like a teaming mob." Thus, the expression *horizontal décalage* serves as a label for such inconsistency but not as an explanation. However, Case's notion of substages within each major period permits him to rationalize the apparent inconsistency in children's thought processes. For instance, in the early unifocal-coordination phase of the preoperational stage, (ages 5 to 7), the child focuses on separate factors of physical objects (such as dimensions of height, width, weight, mass), with the understanding of each occurring at a different time. Only by phase three (elaborated coordination) do all of these separate insights become integrated into a general,

---

[*] As noted earlier, in Piagetian nomenclature, the term *conservation* refers to the aspects of a phenomenon that remain unchanged when other aspects change. For example, when a pint of water is poured out of a quart bottle, the chemical composition of water (H_2O) has remained the same (been conserved) even as the quantity has changed. And when a group of 8 apples is divided into two groups of 3 and 5, the total quantity has been conserved even though the grouping has changed.

qualitatively distinct mode of thought governing a broad spectrum of mental activities.

More recently, Case proposed a feedback loop between the specific knowledge acquired in specific contexts and the more general knowledge represented in the child's major conceptual structures. When intense experience in a given domain hastens progress in that area, the resulting change also feeds "up" to the central conceptual structure, nudging that structure toward the optimal level permitted by the current maturational potential of the system. This resulting increased sophistication of the central structure in turn feeds "down" to other specific contexts in which the child may have less experience, thereby urging improvement in those areas as well. The result is a much more even level of development than one would otherwise expect. For instance, consider the quantitative domain and three of its constituent subcategories—school math, time, and money.

> The diligent schoolchild who invests a great deal of attention in learning the math taught by her teacher, the lazy schoolchild whose prime interest is in checking the clock to see how soon his lessons will be over, and the unschooled child who sells candy in the streets of Brazil—each lives in a highly distinctive environment. Nevertheless, each must work at understanding the same general numerical system. Moreover, as progress is made in understanding this system, the progress should in each case inform the child's performance in a broad range of contexts, including those to which they have relatively little exposure or to which they have not bothered to apply themselves. In effect, different developmental pathways should all lead to the same general end point, namely, that all three children should be able to answer novel questions at the same developmental level in all three task domains (school problems, time problems, and money problems). (Case & Okamoto, 1996, p. 160)

Case proposed that in very young children, the development of a central conceptual structure is heavily dependent on genetic factors—on an inherited biological clock. However, with advancing age,

> The experience that is relevant to the formation of central conceptual structures becomes less universal, and more highly dependent on technologies and bodies of knowledge that are unique to the culture in which they were developed. . . . [As age progresses] social institutions, such as schooling, play an increasingly important role . . . in providing this experience . . . [by familiarizing] children with the culture's symbol system and the concepts and conventions underlying their use. (Case, 1992a, pp. 367-368)

In summary, the idea that cognitive development involves domains (specific) that are built up within a central conceptual structure (general) has enabled Case to explain the apparent contradiction between specific-stage and general-stage theories. He sees mental activity as a combination of specific and general tiers of intellectual functioning.

SOCIALLY CONSTRUCTED EMOTIONS

The model offered by psychotherapist Henry Dupont (Atlanta Area Psychological Associates) to explain human emotional development is an example of a theory designed to extend a line of thought that Piaget introduced. Dupont writes that Piaget on occasion focused attention on emotions but then "lost interest in affective development. I have tried to pick up this topic where he dropped it" (Dupont, 1994, p. xiii).

Dupont disagrees with Freud's assertion that people's emotions are instinctual, innate, fully formed at the time of birth, and residing in the unconscious, from whence they influence behavior. In contrast, Dupont has suggested that emotions, in their multiple forms, are not inborn but, instead, are social constructions—personality components that individuals create by means of their encounters with other people during their growing years. Dupont's neo-Piagetian theory postulates that

> both our feelings and emotions, which are assumed to be constructions, are informed by our needs and values, and that our feelings and emotions change considerably in the course of our development. It also postulates that our consciousness is constructed as a product of our social experience, and that its acquisition plays a crucial role in the development of our emotional maturity. (Dupont, 1994, p. xiv)

Dupont begins with Piaget's conception of *needs* and *homeostasis,* asserting that all thought and behavior is the result of some event occurring within the person or within the environment that shifts the person out of balance. The disequilibrium resulting from this shift generates a need that stimulates the person to search for something to satisfy the need and reestablish equilibrium. Then all "action terminates when [the] need is satisfied" (Piaget, 1967, p. 6).

Dupont sees feeling as an energizer and sees emotion as a resultant action called into the service of a need. He distinguishes between feelings and emotions by proposing that feelings are *energy-regulating evaluations* and emotions are *sequences of behavior deriving from those feelings.* In Piagetian terms, emotions are thus cognitive constructions or *action schemes.* Hence, feelings mobilize energy, then emotions put that energy to work (Dupont, 1994, pp. 6, 14). Dupont uses the term *affect* or *affective development* to encompass both feelings and emotions.

In discussing energy-regulating evaluations, Dupont implies that *values* are judgments—originally intuitive and later intentional—about the desirability or propriety of events, objects, or people. These are judgments of good versus bad, right versus wrong, love versus hate, kindness versus malevolence, and more. How people feel about (evaluate) something regulates how they will invest their energy in regard to that something. Emotion is the translation of a feeling into a cognitive construction or action.

Dupont follows Piaget's lead in visualizing affective development as a series of stages. For Piaget, persons' feelings about themselves (intra-individual) (a) begin at birth with hereditary organizations, (b) are increased during early childhood with acquired feelings, and (c) ultimately assume the form of conscious regulators of intentional behavior. Feelings about other people (interpersonal) (a) start with intuitive responses, (b) during childhood take the form of the surrounding culture's normative version of affects, and (c) may ultimately achieve the status of idealistic feelings (Piaget, 1981, p. 14).

Similar to Piaget, Dupont believes that people do not inherit such particular feelings and emotions as jealousy, envy, anger, guilt, shame, sadness, pride, and happiness. Instead, the neonate comes into the world with no more than a vague sense of distress or of well-being along with the capacity to separate these vague feelings over the coming years into more distinct types as a consequence of (a) the increasing maturation of the child's cognitive system and (b) the child's experiences with other people.

Thus, in Dupont's scheme, affective development begins at birth with a few elementary inborn feelings. From then on, children's interactions with the important people in their lives stimulate them to differentiate their amorphous, general feelings into more precise types, particularly those types commonly defined and endorsed by their culture. Children, thus, mentally construct beliefs about how their culture expects them to feel under different circumstances and what behavior they should exhibit in expressing those feelings. Because cultures are not all alike in the affective expectations they hold, the kinds of events that should elicit shame, guilt, delight, and pride—and how those feelings are properly expressed—can vary from one culture to another. Consequently, the way children build feelings and emotions into their personalities will differ by cultural background.

A further step in affective development involves the individual constructing his or her own version of the culture's conception of feelings and emotions.

> Emotional maturity requires us to develop a personal psychology that is congruent with the psychology of our culture. Indeed, our personal psychology has meaning only within the context of our culture's folk psychology. (Dupont, 1994, p. 24)

And as people advance to higher stages of emotional development, their level of logical thought becomes increasingly important.

> Our intelligence and our consciousness are essential for our emotional development. At maturity, we are conscious of and clear about our feelings and conscious of the logic of our choice of action upon our feelings. And, at the highest levels of equilibrium (social equilibrium) we must also be conscious of how others are reacting to our emotional actions, and the probable consequences of our actions or any new actions that we might initiate. . . . We cannot achieve this level of self-reflective consciousness without social experiences. . . . We are de-

pendent on . . . the dialogue we have with others to achieve this highest level of consciousness. (Dupont, 1994, p. 22)

CHILDREN AS MINDREADERS

Whereas Dupont portrayed his theory of emotional development as a direct continuation of original Piagetian thought, the following model is one whose connection with Piaget's proposals is more remote. In this case, Henry M. Wellman, a University of Michigan professor of psychology, has developed a theory founded on Piagetian assumptions about how children construct the contents of their minds; however, Wellman's model focuses on an aspect of cognition that Piaget did not address so formally nor in such detail. That aspect concerns how children acquire the ability to estimate other people's mental states. This is the field of investigation typically referred to as *theory of mind.*

Carol Feldman has suggested that

This new research represents a Kuhnian (1970) paradigm shift for post-Piagetian developmental psychology. It preserves a view of the child as an active seeker after knowledge, as building mental models that undergo successive qualitative reorganization in more abstract and powerful terms over time. Thus, it preserves the central gains of the Piagetian era over the theoretical view of childhood that preceded it. . . . The new paradigm creates a more inclusive and powerful model of cognitive development by incorporating important achievements of the earlier era into a larger structure. Piaget's active, thinking, and reasonable organism was alone in a world with uninterpreted objects to be explored. The new literature on theory of mind contextualizes Piaget's solitary thinker in a social world composed of encultured and communicating human adults. (Feldman, 1992, p. 107)

There seems to be widespread agreement that Premack and Woodruff's 1978 article "Does the Chimpanzee Have a Theory of Mind?" was the original impetus behind the spate of theories and empirical studies that appeared in the 1980s and 1990s to explain when and how children come to imagine that other people have minds whose operation and contents may in some ways be similar to, and in other ways be different from, their own. Among investigators in this field, there seems to be considerable agreement that by age 4, children come to an initial realization that there is a difference between "an *actual* event" and "what people *think about* an event." As a typical way of determining if children can distinguish between events and people's thoughts about events, an experimenter conducts a *false-belief test* that consists of (a) telling a young child a story about a character named Maxi who sees some candy in one place, (b) explaining that while Maxi is not looking the candy is moved somewhere else, and (c) then asking the child, "Where will Maxi look for the candy?" In studies reported by Perner (1991), children younger than age 4 believed Maxi would look where the candy really was after it was moved. But at around age 4, children suggested that Maxi's (false) belief would lead him to look in the candy's first location. "This recognition of the difference between Maxi's false belief and the reality of the matter was said to be the critical indication that the 4-year-old child has, while the 3-year-old child lacks, a theory of mind" (Feldman, 1992, p. 110).

A number of critics have objected to crediting a young child with such a formal mentalism as a *theory* of mind. They would reserve the term *theory* for the adolescent's more sophisticated conception of other people's mental states, a conception made possible by reaching Piaget's formal-operations stage of cognitive development. Thus, some investigators prefer to identify the 4-year-old's newly acquired ability as *mindreading* rather than as a *theory of mind*. In any event, both *theory of mind* and *mindreading* are used to label this recent field of interest.

Wellman's model is founded on the dual assumption that (a) children's ability to estimate other people's mental states is acquired rather than inherited and (b) that such ability comes earlier in life than Piaget imagined.

> I do not propose that an understanding of mind is innately given (as does Fodor, 1987); it is not available at birth, nor does it simply emerge by maturation. An understanding of mind is constructed by the child in the course of development. But at the same time I do not think that past developmental accounts are correct. [For instance,] Piaget's [accounts] have gotten the developmental story wrong[*] [because] quite young children are [actually] mentalists. I argue that while infants do not have a theory of mind, young preschoolers do. (Wellman, 1990, p. 5)

A further conviction undergirding Wellman's scheme is that people's (including children's) everyday understanding of mind does indeed constitute a theory since it fulfills the three principal requirements that, in Wellman's opinion, a theory must satisfy:

- an interconnected coherent body of concepts, which in this case consists of thoughts that include dreams, beliefs, desires, memories, imagination, fantasies, and more,
- ontological conceptions, that is, convictions about the nature of *reality*, including being able to distinguish between (a) events that actually occur in the world and (b) people's ideas about events, and
- a causal-explanatory account of a domain of phenomena. In the case of a theory of mind, the domain is that of human action and thought.

Because Wellman's studies of children's reasoning have convinced him that the thinking done by preschoolers age 3 and older fulfills his three criteria, such children can be credited with possessing a *theory of mind*. "It is a naive theory, not a developed or disciplined scientific theory, but a theory nonetheless" (Wellman, 1990, p. 8).

---

[*] Piaget (1929, p. 100) wrote: "Care must be taken not to endow the child with a systematic theory."

Wellman sees the child's theory of mind evolving through the following series of increasingly complex phases.

Two-Year-Olds

Even though prior to age 3 children's thinking does not reflect all three characteristics required for attributing to them a theory of mind, at age 2 they do possess an ability considered to be a precursor of mind theory—a building block on which a theory of mind can be erected. Wellman identifies this precursor as an understanding that people have simple desires, but there is yet no understanding of beliefs, "that is, no understanding that persons possess internal mental representations—convictions—as to how the world is" (1990, p. 9).

Two aspects of mind theory on which Wellman focuses are (a) the hypothetical or imaginary and (b) the causal. The hypothetical aspect involves distinguishing between *thoughts* and *things of the world,* that is, separating *mind* from *reality.* The second aspect, the causal, involves recognizing that when a person has a belief linked to a desire, that belief-desire combination can lead to action. In effect, it consists of recognizing the causal relation between mental states and real-world actions. Thus, our understanding the cause of others' behavior can involve estimating what beliefs and desires they "have in mind."

According to Wellman, the average 2-year-old can conceive of other people having desires for visible objects—a doll, a toy truck, a piece of chocolate. However, 2-year-olds do not conceive of others having in mind representations of objects. Thus, in Wellman's view, 2-year-olds recognize other people's direct desires—wanting a seeable object— but they do not yet envision others having a belief (idea, concept, expectation) of objects or events "in mind." Consequently, Wellman proposes that 2-year-olds have the start toward one component of a theory of mind—that desire leads to action. But they lack the remaining component needed for a beginning version of a mind-theory—an understanding that people have beliefs "in mind" that are distinct from the things of the world. Two-year-olds do not yet realize that a belief (a conception or symbol of doll, truck, and chocolate that is not presently visible) when linked to a desire can lead to action. In Wellman's opinion, that realization usually comes after the child's third birthday.

Three-Year-Olds

Wellman concludes that around age 3, children begin to recognize that people have beliefs about their world—ideas about things that are not the same as those things. These beliefs are symbols or representations of the world's objects and events. Such beliefs may also represent things that do not exist in the world outside the child's body, such as dreams, fantasies, imaginings. At age 3, this initial theory of mind is quite simple and undeveloped, so experts who investigate such matters have disagreed about whether the 3-year-old's perceptions do, indeed, qualify as a theory of mind.

I believe that three-year-olds have a basic sense of mental representations; it is part of their rudimentary conception of belief and hence part of their beginning theory of mind.   Perner (1988), Flavell (1988), and Gopnik (Forguson and Gopnik, 1988), however, believe that this is not achieved until four or four-and-a-half years.   In spite of our differences, we all agree that this is a fundamental achievement attained between three and six. (Wellman, 1990, p. 243)

The basis for the disagreement among researchers is often found in their having employed different ways of appraising children's thinking. For instance, in Perner 's (1991) use of the *false-belief task,* 3-year-olds did not judge that Maxi would look for the candy in the first location (the place Maxi had last seen the candy). Only by age 4 would children base their judgments on their conception of what Maxi would "have in mind." However, Wellman used a *not-own-belief task* to test children's thought processes. A typical not-own-belief task consists of first telling a girl, "Sam wants to find his puppy. It might be in the garage or under the porch. Where do you think the puppy is?" This initial step is taken to ascertain whether the child already has a belief about where the puppy would be, such as under the porch, on the basis of her own experience. Then, once the girl offers her opinion, the experimenter seeks to separate the girl's own belief from the decision about Sam's expectation by saying, "That's a good guess, but Sam thinks the puppy is in the garage. Where do you think he will look for the puppy?" Wellman found that 3-year-olds could draw the correct inference that Sam would hunt in the garage.

Because Wellman's 3-year-old subjects passed his not-own-belief test as well as a variety of similar puzzles, yet failed Perner's false-belief tasks, Wellman and his fellow pathfinders in this theory-of-mind domain are left with the job of more precisely teasing out the complex features that characterize child thought at ages 3 and 4.

From Age 3 to 6

According to Wellman's speculation, from age 3 to age 6 the typical child's theory of mind changes in two major ways: (a) in the conception of the nature of mental representations (moving from copy to interpretation) and (b) in the child's proficiency in processing information and manipulating beliefs (moving from inconsistent to consistent responses).

In 3-year-olds' theory of mind, the things they see and hear are recorded and maintained in their heads as exact copies of those things. They believe that their mother, their tricycle, and their morning in nursery school are all represented in mind as true pictures of those items or happenings. However, as children progress through ages 4 and 5, they increasingly recognize that different people can have in mind different impressions of the same event. Therefore, mental representations are not exact copies of perceptions but, rather, are interpretations of objects and events. Those interpretations are not solely pictures in the mind but, rather, can be in the form of visual and auditory icons as well as words or other symbols. Wellman characterizes this transition in conceptions of the mind's function—from copying to interpreting—by adopting the analogies of *container* and *homunculus*.

In the 3-year-olds' view, mind is like a passive container in which representations of the world—pictures—are collected to remain in the mind as copies to be consulted whenever the child is stimulated to think about them. But by age 6, children come to understand mind as an active constructor of interpretations of things they witness in their world and of things they can imagine. So Wellman proposes that by age 6, children feel as if the mind is rather like a homunculus, an active little person making judgments.

> By analogy, the mind can be viewed (in a crude but useful way) as a person in the head: a person who can be fooled, leading to misinterpretations; a person who can direct and order, leading to actions; an inner person who works with ideas, crafting them, constructing them, sorting them out, just as outer persons work with objects. . . . People know that the mind is nonphysical; they do not actually think of minds as physically-spatially personified in any sense; they see mental activity only as psychologically personified. (Wellman, 1990, p. 269)

Wellman's second postulated major advance in children's mind-theory over the years 3 to 6 is in the improved efficiency with which the young make decisions in their mindreading activities, in their estimating how and why other people think as they do. This progress is noted in the speed and accuracy with which children solve the reasoning problems that psychologists pose for them—identifying false beliefs, separating their own knowledge from the knowledge others are likely to have (not-own-belief task), and similar tests.

Summary

The model proposed by Wellman is his response to the tripartite question: "Do young children have a theory of mind; and if so, what is its nature and how does it evolve?" Wellman's answer is: Yes, the young do have such a theory, in the sense of a systematic notion about how other people and themselves "think." To qualify as a theory of mind, in its simplest form, the child's notion needs to include a conception of *desires* and *beliefs* that combine to produce people's *actions*. Children achieve such a conception around age 3, an accomplishment built on their understanding of *desire* around age 2, but at that age the typical child has not yet reached the *belief/desire→action* stage. Between ages 3 and 6, children's conception of mind progresses from a container model (the mind's contents are true copies of objects and events deposited for later consultation) to a homunculus model (a process that is like an active person in the head interpreting objects and events—constructing, evaluating, altering, and creating representations in symbolic form). This theory of the mind as an interpreting and creating functionary will continue to develop into increasingly complex forms throughout later childhood and adolescence.

REMAINING CHALLENGES

The authors' intent behind the three theories described in this chapter was to provide answers to questions that had remained unresolved in Piaget's own work. And whereas the authors did, indeed, furnish new insights into their target questions, they, too, left further problems inadequately solved. Here are a few of the remaining puzzles that serve as opportunities for theorizing and data collection.

Case's revision of Piaget's cognitive development stages was tested on children in the age range 4 to 10 years. Case has since imagined that "it seems at least possible that [this revised stage structure] may provide an equally good fit to the waves of structural learning that take place later (during the teenage years) or earlier (during the preschool years) in the overall sequence of children's conceptual development" (1998, p. 790). Thus, additional empirical studies are needed to determine how well Case's theory accounts for the growth of intelligence among preschoolers and adolescents. Additional explanation is also called for to clarify the process by which children advance from one major stage to another and progress from one sublevel within a stage to a higher sublevel. And the claim that the same quality of mental functioning applies to all sorts of mental activities at the elaborated-coordination level of a stage has so far been tested for only a limited variety of cognitive operations. What is now desired is evidence that such a claim does indeed hold true for diverse sorts of mental activity, such as the types postulated in Howard Gardner's *Frames of Mind* theory (Gardner, 1983). Gardner's seven kinds of intelligence focus on (1) language usage, (2) logical-mathematical analysis, (3) spatial representation, (4) musical thinking, (5) the use of the body to solve problems or to make things, (6) an understanding of other individuals (a form of social intelligence), and (7) self-understanding. So, does the child operate simultaneously at the same cognitive stage in all of these types of intelligence?

In Dupont's theory of emotional development, he asserted that different types of feelings and emotions are not inborn but are learned, differentiated out of a initial vague sense of distress or of well-being to gradually assume specific types of affect. But critics can ask how feelings and emotions are generated solely out of experience in the world without being rooted in basic biological processes that are apparently shared with other living beings. In effect, the question of genetic and physiological components of emotional development calls for a more complete explanation. That explanation can usefully include clarification of which emotions are common across cultures and which are unique to a given culture and why.

In Wellman's theory, the most obvious issue to be clarified is the question of at what age does the child's conception of how others think actually qualify as a theory of mind. Settling this controversy requires greater agreement among investigators about (a) the characteristics of thought that exemplify a theory of mind and (b) the methods of investigation that provide convincing evidence that children are employing such a theory. A question also arises about how much the attainment of a mind theory depends on genetically timed maturation and how much depends on learning. Furthermore, do some types of experience hasten the development of a theory of mind more than other types? If so, what are key characteristics of the more effective experiences? Then, through what stages of development do children's theories of mind evolve during later childhood and adolescence? And are those stages common to all children, or can they differ from one child or one culture to another; and if they can differ, why?

.

6

Beyond Vygotsky

Like the Swiss developmentalist Piaget, the Russian developmentalist Lev Semenovich Vygotsky (1896-1934) exemplifies an early 20th-century theorist whose work continued to stimulate extensions during the 1980-2000 era. The theories described in this chapter illustrate three ways Vygotsky's proposals from the early decades of the century affected recent theorists' models. The schemes I selected from among numbers of possibilities are (a) Valsiner's cultural-historical development theory, (b) Siegler's microgenetic data-gathering proposal, and (c) Kemler's revision of a traditional differentiation hypothesis.

A CULTURAL-HISTORICAL PERSPECTIVE

Jaan Valsiner is a highly productive developmental psychologist who was born and schooled in Estonia when that country was still part of the Soviet Union. After earning a doctorate in psychology at Tartu University in the 1970s, he immigrated to the United States to hold professorial positions in a series of universities, first at the University of Minnesota, then at the University of North Carolina in Chapel Hill, and more recently at Clark University in Massachusetts.

Valsiner's theory first appeared in 1987 as *Culture and the Development of Children's Action,* then was published as an updated version in 1997. As significant progenitors of his model, Valsiner has acknowledged contributions by several psychologists from earlier in the 20th century—Russian Lev Vygotsky, Americans James Mark Baldwin and George Mead, Swiss Jean Piaget, French Pierre Janet, and Germans (later to become Americans) Kurt Lewin and Heinz Werner. Among these pioneers, Vygotsky was particularly influential in forming Valsiner's opinions about (a) the impact of a culture's history on individuals' development, (b) the significance of the *zone of proximal development,* and (c) the importance of children's actions in forming their mental life.

The Impact of a Culture's History

Among the multiplicity of ways that *culture* has been depicted, White's version seems well suited to Valsiner's use of the term.

> Culture may be defined as behaviour peculiar to *Homo sapiens*, together with material objects used as an integral part of [their] behavior; specifically, culture consists of language, ideas, beliefs, customs, codes, institutions, tools, techniques, works of art, rituals, ceremonies, and so on. (White, 1994, p. 874)

Any society's culture is assumed to be the product of a historical progression of events that have directed or *canalized* life into a selected pattern referred to as the group's culture. In other words, out of a great variety of possible ways of life, a given people's history has determined which of those ways is actually adopted by the general public and taught to succeeding generations. The historical factors that determine the form of a culture at a particular time include: (a) the physical features of a region (climate, nature of the terrain, predators, natural resources), (b) technologies people have invented to make life more tolerable and efficient (housing, clothing, foodstuffs, tools, modes of communication, modes of transportation, ways of producing and distributing goods and services), (c) beliefs and rituals intended to explain life's mysteries (religion, philosophy, science), (d) pastimes and entertainments, and (e) types of artistic expression (poetry, stories, pictures, sculptures, music, dance, drama, and the like). The pattern that a culture assumes is heavily influenced by the efforts of highly creative and persuasive individuals who offer new variations of lifestyles and convince people to adopt those variations.

Because cultures can differ markedly from each other, a newborn child does not enter a physical-social environment that provides all sorts of possibilities for development. Instead, as Valsiner (1997, p. 313) observes, "Children within a culture are socialized to become adults within that culture." Thus, the people who wield control over children's experiences typically limit learning opportunities to ones in keeping with cultural tradition, and they also administer rewards and punishments in ways intended to encourage the young to adopt that particular shared tradition as their own.

The historical-cultural factors that are assigned a central role in Valsiner's scheme operate at three levels. At the most general level, people within a society share influential physical settings (buildings, mountains, oceans, deserts), objects (houses, tents, autos, camels, books, computers), customs (eating habits, modes of greeting, language, ways of settling disputes, forms of education), bodies of knowledge (social, religious, scientific), and values (moral, economic, aesthetic). These broadscale features of a culture provide the extensive, yet somewhat canalized, cafeteria of stimuli from which the growing child can draw.

A second, more restricted range of influences is found in the cultural characteristics of the people who manage children's environmental encounters. Those influential persons include parents, teachers, club leaders, peers, and models conveyed by mass-communication media (books, periodicals, television, the Internet). Such influential persons are themselves products of the history of their own upbringing within the broader culture. Hence, their personal histories include not only cultural factors common to nearly everyone in the society but also additional factors (or variants of common cultural features) somewhat unique to their own families, schools, churches, and companions. As a result, the individual child's experiences are further canalized by caregivers' own developmental backgrounds.

At the most individualized level, the growing child is daily accumulating a personal history affecting what that individual becomes in the years ahead. At any juncture in a person's development, the accumulation of past experiences—stored as knowledge, skills, and attitudes—helps define which environments the person will encounter in the future and how those encounters will be interpreted.

In summary, the way a given child develops is constrained by (a) the historical causes that have fashioned the surrounding culture, (b) the child's caregivers' own past experiences that have influenced the skills and beliefs they bring to their childrearing tasks, and (c) the child's own history of experiences which has influenced the child's present skills and beliefs and which further constrains the child's future engagements with environments.

Zones and Development

One further way Valsiner portrays the process of development is in terms of three interrelated zones—the *zone of free movement* (ZFM), the *zone of promoted action* (ZPA), and the *zone of proximal development* (ZPD) (Valsiner, 1997, pp. 188-203).

The Zone of Free Movement

The zone of free movement contains the set of items available to influence a person's actions within a particular environmental setting at a given time. The term *items* in this context refers to the areas of the environment and the objects present (including humans), as well as ways the person can interact with those items. The culture and the child's caregivers combine to delineate the characteristics of this zone by influencing the opportunities for action available to the child on each occasion. Caregivers identify language that can be used, how to treat other people, and acceptable ways of using objects. This zone will differ from one time and place to another. The range of free movement will not be the same when the schoolchild is playing soccer during recess, eating lunch at home, eating lunch in a restaurant, behaving toward peers of the opposite sex in school, behaving toward peers of the opposite sex during neighborhood play, and more. During the process of development, children learn the nature of the zone of free movement for each context they inhabit, and they internalize that knowledge, incorporating it into their understanding of the world.

> The ZFM is . . . set up to organize child-environment relationships, and through that organization, to canalize the development of the child in directions that are accepted in the given culture at large. As a means, a particular ZFM can become obsolete, once the child is past a certain age and his or her relationships with the environments are changed. (Valsiner, 1997, p. 190)

Thus, the playpen in 'which the crawling infant is confined is abandoned when the infant becomes a toddler and has learned to abide by parents' rules about the places toddlers are permitted to explore. Later, the rule against trying to drive the family automobile is lifted once the 16-year-old has passed a driver-training course.

For historical reasons, societies can differ markedly in how liberally they define the ZFM that children and youths are permitted. For example, a greater diversity of alternatives is available in Britain's or Canada's present-day multicultural society than in Iraq's or Iran's highly cohesive Moslem cultures.

> The structure of the ZFM is dynamic; given the change in goals or conditions, the boundaries of ZFM are constantly being reorganized. That reorganization may be introduced either by the child or caregivers, or by all of them at the same time. (Valsiner, 1987, pp. 231-232)

Differences in the breadth of the zone of free movement as the result of a child's continually moving into different behavior settings are illustrated in Figure 6-1, where the size of the ZFM is shown by the amount of gray area in each diagram. The two illustrative realms of behavior pictured are those of language usage and physical displays of affection. The ZFM size can change as a child passes from home to school and to unsupervised play activities with peers. The way the zone pattern for one child can differ from that of another is suggested in the comparison between two hypothetical 12-year-old boys. In the realm of language usage, Boy A is from a home in which only English is spoken, a variety of English similar to—though not identical to—the English used in school. In contrast, Boy B is from a home of recent immigrants who speak Spanish almost exclusively at home, but only English is used at school. Thus, in Boy B's experience, there is almost no overlap between the language ZFM at home and the language ZFM at school.

The ZFM for physically showing affection (touching, hugging, caressing, kissing) also differs for the two lads. Boy A is from a home in which parents discourage expressions of feelings; but in Boy B's home, hugging, patting, and kissing among family members is common. At the school the boys attend, occasionally patting others on the back or shaking their hand is permitted, but hugging and kissing are not. In effect, for both boys, the range of the ZFM in school is quite limited. And because for Boy A the same school restrictions apply among his companions at play, there is considerable consistency across behavior settings in his ZFM of affectional displays. But for Boy B, the ZFM for expressing affection varies by context.

Figure 6-1

**Two Cases of Zones of Free Movement for
Language Use and Displays of Affection**

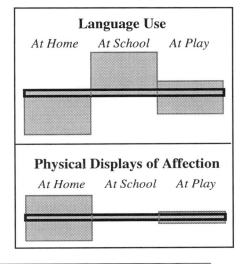

The horizontal, black-line rectangle in each diagram identifies the amount of the zone of free movement that is unchanged across the three settings. We can then envision a principle governing the relationship between (a) the consistency of the ZFM across contexts and (b) the difficulty a child may experience in complying with cultural expectations. The principle is this: The smaller the portion of a zone of free movement that extends across different behavior settings, the greater the demands on the child's ability to adjust readily to cultural standards in all settings. This suggests that Boy B faces a greater challenge than does Boy A in adjusting to home, school, and peer expectations because so little of the ZFM in one of the settings is identical to the ZFM in the other two, particularly in the case of language use.

The Zone of Promoted Action

The second zone in Valsiner's scheme focuses on those modes of action that caregivers encourage or demand within the zone of free movement. Cultures and individual families vary in how restrictively they delineate what constitutes proper or acceptable action in the successive contexts a child moves through day after day. The most controllable situation of parent-child interaction occurs when the zone of free movement is very narrow (with the society permitting the child to act in only one way) and is identical to the zone of promoted action. The decision-making role of parents and teachers is much simplified in such a society, since they merely need to urge their offspring to act in the culture's single permissible manner.

A very different child-development situation results when the zone of free movement is extremely broad, and the zone of promoted action is equally broad. That is, the society offers many options for how to act in different behavior settings, and caregivers fail to favor and promote selected options. Many alternatives for belief and behavior are available in the contexts the child occupies, with little or no guidance offered by caretakers regarding which options might yield the most desirable long-term results. The rationale behind such caregiver behavior can reflect parents' or teachers' conviction that children grow up best if they follow their "natural instincts." This is the notion that the young, when left to their own devices, intuitively know what's good for them. However, in other instances children are permitted much liberty of choice simply out of parental or teacher neglect, as caregivers who are unduly distracted by their own interests pay little or no attention to childrearing responsibilities.

The Zone of Proximal Development

Valsiner defines the last of his three zones as "the set of actions that the child can perform when helped by another person, but which are not yet available to the child in his individual acting" (1987, p. 233); and he explains that "The notion of a Zone of Proximal Development (ZPD) was borrowed from the intellectual heritage of Lev Vygotsky but reconstructed in an attempt to fit it with the other two zone concepts" (ZFM/ZPA) (1997, p. 199).

Piaget proposed that before children can learn something new, they must have reached a level of cognitive growth that enables them to acquire the new learning on their own. Vygotsky labeled this the *actual developmental level*, which could be assessed by means of the reasoning tasks that Piaget invented to evaluate mental growth. But Vygotsky also contended that there was a prior level or zone within which the child could nevertheless solve problems if aided. In other words, when children's cognitive ability is approaching (is proximal to) the actual developmental level, they can learn a new concept or skill if given assistance. As Vygotsky had explained:

> The zone is the distance between the actual developmental level as determined by independent problem solving and the level of potential development as determined through problem solving under adult guidance or in collaboration with more capable peers.
>
> [So] the zone of proximal development defines those functions that have not yet matured but are in the process of maturing, functions that will mature tomorrow but are currently in an embryonic state. These functions could be termed the

"buds" or "flowers" of development rather than the "fruits" of development. The actual developmental level characterizes mental development restrospectively, while the zone of proximal development characterizes mental development prospectively. (Vygotsky, 1978, pp. 86-87)

Valsiner has integrated this notion with his zones of free movement and promoted action to suggest how caregivers can hasten children's acquiring more advanced modes of thought before children discover those modes on their own.

Cycles of Action and Thought

As noted in Chapter 1, Karl Marx contended that people's thoughts—their mental life—were generated out of their society's pattern of production and consumption. A feudal system, with landlords using serfs to produce goods and services, led to one mode of thought, whereas capitalistic and communistic systems led to other modes. In keeping with such a philosophy, Vygotsky and his colleagues proposed that individuals' patterns of thought are generated by their actions. In effect, people's intentions and goals are products of behavior. But things do not stop there. After acting on the world, people ponder how the outcome of their actions has affected their welfare, and they thereafter intend either to continue acting in the same fashion in the future or to alter their actions to achieve better results. Their future actions are thus influenced by their thoughts. Consequently, people's lives consist of continuing cycles of action and thought.

In regard to Vygotsky's proposal, Valsiner (1997, pp. 209-214) noted that psychological theories are frequently based on the teleological assumption that people's actions are always the result of people's intentions, that is, the result of their goals. Hence, thought in the form of aims determines actions. While he did not deny that such is certainly often the case among adults, he postulated that the thought/action cycles originated in infancy by the infant's spontaneous actions being constrained by caregivers. So it is not that the child sets a goal and then acts in an effort to achieve it. Rather, the child acts, with those actions then canalized into culturally accepted directions (the zone of promoted action) by caregivers who encourage and permit some sorts of behavior while discouraging other sorts. The child thus acquires cultural goals and thereafter can select actions intended to serve those ends.

Children's actions (observable behavioral episodes) and acts (culturally meaningful events) are *constructed in the process of transaction between the developing child and his or her social others, as that transaction regulates the relationship of the child to the particular environmental context.* In the process of such transaction, the directedness [intention] of the social others of the young child can be assumed from the beginning, but the child's intentionality and goal-direction constitute emergent developmental phenomena. In other words, the development of a child's actions starts from a state of no intentionality and goal-directedness and is gradually canalized toward culturally acceptable and prescribed forms of goal setting and goal attainment, as well as toward the cognitive construction of intentionality as a psychological device that underlies human actions in their adult form. (Valsiner, 1997, p. 212)

In summary, as the foregoing examples demonstrate, Valsiner has adopted key concepts from Vygotsky's work and recast those concepts in a form that renders them suitable for his own theory of development.

MICROGENETIC DATA-GATHERING METHODS

Robert S. Siegler's analysis of ways to collect information about development illustrates the symbiotic relationship that obtains between a development theory and the methods of collecting information relevant to that theory. This interdependence of theory and data-gathering techniques is reflected in the observations that (a) the kind of information compiled about development constrains the form of theory appropriate for interpreting that information and (b) the nature of the theory determines to a great extent the methods used for gathering suitable data. In other words, a theory and its data-gathering methods assume a cyclical chicken-and-egg relationship.

Siegler, a professor of psychology at Carnegie Mellon University, credited Vygotsky's ways of studying children's development as an important influence on his own version of microgenetic methodology. Vygotsky's complaint about traditional approaches to studying development—a complaint that Siegler adopted—contends that

> A key characteristic for any method aimed at studying change is that it examine changes *while they are occurring*. Most methods used to study cognitive development do not meet this requirement. They are based on a strategy of trying to infer how a change occurred by comparing behavior before and after the change. Unfortunately, this indirect strategy leaves open a very large number of possible pathways to change. . . . Thus, learning about the endpoints of change, though useful, is no substitute for detailed examination of [a child's] changing competence [as it evolves]. (Siegler, 1996, p. 178)

As Vygotsky had remarked decades earlier when introducing his own new methods of analyzing change-in-progress, "Previous investigators have studied reactions in psychological experiments only after they have become fossilized" (Vygotsky, 1978, p. 68).

In place of traditional data-collection approaches, Siegler advocated *microgenetic* techniques, ones that exhibit three key characteristics:

> (a) observations span the period of rapid change in the competence of interest; (b) the density of observations is high relative to the rate of change in the competence; and (c) observations are subjected to intensive trial-by-trial analysis, with the goal of inferring the process that gave rise to the change. (Siegler, 1996, p. 178)

As the term *microgenetic* implies, the aim of intensively studying children's thought and behavior during a limited period of development is to identify the nature of small changes as they are being born.

In Vygotsky's investigations of children's cognitive development, he was dissatisfied with the standard method of presenting children with a stimulus (such as a test question or problem to solve) and then noting how closely their responses matched the correct answer. Such a method would show only whether the child gave the desired response. Instead, what Vygotsky wanted to learn was the detailed pattern of changes in children's actions and thoughts as children grappled with a task and, in the midst of grappling, advanced their mental development. So the child's procedure in constructing answers was what interested Vygotsky, not whether the answers were correct. Therefore, an alternative method he devised was that of placing a child in a problem-solving setting, then carefully tracking the course of the child's actions and listening to the child's running commentary during the attempt to solve the problem. From the resulting record, he drew inferences about what sort of intellectual development had occurred during the problem-solving episode (Valsiner, 1988, pp. 134-140).

Siegler extended Vygotsky's conception of suitable methodology by proposing five dimensions along which development occurs. In the following paragraphs, we first identify the five dimensions, then illustrate how they can be applied in a microgenetic analysis of a study of children's mathematical reasoning.

Dimensions of Microgenetic Analysis

Siegler identified five perspectives that a theory can profitably include if it is to delineate the process of change that development involves. The five are called *path, rate, breadth, variability,* and *sources* of change.

Path of Change

When people are persuaded to "think aloud" during their problem-solving, it becomes apparent that two individuals who offer what is essentially the same answer have often arrived at that solution by quite different routes. One person may adopt a single strategy and stick with it to the end. Another may consider an initial strategy, abandon it in favor of a second, then reconsider the first approach, and eventually replace it with a third that produces the final solution. And the cognitive trails carved out by additional people may be even more individualistic.

> Development often follows paths that no one would imagine beforehand. Regressions in thinking about a given task are not uncommon. Densely sampling behavior while it is rapidly changing and assessing behavior on a trial-by-trial basis can help in documenting the prevalence of such (often brief) regressions, can indicate the conditions under which they occur, and thus can suggest why they occur. (Siegler, 1996, p. 183)

Rate of Change

Whether changes in thinking patterns occur suddenly or gradually can be revealed by microgenetic methods, particularly when those methods involve presenting a task repeatedly to the same individuals in sessions close enough together in time to furnish highly detailed information about the rate of change.

Different conceptions of the pace of change are reflected in various theories of the early and middle 20th century. Stage theories (Piaget, Vygotsky, Freud) portray development as a succession of phases, with each phase consisting of a very rapid change—a large step—followed by an extended period of little or no change—a plateau. Whereas the investigative methods employed by proponents of stage theories usually involve gathering data about individuals at widely separated intervals (semiannually, annually, biannually, every five years, or longer), the periods at which information is sought in microgenetic methods are dramatically shorter—ranging from intervals of seconds to ones separated by minutes or, at most, a few hours.

In contrast to typical stage theories, learning theories (Skinner's behaviorism, Bandura's social-cognition) view development as a continuous series of slight, gradual advances, such as those that can be found through the use of microgenetic approaches.

Breadth of Change

Flavell (1971) coined the phrase "the concurrence assumption" to identity the belief that a variety of cognitive skills which logically appear much alike are all acquired at about the same time. A person subscribing to that assumption will thus expect that a girl who discovers a reasoning strategy while working on a problem involving fractions will subsequently apply that strategy to other problems that seem to belong in the same domain. However, Siegler noted that research focusing on this issue of how broadly children generalize a new way of thinking has, in many instances, failed to support the assumption. He contended that microgenetic methods of data gathering are particularly well suited to discovering the conditions under which a new mode of thought that is acquired while solving a problem in one context will be applied to other problems in other contexts.

Variability in Change Patterns

The variability dimension focuses on the question of how the pattern of change reflected in one person's mode of problem solving compares with the pattern of change in another person's. In Siegler's view, this matter of differences between children in their development patterns has been handled rather poorly in most investigations of the growth of concepts and problem-solving skills. He charged that researchers too often "ignored variability among individuals . . . [and] characterized changes in unqualified terms that imply that the path, if not the rate of change is universal [among children]" (Siegler, 1996, p. 184).

In Siegler's opinion, this flaw in studies of children's reasoning styles can be corrected if researchers adopt microgenetic methods, because such methods reveal the similarities and differences among individuals in the patterns of path, rate, and breadth changes that occur during their problem-solving efforts.

Change Sources

Siegler's fifth dimension concerns the question of what impels people to change their way of thinking during problem solving. In studies Siegler conducted, children were given training sessions in problem solving, with each session involving an investigator posing problems the child was to solve and encouraging the child to describe how he or she was thinking while wrestling with the task at hand. Children's responses to this approach revealed a variety of experiences that could effect changes in their problem-solving strategies—such experiences as receiving rules and feedback from the experimenter, observing someone else solve a problem, interacting with peers, discovering conflicts in their own thinking (cognitive dissonance), and more.

In summary, Siegler defined five dimensions of developmental change that could be illuminated by microgenetic data-collection methods, and he incorporated those dimensions into the theory he created for interpreting the data.

An Instance of Microgenetic Analysis

The way a microgenetic approach can yield information along Siegler's five dimensions can be illustrated with a study of nursery-school children. The purpose of the study was to learn (a) the strategies young children used to solve simple addition problems and (b) how changes in their strategies came about. The children participating in the study could already count from 1 to 10, but they had not formally faced the task of summing two amounts, as in 2 + 5 or 3 + 4. Over a period of weeks, an experimenter met periodically with each child to pose addition questions and observe how the child went about providing answers. Here is a sample exchange between an experimenter and a child:

Experimenter: "How much is 2 plus 4. I mean, if we have 2 apples and then we get 4 more, how many do we have all together?"
(*Child ponders, then answers:*) "6."
Experimenter: "That's right. Good job. How did you know that?"
Child: "I counted 1, 2. " (*Holds up 2 fingers.*) And I counted 1, 2, 3, 4." (*Holds up 4 fingers on the other hand.*) And I put them together like this—1, 2, 3, 4, 5, 6."

The reasoning strategy in this example was identified as the *standard sum approach of counting.* A different strategy that virtually all children eventually discovered during the weeks of the experiment was called the *min approach.* In the min strategy, the child stated the larger of the addends (4 in the case of 2 + 4), then counted out (added) the amount of the smaller addend (2) to arrive at the sum. So the thought process went 4—5, 6. A third strategy that appeared during the study was labeled the *shortcut approach,* a condensed version of the standard sum technique, with the child combining the two addends in one counting motion—1, 2, 3, 4, 5, 6—without first stating the two addends as separate amounts (Siegler, 1996, p. 189).

The experimenters, by applying their microgenetic approach in a series of trials with each child over several weeks, were able to identify both (a) marked differences among individual children's modes of thought along each of the five dimensions and (b) tendencies of cognitive development for the children as a group. Here are two samples of group trends Siegler extracted from the study's results.

> *Generalization:* Once children discover a strategy, they still need to extend it to the full range of problems on which it is useful. In the case of the min strategy, generalization was slow. Most children rarely used it in the sessions following the discovery.
>
> *Transition strategies:* The shortcut sum strategy may mediate many children's discovery of the min strategy. (pp. 188-189)

PERCEPTION: HOLISTIC VERSUS ANALYTIC

Theoretical innovations often result from a researcher creating a more detailed, sophisticated version of some aspect of an earlier theorist's proposal. A case in point is the revision of Vygotsky's differentiation hypothesis offered by Deborah G. Kemler of Swarthmore College.

The issue addressed by Kemler was the question of holistic versus analytical ways people perceive events. When a person is asked to compare two objects to determine whether they are alike or different, does the person judge the objects on the basis of their general, holistic appearance? Or, in contrast, is the decision based on one or more selected dimensions of the objects, such as their size, their color, their shape, their function, their cost, their age, or some other attribute? In other words, to what extent are individuals' opinions about the similarity of objects or events based on chosen criteria (analytic approach) rather than on the overall impression produced by those phenomena (holistic approach)?

Kemler's interest in studying the holistic/analytic issue derived from her curiosity about the traditional view of how those two ways of perceiving events develop over the years of childhood. Vygotsky (1962) had subscribed to the traditional view that

> Young children who do not classify in the same way as adults [analytically] are incapable of entertaining the same concepts as adults, for the adults' concepts are uniformly structured by the extraction of consistent criterial properties [attributes, dimensions], which young children cannot or at least do not spontaneously do. (Kemler, 1983, p. 81)

Kemler carried out a series of studies to determine more precisely the conditions under which Vygotsky's generalization—referred to as the *differentiation hypothesis*—proved true. Her method of investigation consisted of (a) showing children of various ages two objects, such as two identical sheets of paper, (b) altering one object along a single dimension (coloring the sheet or cutting it with scissors), and (c) asking her subjects whether the objects were still the same. When children answered that the two were still the same, Kemler concluded that such children were perceiving the objects holistically—believing that the items were *generally* unchanged. But when children said the items were now different, and they identified the attribute that differentiated the items, she credited them with analytic perception. On the basis of her studies, she was able to revise the traditional differentiation hypothesis to include the following adjustments.

Whereas preschool children do, indeed, tend to perceive objects and events holistically rather than analytically, on a few occasions they may judge things analytically, especially if their attention is directed to selected aspects of the things being judged. And whereas adolescents and adults tend to base their comparisons on chosen qualities of objects and events, they too on occasion may exhibit a holistic viewpoint.

> Thus the bias of young children toward the undifferentiated [holistic] mode does not necessarily preclude the *ability* to employ the differentiated [analytic] mode. In this sense, development differences might be quantitative, even though the difference between differentiated and undifferentiated modes is qualitative. Development may consist in an ever greater likelihood that the differentiated mode is deployed in a wider and wider range of situations. (Kemler, 1983, p. 84)

Furthermore, the nature of the task at hand—the context in which a comparison is called for—may influence which mode of perceiving is used. "Both children and adults are more likely to be analytic—to analyze wholes into properties and relate them by shared components—when the task calls for deliberate problem-solving activities than when it does not" (Kemler, 1983, p. 94). This especially occurs under an *intentional condition*, meaning a situation in which the individual knows that a categorization is to be learned. In contrast, an *incidental condition* is

> one in which the subject is exposed to the category information [such as size, shape, weight, color, expense, complexity, or the like] but is unaware that the information is being acquired, which is possible by attuning the subject to a different task. Thus, whatever is learned about categories [under incidental conditions] is learned without intention. Only the [intentional] condition should elicit deliberate problem-solving activities, directed toward learning the structure of the category distinction. (Kemler, 1983, p. 96)

In short, when people are viewing events in only a casual manner, they are more apt to draw holistic comparisons. When they are intently trying to solve a problem involving comparisons, they are more apt to identify which attributes distinguish one item or event from another.

As illustrated by Kemler's modification of Vygotsky's differentiation hypothesis, the impetus for a researcher to offer a new or revised theory often derives from the researcher's desire to refine and embellish an earlier theorist's proposal.

REMAINING CHALLENGES

A variety of matters that warrant further study can be inferred from Valsiner's expansion of Vygotsky's sociohistorical theory of development. For example, what analytical principles are most useful for explaining how the history of one group of people has produced a different cultural setting for child development than has the history of another group? In other words, what historical factors have been most important for determining how children become socialized into their particular culture? And because individuals within the same culture are not identical in terms of their beliefs and attitudes, what factors are most significant in accounting for the observed differences between individuals? What useful generalizations can be drawn about the effect on people's lives of different combinations of Valsiner's three zones—the zones of free movement, promoted action, and proximal development? For instance, what influence on a person's developmental outcomes can be expected if that individual grows up within a broad zone of free movement, a narrow zone of promoted action, and with no attention paid to the potential of the zone of proximal development?

Several questions about Siegler's microgenetic research methods call for more adequate answers. Because every event in a person's life can be inspected from different viewpoints, how does a researcher determine which viewpoints or aspects of people's behavior during an event should be the focus of attention. That is, how does a researcher decide whether to concentrate on what people say, their body movements, their facial expressions, their unexpressed thoughts, changes in their heart rates, their apparent effect on others' behavior, or what? How does the selection of one set of aspects rather than another set influence the theory that an investigator uses to interpret the developmental effect of an event studied by microgenetic methods? How should the results of microgenetic studies be compiled to produce an overall, long-term interpretation of human development?

Kemler's refinement of Vygotsky's differentiation hypothesis also leaves a variety of questions to be investigated. For instance, to what extent does instruction in differentiating phenomena analytically—rather than holistically—influence the way individuals compare similar types of objects and events in the future? To what degree does training in analysis transfer to situations unlike those faced during training sessions? What age trends are found in persons' ability to apply and to transfer analytical skills? Which attributes of objects and events are easy to teach people as bases of analysis, and which attributes are difficult to teach? For example, can children more easily learn to base comparisons of objects on such attributes as size, color, and shape than on function or complexity? Why or why not? In how many ways can objects or events differ and people still consider them holistically alike?

7

Models of Interaction

As noted in Chapter 1, the term *theory* is used throughout this book to identify any proposal about (a) which components or variables are important for understanding human development and (b) how those components interact to account for why development occurs as it does. Although the matter of interaction has always been of concern to developmental psychologists, it attracted particular interest during the closing decades of the 20th century, with theorists offering multiple versions of interaction in their explanations of how and why people grow up as they do. The introduction to Part I summarized some main lines of thought about interaction as viewed through the lens of an Altman and Rogoff typology (Altman & Rogoff, 1987). The purpose of Chapter 7 is to illustrate four of the diverse forms that interaction assumed in representative theories of the 1980-2000 era.

Any attempt to prepare a narrative that describes interactions among components of a theory suffers from the linear nature of prose. Narratives advance in a step-by-step fashion, one idea after another. As such, narratives cannot simultaneously reveal all of a theory's components and the multiple links among them. But this disadvantage can be surmounted if a verbal description of interactions is accompanied by graphic models that offer a synchronous display of a theory's units and their interconnections. Throughout this chapter, in an effort to cope with narratives' linear limitation, I have sought to enhance the clarity of the presentation by adding graphic renditions of the theorists' proposals.

The chapter summarizes four theories that differ in their portrayals of interaction: (a) Kreppner's family-system scheme, (b) Lazarus's version of emotional development, (c) Heckhausen and Schulz's explanation of selectivity in life-span development, and (d) Granott's model of ways people collaborate in activities they pursue together.

INDIVIDUALS DEVELOPING WITHIN FAMILY SYSTEMS

Sometimes a theory is built with components borrowed from other theories and assembled to form a novel composition intended to explain some developmental process. An example of such a model is Kreppner's scheme for explaining the reciprocal relationship between (a) how individuals' development is influenced by their family's structure and (b) how those individuals, as elements of the family, influence the form and function of their family. From this family-systems perspective, a family is seen as an ever-shifting and adjusting (*dynamic*) kaleidoscope of interactions among family members. Consequently, with the passing of time, neither the individuals nor the family as a whole remain unchanged. The individuals and the family configuration are in a continual state of transition.

Each family member as well as the family as a unit exhibits a life course. For the typical member, that course begins with conception and birth, advances through childhood and adolescence, continues during the stages of adulthood, and ends with death. The lifespan of the typical family (a) begins with adults living together (within or without formal wedlock), (b) expands with the birth of offspring and/or the importation of outsiders who significantly alter the original family pattern, (c) contends with problems of relationships within the family and of difficulties imposed on the family from without, (d) diminishes in size and composition with the departure of members, and (e) eventually dissolves as the result of the members' separation or death.

Kurt Kreppner of the Max Planck Institute for Human Development and Education in Berlin proposed a model for understanding the family processes of socializing their individual members. The model's three major components (or *concepts*, as Kreppner calls them) derive from earlier theorists' proposals about (a) family developmental tasks, (b) an internal working model of the family, and (c) family members' nonshared environments (Kreppner, 1989).

Family Developmental Tasks

Robert Havighurst of the University of Chicago is usually credited with popularizing the notion of *developmental tasks* as a tool for understanding the demands on individuals' development at successive stages of their growing up. According to Havighurst, the developmental tasks of an individual's life course are pursuits that

> constitute a healthy and satisfactory growth in our society. They are those things a person must learn if he is to be judged or to judge himself to be a reasonably happy and successful person. A developmental task is a task which arises at or about a certain period in the life of an individual, successful achievement of which leads to his happiness and to success with later tasks, while failure leads to unhappiness in the individual, disapproval by society, and difficulty with later tasks. (1953, p. 2)

Developmental tasks across the lifespan can be identified for different aspects of life, such as tasks of (a) achieving an appropriate dependence-independence pattern, (b) relating to changing social groups, (c) learning one's psycho-socio-biological sex role, and (d) learning to understand and control the physical world. Each of these general types of tasks assumes a more specific form at different stages of development. For instance, the general task of relating to changing social groups has been envisioned as involving the following demands between infancy and late adolescence :

Infancy (birth to 1 or 2): Becoming aware of the alive as against the inanimate, and the familiar as against the unfamiliar. Developing rudimentary social interaction.

Early childhood (2-3 to 5-7): Beginning to develop the ability to interact with agemates. Adjusting to family expectations for the child as a member of the social unit.

Late childhood: (5-7 to pubescence): Clarifying the adults' world as against the child's world. Establishing peer groupness and learning to belong.

Early adolescence (pubescence to puberty): Behaving according to a shifting peer code.

Late adolescence (puberty to early maturity): Adopting an adult set of social values by learning a new peer code. (Tryon & Lilienthal, 1950, pp. 77-79)

Following Havighurst's lead, several authors subsequently applied the notion of individuals' developmental tasks to the analysis of families by proposing that families are obliged to perform developmental tasks at successive periods in their life course (Aldous, 1978; Duvall, 1977; Rodgers, 1973). Duvall, for example, described "stage critical developmental tasks" for eight stages of the family's life cycle, starting from "married couple without children" (Stage 1) and continuing to "aging family members" (Stage 8). Typical tasks at two of the eight stages include (a) at Stage 5 (teenage-children period) the family's "balancing freedom with responsibility as teenagers mature and emancipate themselves" and (b) at Stage 7 (middle-aged parents whose children have left home) "rebuilding the marriage relationship" and "maintaining kin ties with older and younger generations" (Duvall in Kreppner, 1989, p. 40).

Kreppner thus adopted the concept *family developmental tasks* as a component of his model because he found such a concept particularly fruitful for understanding individual and family development during periods of transition and for analyzing problems of changes in family members' relations.

Internal Working Model

Kreppner's second borrowed component was the belief that each person creates an internalized model of family structure and dynamics. The inclusion of such a concept is founded on the conviction that children use their experiences with other family members to construct a mental template or pattern of what a family is and how it operates. This internal working model then becomes the guide to how children will engage in new social relationships.   They generalize this model, as built from their own family experiences, to influence the way they picture what relationships outside the family should be like.   Kreppner's version of an internal working model derived principally from proposals by Bowlby (1969); Main, Kaplan, and Cassidy (1985); and Sroufe and Fleeson (1986).

> The concept of an "internal working model" representing the accumulated experiences of social relationships appears to be a helpful prerequisite for grasping the complex interplay between the growing individual and the family's relational network.   However, the original dyad-oriented concept needs to be expanded to a model in which all family members are represented in a polyadic pattern.   With such an expansion, these inner representations of relationships within the family may create what an observer of family interaction would call an "enduring pattern" of turn-taking rituals and communication exchanges. (Kreppner, 1989, pp. 40-41)

Thus, as Kreppner adopted the idea of an internal model, he expanded the notion of family members' interactions beyond that of a dyad (mother-infant, father-daughter, sister-brother) to encompass all family members simultaneously. He thereby focused attention on the importance of recognizing, for example, that the interaction between father and teenage son regarding use of the family car could readily be affected by the mother's opinion about such matters and also by the teenage sister's views.

Nonshared Environment

Kreppner noted that members of the lay public, as well as authors who write about development, often appear to assume that children who grow up within the same family share an identical physical, social, and psychological environment. However, he pointed out that such an assumption is only partially true and that, in explaining individuals' development, it is important to recognize ways in which family members' "experienced environments" are not alike. The notion of nonshared environments was imported from the field of behavioral genetics, where studies have demonstrated that a substantial amount of a family's environmental influence on the child

> ought to be interpreted as being "nonshared," that is, unique to the individual, not experienced in the same way by any other family member.   In contrast to other conceptions of emphasizing the influence of the "shared environment" of a family on individual development, here the nonshared segments of a child's experience is taken as an argument for explaining why children become so different in the same family. (Kreppner, 1989, p. 41)

The Process of Interaction

Although Kreppner did not directly describe the pattern of interactions to be expected among his theory's three components, his analysis of examples from a longitudinal study of 16 families seems to imply the pattern of interaction suggested in the following paragraphs. In this interpretation, I have taken the liberty of expanding the application of Kreppner's proposal to include differences across cultures.

First, consider the family-developmental-tasks component. Tasks can usefully be analyzed in terms of the role assignments or role expectations held for the various family members at each stage of the family's life course. At any point in a family's lifespan, each member's role can be defined in terms of that person's responsibilities. For instance, one task that extends throughout the life of the family is that of fostering the health and safety of family members. But the division of responsibilities among members for performing that task varies from one stage of life to another. Thus, the assignment of responsibilities for promoting health and safety in a family composed of two parents and one child will differ when the child is an infant than when the child reaches later childhood, adolescence, young adulthood, and middle age. Furthermore, the division of responsibilities varies with family size and complexity. The behaviors expected of different members for maintaining health and safety in a one-parent (mother) family that has six children (age range 2 through 11) will not be the same as in a two-parent family that has two children (ages 18 and 21).

Even though all cultures share some basic family tasks in common, certain tasks can be unique to a culture. For most families in advanced industrial societies, the task of specific vocational preparation is not a family responsibility but is relegated to other agencies in the society—schools, job-training programs, on-the-job experience. But in subsistence-agriculture societies, vocational training is a key family function. Furthermore, the approved methods of performing a given task can differ from one culture to another, with some methods, by virtue of tradition, being more acceptable in one culture than in another. A rapidly evolving practice in North American culture is that of women being employed outside the home. Thus, the task of caring for young children is increasingly performed by nonfamily personnel—babysitters, child-care centers, and nursery schools. In contrast, in such varied cultures as those of Islamic Saudi Arabia and Shintoist Japan, mothers continue to serve dominantly in the child-care role.

People who adopt traditionally preferred methods of task performance can enjoy social approval, whereas those who deviate from accepted practice can suffer negative sanctions. Hence, a culture's modes of reinforcement and punishment encourage members of the younger generation to adopt traditional family tasks and methods and to eschew deviations from tradition.

As a consequence of the foregoing process, family tasks—including approved methods of performing them—interact with Kreppner's internal working model in the following cumulative fashion. Parents carry in mind a model of how family tasks should be performed and they use that model to guide their child-rearing practices. Those practices then contribute to the children's internal working models of how responsibilities are assigned for performing developmental tasks. Subsequently, those offspring, when grown and raising children of their own, are guided by their acquired model of what a family should be, with this process linking successive generations' conceptions of proper family behavior. "Thus, parents . . . can be seen along with their own children as carriers of 'internal working models' founded in their families of origin and reactivated as they become parents themselves" (Kreppner, 1989, p. 60).

The mode of transmitting internal models from one generation to the next contributes to similarities of belief among members of a family as well as to similarities across generations. However, even if siblings are somewhat alike because of sharing common family experiences, no two are identical in personality or in their internal working models of what constitutes a family. According to Kreppner's scheme, the differences between siblings are to a considerable extent the result of the nonshared environments that their family has provided. For example, the context within which a 2-year-old girl develops is not the environment that was experienced 6 years ago by her 8-year-old brother when he was 2. Not only did the brother at age 2 lack siblings, but the parents now perform their developmental tasks rather differently than they did 6 years ago. A family's configuration is always in a state of transition as members' attitudes, abilities, and interests change with the passing of time and as new members arrive and old ones depart. Thus, each individual's internal working model and resulting perception of developmental tasks (convictions about who bears what responsibilities and why) is affected by a combination of shared and nonshared family environments. As a consequence, family members' internal models are in some ways similar and in other ways different from each other.

A Graphic Illustration

The way family members' internal working models can change with the advancing years is suggested in Figure 7-1, which depicts a hypothetical family's composition at five junctures in the family's lifespan, progressing from (a) the parents as newlyweds, (b) their relationship with their 2-year-old son 5 years later, (c) the four-member family in its 11th year, when the son is age 8 and a recent daughter is age 2, (d) the family in its 26th year, when the daughter is 17 and the 23-year-old son is no longer at home, and (e) the family in its 36th year, as the parents are the only residents left in the home, but they still interact with their daughter and son who have started their own families.

In Figure 7-1, each family member's internal working model is pictured in a lightly shaded square. Then, within each working model, the small squares and circles symbolize the contents of an individual's conception of a family and of a family's developmental tasks (members' responsibilities and ways of carrying out those responsibilities). As shown for the newlyweds in Year 1 of the family's life course, the dark-shaded small squares signify working-model contents that are identical or highly similar for both parents. In effect, the parents agree with each other in their conceptions of what a family is or should be in terms of those particular dark-shaded squares. One square may focus on financial matters, another on the division of labor in carrying out family tasks (who is responsible for what), a third on sexual relations, a fourth on the nature of the family's living quarters, and so on. Thus, the two parents in this example are in considerable agreement about most elements of their mental working models. Such a high level of accord is likely due to the similarity of their family backgrounds that led to similar images of family acquired during their childhood. Similarities are most likely to occur when the couple are from the same culture, influenced by their comparable social-class, religious, and ethnic environments.

Nevertheless, the pair enter marriage disagreeing about several features of family, as suggested by the small white squares within the two mental models. It seems obvious that the greater the proportion of white squares in family members' models, the greater the likelihood of misunderstanding and conflict within the family. The double-pointed arrow linking the wife and husband represents their mutual influence on each other's conception of family.

When we advance to Year 5 in the family's life course, we see that the wife's and husband's models have changed somewhat over the past 5 years, with fewer discrepancies between them (a smaller proportion of white squares) than when they were first wed. Part of this change has probably been effected by the arrival of an infant son, now age 2. As the parents have learned to cope with this new family member, they have been obliged to agree on many aspects of how they manage their recent family responsibilities. As for the young child, he is newly developing a mental model of family, but one far simpler than his parents'. The dark-shaded squares indicate that the boy has adopted some of his parents' beliefs about family. However, in the child's mind, other aspects of family differ from his parents' notions, as suggested by the white circles which symbolize childish conceptions that differ from either parent's beliefs.

In Year 11, the family now includes a 2-year-old daughter, whose working model differs from that of her brother when he was 2 in Year 6, because the environment in which the daughter has been raised is not identical to that from which the brother constructed his model of family. Again, the shaded squares in the two children's models show elements of the children's conceptions of family that match their parents' models. The dark-shaded circles signify ways that the two children's mental models are alike, but are different from both parents' conceptions. That is, in some ways the two siblings concur in how they envision family life, with those ways different from their parents' ideas. The white circles symbolize elements of children's models that differ from any other family member, either the parents or siblings. Therefore, each member's model is a combination of elements that are in some ways similar to, and different from, other members' models. As the double-pointed arrows in Year 11 suggest, with the addition of each new member of the family, the complexity of interactions multiplies.

Figure 7-1

Family Members' Internal Models of Family Functions

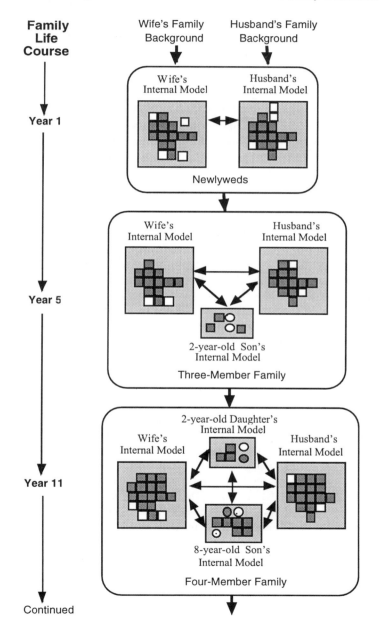

Figure 7-1 continued

Family Members' Internal Models of Family Functions

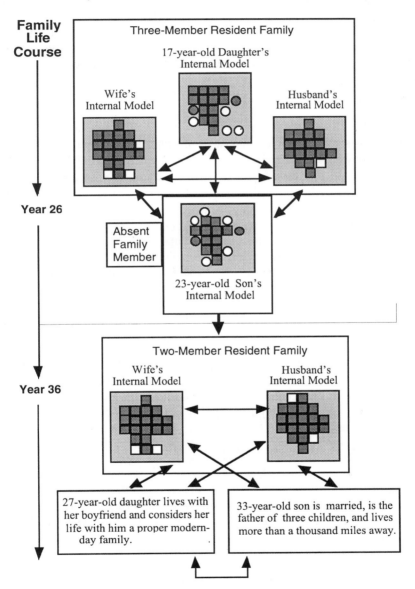

The continuation of Figure 7-1 shows two further periods in the family's life course—Years 26 and 36—when members of the younger generation move away but still interact with the parents and with each other, although no longer in the intimacy afforded by living together in the same house.

Comparing the configurations of family members' models across the time shows that (a) no member's model ever remains entirely the same from one period to another and (b) there is always a combination of agreement (shaded squares and circles) and of disagreement (white squares and circles) among members at any given time.

Conclusion

Interactions among the three components of Kreppner's scheme appear to produce the following pattern:

- Family developmental tasks as practiced by parents and other family members provide the environmental experiences from which children construct internal working models of how a family operates.
- Some of the provided environments are experienced in very similar ways by different family members, thereby contributing to agreement in those members' internal models. But many of the environments—which at first glance may appear identical—are not experienced in the same way by different members, so that such environments contribute to differences in members' models. It should not be surprising, then, that children reared in the same home can differ in their perceptions of what constitutes the appropriate conduct of a family.
- Internal working models should not be regarded as immutable mental constructs. Rather, both adults' and children's models are subject to change as the result of how well methods used for performing developmental tasks appear to succeed. Parents who discover that a given childrearing procedure has not worked out as they had hoped may alter their model of (a) how responsibilities for a given task should be assigned among family members and (b) what constitutes appropriate methods of imposing the assignment. For instance, when a teenager runs away from home after her father has slapped her, the father may change his notion about the best way to carry out the task of maintaining order within the family. Consequently, children's responses to adults' child-raising methods can serve to alter the adults' conceptions of family tasks. Furthermore, children's models can be expected to be even more labile than adults' because children have had far less experience on which to base their convictions.

A RELATIONAL THEORY OF EMOTIONAL DEVELOPMENT

An illustration of a theory involving a large number of interacting components is the depiction of emotional development proposed by Richard S. Lazarus, an emeritus professor of psychology at the University of California, Berkeley. Lazarus's scheme is founded on his belief that

> we cannot understand the emotional life solely from the standpoint of the person *or* the environment as separate units, . . . especially in simple input-output analyses, [but we must give attention to] what relationship means in the context of emotion. (Lazarus, 1991, p. 89)

The nature of Lazarus's theory is most clearly revealed during encounters that evoke such emotions as anxiety, anger, and pride. An encounter can consist of any incident in which a person engages directly (face-to-face conversation) or vicariously (receiving a letter, viewing a television program) with other people, animals, or the physical environment (snowstorm, avalanche, ocean waves). The central focus of the theory is not on the person as an individual nor on the environment as a behavior setting (which includes the people who inhabit it) but, rather, on the quality of the relationship produced when the individual is involved with that environment. An encounter that produces a relationship experienced as threatening elicits anxiety. An encounter experienced as insulting elicits anger. An encounter interpreted as ego-enhancing evokes pride.

Figure 7-2 summarizes in graphic form what occurs during an encounter, as seen from the vantage point of the Lazarus model. Four phases of an emotion-generating episode are portrayed. The first phase consists of influential factors brought to the incident by both the individual and the environment. Lazarus calls these precursors of an encounter *causal antecedents*. The second phase is the actual engagement during which the person (a) appraises the situation and (b) seeks to cope with the interpretation produced by that appraisal. The third phase involves immediate effects of the encounter, whereas the fourth concerns long-term effects. To analyze the model, we can start by identifying the components of each phase, then suggest how the phases fit together.

Phase 1: Causal Antecedents

For convenience of analysis, the influential background characteristics brought to the episode can be divided between (a) the individual's personality components and (b) characteristics of the environment. However, these personal and environmental variables do not act separately. Instead, they combine to form an amalgam which produces the relationship that arouses a given emotion or set of emotions.

Personality variables

A crucial factor that the individual brings to social encounters is *motivation*, which is generated from *goals* the person pursues, with the goals influenced by *beliefs* and *values*. Beliefs concern the person's convictions about *reality*— what is true about the world and how and why things happen as they do. Values are judgments about which things are good or bad, proper or improper.

Figure 7-2

Interacting Components in Emotion-Generating Encounters

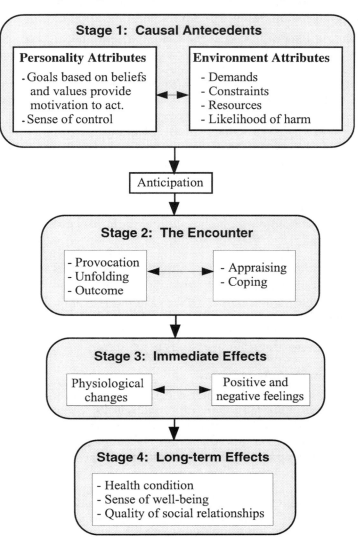

Motivation is essential in determining the activities in which a person engages and the amount of interest and energy invested in those activities. From the viewpoint of emotion, a central goal that subsumes all others is that of enhancing and defending one's *sense of self* or *ego-identity*.

> A self or ego organizes motives and attitudes into hierarchies of importance. . . .
> Threats to any personal goal are, at bottom, threats to oneself. Thus, the self or ego-identity is in large part a motivational concept, and goal hierarchies are organized by an executive agency of the personality, which coordinates and regulates in action what a person desires. (Lazarus, 1991, p. 101)
>   There would be no emotion if people did not arrive on the scene of an encounter with a desire, want, wish, need, or goal commitment that could be advanced or thwarted. The stronger or more important the goal, the more intense is the emotion, other things being equal. (Lazarus, 1991, p. 94)

A further personality component is the person's *sense of control*—the impression of how well the individual can manage the episode to his or her own benefit. The weaker the individual's sense of control, the more likely the episode will produce negative emotion.

Environmental variables

Key factors of the environment are (a) demands, constraints, and resources the person perceives in the situation and (b) the ambiguity and imminence of harm.

Demands are the person's perceptions of requirements that the environment imposes on the individual, such as a school's personnel expecting pupils to arrive on time, a snow storm's making the streets slippery for drivers, a physician's cautioning a patient to avoid alcohol, and a wife's ordering her spouse to stop engaging in extramarital relations.

Constraints are conditions that limit the range of options that people believe are available for coping with problems in their lives. Examples of constraints include (a) a man's lacking enough money to pay his income tax, (b) a mother's being confined to her home in upstate New York at the time her daughter falls ill in Egypt, and (c) a young Chinese woman's being bound by Confucian tradition to accept her parents' choice of the man she is to marry.

Resources are the people, kinds of information, tools, and methods individuals recognize as useful for managing emotion-evoking encounters. An 8-year-old summons his 16-year-old brother when threatened by a 10-year-old bully. An investor searches the Internet for data about the performance of the stocks his broker has recommended. A waitress who must walk several blocks from her work to a public parking lot late at night buys a pistol for protection from muggers. A neophyte high school teacher attends group-counseling sessions to become more self-assured and assertive in his methods of controlling a classroom of students.

The environmental factor called *ambiguity and imminence of harm* is an individual's impression of the potential threat posed by features of the context in which an encounter takes place. The waitress who must walk to her car late at night will probably have a greater sense of threat if the streets are dark and deserted than if the area is brightly lighted with many passersby, especially if the passersby are well-dressed and going about their business rather than not well-dressed and loitering.

Phase 2: The Encounter

Lazarus postulates four emotion-laden phases through which episodes typically pass—*anticipation, provocation, unfolding,* and *outcome.*

As people look forward to an encounter, they often anticipate what might occur and how such a possibility could affect their welfare. Anticipation can itself produce affect in the sense of an emotional set—an expectant anxiety, fear, or joy—that is carried into the episode and influences how the participants will behave. Thus, anticipation serves to link the causal antecedents to the encounter.

Provocation is any change in either the environment or the person that the individual interprets as altering the person-environment relationship so as to increase the likelihood of harm or benefit now or in the future.

The unfolding phase begins with an emotional reaction in person *A* (anger, affront, fear, pleasure) eliciting a visible response by person *B* (apology, shame, anger, disappointment, distress, indifference, warmth) which, in turn, evokes a further response by *A,* with that response drawing a subsequent reaction from *B.* Thus the pattern of exchanges continues, like volleys in a tennis match. As the incident unfolds, emotions can alter in both kind and intensity with each verbal exchange.

Outcome refers to the ultimate emotional state deriving from how the individual has appraised the episode in terms of her or his personal well-being.

Embedded in the four phases are two kinds of intellectual activity—*appraisal* and *coping.* Lazarus disagrees with those theorists who contend that emotions are noncognitive, visceral reactions that don't involve a person engaging in conscious reasoning.

> If there has been a single, central theme in my treatment of emotions, it is certainly that there is no appropriate sense in which emotion and reason are opposed to each other. Although people seem to assume that emotion is irrational, quite the contrary, emotion depends on reason. (Lazarus, 1991, p. 466)

Appraisal is the person's evaluation of *what might be thought or done* by oneself and by others during the incident. Coping is what a person *actually thinks or does* to manage the emotional encounter. Thus, appraisal consists of cognitive analysis, whereas coping consists of acting (or intentionally not acting) in a way the person believes will minimize the harm suffered or increase the benefit enjoyed.

Phases 3 and 4: The Aftermath

Lazarus proposes two final stages of emotional encounters—immediate effects and long-term effects.

The short term

Emotionally charged engagements can result in physiological changes as well as lingering positive and/or negative feelings.

Immediate physiological residues of unpleasant episodes may include increased blood pressure and heart rate, dry mouth, perspiring, disturbed digestion, headache, tremors, increased stomach acidity experienced as "heartburn," breathing difficulties, lethargy, and/or insomnia. Physiological remnants of pleasant episodes can be either the regular operation of bodily functions or changes associated with the excitement of enjoyable emotions, such as the feelings evoked in making love, winning a contest, or receiving effusive compliments. Physiological changes occasioned by pleasant incidents can include heightened adrenaline output, elevated blood pressure and heart rate, rapid breathing, and perhaps sleeplessness as the person continues to revel over his or her good fortune.

Immediate positive or negative feelings are usually the dominant kinds of affect generated during the encounter and that remain when the incident is over.

The long term

Long-term physiological results are often the continuation of certain immediate outcomes, such as recurrent headaches, digestive disturbances, and heart palpitations whenever the distressing encounter is recalled. Likewise, the bodily symptoms that may accompany recollections of a past enjoyable incident may also be similar to those experienced at the time of the incident, perhaps relaxation of tension or else the opposite, such as a surge of energy accompanying the increased adrenaline output that the memory elicits.

Not only may there be long-term physiological remnants of earlier emotionally charged episodes, but individuals' long-term sense of well-being is usually also affected. An intensely fear-evoking episode may cause a person continually to anticipate similar episodes and therefore suffer from persistent anxiety. In contrast, a highly enjoyable incident may enhance an individual's general sense of optimism and hopefulness that is carried into subsequent episodes.

The consequences of encounters can be expected to influence, in either large or small ways, the quality of people's future social relationships, since individuals are laden with the emotional baggage of past incidents as they anticipate the likely emotional results of each new encounter. Therefore, emotional development over the lifespan involves an accumulation of types of affect that rose during the individual's encounters with environments, encounters that have left remnants of emotions to influence the person's feelings and actions in the years ahead.

Applying the Theory

To lend Lazarus's theory a sense of verisimilitude, we can follow a 19-year-old college sophomore English major through the phases of an encounter with three professors, organizing our analysis in the sequence of stages depicted in Figure 7-2. This example is based on a case whose principal features are from an episode I witnessed some years ago. The emotions cited in parentheses throughout the description are ones I inferred from the youth's responses and demeanor during the incident. I'll refer to the student as Sheldon Gray.

Phase 1: Causal antecedents

Personality attributes—values, beliefs, motives. Among his values, Sheldon much admired people prominent in artistic endeavors, particularly novelists, dramatists, and actors. He yearned to be esteemed in the college community as a gifted intellectual—a talented author and actor—and thus he dedicated much time to the activities of the campus drama club. He was the center of a coterie of friends with similar ambitions, and he made a special effort to court the approval of faculty members of the English and drama departments.

His sense of control in such an academic atmosphere varied between confidence and self-doubt. He sometimes feared that his talents could not match those of many of his classmates. He felt pressed for time to accomplish all that he hoped for, and he often suspected that he might be trying to "juggle more plates in the air" than he could safely manage.

Environment attributes—demands, constraints, resources, likelihood of harm. Both the English and drama departments had the reputation of being very competitive and well respected throughout the Midwestern United States. Each department attracted able students, and each demanded that students maintain a high level of productivity. Hence, if they were to succeed, students had to plan their time well, in view of their heavy class schedule and the requirement that their work be of good quality. These conditions served as constraints influencing students' investment of time and energy. Resources at their disposal included a well-stocked college library, opportunities to display their talents publicly (drama club performances, a semiannual literary journal), teaching assistants willing to give extra help, and capable peers. Students who commanded no more than modest talent and motivation were at risk of failing, or at least they risked lagging behind their classmates and thereby losing the respect and comradeship of peers and teachers alike.

Phase 2: The encounter

Anticipation. The secretary to the chairman of the English department phoned Sheldon, asking him to come to the office at 10 a.m. the following Tuesday. Sheldon agreed. In the days leading to the meeting, he periodically wondered what the chairman intended to talk about. As he mused about these matters, he experienced a mixture of *curiosity* and *anxiety* as well as *pride* at being chosen to meet with the chairman.

Provocation, unfolding, and outcome that involved appraisal and coping. During the meeting in the department chairman's office, Sheldon would engage in cycles of appraising each step of the participants' exchanges and of devising actions for coping based on his appraisal of (a) what the others were thinking, (b) what actions they were likely to take, (c) what response he should mount to best achieve his goal of being seen as a talented, pleasant, responsible individual, and (d) what consequences he could expect from different coping methods. The nature of the episode is reflected in the following conversation.

When Sheldon was ushered into the department chairman's office, he found himself (with *increased anxiety*) facing three people—the chairman, Dr. Helen Friesen (who taught "Creative Writing"), and Dr. Mario Martinez (who taught "Current World Literature" and "The Modern American Novel").

Chairman: "Sheldon, I believe you know Ms. Friesen and Mr. Martinez."

Sheldon (*anxious but in control*): "Yes. I've enjoyed their classes."

Chairman: "We asked you to come so we could speak with you about your short story in the college's literary journal, *Visions*. The story was remarkably well written."

Sheldon (*relief, pleasure*): "Well, thanks. I was happy it was chosen."

Chairman: "I understand you'd submitted it as an assignment in Ms. Friesen's creative writing class last semester."

Sheldon (*growing anxiety*): "That's right."

Chairman: "We've had a curious coincidence arise, and we are interested in hearing how you might account for it. Mr. Martinez can explain."

Dr. Martinez: "When I was reading *Visions* last week and came across your story, I had the strange feeling that I'd already met the plot, setting, and characters sometime in the past. And since your story was set in Hawaii, I suspected I'd read something like it a few years back in a little-known magazine published in Honolulu—*Island Paradise*. For the classes I teach, I read lots of stories and novels, often from obscure sources. So I hunted up my old copies of *Island Paradise*, and there it was—the very same tale as in your *Visions* piece, but the original author was someone else, not you."

Sheldon (*intense fear, confusion, does not know how to respond, glances from one professor to another*).

Chairman: "So what would be your explanation?"

Sheldon (*very fearful*): "Oh, I guess a strange coincidence."

Chairman: "Have you ever lived in Hawaii, or even visited there?"

Sheldon (*fearful, but gaining control and confidence as he generates his reply*): "Well, not exactly."

Chairman: "What does 'not exactly' mean?"

Sheldon (*fear diminishes, feels pride in his ability to cope extemporaneously*): "A teacher I had in high school moved to Hawaii, and he sent me letters telling his experiences there. I took some of the incidents he told me and put them together in a story."

Dr. Martinez (taking a copy of *Visions* and a copy of *Island Paradise* from his briefcase): "But what I find strange is how the wording throughout your story—except for part of the first paragraph—is identical to the wording in this magazine."

Sheldon (*increased fear, rapid pulse, perspiration—does not reply but stares at the floor*).

Dr. Friesen: "Sheldon, I suspect that when you had the assignment to write a short story for my class, you took the easy way out—copied from a source you imagined no one here could ever discover. And perhaps you didn't foresee it might be chosen for *Visions*."

Chairman: "Sheldon, we're not interested in ruining your college career by making this a public matter. But I do expect you to tell the truth about what you've done. If you lack the courage to admit what seems obvious, Dr. Martinez suggests that we attach both *Visions* and *Island Paradise* next to each other on the bulletin board outside the department office, with both opened to the first page of the story. It might be a useful lesson for other students."

Sheldon (*intense fear*): "If I say I copied it, you won't post them?"

Chairman: "That's right. We're interested in your at least verbally owning up to what you've done and not trying to maintain this false facade of innocence."

Sheldon (*decreased fear, increased shame*): "So I did. I did copy it—or most of it—but just because I didn't have time to write one of my own when I had a long script to memorize for last spring's drama festival."

Chairman: "For future reference, I imagine you see what it led to. We'll not make it public. But what you should recognize is that you never know who's watching."

Sheldon (*diminishing anxiety; increased shame, guilt, relief*): "May I go now?"

Phases 3 and 4: Aftereffects

Estimating the nature of other people's emotions is clearly a very risky venture. Apparently our estimates are based on viewing others' actions and then imagining how we would feel in their circumstances. Therefore, it's difficult to know how the original youth on whom I've modeled Sheldon Gray felt during and after his encounter in the department chairman's office. But I did note that he carefully avoided ever enrolling again in a class taught by any of the three faculty members who were involved in the encounter. It seems likely that his avoidance was motivated at least partly by shame, guilt, and fear. Probably the three professors would always symbolize to him the sting of embarrassment and anxiety suffered during that painful episode. And he could never be sure that the story of the event would be kept secret. However, throughout the remainder of his college career, he did continue his activities in the drama department with some distinction.

Even more difficult than judging the short-term emotional effect of that one incident is the task of judging how the episode influenced the young man's later life. I would guess that he was always burdened with guilt and shame at having been discovered. And perhaps he suffered some chronic anxiety at never knowing "who was watching." Following graduation, he became a junior high school drama teacher, soon to be diagnosed as suffering from diabetes. Five years after leaving college, he shot himself to death.

SELECTIVITY IN DEVELOPMENT

As noted in Chapter 2, honeybees and ants have very few decisions to make about how they will act, since their behavior is pretty much hard-wired into their genetic structure. To a great extent, bees and ants simply act the way their genes dictate. Not so with humans. Their genetic endowment obliges them to select a pattern of life from a great multitude of potential options—occupations, physical activities, methods of communicating (spoken and written languages), sources of information, kinds of transportation, philosophical and religious persuasions, types of recreation, places of residence, modes of dress, eating and drinking habits, and more. Without help in choosing from among this overabundance of options, people would be overwhelmed by their decision-making tasks. That help—according to a theory of selectivity proposed by Jutta Heckhausen (Max Planck Institute for Human Development in Berlin) and Richard Schulz (University of Pittsburgh)—is provided by selection constraints inherent in three sorts of influence on development—the biological, the social-cultural, and the individual. A *constraint* in this instance is a function that (a) defines the borderlines within which development can take place and (b) identifies the possibilities within those limits.

The manner in which the three sources of selective influence are thought to interact over the lifespan is sketched in Figure 7-3. The sketch suggests that the human life course is analogous to a wide river that begins at a narrow inlet, widens dramatically, only to narrow to a constricted outlet at the end. In people's lives, the river's banks are defined by individuals' genetic endowment—by biological borders within which development can take place. Then, well within the riverbanks, the particular culture in which a person is reared further restricts the options available for development. That society/culture is like a central channel coursing down the river's center between the sandy shallows that extend to the bordering banks. Finally, inside the channel, a paddler in a canoe—the developing individual—wends along a self-chosen route, turning this way and that as guided by judgments about which route within the channel will be most efficient for reaching the intended destination.

The following paragraphs summarize Heckhausen and Schulz's notion of how the biological, the social/cultural, and the individual factors interact. To illustrate

Figure 7-3

**Interacting Biological, Social/Cultural, and Individual
Constraints on Lifespan Development**

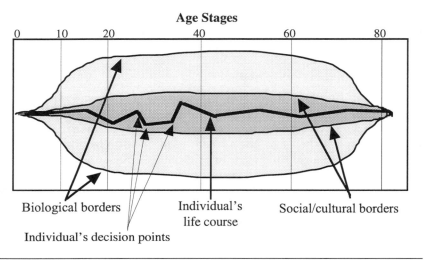

the operation of the those factors, I cite examples from three realms of human behavior: (a) eating and drinking practices, (b) modes of communication, and (c) recreational pursuits.

Biological Constraints

Obviously, a baby's task of selecting suitable behaviors from among the universe's myriad options is much simplified by the strict limitations imposed by infants' biological condition on the kinds of thought and action that infants can perform. Newborn humans' biological capacities are so restricted that decisions about what to eat and drink, how to communicate, and what to do for amusement are left mostly to their caregivers. But it is apparent during the first two decades of their lives that biological maturation rapidly multiplies children's available options for how to think and act. In terms of our river analogy, the banks that encompass the range of choices for mental and physical actions widen at a fast rate from birth through adolescence. Not only do the young recognize more alternatives as the years advance, but also they become physiologically and mentally more adept at taking advantage of those alternatives. In communicating with others, the typical 10-year-old not only can speak with a larger and more precise vocabulary than can the 3-year-old, but can read, write, and skillfully use such instruments as computers and the Internet. The 14-year-old is obviously larger, stronger, more agile, better coordinated, and can think in more complex ways than the 4-year-old.   Consequently, in recreational pursuits adolescents are better than young children in sports that require coordination, strength, agility, and assigned roles on teams. Furthermore, in all these matters the typical 20-year-old is more competent than either the 10-year-old or 14-year-old.

The changes in people's biologically determined capacities between birth and young adulthood are so much alike throughout the human species that it is common in all societies to view biological constraints in terms of age stages, with the progressive changes in abilities more evident early and late in life than during the middle years. The human biological condition from about age 25 to about age 60 does not vary dramatically for most people, but at both ends of the lifespan biological constraints change quite visibly—expanding rapidly in youth, declining markedly in old age.   Thus, during their first 20 years on earth, the young experience a striking increase in the options for thought and action available to them; and this increase imposes on them an ever-growing burden of selecting among options.   At the other end of life, old folks' declining capacities simplify their task of selecting how to think and act.   Their biological condition (reduced energy, nagging ailments, crippling, slow reaction times, untrustworthy memory) eliminates alternatives that were available in their earlier adulthood. They need not select among former alternatives, because their present biological fate renders those alternatives unavailable.

These generalizations about the extent of biological constraints obviously apply to humans as a species—to "the average person."   But it is apparent that within the broad scheme of development, individuals can vary from the average. Therefore, it is useful to distinguish between (a) specieswide or societywide biological limits on available choices and (b) individuals' particular limits that can deviate from "the norm."   One person's biological riverbanks are rarely quite the same as those of people of similar age and gender.

Whereas biological factors delineate the realm of possible choices, there still remains within this realm a seemingly infinite number of alternatives from which people must choose in directing their lives.   Much additional help in reducing those options comes from the traditions of the cultural environments within which people are reared.

Social/Cultural Constraints

For present purposes, a *society* can be defined as consisting of a collection of individuals living as members of a community.   That community may be limited in size, comprising a *village society,* or very broad in scope, such as *American society.*

Culture can be defined as

behavior unique to human groups, including material objects involved in such behavior, as well as language, ideas, beliefs, customs, strategies, codes, institutions, tools, techniques, works of art, rituals, ceremonies, pastimes, and the like.   Culture reflects the collective programming of the mind which distinguishes the members of one human group from another. (Hofstede, 1980, p. 25)

A society can be *monocultural,* with virtually all its members conforming to the same cultural traditions, or it can be *multicultural (plural society)*, with its members displaying cultural characteristics that vary from one subgroup of the society to another.

Every society's instructional and regulatory activities are designed to specify which beliefs, values, and modes of action are espoused—or even tolerated—by the society's members. In the realm of instruction, most child-raising activities within the family consist of teaching the young which thoughts and behaviors they should adopt and which they should avoid. Schooling serves the same purpose, as do the activities of the police, legislatures, government inspection agencies, religious groups, fraternal societies, business associations, and more. This process of influencing people to select the group's preferred choices as the proper, true, most desirable ones is often referred to as *socialization.* People who are successfully socialized accept their society's particular selections from among the multiple biologically possible alternatives and reject or simply ignore the remaining alternatives.

Thus, while humans have the advantage of being highly adaptive so that they have an abundance of potential beliefs and behaviors from which to choose, that advantage needs the support of the regulatory functions of social groups so that the daunting task of selecting ways of life will be bearable.

> Being part of a social group releases some of the regulatory load and provides reassurance to the individual about his or her own behavior by way of group approval.   Modern cultural anthropologists argue more specifically that social conventions become transformed into institutionalized [culturally embedded] ways of thinking. When it comes to implicitly regulating individuals' behavior, institutional [unwritten customary] ways of thinking are superior to explicit social conventions [laws, regulations] because conventions as pragmatic rules for social interactions are too transparent and therefore vulnerable to conflicts of interest between social agents.   In contrast, institutionalized ways of thinking are powerful shapers of individuals' beliefs because they appear to be grounded in nature itself. (Heckhausen & Schulz, 1999, pp. 79-80)

In way of illustration, consider the following examples of the way cultures channel people's choices for communicating with each other and for amusing themselves.

Humans' biological construction equips them to make a great diversity of sounds, ones that often differ from each other only in very subtle ways. Of all these potential sounds, only a few have been adopted over the ages as elements of any specific spoken or gestured language. Furthermore, different cultural groups have assigned particular meanings to selected sounds, thereby producing their language's vocabulary. Each language also involves an agreed-upon sequencing of sounds (syntax) and way of combining them (grammar). Consequently, the overwhelming task of selecting among all biologically possible sounds for communicating with others is greatly simplified when people learn their culture's accepted patterns.

Ways people amuse themselves are likewise channeled by cultural tradition, with each culture not only displaying a selected number of potential pastimes but also encouraging some types and discouraging or outlawing others. In a study of villagers' opinions of recreational pursuits on the Indonesian island of Java, respondents ranked 37 pastimes in terms of their prestige or social acceptability. The five most prestigious were soccer, badminton, classical Sundanese singing, going on a holiday excursion, and attending traditional puppet shows. The least respected were cock fighting, quail fighting, ram fighting, squat wrestling, and dueling with whips (Thomas, 1975, pp. 126-127). In some societies, such activities as cock fighting and ram fighting are considered so reprehensible that they are officially banned, with people who engage in those activities subject to fines and/or imprisonment.

Societies can differ significantly in the quantity of acceptable options they offer or endorse from among the biologically possible choices for thought and action. In general, highly industrialized societies that are populated by numerous ethnic, religious, and social-class communities tolerate a greater variety of beliefs and behaviors than do subsistence agricultural and hunter-gatherer societies whose members represent a limited range of ethnic, religious, and social-class diversity. In other words, the channels down the center of the life-span river are broader in some societies than in others.

But even within societies that offer a restricted range of choices, individuals are still obliged to select among the available options. We now address this matter of individual choice.

Individual Constraints

The dark line extending from left to right in the center of Figure 7-3 symbolizes the route from birth to death traveled by a hypothetical person. At each age stage, that person has adopted for himself or herself a limited set of beliefs and behaviors available within the society's cultural borders. By means of their personal decisions, individuals constrain the beliefs and actions that comprise their life pattern.

Periodic junctures along an individual's life course produce critical incidents that function as important decision points. Typical critical incidents include such events as suffering a serious accident or illness, witnessing the death of a parent, moving to a different city, entering a new school, dropping out of school, taking a job, being dismissed from a job, changing occupations, engaging in a love affair, marrying, bearing children, suffering the death of a child, and becoming divorced. In Figure 7-3, critical incidents are signified by sudden changes in the life course. At each such juncture, a sharp shift occurs in the options the person selects for the next phase of the lifespan.

As the pattern of the individual's lifeline in Figure 7-3 suggests, more dramatic changes in the life course are likely to occur earlier in life than later, because each time an individual makes a significant selection, the available options for future choices are reduced. A boy who drops out of high school eliminates a variety of future vocational opportunities that would have been available if he had graduated and attended college. A young woman who marries thereby restricts her future options among men or women with whom she can spend her life. The man who trains for a career as a stockbroker and enters a brokerage house restricts the vocational alternatives from which he can now choose. Therefore, as the years of adulthood advance, the task of selecting among options becomes simpler, since each important decision diminishes the alternatives from which to choose in the future.

The options open to individuals differ at different age stages as a result of both biological and cultural constraints. In learning to speak, young children are constrained by their biologically limited ability to utter their culture's language sounds correctly, resulting in the deviant enunciation, syntax, and grammar of "baby talk." In amusing themselves, people are constrained by their society's traditions regarding what sorts of rights and responsibilities are appropriate at different age levels. Even though an 8-year-old is biologically equipped to steer an auto and drink beer, social convention may dictate that driving privileges be available only at age 16 and alcohol-drinking privileges at age 18.

Three Guiding Principles

Finally, to aid people in directing their lives successfully and in reducing their burden of having to select among alternatives, Heckhausen and Schulz suggest three *principles of developmental optimization.*

The *age-appropriateness* principle

> implies that the individual selects his or her developmental goals to strive for when opportunities provided by the biological resources and the societal support systems (e. g., education, parent, or state support) are at their maximum. . . . Age-appropriate goal selections not only maximize access to relevant resources for goal attainment, they minimize the regulatory burden for volition. (Heckhausen & Schulz, 1999, p. 87)

In effect, you will have a better chance of getting what you want, and you can expect easier decisionmaking if you abide by your culture's expected pattern of how and when to pursue different developmental tasks (such as Havighurst's developmental tasks mentioned earlier). So, being willing to fit into your culture's age-and-gender schedule for acquiring knowledge, skills, rights, and responsibilities reduces your burden of making choices at progressive stages of your life course.

The *positive-negative-tradeoffs* principle concerns the consequences of investing energy and resources in a particular venture, such as in selecting an academic major in college, going into debt to own an expensive car, getting married, bearing children, enlisting in the navy, or emigrating to another country. What may look like a wise choice in the short term can turn out to yield undesired results in the long run. Therefore, the aim in wisely selecting actions is to make choices that have the best chance of producing positive tradeoffs in both the short and long run. This aim can most often be achieved

> when the goals involve general-purpose abilities. An example is education in terms of basic abilities and skills, such as reading, writing, algebra, and languages. It is hardly surprising that this principle of developmental optimization is not left to the individual but institutionalized in modern educational systems. It has become part of the societal canalization of developmental growth. (Heckhausen & Schulz, 1999, p. 88)

The *diversity-of-developmental-potential* principle is linked to the trade-off principle. This diversity rule suggests that, even as you appreciate biology's and culture's simplifying your job of selecting among life's alternatives, you still need to keep a variety of options accessible in case some of the choices that you might make would not be the wisest for your welfare.

> The principle of maintaining diversity embedded in optimization protects the individual from excessive narrowing down of developmental pathways. Although selectivity in resource investment is necessary, it has the potential of becoming dysfunctional if pushed to the extreme. (Heckhausen & Schulz, 1999, pp. 88-89)

THE INTERACTION BETWEEN COLLABORATION AND EXPERTISE

Nira Granott of the Massachusetts Institute of Technology proposed a theory to account for how the development of people's knowledge and skill is affected by individuals engaging in collaborative activities to which each person brings a particular level of expertise (Granott, 1993).

Granott credited Vygotsky, Piaget, and Bandura with providing key assumptions on which she built her model. From Vygotsky and Soviet psychology she adopted the conviction that cognitive change does not result from an individual's being in isolation. Rather, change results from individuals' social encounters, as in parents or teachers interacting with children or in youths interacting with agemates. From Piaget, she adopted the belief that cognitive development does not consist of passively absorbing knowledge but, rather, development involves persons constructing knowledge through acting physically or mentally on their world. "When considering social interaction, the Piagetian school emphasizes cognitive conflict [leading to the restructuring of knowledge] resulting from interaction among peers" (Granott, 1993, p. 184). From Bandura, Granott drew the proposal that much social learning consists of individuals observing the behavior of others, then modeling their beliefs and actions on those observations.

Granott's model features two sorts of interaction: (a) people interact with each other while engaged in an activity and (b) during this social relationship, participants' degree of collaboration interacts with their levels of expertise to determine how they perform the activity at hand. To understand how Granott views the interaction between collaboration and expertise, we can start with her conception of *degrees of collaboration* and *relative expertise.*

The Collaboration Dimension

In Granott's scheme, the degrees-of-collaboration dimension assumes the form of a scale ranging from *highly constructive collaborative activity* at the positive end to *highly inter-disruptive activity* at the negative end.

An event located at the midpoint of the scale is one in which two or more participants are independently engaged in an activity, neither cooperating nor conflicting with each other. Positions between the midpoint and the highly collaborative end of the scale range from slight to extensive collaboration. Positions between the midpoint and the highly inter-disruptive end of the line extend from little conflict to much contention between participants.

--	-	0	+	++
High Level of Inter-disruption	Moderate Inter-disruption	Independent Activity	Moderate Collaboration	High Level of Collaboration

Throughout her presentation, Granott's use of the term *collaboration* implies participants acting together in a generally amicable manner that leads to cognitive growth. In contrast, *inter-disruption* implies a relationship that is abrasive, awkward, or disordered and therefore less apt to foster cognitive development.

The Expertise Dimension

In an activity that involves two or more participants, some individuals may have greater skill or knowledge than others for pursuing the task. That is, participants can vary in their expertise. In Granott's model, an expertise scale interacts with the collaboration scale to determine the nature of participants' relationship. I've used black circles to suggest the comparative expertise that two participants might bring to a given activity. At one end of the expertise scale, two circles of equal size represent participants having the same degree of knowledge or skill for pursuing the task (called *symmetric* expertise). At the opposite end, two circles of dramatically contrasting size suggest that one participant brings to the activity far greater knowledge and skill than does the other (*asymmetric expertise*). Stations between the extremes identify intermediate levels of difference between individuals in their knowledge and skills. It should be apparent that the two small circles at the left end of the line (which here symbolize two novices) could just as well be medium-size or large circles and still represent symmetric expertise. In other words, the partners in a venture could both be moderately or highly experienced and their relationship still qualify as symmetric expertise so long as there was little or no difference between them in their ability to perform the task at hand.

Symmetric Expertise   Asymmetric Expertise

Dimension Interactions

Figure 7-4 combines Granott's two dimensions by casting the collaboration scale on the horizontal axis and the expertise scale on the vertical axis. In the right-hand half of the diagram, the boxes display the names of nine types of collaboration that Granott suggested are the result of how collaboration levels intersect with expertise levels. The nine varieties form three vertical groups that extend from a simple, low-level of collaboration (imitation, swift imitation, parallel activity), through a medium degree of cooperation (guidance, asymmetric counterpoint, symmetric counterpoint), to a high degree of complex collaboration (scaffolding, asymmetric collaboration, mutual collaboration).

Within the first vertical group, *imitation* appears as the form of collaboration that occurs when (a) one member of a pair of individuals (or one or more members of a group) has far more knowledge and skill than does the other member for performing an activity and (b) the less expert of the pair copies the behavior of the more knowledgeable one without the more expert member actively aiding the observer in adopting the copied behavior. In effect, the two individuals act independently rather than cooperatively, with the more knowledgeable one passively influencing the other's behavior. The influence goes in only one direction—from the model to the imitator. And there is a marked discrepancy between the individuals in their levels of competence (high degree of *asymmetric expertise*).

Swift imitation involves peers—who are only moderately different in their level of expertise—pursuing the same activity but in a manner mostly independent (noncollaborative). The individuals' independent efforts are interspersed with short periods in which the less expert member copies the more competent one. "The information flow, whether verbal or visual, is mostly unidirectional and asymmetric" (Granott, 1993, p. 193).

The label *parallel activity* applies to situations in which peers who have similar degrees of skill and knowledge are independently performing a task with no more than brief, occasional exchanges of opinion or information. Those exchanges, often unidirectional, can alter the recipient's knowledge structures.

Within the second vertical grouping of types, *guidance* or *apprenticeship* consists of persons who have significantly more expertise giving advice, direction, and training to participants who have less experience with the activity. The guide is often a parent, teacher, coach, club leader, or an especially knowledgeable agemate. The guidance is unidirectional, with the guide always the one offering suggestions to the apprentice. The periods of giving guidance are interspersed with periods during which the apprentice works alone.

Figure 7-4

Interaction Between Levels of Collaboration and Expertise

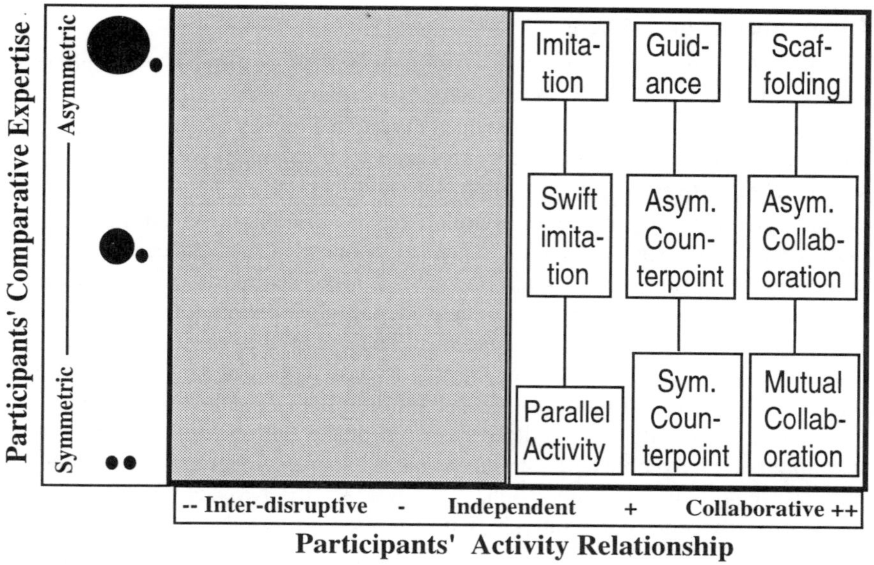

Participants' Activity Relationship

Asymmetric counterpoint is a partially collaborative effort among agemates whose level of expertise is somewhat different. The partners share information and evaluations of their progress, each offering ideas but with the more capable member usually directing the activity. "The process of knowledge construction is unsynchronized, and the interaction reflects previously or independently constructed knowledge of the more capable partner" (Granott, 1993, p. 189).

Granott applied the label *symmetric counterpoint* to the third type within the moderate-collaboration group. This mode of interaction features peers of a similar level of ability working together, with each taking a dominant role at some stage of the project. "For example, during a problem-solving activity, typically one participant at a time tries a solution while the others watch. Another example is a group discussion in which one participant talks at a time while the others listen" (Granott, 1993, p. 188).

The highest degree of collaboration occurs in the third vertical grouping, where the greatest discrepancy in participants' expertise can produce a *scaffolding* mode of participation.

The guiding partner assists the other's construction of knowledge. In a supportive and approving manner, the guide subtly directs the other's observation and activity step by step, while accommodating to the other's wishes and ability. (Granott, 1993, p. 193)

Asymmetric collaboration involves peers of moderately different levels of expertise working together, with a more experienced member dominating the decisions about the activity and giving directions and aid to the less experienced. There is constant sharing of information and opinion throughout the activity, but the extent to which participants display initiative and direct the activity is unbalanced in keeping with the differences among the participants in the skill and knowledge needed for performing satisfactorily. In sharing their knowledge and suggestions, the participants co-construct their understanding of the task.

Finally, the most extensive cooperation between peers of equal expertise is *mutual collaboration.* The interaction is continuous and reciprocal, with each participant introducing ideas, assessing the contributions of the others, and agreeing on plans of action. The members co-construct their knowledge by continually sharing their perceptions and profiting from their peers' contributions.

Such is the nature of Granott's nine types of collaboration. Then to what use can such a scheme be put? I believe the model can be helpful to teachers, parents, club leaders, employers, and supervisors who are responsible for placing individuals in pairs or in groups to pursue activities intended to promote learning—that is, to foster their construction of skills and knowledge. The teacher or supervisor, by identifying the levels of expertise participants bring to an activity, can estimate which of Granott's nine types of relationship might be most suitable for both (a) achieving the activity's goal (winning the game, producing a viable plan, improving a product, increasing work efficiency) and (b) enhancing the participants' skills and knowledge. On the basis of this estimate, the supervisor can structure the activity (assign responsibilities and suggest a manner of working together) that is likely to produce the desired two-part outcome of attaining the group's goal and enriching the individuals' skills and knowledge.

More Dimensions?

In Granott's graphic presentation of her scheme, she identified only the nine types of collaboration pictured in the right sector of Figure 7-4 and left the shaded sector blank. Rather than specifying types, she simply noted that the left region represented *negative relationships* or *inter-disruptive activity,* then proposed that

Disruptive interactions form a mirror image of the collaborative interactions. Disruptive interactions range from highly inter-disruptive interactions (with extremely interlocked, interfering activities), through moderately interlocked, disruptive activities, to least inter-disruptive interactions (represented close to the [center] intersection of the dimensions) that are mostly independent. (Granott, 1993, p. 202)

This abrupt and seemingly off-hand dismissal of the left region of the model aroused my curiosity. I wondered if there was not a better way to account for what Granott called the *negative interactions* that characterize the shaded sector. One possibility that occurred to me is that a factor called *emotional and motivational climate* might go a long way toward clarifying the difference between the model's collaboration and inter-disruptive halves. The following line of reasoning explains the nature of such a possibility.

First, it should be recognized that the horizontal scale in Figure 7-4 is not a single-dimension scale as Granott's version implies. The reason it's not a single dimension is that the right half concerns *extent of collaboration* whereas the left half evidently concerns *disruptions of progress toward the goal (or goals) of the activity.* In other words, the left side is not the lower end of an *extent of collaboration* scale but, rather, seems to be a separate *efficiency of progress* dimension that interacts with Granott's original pair. I would suggest that a factor strongly influencing the efficiency of progress is the emotional/motivational tone of the interactions among participants in an activity. In Figure 7-5, I've displayed some typical emotions/motives that could affect the success participants achieve in the sorts of collaborative arrangements that Granott's nine types involve. But my simply listing illustrative emotions/motives is clearly not an effective way to show how the system of interactions really operates. A different narrative and graphic rendition is required.

If, indeed, the left sector of the original diagram does concern progress toward the aims of collaborative activities, then it's important to identify what those aims might be. Although the aims are not stated outright, two principal ones to be inferred from Granott's discussion are those of (a) generating the visible *product* that was to be the outcome of the activity (such as win a game, devise a plan, settle a dispute, define a concept, choose a leader, and far more) and (b) enhancing the participants' *knowledge structures.* Each of these goals can assume the form of a dimension represented as a scale, as shown in Figure

Thus, I'm suggesting that the left sector of Figure 7-4 should consist of a pair of dimensions which define the *efficiency of progress* that seems to be implied in Granott's scheme. In Figure 7-5, I've simply listed those two dimensions at the bottom, since they cannot easily be incorporated into Figure 7-5's basic two-dimensional display.

Consider, now, a likely difference in how each of these postulated dimensions relates to Granott's nine collaboration types. In the interaction between the quality-of-product dimension and Granott's extent-of-collaboration scale, the product resulting from a high degree of collaboration (scaffolding, mutual collaboration) is likely to be a single, shared product (every child contributed to painting the mural, every member of the jury contributed to a single final decision). But at the low-degree-of-collaboration end of the scale (imitation, parallel activity), each participant is likely to create his or her own product (each child draws a picture of his or her own family, each employee works on his or her own computer).

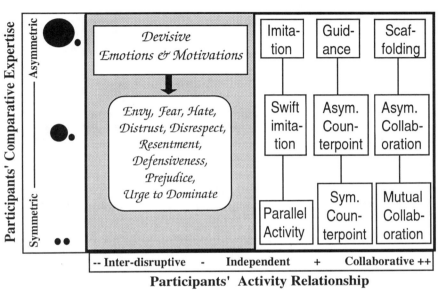

Figure 7-5

Causes of Inter-Disruptive Relationships

Quality-of-Product Scale

| Complete failure | Finished but many weaknesses | Moderately successful | Quite good, very few weaknesses | Excellent job |

Knowledge-Enhancement Scale

| No change | Slight enhancement | Moderate growth | Considerable enhancement | Extensive enrichment |

Therefore, the task of assessing product quality will more often require individualized evaluations for low-level types of collaboration than for high-level types. But assessing the effects of different levels of cooperation on knowledge enhancement will more often require individualized evaluations because the type and extent of change in one participant's skills and knowledge as a result of the activity is likely to be different from that of others', no matter which of the nine working arrangements is involved.

Next, consider the emotional/motivational factor which I believe exerts significant influence on how efficiently a given type of collaboration furthers the quality of products and knowledge acquisition resulting from an activity. Each kind
of emotion/motive noted in Figure 7-2 can itself be envisioned as a dimension
ranging from strong to weak. I would speculate that, as a general rule, stronger
negative emotion/motivation will exert greater inter-disruptive influence in high-
level collaboration (scaffolding, mutual collaboration) than it will in low-level
cooperation (imitation, swift imitation, parallel activity). For instance, hating,
fearing, distrusting, or disrespecting fellow participants is likely to retard product
creation when a group's members are expected to play equally important roles
(mutual collaboration, symmetric counterpoint) than when their interaction is
minimal and unidirectional (imitation, parallel activity).

Furthermore, the change in participants' knowledge structures is likely to be
different if their relationship involves strong negative emotions/motives than if
the relationship is infused either with weak negative affect or with a degree of
positive affect.

In sum, I am assuming that the emotional/motivational character of the relationship among participants in group efforts will influence both the (a) visible
outcome or product of their venture and (b) the invisible ways that participants'
knowledge structures change—or fail to change—during the activity.

Conclusion

The dual purpose of the foregoing discussion has been (a) to introduce Nira
Granott's model of interaction between degrees of collaboration and the extent of
expertise of the participants in group activities and (b) to illustrate one way that
a model of interactions can be expanded by the addition of more dimensions to
increase the accuracy of the model's explanations and predictions.

REMAINING CHALLENGES

While writing the present chapter and attempting to describe—both verbally
and in graphic form—the interactions implied in the chapter's theories, I recognized more clearly than ever that the available methods for depicting the relationships among theories' components are very inadequate. The methods are
especially unsatisfactory for comparing one theory's structure and functions with
another's. Typical typologies, such as the five-category system summarized in
the introduction to Part I (*trait, consequences, interactional, organismic,
transactional*) are much too general—far too vague—to characterize a specific
theory in a manner that clearly reveals how its conception of interactions is
similar to, and different from, other theories' conceptions.

As I sought to convey the notions of interaction in this chapter's four theories
in graphic form, I was obliged to adopt four separate graphic "vocabularies" and
"grammars." As a consequence, the graphic versions of the four models cannot
be compared in terms of a common coin. It seems to me that this need for both

a sufficient verbal taxonomy and a sufficient graphic taxonomy for delineating component interactions poses a worthy challenge to developmentalists' creativity in the years ahead.

8

A Potpourri of Theories

This chapter describes five theory types that did not fit conveniently into any of the previous chapters but were ones I thought deserved attention. Each model illustrates a different set of problems in relation to development, a different type of development, and/or a different approach to theory construction. The first example focuses on the age-old problem of determinism, now clad in modern garb. The second concerns how people mentally represent events. The third proposes stages through which friendships evolve. The fourth is designed to explain personality development over the lifespan. The fifth centers attention on what its authors characterize as a "neglected function of play."

DETERMINISM, INDETERMINISM, CHAOS, AND COMPLEXITY

A never-settled issue in the sciences and humanities is the question of determinism. Is everything that happens in the universe the result of a combination of causal factors? In other words, can every event be accounted for by factors (causes) whose operation produces events (effects)? And if all events are predestined by previous factors, then exactly how does that process work? Or, on the contrary, can events just occur without causes?

This perennial cause/effect puzzlement also involves the question of *free will*. In decision-making situations, to what extent are people free to choose which course of action they will pursue, unconstrained by earlier events? Or is the notion of a *free will* merely a delusion, so that our decisions are all preordained by unrecognized prior events (causes) which have dictated the option (effect) that we think we have freely picked?

Such questions have been pondered by philosophers from early times. Siddhartha Gautama—the Buddha—in the fifth century B.C.E. avoided proposing that earlier events caused later ones by simply noting that two phenomena can consistently occur coincidentally. The Buddha's correlational principle of causality states that

"When this is present, that is present; when this arises, that arises; when this is not present, that is not present; when this ceases, that ceases." This causal formula was the Buddha's answer to both those who held that events were strictly determined and those who posited that things happened by chance. The formula does not talk about first causes [of the world] nor about such metaphysical entities as God or Soul [with its karma] that supposedly have totally determined the future course of events; and it denies the element of chance. (Marek, 1988, p. 86)

The early American theologian Jonathan Edwards (1703-1758) revealed his determinist position by asserting that "nothing ever comes to pass without a cause." The same conviction had been espoused by the Dutch philosopher Baruch Spinoza (1632-1677), who contended that "nothing exists from whose nature some effect does not follow" (Lerner, 1965, p. 2).

In contrast to the determinist stance is the opinion expressed by such thinkers as Bertrand Russell (1872-1970), the English philosopher of science who observed early in the 20th century that "the Law of Causality . . . is a relic of a bygone age, surviving like the [British] monarchy, only because it is erroneously supposed to do no harm" (Lerner, 1965, p. 5). In agreeing with Russell's opinion,

many influential scientists and philosophers have argued that the notion of cause plays a diminishing role in modern science, especially in the more advanced branches of it, such as mathematical physics, and that the notion is . . . a primitive, anthropomorphic interpretation of the various changes occurring in the world. It is beyond serious doubt that the term "cause" rarely if ever appears in the research papers or treatises currently published in the natural sciences, and the odds are heavily against any mention in any book on theoretical physics. (Nagel, 1965, pp. 11-12)

Instead of the traditional cause-and-effect relationships postulated in most of the human-development models described in this book, such scientists offer only a statement of the probability that two or more conditions or events occur together. This is a statistical refinement of the Buddha's utterance 2,500 years ago. According to the scientists, the fact that two or more variables interact in a consistent manner equips us to predict changes in one by knowing what changes are occurring in the other. Hence, we need not speculate that one of the variables caused the change in the other, nor that a third factor caused the changes in the original two.

As philosophers and scientists have struggled with the determinism issue, they have come up with several lines of reasoning. One is the mathematical physicist's *functional relationships* position, which actually may avoid the issue rather than resolve it. The astrophysicist who does not accept the notion of causality in the physical world, still appears to display belief in cause-and-effect in his daily life. When his 10-year-old daughter turns on a pornographic television program, her scientist father can be expected to turn the set to a different channel, on the grounds that such raunchy fare "is a bad influence." And when the TV and room lights suddenly go off, the astrophysicist can be expected to grope for a flashlight so he can find the circuit-breaker box where he suspects the problem might be remedied.

A second variety of response to the determinism issue has been reflected in recent years in *chaos theory,* a neologism created in 1975 by a mathematician, James Yorke, as he sought to account for the disappointment that scientists experienced in trying to predict such things as the movements of heavenly bodies and the weather. Experts were able to create computer models of such phenomena and thereby quite accurately predict how the phenomena would behave in the short run. But reasonable short-term predictions turned into incomprehensible chaos when projected farther into the future. However, careful analysis of the prediction process suggested that the results gave the impression of chaos merely because the scientists (a) had not identified all of the multiple causal factors affecting objects in outer space nor all of the factors influencing weather conditions or (b) had failed to measure the factors' interactions accurately enough or (c) had not recognized that a very minuscule influence of a factor (when it was in its original condition) could, over time, multiply so dramatically that it would lend the outcome a chaotic appearance. As Edward Lorenz wryly suggested in reference to weather prediction, because of the long-term cumulative effect of an extremely slight initial influence, a butterfly flapping its wings in a weather system over San Francisco might result in a thunderstorm over Denver some days later. Thus, the observed chaos that casts doubt on the doctrine of absolute determinism could be interpreted as resulting from scientists' lacking adequate methods of identifying and measuring the entire array of causal influences. So, by recognizing a long-term outcome's "sensitive dependence on initial conditions," we might keep a belief in determinism intact (Bütz, 1997, p. 7).

The notion that causal relationships are often too complicated for people to understand has led to another set of interpretive models under the rubric *complexity theory.* The self-assigned task of complexity theorists is to identify all of the causal components involved in an event and to describe how the components interact. Complexity theorists' object to the linear causality of traditional science mentioned in Chapter 3. Complexity theorists, like other dynamic-systems proponents, reject the notion that a single causal factor—or even a combination of factors—directly produces a later event (an effect). Instead, they propose that components engage in reciprocal *dynamic interactions* that influence all of the components in a kind of mutual causality. To illustrate this concept in a simple fashion, Ford and Lerner cite the example of a child swallowing a pill.

One can ask, "What effect does the pill (P) have on the child (C) (e.g., does it increase stomach acidity or blood pressure?), that is, PÄC. Or, one can ask, "What effect does the child (C) have on the pill (P)" (e.g., how do digestive processes affect changes in and absorption of the pill?), that is, C → P. The fact is that both processes are occurring simultaneously; for example, the pill is affecting the child, while the child is affecting the pill (C ↔ P) and the dynamics of their interaction changes over time. . . . [The resulting] networks of interdependent variables [components] might be called a *causal field.* In a causal field a change in any variable is understood as a consequence of the operation of the entire field of variables. (Ford & Lerner, 1992, pp. 56-57)

In summary, investigators who style themselves as chaos theorists, complexity theorists, and dynamic-interaction theorists typically seem committed to a deterministic explanation of events. However, they recognize that completely identifying and measuring the transactions among variables is a daunting task, one that perhaps can never be performed perfectly, so accounts of cause will always leave a residue of unknown and inadequately measured components. Those unrecognized components are typically lumped into a category that hints at the investigator's admission of ignorance—a category labeled *chance, error, random behavior, indeterminate functions,* or *miscellaneous.*

A third response to the determinism/indeterminism conundrum is that offered by theorists who assert that events can be partially determined and partially not. An instance of this in the field of human development is Alan Fogel's (University of Utah) proposal about the nature of people's daily transactions with each other and with their physical environments.

My answer to the question of the balance of indeterminism vs. determinism is conceptualized within the frame of a continuous process model of relationships. Rather than thinking of some actions and events as fortuitous and others as determined or predictable, I believe that virtually every action and event is partly determinate and partly indeterminate. Events are partially indeterminate in the sense that the information we create about them is always changing [showing that our belief system and life trajectory are not immutable], and partially determinate in the sense that [events] are perceived as part of ongoing action within a frame [of an established life pattern] that constrains our degrees of freedom [by limiting the options and paths we can follow]. (Fogel, 1993, p. 178)

In attempting to understand Fogel's line of reasoning, I find it a challenge to grasp the logic that development is both determinate (the result of causal factors) and indeterminate (simply happening without causal factors). I could more easily understand Fogel's position if what he really meant was that the practical task of identifying the entire array of causal factors (including the butterfly over San Francisco) is so far beyond human ability that we are obliged to accept the fact that we can never "know it all." Thus, we must be content with failing to account for "it all" and are compelled to accept—but not be able to specify—the factors that make up what we choose to call *indeterminacy, fortuity, chance, luck, error,* or *fate.*

Yet there are those who contend that chance and indeterminacy cannot simply be dismissed as a lack of identifying all components or as poor measurement. They buttress their argument with developments in the field of physics where "the erosion of determinism was subverted by statistical regularities . . . and credibility was assessed in terms of probabilities" rather than a linear conception of cause and effect (Gulerce, 1997, p. 46).

Paul van Geert, a developmental psychologist at the University of Groningen in the Netherlands, has rejected strict determinism by leaving some room for the operation of people's free will and unexpected events in accounting for human development. But, at the same time, he contends that present events are to a degree determined by past events. In effect, he has set the boundaries of what he defines as the territory within which reasonable debate over determinism/indeterminism should take place.

> In its original form, *determinism* is the philosophical doctrine that every event, act, and decision, is the inevitable consequence of antecedents that are independent of the human will. Nobody, with the exception of a few weirdoes maybe, will seriously endorse philosophical determinism in this particular form. However, there exist forms of physical and statistical determinism that still color the scientific discussion about how human development comes about, and to what extent development is determined by either natural [hereditary] or nurtural [environmental] factors.
>
> The verb *determine* comes from the Latin *determinaire,* which means *to limit.* In view of its etymology, determinism boils down to the doctrine that antecedents limit the range and properties of consequent events, or that events are constrained by their past. It is hard to imagine that anyone would seriously object to this particular form of determinism.
>
> In summary, there is a form of determinism that no one would endorse, and there is a form of determinism that no one would seriously reject. The fight over developmental determinism must take place somewhere between these two poles. (van Geert, 1997, pp. 13-14).

As the foregoing discussion suggests, interest in the determinism/indeterminism issue continues in force, with no consensus in sight. Recent versions of the controversy are enlivened with arguments stemming from dynamic-systems theory, chaos theory, and complexity theory as they have been imported into developmental psychology from their original homes in such disciplines as mathematical physics and meteorology.

HOW EVENT KNOWLEDGE IS GENERATED

The inspiration for theorists to create a new model or revise an existing one is typically provided by puzzling happenings, that is, ones that prove difficult to interpret. Such was the inspiration behind the general-event-representation (GER) theory devised by Katherine Nelson (City University of New York) and her colleagues. Their curiosity was aroused by noting that young children who failed to solve such reasoning problems as those created by Piaget for studying cognitive growth could adequately perform equally demanding reasoning tasks in their daily lives. To account for this enigma, Nelson and her associates devised a version of script theory that enabled them to explain the mystifying observations that had launched their hunt (Nelson, 1986b).

The following description of Nelson's model first describes the theory's foundational assumptions, then illustrates how the theory can be applied to interpreting the development of children's modes of thought.

Assumptions Undergirding Event-Representation Theory

Nelson's theory was founded on the following beliefs about the form and sources of the contents of people's minds.

People's knowledge (the accumulated contents of their minds) derives principally from episodes that people have witnessed and/or helped produce. Everyone's daily life is composed of an abundant succession of such episodes. The resulting knowledge consists of mental *representations* in the form of symbols that stand for beliefs or constructs at two main levels of abstraction.

Level 1. Contents at the most basic level are *perceptions*—mental impressions or records of (a) a particular episode's objects and people and (b) what happened during the episode. These direct impressions serve as the material from which increasingly abstract, broadly applicable representations are subsequently built on Level 2.

Examples of particular episodes: The New York Yankees and California Angels baseball game on August 9. The South High School junior prom on May 27. Johnny Green's ninth birthday party. The First Baptist Church's Sunday service the morning of January 11. A State College freshman American history class on October 29.

Level 2. Separate specific episodes often display the same essential elements in common, even though the details of those elements differ from one incident to another. In other words, there are certain *types* of incidents whose general patterns are identical. In Nelson's theory, these types are called *events*. When a given symbol stands for a kind of event that encompasses a variety of episodes, it is called a *general event representation* (GER).

Examples of events: A baseball game. A high school prom. A child's birthday party. A Sunday church service. A college history class.

At this level, the symbolic forms are not verbal concepts, like the meanings intended by such words as *poodle, leaping,* or *investments* nor by such phrases as *elephants in the forest* or *theories of human development.* Rather, the symbols assume the character of *schemas.* A *schema*, as typically intended in cognitive psychology, refers to mental structures that organize information in configurations. A configuration, in contrast to a concept or a category, depicts the components of an event in their temporal and spatial relationships.

A schema is formed on the basis of past experience with objects, scenes, or events and consists of (usually unconscious) expectations about what things look like and "what goes with what." (Mandler, 1979, p. 263)

One way to depict schemas that act as general-event-representations is to cast schemas as *scripts.* A script in Nelson's model is

an ordered sequence of actions appropriate to a particular spatial-temporal context and organized around a goal. Scripts specify the *actors, actions,* and *props* used to carry out those goals within specified circumstances. The script is made up of *slots* and requirements on what can fill those slots. That is, the script specifies roles and props and defines obligatory and optional actions. For each of these slots there are *default values* that are assumed if the person, object, or action is not specified when the script is instantiated in a particular context. (Nelson, 1986a, p. 13)

Space limitations prevent me from identifying all of the components of the scripts for the five examples of events—the ball game, the prom, the party, the church service, and the history class. But my identifying brief segments of two of those events—baseball games and birthday parties—may suffice to suggest how scripts are composed.

- *Examples of complexity:* The script of a formal baseball game is far more complex than that of a child's birthday party. Because the details of the baseball representation are so numerous and so complicated, they have been cast as detailed written rules of the game that explain the meanings assigned to a host of such terms as *innings, hit, out, base runner, steal, balk, slider, infield,* and far more. The components of a birthday party are unwritten and few in number—*cake, candles, the singing of Happy Birthday, presents,* and *the opening of the presents.*

- *Examples of obligatory and optional components:* Obligatory elements of a baseball game include a ball of specified diameter and composition, bats of defined shape and composition, bases, a pitcher, outfielders, and more. Optional elements include a printed roster called a "program" as well as a public-address announcer. Obligatory elements of a child's birthday party include a child who has reached a new age, guests who help the child celebrate, gifts for the child, and a cake with as many candles as the child's age. Optional elements include hired entertainers, such as a clown or magician, and lesser gifts called "favors" that are provided for the guests.

- *Examples of slot fillers:* A *slot* is a role, type of equipment (prop), place, or time period that is filled on different occasions with different specific people, props, contexts, or time lengths. In baseball, the role of *player* is filled by different people on different teams. Furthermore, a principal slot can be divided into constituent subslots. For instance, the *player* slot subsumes such subslots as *catcher, pitcher, shortstop,* and *left fielder,* with each of

Figure 8-1

The Process of Generating Event Representations

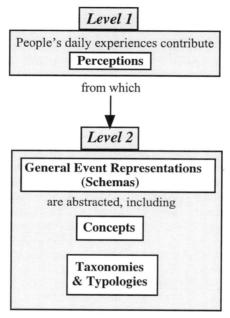

these roles filled by different individuals on different occasions—or even different individuals during the same game when *substitutes* are inserted into the *lineup*. In baseball, the *spatial slot* can be filled by different fields on which the game is played. The contents of the temporal slot can vary according to such conditions as the number of hits during *innings* (many hits extend the time) and whether the score is tied at the end of nine innings and the game extends into *extra innings*.

Each slot in a birthday-party script can also be filled by different alternatives—the birthday child (different children), guests (different guests), cake (chocolate, angel food, one layer, three-layer), presents (money, a doll, a video, a computer game), opening of presents (before serving the cake, after serving the cake). The *spatial slot* can be filled by various locations (the child's home, the child's backyard, a restaurant, a school gymnasium, an amusement park), and the *temporal slot* can vary from short to long (half an hour, one hour, three hours, an all-night sleep-over).

As Nelson explains, event representations can include different kinds of abstractions derived from a person's perceptions of daily life episodes (Figure 8-1).

> Although schemas are abstractions from experience, they are not the only abstractions. Elements that occur in events and scenes—i.e., objects, people, actions—become represented in their own right as concepts that may participate in other representational structures besides the schemas in which they are originally embedded. At a still more abstract level, these concepts may be organized into hierarchical structures, such as taxonomic [and typological] categories, or into logical or mathematical systems. (Nelson, 1986a, p. 9)

Kinds of abstraction can be illustrated in the cases of baseball and birthday-party event knowledge.

First, consider concepts, with the term *concept* defined as a labeled quality shared by diverse phenomena. *Hit* is not only an action abstracted from baseball games, but the concept *hit* also participates in events outside of baseball—a car hits a fence, one clown hits another with a custard pie, and a boxer hits his opponent. The concept *cake* is not limited to birthday celebrations but can appear as a component of other kinds of events, such as dessert during a picnic or as the main item of lunch in a cafeteria.

Next consider taxonomies, with *taxonomy* defined as a hierarchical system of categories that displays ways in which items in a designated class of phenomena are similar to, and different from, each other. In the case of baseball, we might envision the upper four levels of a *games taxonomy* within which baseball could be located (Figure 8-2). This would equip us to systematically compare baseball with other sorts of games. The structure can begin at the top with the most abstract, broadly encompassing *games.* The next level down divides games into competitive and noncompetitive varieties, with competitive games involving human adversaries. Examples of competitive games are baseball, chess, and poker. Noncompetitive games include crossword puzzles and the card game solitaire. The third level in descending order concerns types of competitors—teams or individuals. Baseball, volleyball, and tug-of-war are typically team sports. Golf, singles-tennis, chess, and poker usually pit individuals against each other. A fourth level can focus on key equipment whose movement earns points. In baseball that equipment is a baseball, in chess it's a token, in ice hockey it's a pellet (puck); and in crossword puzzles there is equipment but no points. Hence, in such an ever-descending fashion as this we could continue to move to additional levels that focus on other attributes of games, recognizing that the games assigned to a given category share more characteristics in common the farther we move down the structure. From the viewpoint of event-knowledge theory, the more extensive the taxonomy and the better we understand it, the more complex our event knowledge becomes.

With the foregoing model of general event representations in mind, we next consider some ways event knowledge develops during childhood.

Figure 8-2

Segment of a Games Taxonomy

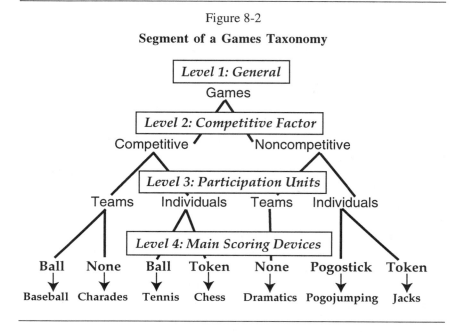

Typical Features of Event-Knowledge Development

As explained at the beginning of the presentation of event-knowledge theory, Nelson and her colleagues set for themselves the dual task of

- testing the accuracy of their impression that children reason in a more mature fashion when faced with practical problems in their daily lives than they do when confronted with problems posed for them by psychologists, and
- gaining detailed insight into how and when children's event-knowledge develops.

In pursuit of this pair of aims, Nelson's group conducted a series of studies of children's event reasoning, designing the studies around the version of script theory described above The studies did, indeed, confirm the investigators' earlier impression that children reason in more sophisticated ways about events in their daily lives than they do about events described to them under laboratory conditions. Nelson estimated that this discrepancy in the quality of children's thinking between daily-life and make-believe contexts was caused, at least in part, by children's greater ability to reason about (a) information that is part of their own prior experience than information in a more abstract form and (b) information related to their own social and cultural world rather than information in an abstract cultural setting (Nelson, 1986a, p. 4).

Three examples of further conclusions drawn by Nelson from her research illustrate the sorts of results yielded by her empirical application of event-knowledge theory.

- Children as young as age 3 "are sensitive to the temporal structure of events and are able to report sequences of familiar events virtually without error. This contrasts with earlier reports [from laboratory studies] that young children's memories are all jumbled up" (Nelson, 1986a, p. 231).
- Young children don't merely file in memory specific episodes they witness. Although they may, indeed, remember specific episodes, they also use a series of episodes—or even a single one—to form a general schema of the type of event into which such episodes fit. In other words, it's natural for young children to generate general event representations out of their perceptions of specific daily life incidents.
- As children experience an increasing number of similar incidents, their memories of those incidents become more abstract and general; and the details associated with particular incidents become confused. Thus, what children remember best is the basic framework and components of a schema, a habit that leads to the construction of a general event representation (GER).

This suggests that, as the GER develops . . . specific memories become fused in general representations, becoming memorable in themselves only when they depart in some "weird" way from what can be expected in the general case. (Nelson, 1986a, p. 232)

Conclusion

From the vantage point of event-knowledge theory, of what does human cognitive development consist? It consists of individuals accumulating in mind the event representations to which members of their culture typically subscribe. Children acquire these mental scripts through witnessing episodes in their daily lives and through receiving instruction from parents, teachers, peers, pastors, coaches, club leaders, and others. Some of the child's observations are *direct, real-life* experiences, as when a girl plays cornet in an orchestra, a boy sees his father lead a prayer meeting at church, or a youth takes a job in a fast-food restaurant. Other observations are *mediated*, consisting of episodes in the form of tales and documentaries presented via television, radio, newspapers, magazines, books, stage dramas, and the Internet.

STAGES IN THE DEVELOPMENT OF FRIENDSHIP

Among researchers, attention to the development of friendships during childhood and adolescence has increased in recent times and has yielded a growing variety of theories about how friendships are formed, are sustained, and function in individuals' lives. The following example illustrates a friendship-stage theory extracted by Jeffrey G. Parker (University of Illinois) and by John M. Gottman

Table 8-1

Friendship Stages: Early Childhood Through Adolescence

Age Stage	*Central Function of Friendship*	*Conversation's Principal Roles*	*Friendship's Effect on Emotional Growth*
Early Childhood Ages 2-5	Gain pleasure in play	Coordinates play; resolves conflict	Regulates arousal in interactions
Middle Childhood Ages 6-12	Gain acceptance by peers; present oneself acceptably	Gossip that negatively evaluates others	Teaches rules for displaying feelings; urges rejection of sentiment
Adolescence Ages 13-17	Explore and define one's self	Discloses oneself; solves problems	Integrates logic and emotion; teaches implications of affect for social relations.

SOURCE: A revised version based on Parker and Gottman, 1989, p. 104.

(University of Washington) from conversations between friends at different age levels.

Their model is an instance of inductive rather than deductive theory building. The authors did not begin by postulating principles of friendship formation and subsequently testing the principles by observing interactions between friends. Instead, they started with no preconceptions as to the likely nature of friendship patterns; they simply made audiorecordings of conversations between pairs of friends who ranged in age from 3 through 17 years. The recordings were then analyzed to identify themes that might distinguish one age level from another. This process resulted in a proposed model that pictured friendships as advancing through three major stages of social/emotional development from early childhood into adolescence—stages of (a) enjoying playing together, (b) seeking peer acceptance, and (c) confirming one's self-concept. The stages are summarized in Table 8-1 in relation to each period's central friendship function, the period's key focus of conversations between friends, and friendship's contribution to emotional development. Parker and Gottman did not present their scheme as a finished product but, rather, as a start "toward a model of friendship and social/emotional development" (1989, p. 99).

Friendships in Early Childhood

Our observations indicate that what concerns children in early childhood is maximizing the level of enjoyment, entertainment, and satisfaction experienced in their play. It has been recognized for some time that young children place a premium on a child's potential as a playmate. (Parker & Gottman, 1989, p. 104).

The authors concluded that the amount of pleasure attained in play depends almost entirely on the degree of coordination that the play involved, meaning "the extent to which the children fit together their separate lines of action into jointly produced, jointly understood discussions or activities. . . . The level of coordination is defined by the amount of social involvement and attention required of the participants" (Parker & Gottman, 1989, pp. 104-105). By applying this standard, Parker and Gottman were able to rank types of play according to the extent of coordination involved. The least coordinated kinds were seen as yielding the slightest rewards in participants' satisfaction and social development.

Three tiers of play were identified—parallel, joint, and fantasy.

The lowest level of coordination occurs in *parallel play* that involves two or more children engaged in the same activity, side by side, without any interaction that would affect how they pursued their tasks. A pair of agemates could be painting pictures, climbing on a jungle gym, or pushing toy cars. They would speak to each other, but what they said would have no influence on what they were doing. The conversation would be activity based, conflict free, and not intense (Parker & Gottman, 1989, p. 105).

The next higher tier features *joint activity* in which the participants exchange comments that can influence each other's work. The painters might give suggestions to each other about what colors to use, how to hold the brush, or what subject matter to paint. The jungle-gym climbers might offer opinions about each other's agility—or lack of it—or about what tricks they should try. Although joint activity runs the risk of greater conflict and disagreement than does parallel play, it offers greater potential for camaraderie, humor, and excitement.

The highest level of coordination occurs with *fantasy play* in which participants spontaneously create a drama in the form of a progressive dialogue of suggestions and replies. In Parker and Gottman's opinion, fantasy activity is the most effective form of play for promoting both pleasure and social/emotional growth by serving as "a laboratory for the rehearsal of adult roles and relationships [and for] working through major concerns and fears" (1989, p. 106).

Young children are generally not adept at controlling their emotions. But social play can help them learn to modulate their feelings through showing them how emotional outbursts and displays of raw affect can influence friendships.

Friendships in Middle Childhood

As children enter elementary school, their social contacts become more varied. They often meet classmates representing a wider range of social-class backgrounds and personality types than they had encountered earlier. In the school setting, they soon recognize the social-status hierarchy of child society, with some classmates clearly more popular than others. They also form cliques and discover that some cliques are more highly valued than others. Being a member of an in-group becomes increasingly important, particularly being a member of a high-status in-group.

> Gossip is far and away the most salient social process in friendship interaction at this age. Not only does gossip, primarily disparaging gossip, make up the great bulk of the content of conversation among middle childhood friends, but other social processes, such as information exchange, exploration of similarities, humor, and self-disclosure, occur almost exclusively in the context of gossip. (Parker & Gottman, 1989, p. 114)

Gossip satisfies several key needs at this time of life. It defines social norms and values, identifies behavior that violates those norms, reveals the consequences of abiding by or violating group values, and distinguishes between those personality characteristics that lead to peer approval and those that lead to peer rejection.

In middle childhood, both boys and girls find overt sentimentality embarrassing and to be avoided, even among friends. They prefer to appear "cool," reasonable, rational, calm, and under emotional control. At least part of their rejection of sentimentality results from a desire to protect themselves from peer teasing and criticism. Their cognitive growth equips them to be increasingly logical, a skill they employ in arguing with agemates.

Friendships During Adolescence

The physical and sexual development brought on by puberty is coupled with increased cognitive skills. These advances serve to focus adolescents' attention on their personal identity, the opposite sex, philosophical matters, and their future as adults. "Our observations make it clear that this process of defining who one is and who one will become is the underlying theme of friendship at this age" (Parker & Gottman, 1989, p.118).

Conversations are marked by intimate self-disclosure that employs humor, gossip, problemsolving, social comparisons, and estimates of other people's thoughts as a means of exploring and revealing "who I really am" and "who you really are."

Gossip at this age is not intended simply as a device for promoting in-group solidarity and identifying the norms of one's own sex group, as was the case in middle childhood. During adolescence, gossip serves the additional aim of self-exploration, of discovering "my true self" as compared to others' conceptions of their true selves.

Teenagers display a growing ability to control their emotions, to recognize the likely consequences of acting thoughtlessly on the basis of emotion, and to openly admit their feelings. Yet many still have trouble managing their emotions, particularly in relations with adults in authority—such as parents—and with peers.

Conclusion

The above brief sketch of the Parker/Gottman model has been intended to illustrate the main thrust of the authors' initial version of a theory of children's friendship as derived from recorded conversations of subjects between ages 3 and 17. In the theorists' opinion, their model is more adequate than other models of childhood friendship patterns in its

- Identifying changes in the functions of friendship from one age stage to another.
- Revealing connections between social development and emotional development.
- Showing how children's advancing cognitive skills affect their social/emotional concerns at different age levels.
- Illustrating the value of recorded conversations for revealing "many surprises, phenomena, and mysteries" about the nature of young people's friendships (1989, p. 125).

Parker and Gottman describe their scheme as "provocative" and "unabashedly speculative," inviting confirmation and/or revision on the basis of conversations gathered from children from cultures other than that of the white, middle-class American children they studied.

LIFESPAN PERSONALITY DEVELOPMENT

A growing trend over the final years of the 20th century was that of theorists encompassing the entire lifespan in their accounts of development rather than focusing on only one or two stages, such as childhood, adolescence, or old age. In terms of the quantity of published theories and of empirical studies, the most neglected segment of the life course had been middle age. Therefore, the recent attention theorists have accorded the full range of ages from the prenatal period to the final years of life has served to correct the neglect of certain stages and has more adequately revealed the manner in which one phase of life merges into another.

An example of a life-span theory is the model of personality development devised by Luciano L'Abate, a professor emeritus at Georgia State University. At the outset of his presentation, L'Abate defines *theory* as "an attempt at interpretation and explanation of reality as one sees it" (L'Abate, 1994, p. 5). He then defines *personality* as the sum total of a person's competencies as displayed in three contexts (home, work, leisure settings) when competencies are specified as the "minimal task requirements or responsibilities demanded of each individual in that setting. This definition posits a developmental competence-and-setting interaction in the three [contexts] that account for most of our waking time" (L'Abate, 1994, p. 31).

Competencies are divided into two major varieties, (a) the ability to love and (b) the ability to negotiate. The term *love* refers to "being emotionally available to self and to significant others" and engaging in relationships of affection and intimacy with valued others (L'Abate, 1994, p. 7). The concept *negotiate* encompasses a wide diversity of skills for exchanging services and information and for producing goods and services. The dominant settings in which such competencies are developed are the home, the work site, and places of leisure activities. The home is the main source of the ability to love, whereas the work site and leisure settings are the main sources of negotiation skills.

The concept *development* is defined as a process of competency attainment and of self-differentiation in the sense of progressively distinguishing oneself from the environment and from other people in order to create a unique self-identity.

> Personality development is a sequential process [viewed] in terms of three major *phases* in skill development [with advancing age]: (a) nonverbal, (b) verbal, and (c) written; and four major *stages*: (a) dependence, or childhood; (b) denial of dependence, or adolescence; (c) autonomous interdependence, or adulthood; and, finally (d) a return to dependence in old age. Adulthood means achieving three different goals: (a) personhood, (b) partnership, and (c) parenthood, not always in this sequence. (L'Abate, 1994, p. 55)

Stages of Development

L'Abate divides the lifespan into seven major stages, with the years of adulthood further divided into substages that reflect particular developmental concerns (1994, pp. 55-78). In effect, L'Abate's model addresses adulthood in greater detail than childhood, perhaps because he developed his theory from his clinical experience over several decades of marriage and family counseling.

Stages of childhood and adolescence

The theory's first four stages extend from birth through age 19 and bear the labels *infancy, childhood, latency,* and *adolescence.*

The tasks of personality development during infancy (ages 1-4) are those of beginning to overcome dependence on parents and other family members and of establishing initial self-awareness, that is, recognizing oneself as unique.

Childhood (ages 5-8) involves gaining physical independence (learning to do things by oneself) while maintaining emotional dependence on others.

During the latency stage (age 9-12), children increasingly learn to give and to receive help, trust, and affection.

Adolescence (ages 13-19) is characterized by teenagers developing individuality, no longer dependent on peers for a sense of worth and identity.

Early and middle adulthood

The years of early and middle adulthood (ages 20-50) are divided into three subperiods. The first is a transition phase from adolescence (ages 17-20) called "pulling up roots," during which youths typically leave the sheltering care of high school and the family in order to experiment with various life courses (ages 20-28). This stage poses problems of work, marriage, and perhaps childbearing.

The second subperiod—the early phase of middle adulthood (ages 31-40)—confronts individuals with the choice of developing either a generative or a stagnated personality. In keeping with usage introduced by Erik Erikson (1963, 1964), *generativity* refers to a person's wish to combine his or her personality with that of a love partner in producing and caring for offspring. Stagnation, the opposite of generativity, consists of individuals being self-absorbed, that is, concerned solely with their own well-being. Within middle adulthood, important developmental tasks include that of settling down (ages 32-38), which includes managing a career and managing a household.

As the third subperiod, the latter years of middle adulthood (ages 40-50 or so) confront people with the tasks of evaluating their past achievements and/or failures, becoming increasingly "one's own person," guided more by one's own ideals and standards than by other people's opinions. Now on the verge of late adulthood, individuals face a midlife crisis of recognizing that their years of youth have passed, their sex life is decreasing, their skills may soon diminish, and their choices among partners and occupations are progressively reduced.

Old age

L'Abate again draws on Erikson's psychosexual personality theory in characterizing old age as a period in which people's decline in physical abilities and opportunities confronts them with a choice between *integrity* and *despair*. The older person who achieves integrity is one who accepts and "is ready to defend the dignity of his own life cycle against all physical and economic threats" (Erikson, 1959, p. 98). The elderly who settle for despair face the final period of their life in a continuing state of gloom, hopelessness, and desperation.

L'Abate has divided the final years of the lifespan into early and late old age. The early phase is a transition period from middle to late adulthood (years 51-65) marked by individuals gradually redirecting their energies from traditional occupations and childrearing, accepting a new role in life, and developing an attitude toward their declining years. The final phase (year 65 to death) finds people choosing the manner in which they will invest their final years on earth. Once more, L'Abate borrows from Erikson's theory in portraying the choices open to the elderly as those of spending the remaining years (a) engaged in activities rather than passively letting life slip away, (b) becoming involved with other people rather than isolating themselves from social contacts, and (c) "getting on" with their lives rather than giving up and simply waiting for death to end their sojourn on earth.

Three Personality Modalities, Three Settings

L'Abate proposes three personality modalities that develop from people's ex-periences in his three dominant behavior settings—home, work, and leisure sites. He labels the modalities *Being, Doing,* and *Having.* The ability to love, developed primarily in the home, leads to Being, which is the person's capacity to exchange love and status-enhancement with others. The ability to negotiate leads to Doing and Having.

> Doing is measured by *how well* the person performs on various roles and tasks at home, as a provider, partner, and parent; at work, as an employer or employee; and in leisure-time activities, such as hobbies, avocations, games and sports. Having is made up by exchange of resources in goods and in money and is ex-pressed through production. Having is measured by *how much* one produces at home, at work, and in leisure-time activities. (L'Abate, 1994, p. 7)

At each stage of life the developmental tasks defined for that stage by the sur-rounding culture identify the learnings individuals are expected to acquire in order to be considered successful and well-adjusted. In the years of childhood and ado-lescence, such caregivers as parents, other relatives, teachers, priests and pastors, club leaders, and older companions bear the principal responsibility for guiding young people's personality development. In adulthood, individuals themselves, along with their love partners, bear the main burden of personality growth.

When L'Abate compares his model with other personality theories, he charges that past theories have failed to give sufficient credit to the family for personality development, particularly to the family as a system in which individual members are affected by the family's structure while that structure itself is being altered by the members' behavior.

> The task of the family is to allow for change in its members while still maintain-ing a sense of continuity. The task is not easy because change often is not a smooth process. Sometimes, it appears that every step a family member takes developmentally can disrupt the family structure. . . . The family is momentarily disrupted as old solutions no longer work and thus need to be altered. . . . The key to successful change in the family and in its individual members is flexibil-ity. (L'Abate, 1994, p. 167)

L'Abate further claims that theorists in the past have ignored the roles played by work settings in affecting the competencies that comprise personality. He wonders at this oversight, in view of the fact that such a large part of people's lives are spent at work. It is primarily in work sites that people develop two sorts of competence: (a) specific skills required in a particular job and (b) general skills that contribute to effective social relations and work-related attitudes (being prompt, hardworking, honest, loyal).

Likewise, L'Abate's accords far more importance to leisure activities—*discretionary pursuits*—than do other personality theorists. Personality com-ponents that L'Abate suggests are aided by leisure pursuits include (a) intiative

Figure 8-3

Steps in Personality Development

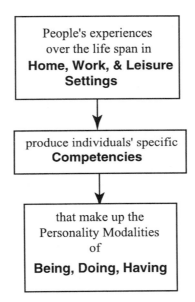

People's experiences
over the life span in
**Home, Work, & Leisure
Settings**

↓

produce individuals' specific
Competencies

↓

that make up the
Personality Modalities
of
Being, Doing, Having

(children devising activities free from adult direction), (b) a sense of mastery and accomplishment, (c) creativity (expressing fantasies), (d) social skills (as needed in games), (e) stress-release techniques (diversion from worrisome cares), (f) boredom reduction, and (g) self-definition (recognizing and developing formerly unidentified talents and interests) (L'Abate, 1994, pp. 179-180).

Conclusion

As summarized in Figure 8-3, L'Abate's theory pictures personality development progressing through three phases: (a) people's experiences over the lifespan in home, work, and leisure contexts (b) produce individuals' specific competencies that (c) make up the personality modes of Being, Doing, and Having.

In pointing out the advantages of his model, L'Abate has claimed that other theories have seriously neglected the influence of events in the home on personality development. In the eyes of psychoanalytic and family-system theorists, that claim must seem rather ill informed in view of the central role they assign to family influences in their own theories. A review of literature on personality development suggests that L'Abate is on sounder ground in charging that other theorists have failed to recognize the importance of work settings and leisure settings in personality formation.

PHYSICAL PLAY'S CONTRIBUTIONS TO DEVELOPMENT

Some authors create theories by first observing, interviewing, or testing people, then constructing explanatory models intended to clarify how and why people act in such ways. Those types of theories are sometimes called *grounded* or *data-based* models. Other authors not only generate models out of their own empirical investigations, but they also draw additional ideas from studies found in the professional literature. Still other authors depend entirely on published studies for their evidence. The following example is a variant of the second of these types—a scheme built from a combination of the authors' own studies and other investigators' reports and interpretations, with the others' investigations furnishing by far the greater amount of evidence in support of the scheme. The example concerns one form of play—physical activity play. The theoretical scheme is analyzed in terms of (a) foundational assumptions, (b) age levels and types of play, and (c) functions of play.

Foundational Assumptions

Among dvelopmentalists, a widely held conviction is that the basic pattern of how a person's appearance and abilities will arise, mature, and eventually decline over the lifespan has been determined by a timing system embedded in the genes. This preset growth schedule is common throughout the species and thus can be considered a characteristic of human nature. Erik H. Erikson (1968, p. 92) applied the term *epigenetic principle* to this predictable construction program: "Out of this ground plan the parts [of the person] arise, each part having its time of special ascendancy, until all the parts have arisen to form a functioning whole." Heinz Werner (1961) called such a genetically determined growth process *orthogenesis* (*ortho* = correct, *genesis* = development).

From the perspective of evolutionary psychology, across the ages various behaviors have become implanted in people's genetic nature because such behaviors' have enhanced people's chances of surviving in the environments they encountered. Included among such behaviors are those that qualify as *play*. A question for development theorists then becomes: "What functions does play perform to foster the growth and fitness of individuals and to promote the survival of the genetic strain?" This question has been answered in a variety of ways for certain forms of play; but in the opinion of A. D. Pellegrini of the University of Minnesota and Peter K. Smith of the University of London, theorists have failed to give sufficient attention to the nature and function of physical activity play (Pellegrini & Smith, 1998). To remedy this apparent oversight, Pellegrini and Smith have produced the following model.

The Pellegrini-Smith scheme takes the form of a review of the literature on physical activity play, with the review qualifying as an informal development theory organized in terms of (a) age trends in types of physical play and (b) functions of play, particularly in relation to gender.

Age Levels and Types of Physical Play

> Both child developmentalists and animal ethologists agree that play behavior is enjoyable, and that players, typically children or juveniles, are concerned with means over ends, and that the activity appears to be "purposeless," or to occur for its own sake. . . . Physical activity play may involve symbolic activity or games with rules; the activity may be social or solitary, but the distinguishing behavioral features are a playful context, combined with . . . moderate to vigorous physical activity, such that metabolic activity is well above resting metabolic rate. (Pellegrini & Smith, 1998, p. 577)

The authors note that throughout the lifespan, the typical incidence of physical play assumes the form of an inverted U. From a condition of no physical play at birth, the amount rises rapidly over the first two decades of life, then gradually diminishes during the early and middle adult years, only to drop off rapidly in old age.

Within the age span from early infancy through adolescence, Pellegrini and Smith identify three kinds of physical play—rhythmic stereotypies, exercise play, and rough-and-tumble play. Each kind becomes prominent at a different stage of development, with each apparently serving functions important for that stage.

Infants engage in a great deal of rhythmical stereotypic behavior that consists of gross motor movements—such as body rocking, arm waving, and foot kicking—to the degree that the baby's neuromuscular maturation pace permits. These movements begin after birth, peak around the middle of the first year of life, and gradually drop out of children's normal behavior repertoire as they achieve greater control of their muscles.

Exercise play involves such activities as running, chasing, jumping, pushing, pulling, lifting, and climbing. It increases during the early toddler and preschool years, reaches a peak around age 4 or 5, and diminishes during the primary school years.

The term *rough-and-tumble play* refers to the vigorous physical contact involved in the kinds of wrestling, pushing, pulling, grappling, kicking, and tumbling "that would appear to be aggressive except for the playful context" (Pellegrini & Smith, 1998, p. 579). Rough-and-tumble behavior begins during the preschool years, increases into the primary school years, reaches a peak around ages 8 to 10, then declines during early adolescence to account for less than 5% of play activities at ages 11 to 13 and even less thereafter (Figure 8-4).

Functions of Play

Functions of physical play in promoting people's developmental welfare can be viewed from at least three vantage points. First, we can speculate about why the process of evolution over millions of years decreed that physical play—in its rhythmic stereotypical, exercise, and rough-and-tumble forms—should become a part of human nature. Second, we can evaluate play for its contribution to the immediate well-being of the individual child. Third, we can analyze play for its deferred benefits to the individual.

Rhythmic stereotopypes

Studies of the neuromuscular maturation process in infants suggest that as different sets of muscles approach the time of their next step of maturing, rhythmic movements of the limbs and torso apparently hasten the child's gaining voluntary control over those sets of muscles. Therefore, rhythmic play apparently provides immediate developmental benefits by modifying or eliminating synapse formations, thereby furnishing the young child greater control in using muscle systems in intentional ways (Pellegrini & Smith, 1998, p. 582). Because babies are born with far more synapses than will ever be needed, perhaps rhythmic movements may strengthen certain synapses and—by neglect—get rid of irrelevant ones. Such a strengthen-and-eliminate process could have evolved over thousands of generations as nature's way of improving the efficiency of muscular control by improving the most useful synapses and discarding ones that might interfere with purposeful action. For the individual child, the rhythmic stereotypical movements of infancy have the deferred benefit of providing a sound neuromuscular foundation for the more complex physical actions of later childhood, youth, and adulthood.

Exercise play

The running, jumping, leaping, stopping, lifting, throwing, twisting, and turning in which children so often engage during the age period 2 to 8 appear to yield both immediate and deferred benefits for large-muscle coordination, endurance, strength, and skill by fostering muscle fiber differentiation and synapse improvement (cerebellar synapotogenesis). One traditional evolutionary explanation of why exercise play is found in all cultures is that such play is nature's way of preparing the young for adult roles they will fill (a) in the hunting and gathering activities essential for providing food for themselves and their offspring and (b) in protecting themselves and their dependents from predators.

Whereas no gender differences have been observed among infants in the frequency of rhythmic stereotypes, differences in the incidence of exercise play have been found in virtually all cultures that have been examined. Boys engage in more exercise play than do girls. Evidence suggests that at least part of the cause is hormonal, with the higher levels of androgens in males conducive to higher levels of physical activity. However, socialization customs also contribute to differences in exercise activity, as parents typically socialize boys and girls to pursue different amounts of physical play.

Figure 8-4

Age Levels and Types of Play

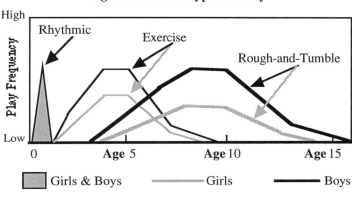

The proposal that exercise play also improves cognitive functioning is a matter of continued debate. Studies have supported the notion that distributed practice at mental tasks—that is, periods of mental work separated by periods of exercise play—can lead to more efficient problem solving. However, whether the improved mental efficiency is due to the interspersed physical play or is due solely to the recess from continual cognitive exertion—or perhaps a combination of both—is still unclear (Pellegrini & Smith, 1998, pp. 585-586).

Rough-and-tumble play

Pellegrini and Smith inspected the functions of rough-and-tumble play from the viewpoints of both physical and social development. A marked gender difference is found across cultures, with boys engaging in far more rough-and-tumble play than do girls.

In terms of physical skill, rough-and-tumble play clearly contributes to some immediate improvement in strength and agility, with those gains providing a foundation on which later physical fitness is built.

The possible social functions of rough-and-tumble play are more controversial. Three proposals in the professional literature concern relationships between (a) combative play and (b) fighting ability, social dominance, and emotional coding.

Traditionally, analysts of play have interpreted boys' rough-and-tumble engagements as evolution-based practice for the fighting (and perhaps hunting) skills needed for survival in primitive societies. However, Pellegrini and Smith question this interpretation on the grounds that such play diminishes markedly in adolescence when, it might be assumed, fighting skills were becoming increasingly important to individuals' survival. In these authors' opinion, a stronger case can be made for rough-and-tumble's function in establishing dominant and submissive relationships in social situations. Evidence from studies of children's positions in hierarchies of dominance/submission (leadership/followership) suggests that rough-and-tumble "is used to establish dominance in early adolescence; once established, the hierarchy reduces aggression [among group members], and R & T decline" (Pellegrini & Smith, 1998, p. 588).

A third hypothesis holds that rough-and-tumble play teaches the young skills of interpreting (mentally encoding) other people's emotions. Some observations of children's play indicated that children who engaged in more vigorous physical engagements were more adept at decoding others' emotional expressions (happiness, sadness, anger, fright) than children who engaged in less rough-and-tumble activity (Parke, Cassidy, Burks, Carson, & Boyum, 1992). However, Pellegrini & Smith question the emotional-encoding hypothesis because estimating others' emotions should be quite as important for girls as for boys, "and they certainly are no worse at it than boys. Yet the gender difference in R & T [which finds boys engaged in combative play far more than girls] is a well established finding" (Pellegrini & Smith, 1998, p. 589).

In summary, Pellegrini and Smith conclude that the principal social function of rough-and-tumble play throughout the elementary-school years is that of providing a means for boys to assess the strength of others for dominance purposes. Possibly rough play also furnishes practice in fighting skills. "Finally, we hypothesize that any benefits for emotional encoding or decoding are incidental benefits of R & T, achievable in other ways, rather than functions" (Pellegrini & Smith, 1998, p. 589).

REMAINING CHALLENGES

From reviewing this chapter's four illustrative theories, I would suggest that the following matters are worthy of further investigation in the future.

The determinism/indeterminism issue remains unsettled, as it has for ages. Thus, the matter warrants further research and innovative theory. As past experience suggests, the problem may be intractable, in the sense that no explanation has been acceptable to all players in the game of "Is everything *caused*?"

In Nelson's event-representation theory, she noted that her group's study of event knowledge, as viewed through the lens of script theory, "has left many questions—even many basic questions—unanswered." For example, how and when event representations are initially formed has remained unclear, "although our observations have led us to the presumption that [ERs] are operative by one year of age and are important to cognitive and linguistic developments during the second year" (Nelson, 1986a, p. 234). In other words, it's not clear whether the young child's event schemas first consist of separate scenes that gradually are hooked together to form a script or else a schema is initially a unit that progressively differentiates into clearer temporal and spatial components.

Parker and Gottman admitted the tentative nature of their model of friendship formation by characterizing it as "provocative" and "unabashedly speculative," calling for confirmation and revision on the basis of evidence gathered in cultures other than that of the white, middle-class American children they studied. Not only should additional studies draw on conversations of children from other cultural and social-status backgrounds, but other methods of data collection besides conversations could profitably be included so as to show how different perspectives toward friendship relate to each other. Such additional methods could include sociometric maps (charting children's expressed choices of friends), observations of children's relationships with friends and nonfriends (dominance/submission, methods of dispute resolution, degrees of intimacy), and individuals' descriptions of the traits they value in friends.

Because L'Abate's theory of personality development involves a host of components that interact in complex ways, there are many aspects of the model to verify, embellish, refine, and possibly revise. For example, what is the comparative importance of home, work, and leisure sites in personality development at each stage of development, and how is such importance measured? How valid are such generalizations as "adolescence is characterized by teenagers developing individuality, no longer dependent on peers for a sense of worth and identity"? To what degree are the personalities of people at a given age level alike, and to what extent are they different? If development involves individuals progressively distinguishing themselves from their environment and displaying increased individuality, what criteria should be used to determine the optimally desirable degree of differentiation from others? In other words, can the drive to be distinct from others produce undesirable social and personal outcomes?

In the realm of physical play, Pellegrini and Smith identified the need for several kinds of further research. For instance, the meager amount of information about age trends in physical play during childhood and adolescence should be enhanced with additional data. In particular, the transition from childhood to adolescence warrants clarification. The immediate and deferred effects of physical exercise on strength and endurance from infancy through adulthood are not sufficiently clear, nor is the influence of physical play on cognitive functioning well understood. Although existing evidence suggests that rough-and-tumble activities assume a role in establishing dominance/submission relationships among boys, that evidence is based on "several untested assumptions" about how boys estimate the relative strength or "toughness" of peers and about how they perceive the benefits and disadvantages of cheating in their attempts to dominate others (Pellegrini & Smith, 1998, p. 590).

Part II

Products of Social Movements

During the last half of the 20th century, two major social watersheds emerged to redirect several societal groups out of their traditional identity-and-power channels and into newly charted sociopolitical passageways. The first watershed appeared after the close of World War II and extended into the 1950s and beyond. The second surfaced in the 1960s, then continued in somewhat altered form throughout the rest of the century.

POSTCOLONIALISM

The first of the pair of movements was *postcolonialism*. In the aftermath of World War II, most of the regions of the world that had been held as colonial territories by European nations, the United States, and Japan won political independence. First were the Asians. Japan's wartime defeat brought freedom to Korea, parts of China, and areas of Southeast Asia that the Japanese had occupied. As early as 1946-1947 the British government transferred control of South-Central Asia to the indigenous peoples of India, with the region soon divided to form the nations of India and Pakistan. During the same period, the United States granted independence to the Philippines. Subsequently, Indonesians won their freedom from the Dutch; the Burmese, Malaysians, and Singaporeans from the British; and eventually the Cambodians, Laotians, and Vietnamese from the French.

Most Africans, slightly later than most Asians, successfully freed themselves from European colonial control between the late 1950s and early 1960s.

In contrast to Asian and African colonies, those in the Pacific were late in declaring for self-governance. Between the latter 1970s and the close of the century, most of the territories comprising Oceania were still engaged in the process of moving from colonial status to that of self-rule. Certain island areas would continue into the indefinite future as possessions of European and American governments.

South America was a different matter. In the early 19th century, a series of revolts against colonialism, led by such activists as Simón Bolívar, had already severed official ties to Spain and Portugal in most sections of the continent. However, throughout much of the 20th century—and in some places during the entire century—large portions of the population in South American nations remained under a form of *internal colonialism,* a mode of political-economic domination imposed by a local elite of European ancestry.

From a theories-of-human-development perspective, postcolonialism in the latter decades of the 20th century resulted in greater prominence accorded to indigenous beliefs about how and why people grow up as they do. Gaining political independence encouraged certain segments of the newly freed societies to reject their former colonial masters' secular and religious explanations of human development and to readopt traditional beliefs. The movement was an attempt to rediscover indigenous cultural roots. For example, in Islamic societies, Western secular explanations of human origins and development were pitted against traditional interpretations based on Islamic doctrine found in the revered scriptures, the *Qur'an* and the *Sunnah.* In India during the 1990s, Hindu nationalists of the Bharatiya Janata Party sought to replace Western science in schools by introducing the ancient science of *vastu shastra* (Thomas, 1998).

The spirit of postcolonialism, which contested the validity of the world's dominant political-economic social order that had lasted from the 17th century until the mid-1900s, would—in the 1960s—also challenge the principles of *rationalism* that had been hallmarks of modern science and of the theories of human development we inspected in Chapter 1. The following pages address those challenges and describe some of the results in the form of newly proposed models of development.

THEORIES' PHILOSOPHICAL AND SOCIAL CLIMATES

The second of the social-movement watersheds appeared in the 1960s. As mentioned in Chapter 1, the anti-Vietnam War protests in the U.S. and elsewhere were accompanied by an even broader rebellion on the part of an influential portion of the youth population—a rebellion against traditional social values. At the same time, unconventional perspectives in the arts, literature, philosophy, and the sciences were emerging in Europe under the label *postmodernism,* a movement that appealed to a noteworthy body of writers (a) who sought to correct what they considered social wrongs from the past and (b) who also objected to traditional rationalist tenets of Western science, tenets bearing on matters of objectivity, the nature of acceptable evidence, the value of controlled experiments, and the discovery of general laws of nature purporting to explain cause-and-effect relationships in human affairs. The social wrongs that advocates of postmodernism hoped to fix included the social status and life conditions of colonized and oppressed persons, especially of (a) persons on the lowest rungs of the socioeconomic ladder (the poor), (b) disadvantaged ethnic groups, (c) women, and (d) individuals whose preferences for sexual partners traditionally had been viewed as unconventional (homosexuals and bisexuals). A substantial portion of the proponents of social reform adopted postmodern conceptions of research and theory-building in the pursuit of their goals. Consequently, over the 1960-2000 era, the halls of academia were filled with animated and sometimes acrimonious debate about which sorts of guidelines should govern research and theory-construction in the social and behavioral sciences. The nature of this debate can be illustrated by comparing the social/intellectual paradigms that bear the labels *positivism, postpositivism,* and *postmodernism.* If we are to understand some important differences between the theories in Part I and those in Part II, it is useful to recognize distinctions among these three vantage points, because most of the models in Part I have been founded on positivist or postpositivist tenets, whereas many in Chapters 9 through 12 have been influenced by postmodern convictions.

Characterizing the three philosophical perspectives with any degree of completeness would require many more pages than this introductory essay permits, because none of the three exists in a singular, cohesive form. Instead, all three appear in multiple versions, because writers within each group often disagree in their proposals. Consequently, the following brief sketch of the three viewpoints represents no more than a single rendition of each and, as such, is bound to displease at least some proponents of such worldviews. In preparing the sketch, my intent has been to identify key features that are not unique to any particular version but, rather, generally distinguish one of the three perspectives from the other two. I believe my representations do no serious violence to the core convictions held by members of the three camps.

Positivism/Modernism[*]

The words *modernism* and *positivism* are so closely linked in much of present-day discussion that the two terms can be considered synonymous. *Positivism,* including the subvariety from the 1920s and 1930s known as *logical positivism,* has functioned over the past two centuries as the principal paradigm guiding the conduct of modern science (Toulmin, 1994). Here are typical assumptions on which a positivist or modernist worldview is founded:

Reality: There is an objective real world beyond the individual's body, and that world can be known and described. (Thus, positivists disagree with both forms of philosophical *solipsism.* Form 1 is the belief that there is no real world outside the person's mind; the only reality is what's in one's mind. Form 2 is the belief that although there is a "real world out there," occupied by objects

---

[*] A similar version of the following discussion appeared in Chapter 18 of R. Murray Thomas, *Comparing Theories of Child Development* (5th ed., Belmont, CA: Wadsworth, 2000) and appears here by permission of Wadsworth and Thomson Learning.

and people, each person carries in mind a subjective image of that world, and it's impossible to know the contents and processes of anyone's mind other than one's own.)

For positivists, all conclusions about reality—about the "truth" of what exists—must be based on empirical observations and measurements, that is, on real-life experiences and not on speculation about things that cannot be publicly verified (seen, heard, touched, smelled, measured) or that cannot be reduced by logical operations to public observations. Logical positivists reject "statements of only emotional significance, as judged by an inability to be verified against a formal analysis involving the facts of experience" (Moore, 1995, p. 53).

The aim of research and theory: The purpose of collecting empirical evidence and interpreting it is to reveal the truth about the physical/social world and how it functions. The aim of a positivist approach to human development is to discover principles or natural laws that are the foundation of development under all circumstances. The principles or generalizations can be organized in the form of theories or models of reality. Models of reality are always tentative, subject to revision on the basis of better methods of data collection, more complete sampling of contexts, convincing statistical analysis, and the application of more adequate logic for drawing interpretations.

Investigators: The people best qualified to carry out scientific studies are ones professionally trained in theory, data collection, information classification, and data interpretation.

Validity: Decisions about whether an account about events is "true" (accurately reflects the real world) are guided by criteria of objectivity (the methods of research are free from the researcher's personal biases), of representativeness (the study's sample of people or episodes accurately represents the characteristics of the broad population to which the generalizations will be applied), and of public verifiability (other researchers could replicate the study so as to verify or disconfirm the results). In effect, the validity of a generalization or theory is fostered by such scientific procedures as (a) conducting research studies with large numbers of participants, (b) replicating the study in different settings and with different kinds of people, (c) using the same interview questions with each participant, (d) checking on how consistently one researcher agrees with another regarding observations, and the like.

Nature and function of results: An increasingly accurate picture of reality (of what the world "out there" is truly like, as based on an ever-expanding quantity of empirical evidence and its logical interpretation) can be portrayed and communicated in linguistic, mathematical, and graphic descriptions. The portrayal assumes the form of principles and theories which are not limited to the things directly studied but can legitimately be applied to understanding similar events that were not studied. For instance, generalizations about how children learn, as derived from observing one group of children, can legitimately be applied to explain learning among other groups of children of similar age and in similar contexts.

Presentation of results: The writing style of positivist theories and empirical studies is "third-person omniscient"—a style intended to give the impression that the account is an accurate, objective description and that no subjective judgments on the part of the theorist or researcher affected the results. There are no such phrases as "We found a few studies in the *PsychInfo* database that seemed to be similar . . ." or "There probably are lots of criteria that could have been used, but the ones that occurred to us were . . . " or "In my opinion, these four children were . . . ." Instead, the description reads, "The extant research in the field supports the thesis that . . ." and "The criteria deemed most appropriate were . . . " and "According to established standards for classifying children, the four participants in this study were . . . ."

Understanding reality: People can learn the nature of reality by studying properly educated scholars' descriptions of empirical findings and their interpretation as viewed through the lens of a particular theory.

Postpositivism

A growing dissatisfaction with the ability of positivist approaches to effectively describe people's lives has led in recent decades to the revision of certain traditional positivist assumptions.

> Most of the social science disciplines have experienced an eruption of internal "crises" over the past several decades. . . . To many in the disciplines, social scientific knowledge seems to have had only limited relevance for understanding societal problems, whether those involve social behavior such as school learning and interpersonal violence, or community and institution conditions such as poverty, unemployment, and racial segregation. Another common theme—of particular concern in psychology—has been the *a*contextual character of research findings, the fact that the accumulated body of knowledge tends not to be situated, not to be conceptually and empirically connected to the properties and texture of the social settings in which it was obtained. A third theme reflecting discontent in the social sciences is the failure to accommodate human subjectivity in inquiry and to attend to the role of meaning in behavior, in development, and in social life. (Jessor, 1996, p. 4)

Problems have also arisen regarding two traditional positivist assumptions— that (a) experimental conditions can be controlled in ways that enable research-ers to precisely identify different variables' contribution to causing events and thereby (b) permit accurate predictions of future events.

Because many of the critics have only revised—not completely abandoned—a positivist perspective, they have been dubbed *postpositivists*. The following precepts typify the postpositivist paradigm (Campbell, 1996; Shweder, 1996):

Reality: There is indeed an objective real world beyond the individual's body. However, no one can offer an objective account of that reality because each investigator's own needs, cultural traditions, training, and biases filter her or his experiences. A theorist's or empirical researcher's version of human development inevitably becomes a combination of the researcher's viewpoint and the viewpoints of the people the researcher has studied. This means that a postpositivist perspective fits Denzin's (1997, p. 3) definition of ethnography as "that form of inquiry and writing that produces descriptions and accounts about the ways of life of the writer and those written about." Investigators who have proper training and recognize the danger of the biases they could bring to their task can more closely approach objectivity than do those who are less aware of factors that prejudice their conclusions. Still, no matter how careful investigators are, each of their accounts necessarily includes a large measure of their subjective selves.

Conclusions about reality—about the "truth" of what exists—should be based on empirical observations and their interpretation from the viewpoints of both the investigator and the people the investigator interviews, observes, or tests. When a researcher performs the data collection and interpretation, the result is a *personally constructed reality*. When numbers of people agree on the interpretation, the result is a shared, *socially constructed reality*. Hence, people's interpretation of life events constitutes their constructed reality.

The aim of research and theory: The purpose of theorizing and empirical research is to produce a description of constructed reality. This aim is pursued by an individual fabricating "my vision of the world out there" and of continually refining that vision on the basis of new experiences and more convincing logic. From a postpositivist viewpoint, the theories described throughout this book are all different people's constructions of the reality of human development.

Postpositivists share the hope of positivists that they can identify general principles that help explain human development in all places at all times. But whereas positivists generally are most interested in discovering principles that explain the likenesses among children, postpositivists are interested as well in explaining how and why individual differences among children make each child unique. Many postpositivists seem to consider it most realistic to search for principles that bear on somewhat limited aspects of development, so they are prone to focus more on minitheories rather than on macrotheories.

Investigators: There are two sorts of investigators or people who produce accounts of human development. First are the so-called *trained experts*, individuals with special academic preparation in theories and research methods— anthropologists, ethologists, psychologists, sociologists, historians, political scientists, economists, human geographers. Second are the people whom the experts study. From a positivist perspective, these people are exclusively the *objects* of study and therefore do not participate in describing or interpreting data. But from a postpositivist viewpoint, these objects are also worthy interpreters whose comments provide valuable insights from the respondents' particular vantage points. The experts include those insights in their reports of the constructed reality of development.

Validity: Hammersley (1992, p. 64) proposes that typical postpositivists evaluate research studies on the basis of how well they (a) generate or test formal theory, (b) are founded on empirical, scientifically credible evidence, (c) produce findings that can be generalized or transferred to other settings, and (d) identify the influence that the researcher and the research methods exert on the findings.

Nature and function of results: Postpositivists share positivists' opinion that an increasingly accurate picture of reality (of what the world "out there" is really like) can be portrayed and communicated in linguistic, mathematical, and graphic descriptions. The portrayal assumes the form of generalizations, principles, and theories which are not limited to the things directly studied but can be legitimately applied to understanding similar events that were not studied. However, it is important not to be content with generalizations but also to portray the individualistic features of the people and contexts that have been directly studied—features that make them unique. As for objectivity, the researcher openly admits to personal bias in selecting interview questions, the people and places that are studied, and theoretical assumptions that influence the interpretation of data. It is important not to feign objectivity but, instead, to inform readers of the sorts of subjectivity that give data and theory their particular character.

Presentation of results: The postpositivist's writing style is a mixture of third-person and first-person descriptions. Examples of third-person phrasing include: "Interobserver agreement among the three judges of the Piagetian stages was r = +79" and "During the videotaping, the group worked in a small room adjacent to their classroom." Examples of first-person expressions include: "We speculated that the most submissive pupil was . . . " and "We would place more confidence in our appraisal of the students' intentions if we had also. . . ."

Understanding reality: When people read an account of human development, they are not learning what "the world out there" is really like. Rather, they are learning an interpretation of what it seems to be like from a particular theorist's or researcher's vantage point; it is one perception of objective reality from one individual's or one group's outlook.

The theories described in Chapter 1 and in Part I of this book all represent positivist or postpositivist conceptions of theorizing.

Postmodernism

The dissatisfaction with positivism since around 1970 led not only to postpositivism but also, among especially rebellious revisionists, to an even more drastic abandonment of positivist convictions, the abandonment labeled *postmodernism* or *poststructuralism* that links such vaguely allied groups as avant-garde artists and architects, literati, critical social scientists, feminists, representatives of disadvantaged ethnic minorities, postcolonialists, anti-imperialists, neo-Marxists, and gay-and-lesbian liberationists. Thus, postmodernism is not a unified, coherent movement but, rather, is what Clark (1994, p. 22) characterized as an "ill-defined melange of attitudes, theories, and cultural criticism." A principal inspiration behind the postmodernism that has become popular since around 1970 has been a series of French philosophers, including Michel Foucault (1982, 1988, 1998; Rabinow, 1984), Jacques Derrida (1976), Jacques Lacan (Benvenuto & Kennedy, 1986), Julia Kristeva (1986), and Jean Baudrillard (1996, 1998).

Variants of postmodernism are found in diverse disciplines—the arts, the humanities, and the social and behavioral sciences. A subcluster within the behavioral sciences is composed of a loosely knit collection of developmental psychologists who trace their inspiration in the United States to the dialectical developmentalist Klaus Riegel (Broughton, 1987, p. 11) and to the Group for a Radical Human Science (1981). The following treatment is limited to social/behavioral-science versions that hold implications for understanding human development.

Because there are far more variations of postmodern belief relating to research and theory than can be described in this introduction, I try to convey the general sense of postmodernism by reducing the varieties to a pair—the *mild* and the *radical*.

The following are typical assumptions on which a postmodernist worldview is founded:

Reality: The conviction that there is an objective "real world out there" can either be questioned (the mild version) or be regarded as blatantly false (the radical version).

The mild version. There apparently is a real world, but people can never know it objectively for the same reasons that postpositivists offer—the investigator's own needs, cultural traditions, training, and biases filter her or his experiences. Consequently, an account of either an individual person's life or the lives of a group of people is a combination "of the ways of life of the writer and those written about."

The radical version. The notion that there is a "real world out there" is not merely held in doubt but is denied. According to the radical position, a person does have experiences, but the source of these experiences is unclear—possibly no more than that individual's imagination. The person continually casts the experiences into symbols, that is, into language—verbal, mathematical, or graphic. The resulting linguistic interpretation becomes the person's reality. Words are assigned meanings but the referents for those meanings are not found in a "real world out there." Rather, the meanings (the *signified*) are simply experiences attached to words (*signifiers*), and those words are then rearranged into combinations that provide new meanings. Hence, reality is nothing more than the manipulation of language (Derrida, 1976; Saussure, 1966). The basis for this belief is that all sorts of descriptions or interpretations can be offered for any experience or imagined event, so—the reasoning goes—there must not be any objective "world out there" that is being accurately portrayed. Otherwise, all of the descriptions would be identical. Ergo, each theory or description is just a maneuvering of language.

In mild postmodernism, research involves collecting, organizing, and reporting people's linguistic reactions to experiences in "the world out there." These accounts are *narratives, tales,* or *stories*—certainly not objective descriptions of the world. They are subjective "glimpses and slices of the culture in action" (Denzin, 1997, p. 8). Each glimpse or slice—such as an observation of two 6-year-olds playing together—is unique. No generalizations extracted from those children's interaction can be applied to explaining the play of any other children. Each narrative stands on its own. It serves as its own validation, requiring no sampling techniques, statistical analyses, interobserver agreement measures, replication, or the like.

> Any given practice [or event] that is studied is significant because it is an instance of a cultural practice that happened in a particular time and place. This practice cannot be generalized to other practices; its importance lies in the fact that it instantiates a cultural practice, a cultural performance (story telling), and a set of shifting, conflicting cultural meanings. Messy texts [in contrast to finely polished positivist theories and research reports] are based on these kinds of empirical materials. (Denzin, 1997, pp. 8-9)

Such "messy texts" require no interpretation or explanation. Their meaning is simply what it seems to be to the observer.

The aim of research and theory: In contrast to the positivists' and post-positivists' goal of describing how the physical/social world "out there" operates, the purpose of postmodernists is frankly political—to expose and remedy injustices suffered by people in situations of unfair social disadvantage. In other words, the goal of postmodernists is to correct society's wrongs (Giroux, 1992).

> [A] critical social science project seeks its external grounding not in science, in any of its revisionist, postpositivist forms, but rather in a commitment to post-Marxism. It seeks to understand how power and ideology operate through systems of discourse. A good text exposes how race, class, and gender work their ways into the concrete lives of interacting individuals. (Denzin, 1997, p. 10)

Investigators: Anyone who expresses a response (narrative, story) to oppressive social conditions is accepted as a qualified investigator. Thus, the tale told by a child living in a poverty-ridden inner-city ghetto is a respected exposition, as are the accounts offered by abused wives in a wealthy suburb. An important task of the professional researcher is that of collecting those narratives.

Validity: In Hammersley's (1992, p. 58) opinion, the character of postmodern studies "implies that there can be no criteria for judging its products," so that each speaker's voice deserves equal regard. "This position doubts all criteria and privileges none, although those who work within it [may] favor criteria such as [respect for] subjectivity and feeling" (Denzin, 1997, pp. 8-9). Each person's narrative is "truth" from that person's perspective and must be respected as such.

Nature and function of results: The most authentic accounts are the unedited records of what was said and done during a given event. These are uninterpreted narratives of what occurred. No generalizations are drawn. No applications are suggested for explaining human development beyond the particular event.

Understanding reality: Each narrative is someone's reality. Reading or hearing a wide variety of narratives reflecting individuals' experiences within the social structure provides an understanding of the reality of social injustice.

Critics' charges: Criticisms of postmodernism have come chiefly from people who subscribe to some version of positivism or postpositivism.

Matt Cherry (1998, p. 20) has commended postmodernism for "exposing biases of human understanding, [thereby] emphasizing a tenet of science that has been too often overlooked—the fallibility of human thought and the need for constant questioning and testing to improve our theories." At the same time, Cherry has chastened "the leading postmodernist thinkers" for

> [going] much farther than simply stressing the difficulty of getting at the truth. They reject the very notion of "truth" itself. They argue that there is no "objective knowledge" and no "facts," only personal interpretation, and that "reason" and "science" are no better than any other "myth," "narrative," or "magical explanation." (p. 20)

In a similar vein, Barbara Ehrenreich (1999, p. 17) has suggested that

> It's the job of the paid thinker—the literary critic expert no less than the physicist—to puncture myths, challenge prejudices, and expose the emperor's unclothed state. The [postmodernists] did some of that, and we should thank them for it. But in denying a reality independent of us, they condemned us to live in our collective [socially constructed] delusions. . . . But there *is* an external reality. If you doubt it, as the old saw goes, kick a rock. The two most venerable systems of human knowing—science and religion—disagree on many things, but both start from the postulate that there is indeed something "out there" that is not of our own making and that it is thoroughly independent of our thoughts.

Alan Sokal, a physicist at New York University, gained notoriety in 1996 for writing a parody of postmodern critiques of science and sending it to a leading postmodern journal, *Social Text,* whose editors failed to recognize the article as a hoax and published it as a serious work. Sokal later explained that his article was a "melange of truths, half-truths, quarter-truths, falsehoods, non sequiturs, and syntactically correct sentences that have no meaning whatsoever." He said he sought to mimic the "strategies that are well-established in the [postmodern] genre: appeals to authority in lieu of logic; speculative theories passed off as established science; strained and even absurd analogies; rhetoric that sounds good but whose meaning is ambiguous; confusion between the technical and everyday senses of English words" (Sokal in Bricmont, 1998, p. 23).

All of the theories in Part II were created out of the same spirit of social reform associated with postmodern social/behavioral science. Furthermore, many of the theories share postmodernists' concern for including in their interpretations the viewpoints of the people who are the objects of research, thus not limiting their conclusions to ones drawn solely from researchers' vantage points. In addition, authors represented in Part II often allude to the writings of such postmodern authors as Foucault, Derrida, and Lacan when offering a rationale in support of their work. However, it is the case that, in the spirit of traditional positivism, the authors have also sought to identify general principles of human development that apply to an entire category of people rather than regarding each person's development as something entirely unique.

THE CONTENTS OF PART II

The chapters that comprise Part II focus on the development of four types of people that were the concern of social reform movements during the final decades of the 20th century—the poor, disadvantaged ethnic minorities, women, and homosexuals/bisexuals.

Chapter 9: Growing Up in Poverty describes three theories about aspects of development of people whose lives are lived within society's lowest socioeconomic strata. The three are (a) Smeeding's model for guiding the study of poor children, (b) Garfinkel and McLanahan's analysis of how increased support payments to single-parent families might influence children's well-being, and (c) McLoyd and Wilson's conception of how stress affects poor children's growth and adjustment.

Chapter 10: Ethnic Minorities describes two models. The first, designed by Cynthia Garcia Coll and her associates, concerns how the disadvantaged status of an ethnic minority in a society affects the competencies displayed by children who grow up in environments of disadvantage. The second model, created by Janet T. Helms, proposes the way people create their ethnic identities, with Helms's illustrative examples being those of blacks and whites in America.

Chapter 11: Feminist Perspectives offers synopses of diverse theoretical proposals from the feminist movement during the final decades of the 20th century.

Chapter 12: Sexual Orientations describes four theories. The first two focus on how people's sexual orientations develop. The last two trace ways people of homosexual and bisexual tendencies come to terms with their sexual identities.

9

Growing Up in Poverty

Portrayals of how and why people in different social-class strata grow up as they do are not unique to the closing decades of the 20th century. Such portrayals obviously have a long history. Even though Jean-Jacques Rousseau (1712-1778) cast his book *Emile* in the guise of a novel, his account was actually a thinly masked prescriptive theory of how boys (Emile) and girls (Gertrude) in economically privileged families should develop. In the 19th century, Charles Dickens'(1812-1870) novels ranged across the English social strata, contrasting the lives of people in poverty with the lives of those in the middle and upper classes. In the United Staes, Horatio Alger, Jr., (1832-1899) penned dozens of idealized tales picturing youths of lower-class beginnings climbing the social-class ladder by dint of honesty, hard work, obedience, and humility. In addition to scores of such stories from a variety of authors of fiction, 19th-century social reformers published numerous tracts exposing the offenses of child labor and the neglect of the poor.

As the decades of the 20th century advanced, philanthropic organizations and governments focused increasing attention on the plight of children in poverty and created a growing array of programs to promote the welfare of the poor. After World War II, such efforts assumed a broader international scope with the establishment of the United Nations Children's Fund (UNICEF) in 1946 and with the endorsement of the U.N. Declaration of Rights of the Child in 1959 by representatives of nearly all nations of the world (Tarrow, 1985, pp. 238-239). In the United States, improved economic conditions contributed to a post World War II decline in rates of children living in poverty, a trend that continued throughout the 1950s and 1960s. But after 1970, poverty among American children increased substantially and progressed at a high rate into the 1990s.

In 1991, 21% of all children under 18 years of age were poor, up from 15% in 1970. Although white children comprise the majority of the poor in absolute numbers, children from Hispanic and African-American families are overrepresented: 46% of African-American children and 40% of Hispanic children live below the poverty line, compared to 16% of white children. . . . When one takes a life-course perspective, asking what is the probability of children being exposed to poverty during childhood, the statistics are even more alarming. Duncan and Rogers (1988) report that approximately 50% of all children hover near the federal poverty line at some point during their childhood, and that nearly one-third drop below the poverty line by age 15. . . . Among African-American children, 24% are likely to spend over 10 to 14 years in poverty on average, compared to less than 1 year for white children. . . . [Such] persistent poverty poses even greater risks to child development than do short, intermittent spells. (Chase-Lansdale & Brooks-Gunn, 1995, p. 1)

News of such distressing conditions was accompanied by heightened interest in the predicament of the poverty child on the part of social workers, religious groups, social-welfare foundations, scholars, politicians, and government agencies. Among the questions that attracted attention were ones about the effects of poverty on children's development and about how children might avoid or overcome the negative consequences of growing up poor. Proposed answers to those questions often assumed the form of theories. The purpose of this chapter is to inspect three typical proposals from the 1980s and 1990s. The authors of two of the theories cast their schemes as formal models—(a) Timothy M. Smeeding's (1995) method of guiding the study of poor children and (b) Irwin Garfinkel and Sara McLanahan's (1995) analysis of how increased support payments to single-parent families could affect children's well-being. The third example—Vonnie C. McLoyd and Leon Wilson's (1991) conception of how stress affects poor children's development—demonstrates that models of development associated with social reform are often not formally posed as theories. Rather, their status as theories is only implied in the authors' estimates of why members of a disadvantaged segment of society have arrived in such an unhappy state and how their condition might be improved.

A MACRO-MICRO MODEL FOR STUDYING POVERTY CHILDREN

Timothy M. Smeeding, a Syracuse University professor, has proposed an "interdisciplinary model of child well-being" intended to incorporate two traditionally separate perspectives toward children's development—the *macrosocial* and the *microbehavioral.* In explaining his reasons for creating such a scheme, Smeeding observed that

Economists, sociologists, and most public policy analysts measure children's well-being indirectly, by focusing on the well-being of their parents, . . . [using] measurable socioeconomic variables that are really inputs into children's well-being: household consumption, income, wealth, and capital goods (e.g., computers, television and video equipment, own room for each child). . . . [However, these] "macro" databases, while quite large and representative of major ethnic, racial, and demographic groups, simply do not deal well with children as individual entities. (Smeeding, 1995, p. 292)

In contrast to investigators who use macro approaches,

Developmental psychologists, educators, anthropologists, and pediatricians come at children's well-being from the other or "micro" end of the spectrum. That is, they employ direct measures of children's well-being: cognitive, social, intellectual, educational, or other development measures for psychologists, educators, and anthropologists; and physical and mental health status for pediatricians. (Smeeding, 1995, pp. 292-293)

To take advantage of the strengths of both the macro and micro perspectives, Smeeding sought to incorporate the two viewpoints within a single model featuring four major components. Three of the components are conceived as input causes (physical-social environment, parent/family processes, and community/life processes) that contribute to the output effect (children's developmental status). As shown in Figure 9-1, the macro component is the broad social/physical environment within which children's families function. Next, two parallel micro components represent the (a) particular child's parent/family situation and (b) characteristics of the particular community that directly affect the child's destiny. Finally, the model identifies the developmental characteristics of the child that result from interactions among the macro and micro inputs.

Although the model can be used for analyzing the development of children in any social-class stratum, Smeeding has applied it specifically to understanding child growth in poverty families. He uses the model as a guide to identifying what to observe and measure when appraising the state of children of the poor. Variables deserving analysts' attention in each of the four domains of the model include the following items, which are a combination of sources of evidence in Smeeding's original list and further sources that I've added to render the list more complete.

Physical/Social Environment

Family characteristics: Child's family's structure (members, roles) and family's well-being (income, housing)

Community environment: (incidence of employment/unemployment, incidence and types of crime, family social networks, available role models)

Social policy environment: (services offered by public and private social agencies)

Social attitudes context: (prevailing attitudes about race, ethnicity, gender, social-class status)

Figure 9-1

A Macro-Micro Model of Child Development

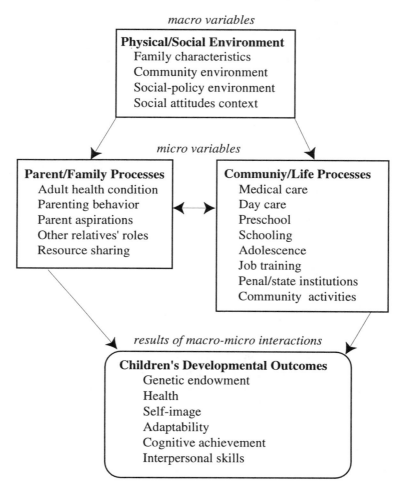

macro variables

Physical/Social Environment
  Family characteristics
  Community environment
  Social-policy environment
  Social attitudes context

micro variables

Parent/Family Processes
  Adult health condition
  Parenting behavior
  Parent aspirations
  Other relatives' roles
  Resource sharing

Communiy/Life Processes
  Medical care
  Day care
  Preschool
  Schooling
  Adolescence
  Job training
  Penal/state institutions
  Community activities

results of macro-micro interactions

Children's Developmental Outcomes
  Genetic endowment
  Health
  Self-image
  Adaptability
  Cognitive achievement
  Interpersonal skills

SOURCE: Adapted from Smeeding, 1995, p. 295.   Reprinted with the permission of Cambridge University Press.

Parent/Family Processes

Adult health condition: Physical and mental health of the child's caregivers

Parenting behavior: Ways caregivers treat the child, amount of time they spend with the child

Parent aspirations: Parents' personal ambitions and what they hope for, and expect of, the child

Other relatives' roles: Which other relatives interact with the child—type of interaction, frequency, emotional quality

Resource sharing: Ways that parents' and other relatives' money, time, and goods are shared with the child and with other family members

Community/Life Processes

Medical care: Type and quality of care available and provided in the past for the child

Day care, preschool, elementary and secondary school: Type and quality of school facilities, and how school personnel treat the child

Adolescence: Community facilities available to the adolescent

Job training: Opportunities for vocational preparation

Penal institutions: Location and type of facilities in which lawbreakers are incarcerated

Community activities: Facilities available for educational and recreational pursuits; types of activities for which those facilities are intended

Children's Developmental Outcomes

Genetic endowment: Inherited physical and cognitive potentials affecting the child's health, energy level, pace of maturation, appearance, and aptitudes for different physical and mental activities

Health: Physical and mental health resulting from a combination of genetic endowment, physical/social environment, and life style

Self image: The child's impression of "what I look like, what I can do well, what I can't do well, how worthwhile I am, how socially acceptable I am"

Adaptability: How quickly and successfully the child adjusts to changing life conditions

Cognitive achievement: How well the child succeeds in school and solves problems outside of school

Interpersonal skills: How amicable the child's relationships are with various kinds of people—parents, other relatives, agemates, school personnel, members of the community

In summary, Smeeding proposed that gathering the foregoing sorts of evidence about a child in a poverty family provides a profile of information unique to that child's life, information representing a sound foundation for recommending steps to take toward improving that child's well-being.

Smeeding offered two proposals about how to apply his diagnostic scheme most effectively. First, he suggested that particular attention be given to life events that typically play a crucial role in child development, such events as physical and mental child abuse; a parent's death, absence, divorce, or remarriage; and criminal activity on the part of the child, a relative, or a close companion. Second, Smeeding recommended that the child be studied over a period of time, since the factors identified in the macro and micro causal factors, as well as in the developmental outcomes, usually change somewhat with the passing of time. Noting the trends of such changes better equips the diagnostician to recognize which interventions may prove most suitable and when those interventions can best be introduced.

FINANCIAL SUPPORT AND CHILDREN'S WELL-BEING

A very simple model proposed by Irwin Garfinkel and Sara McLanahan (1995) qualifies as a microtheory, because it concerns an extremely confined facet of human development. The model's focus is reflected in the question: "What change in the well-being of children in single-parent families could be expected from implementation of the U.S. government's Family Support Act of 1988?" In effect, the model was created as a device for predicting what changes in children's welfare might be expected from such legislation.

To develop the model, the authors (a) identified the legislation's provisions that affected the financial support of children in single-parent families, (b) canvassed the research literature for studies suggesting how such provisions might influence child welfare, and (c) on the basis of the research, speculated about how putting those provisions into practice would likely affect children's living conditions.

A key feature of the legislation was its increasing the pressure on states— through incentives and prodding—to do a better job of establishing the identity of fathers of children who live with their mothers. Such paternity identification enables the courts to require that fathers make child-support payments. First, fathers' child-support payments directly improve the single-parent (mother-only) family's financial security and thus the quality of the child's life (Figure 9-2). In addition, establishing paternity and requiring fathers to furnish child support typically leads to increased contact between fathers and their children. Such contact usually revises the two adult parents' behavior in either positive or negative ways. As a positive result, the father spends more time with the child, which usually improves father-child relations and, thus, contributes to the child's emotional well-being. As a potential negative result, the father also has greater contact with the mother, resulting either in an amicable relationship or in acrimonious conflict—a repeat of the hostilities that led the parents to separate in the first place (Figure 9-2). However, the studies cited by Garfinkel and McLanahan suggest that, overall, increased child-support payments improve children's well-being. The amount of improvement to expect in a given instance

Figure 9-2

**Effect of Level of Financial Support on Child Well-Being
in Single-Parent Families**

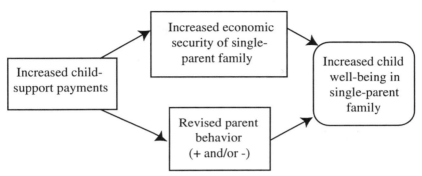

SOURCE: Adapted from Garfinkel and McLanahan, 1995, p. 228. Reprinted with the permission of Cambridge University Press.

depends upon a variety of factors, particularly on the amount and regularity of support payments, the amount and quality of additional time fathers spend with their child, and the quality of interaction between the two parents.

In its form pictured in Figure 9-2, the model can serve as a guide to studies of the actual consequences of the 1988 legislation and thereby lead to the construction of a more detailed, sophisticated theory of the effect of child-support provisions on children's lives.

A THEORY OF THE STRAIN OF LIVING POOR

Vonnie C. McLoyd and Leon Wilson's (1991) conception of how stress affects poor children's development was not cast as a formal theory. Rather, their proposal was presented as a narrative whose content was drawn from research about which conditions in the lives of poverty families contribute to children's suffering anguish and disordered development. In order to lend McLoyd and Wilson's account the semblance of a formal theory, I extracted from their description the components and interrelationships that comprise the stress-and-development model implied in their work. The resulting scheme is depicted in graphic form in Figure 9-3, with details of the model described in the following paragraphs. The product at the final stage of the model is the individual child who is raised in poverty.

The term *stress* refers to anxiety, emotional tension, or a sense of pending disaster that a person suffers. *Stressors* are events and conditions that cause people anxiety.

> Chronic stressors, in combination with an unremitting, rapid succession of negative life events, militate against positive mental health in poor children. Poverty, especially if it is long standing, is a pervasive rather than bounded crisis distinguished by a high contagion of stressors that grind away and deplete emotional reserves. The most glaring ongoing stressors derive from the ecological context—inadequate housing, environmental instability, and, in urban settings, dangerous neighborhoods. (McLoyd & Wilson, 1991, p. 105)

The model is divided into four principal units, each characterized by *significant factors* that define the nature of the unit (Figure 9-3). The first unit *(A)* represents life conditions and events that qualify as *stressors* because they threaten people's sense of well-being. The other three units identify types of people who feel imperiled by the stressors—*(B)* parents and family members who are in frequent contact with the child, *(C)* acquaintances who are outside the family, and *(D)* the child herself or himself. Significant outcomes in the lives of the three types of people include two sorts of consequences of stress: (1) a person's physical, cognitive, and emotional states as the result of stress and (2) a person's behaviors resulting from those states. The four units and illustrative significant factors are as follows:

(A) Life Conditions and Events (Stressors)

Significant factors include:

Inadequate housing: Lack of heat in cold weather, lack of cooling facilities in hot weather, faulty plumbing, insect and rodent infestation, fire hazards, overcrowding, lack of laundry facilities

Inadequate nutrition and health care: Lack of health insurance, hospitals and physicians reluctant or unwilling to furnish free or low-cost treatment, inadequate knowledge of proper nutrition, lack of funds to purchase vitamin supplements

Shortage of funds: No savings to care for emergencies, lack of funds to move to more suitable quarters, debt with high interest payments, temptation to get money by illegal means

Dangerous neighborhoods: Crime, violence, frequent death, unsuitable role models

(B) Parents/Family

Significant factors include:

Poor health: Frequent illness, pain, and chronic medical conditions due to inadequate diet, lack of proper exercise, inability to afford expensive medicines, lack of professional medical and dental attention, and lack of proper prenatal care

Figure 9-3

Environmental Stressors' Effects on Children Raised in Poverty

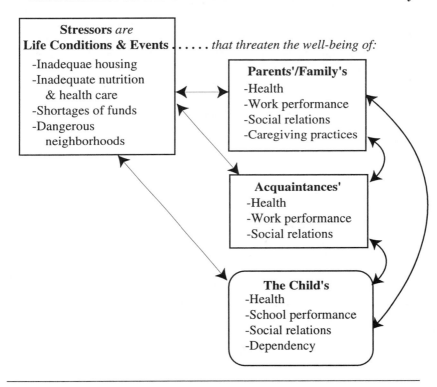

of the pregnant mother; contagious diseases are readily contracted as a result of congested, unsanitary environments

Unsatisfactory work performance: Inadequate preparation for well-paying jobs, difficulties with transportation to desirable job sites, frequent absence from work due to health and family problems

Unsatisfactory personal-social relations: Irritability leading to abrasive interpersonal behavior due to stressors and ill health; habitual abusive, violent techniques for settling differences of opinion

Faulty caregiving practices: Burden of child-rearing in one-parent home leads to fatigue, anger, and abusive verbal and physical treatment of children; parent absence from home due to work responsibilities leads to child neglect

(C) Acquaintances

Significant factors in lives of nonfamily acquaintances who affect children's development include:

Poor health: Frequent illness, pain, and chronic medical conditions due to improper diet, lack of exercise, and insufficient medical attention; contagious diseases readily contracted as a result of congested, unsanitary environments

Unsatisfactory work performance: Inadequate preparation for well-paying jobs, difficulties with transportation to desirable job sites, frequent absence from job due to health and family problems

Unsatisfactory personal-social relations: Irritability leading to abrasive interpersonal behavior due to stressors and ill health; habitual abusive, violent techniques for settling differences of opinion

(D) The Child

Significant factors include:

Poor health: Frequent illness, pain, and chronic medical conditions due to improper diet, lack of exercise, and insufficient medical attention; contagious diseases readily contracted as a result of congested, unsanitary environments

Studies cited by McLoyd and Wilson (1991) attested that children raised in poverty frequently suffered from low self-esteem, nightmares, depression, apathy, hopelessness, withdrawal from social contacts, hate, and aggression.

Unsatisfactory school performance: Frequent absence due to illness, to lack of proper family supervision, and to unsuitable family and acquaintance role models; failure to complete homework due to lack of study space at home, lack of family supervision and help with homework, and lack of study aids (books, computer)

Unsatisfactory personal-social relations: Irritability and anger leading to abrasive interpersonal behavior due to stressors, ill health, and habitual abusive, violent treatment by family and acquaintances that is copied in the child's own treatment of others

Dependency: Forced to remain in a poverty setting because of being a dependent minor, obliged to remain in the family, unable either to strike out on his or her own or be accepted by a more satisfactory family

The interactions among the four units in Figure 9-3 are suggested by the lines connecting the units. Arrowheads at both ends of each line suggest that the affect of one unit on another is reciprocal. Not only do the environmental stressors influence the fates of parents, family members, acquaintances, and the child, but each person exerts some influence on the environment. Usually, the effect of environmental conditions on the three types of people is far greater than the influence of the people on the settings they inhabit. Likewise, the effect of parents' life conditions and childraising practices on their children is typically far greater than the influence of children on their parents' lives. However, at the very least, the fact that parents are obliged to take care of their children has a significant influence on parents' circumstances. And if the children happen to be an unusual bother or expense—which occurs if they are physically or mentally handicapped, or if they behave in socially unacceptable ways—the children exert particularly unwelcome stress on family members. Finally, poverty children and poverty acquaintances often do damage to each other through physical and mental conflicts or by serving as destructive role models. On the other hand, poverty children and their acquaintances may also prove mutually supportive and teach each other skills and attitudes that promote self-confidence and the ability to cope with unfortunate circumstances.

REMAINING CHALLENGES

Perhaps the most obvious future challenge for developers of two of this chapter's theories is the task of describing the interactions among those theories' components. The two theories are Smeeding's macro-micro model and McLloyd and Wilson's proposal about the causes and effects of stress. The authors of each of these schemes has offered an extended series of components of cause and effect. In Smeeding's model, four macro causes are subsumed under the physical/social environment while five micro causes are cited under parent/family processes and eight under community/life processes. Then, six types of effects are listed under children's developmental outcomes. In the McLoyd and Wilson proposal, four types of causes are identified as stressors that derive from unfavorable life conditions and events; and effects of those stressors are proposed for three categories of people—the child, the child's acquaintances, and the child's family (particularly the parents).

However, identifying components gets the job only half done. If the models are to serve as practical guides to analyzing and improving childrearing practices, information is also needed about how the components interact—how components influence each other to produce different results for different children in terms of physical, cognitive, self-concept, and social development. One way that the influence of various combinations of components might be discovered is by investigators first compiling a series of cases in which the postulated components are identified. Then the collection of cases can be analyzed to derive principles that appear to govern the way different patterns of components produce particular developmental outcomes.

The chapter's third theory—Garfinkel and McLanahan's estimate of how a specific government policy can influence children's well-being—calls for verification and refinement based on studies of the application of that policy in various family-relationship patterns. By analyzing cases of family relationships and child well-being before and after implementation of the policy, theorists should be able to revise original theory in ways that make it a more accurate depiction of ways that absent fathers' child-support roles influence children's welfare.

10

Ethnic Minorities

Among members of both the academic community and the general public, there continues to be marked disagreement about what the term *ethnic minority* means, or about what it should mean. Are *ethnicity* and *race* the same, or do the two deserve separate definitions? Is *minority* defined strictly in numbers, so that *minority* designates a group that comprises less than 50% of a population? Or does *minority* apply to any group that's numerically smaller than another group which is referred to as *the majority*? Or can a numerically dominant group still be deemed a *minority* if its members suffer social, political, or economic disadvantages?

In view of this lack of consensus, it's important to recognize at the outset how *ethnic, racial,* and *minority* are intended throughout this chapter. It would be my preference not to use the words *race* and *racial* at all, because (a) there has been so much confusion about which characteristics distinguish one "race" from another, (b) ways of assessing racial differences have so often been unreliable, and (c) the expressions *race* and *racial,* when applied to a group, have so frequently carried pejorative connotations.

Instead of *race,* I would prefer to use the term *ethnic* to designate a group whose members (a) share a distinctive culture that includes such characteristics as customs, language, appearance, and/or religion and (b) are assigned their ethnic identity by other people and/or adopt that identity for themselves. The first part of this description is a typical dictionary definition. I added the second part to suggest that ethnicity is a social and/or individual construction. The addition is founded on the observation that a person's ethnic identity as it functions in daily social interactions has not been decreed by Nature or by a Supreme Being. Rather, it has been determined by groups' and individuals' opinions about which characteristics should define *ethnicity*. In the (b) portion of the definition, the distinction between "other-assigned" and "self-adopted" ethnic identity is important because that distinction helps account for the potential conflict between what "*they* think my ethnic identity is and what *I* think it is." A girl may be categorized by others as Mexican American but identify herself as a nonhyphenated American. A man may be labeled Native American by law but consider himself an Indian-Irish-German American on the basis of his ethnically mixed ancestry.

Thus, in discussing this chapter's first theory—one proposed by Cynthia Garcia Coll and her colleagues—the word *ethnic* will predominate and *racial* will be avoided. However, in presenting the second theory—the Helms racial identity model—I defer to Helms's distinction between *race* and *ethnicity*.

The term *minority* is applied throughout the chapter in a social-disadvantage sense rather than numerical sense. Because blacks in both England and South Africa have suffered social disadvantages, each group would be considered a minority in the way that term is used here, even though blacks in South Africa are numerically overwhelming and blacks in England are relatively few.

A further point concerns the relationship between minority status and different social settings. In American higher-education institutions, youths of Chinese heritage can hardly be considered a socially disadvantaged minority, since they are represented in colleges in considerably larger numbers than the proportion of Chinese Americans in the general society would seem to warrant. On average, Chinese-American students are also more successful academically than are typical members of Anglo, Black, and Hispanic groups. However, in other social contexts, such as in certain neighborhoods and country clubs, people of Chinese ancestry may qualify as a disadvantaged minority when they are denied the freedom of social intercourse available to other groups. In a similar way, blacks could hardly be deemed a minority in professional basketball, football, and baseball, although they can suffer harmful—and officially unlawful—minority status in certain educational, occupational, and social contexts.

The origin and acceptance of theories of human development within a society cannot be divorced from that society's past and present sociopolitical circumstances. Whenever a new conception of how a society should be organized wins adherents, new models of development suited to that conception can be expected to arise. This phenomenon was illustrated in Chapter 1 in the case of the Soviet theory that fit nicely into a Marxist vision of the proper society. A similar phenomenon is witnessed today in the political prominence gained by subgroups of society that have suffered disadvantaged status in the past. One of the most obvious features of present-day nations is their recognizing the multicultural composition of their populations and the rising political power of social minorities. No longer is the United States portrayed as a melting pot in which people of diverse ethnic and national origins become homogenized Americans, that is, become more alike than different from each other. Instead, the analogies of mixed salad, mosaic, and potpourri are adopted to represent a collection of separate groups who happen to share the same territory. Traditionally, some of these groups have enjoyed greater status, privilege, and power than others.   But recent years have brought marked changes to this tradition, with disadvantaged collectivities (African Americans, Hispanics, Native Americans, Pacific Islanders, Asians, and more) seeking to win equal social status—equal respect, equal economic and educational opportunities, and equal political power.

The ascension of this multicultural view of the United States and Canada and of the differential advantages enjoyed by ethnic groups has been accompanied by theories of development featuring intergroup differences.   From the human development literature, two of the more complete theories focusing on ethnic minorities are inspected in the following pages.   The first model envisions the ways minority children develop competencies.   It was created by Cynthia Garcia Coll (Brown University) and six of her associates.   The second theory is a conception of racial-identity development proposed by Janet E. Helms (University of Maryland).

A SCHEME FOR THE STUDY OF MINORITIES' COMPETENCIES

The following description of the model offered by Cynthia Garcia Coll and her colleagues identifies (a) the authors' reasons for creating the theory and (b) ways the model's principal components and subcomponents interact in particular individuals' lives.

The Need for Such a Theory

A new model is needed because, traditionally, the interaction of social class, culture, ethnicity, and race has not been included at the core of mainstream theoretical formulations of child development, . . . even in most of the contextually based theoretical frameworks identified in the developmental literature as organizational, transactional, and ecological. . . . [Our] model is anchored within social stratification theory and emphasizes the importance of racism, prejudice, discrimination, oppression, and segregation to the development of minority children and families. (Garcia Coll et al., 1996, p. 1892)

From their analysis of published studies, the authors concluded that past research has suffered from serious shortcomings—(a) a lack of longitudinal investigations of the typical development of minority children, (b) a focus solely on the outcomes rather than on the processes of minority children's development, (c) interest only in cross-group analyses, with a resultant neglect of within-group comparisons, and (d) minimizing the influence on development of such social-stratification derivatives as racism, prejudice, discrimination, and segregation. The model they propose and the potential applications of that model in guiding research are intended to remedy those shortcomings.

Interactions Among the Model's Components

The manner in which the Garcia Coll scheme can explain the development of minority children is illustrated in the following paragraphs by a case identifying

Figure 10-1

The Route of Influences on Minority Children's Development

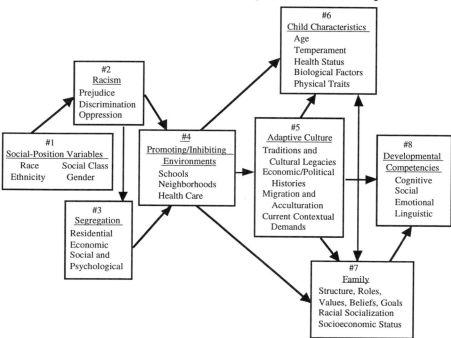

SOURCE: Garcia Coll, C., Lamberty, G., Jenkins, R., McAdoo, H. P., Crnic, K, Wasik, B. H., and Garcia, H. V. (1996). An intregrative model for the study of the developmental competencies in minority children. *Child Development, 67,* pp. 1891-1914. Used by permission of the Society for Research in Child Development, Inc.

patterns of interaction among the model's components (Figure 10-1) in the life of a minority youth.

A Pacific Islander's experience

Tupuai Lolotai is a 16-year-old high school student who has lived in a Southern California seacoast city since his family arrived 5 years ago from the South Pacific Island territory of American Samoa.

Social position variables. The youth's social-class status changed when the family immigrated to the United States. In Samoa, the family had been considered middle class. They owned a plot of land and a typical Samoan house (a *fale*). Tupuai's father worked for the government as a customs inspector, and his mother was employed in a tuna-packing facility. The family were faithful members of a Protestant Christian church.

When the family went to California, their social status declined. Tupuai's father became a laborer loading cargo onto ships and his mother took part-time housekeeping jobs in hotels. The family—parents and four children—settled in a neighborhood populated mainly by Samoans, where the Lolotais occupied three rooms in an apartment house that building inspectors described as "moderately run down."

Outside of the local Samoan community, the social status of Samoans was affected by the ethnic group's reputation for physical violence, heavy consumption of alcohol, and eating habits (or genetic tendencies) that led to overweight. In their island culture, Samoans were accustomed to using physical means of disciplining the young and settling disputes, to enjoying liquor, and to admiring hearty eaters and large body girth. Now, in a city in which people outside of the Samoan community looked down on such behaviors, the Lolotais found their diminished social status to be a new and strange experience. But what outsiders did admire was the performance of physically powerful young Samoans on the football field. However, that admiration did little to raise the ethnic group's general social-class position.

Racism. Outside of the Samoan neighborhood, members of the Tupuai family were often regarded with suspicion that led to (a) difficulties in the parents' receiving credit in stores or a loan at the bank, (b) the children not being invited to the homes of classmates, and (c) the children being considered the likely perpetrators of scuffles with classmates, of vandalism, and of petty theft at school.

Segregation and promoting/inhibiting environments. The Lolotais' intimate social contacts were mostly with other Samoans. There were two main reasons for this. First, when they first came to California, they wished to live near friends and relatives so that adapting to a new environment would be as easy as possible. This meant that they settled into an established Samoan neighborhood. Second, people outside of the Samoan community, by bringing negative prejudicial attitudes to their contacts with these newcomers, tended to alienate rather than welcome the Lolotai family. Consequently, the only settings in which the Lolotais encountered non-Samoans in a continuing relationship were in the parents' work sites and in the children's schools. Nearly all of the remaining time of their day was spent with other Samoans.

Adaptive culture. A variety of differences between Samoan and Californian customs influenced Tupuai's school career. The following four examples concern authority, language skills, *musu,* and cooperative ventures.

In the traditional multilevel Samoan social structure, the most basic unit is the extended family (*aiga*). The person in highest authority in the family is its chieftain—usually a patriarch but occasionally a matriarch. The next higher social structure is the village, consisting of several extended families. The principal village authority and decisionmaker is the village chieftain, aided in his duties by his talking chief, a skilled orator who speaks on the chieftain's behalf. The next broader level is the district—often an entire island—headed by a district chieftain and his talking chief. Finally, the entire collection of Samoan islands makes up the top level in this social-power and privilege hierarchy. Samoan children are taught to obey those in authority, a lesson that serves Tupuai well at school, where he feels obliged to respect teachers and administrative personnel.

At home, Tupuai's family members usually speak Samoan. When at school, Tupuai speaks, reads, and writes only English. However, the fact that he has been expected to master two very different languages (English from the Indo-Euopean group, Samoan from the Malay-Polynesian group) has meant that his English at school is less than perfect. Some of his teachers and schoolmates interpret Tupuai's errors to mean that he is not very smart.

Traditional Samoan society is a communal type. Land isn't owned by individuals but, rather, it's owned by the extended family or the village. This notion of group ownership can extend to other sorts of property as well—buildings, boats, horses, and vocational tools. Because so many of Samoans' material possessions are owned in common, family members often feel free to use other people's belongings without asking permission. This attitude causes Tupuai problems in California, because North American custom strongly emphasizes the sanctity of personal private property. In California, you don't borrow anyone else's pencil, skateboard, or baseball cap without the owner's permission. So when Tupuai, without asking, takes a few sheets of paper from a classmate's notebook and uses one of the classmate's pens, he is accused of stealing and henceforth will be considered a likely suspect when things are missing.

The meaning of the Samoan word *musu* can be approximated in English by an admixture of such terms as *bored, irritable, not up to it, kind of sick, distressed, fed up,* and *dissatisfied.* In islanders' tradition, feeling *musu* is an acceptable reason for getting up late in the morning, being absent from school or work, or avoiding routine responsibilities. In an islander's home culture

> One's musu is a sufficient explanation; it is never questioned by others or justi-
> fied by the person who experiences it. The self-attribution of musu serves, then,
> as a mechanism by which a person can avoid a burdensome situation while at the
> same time not having to admit to the existence of unacceptable feelings.
> (Gerber, 1985, p. 129)

However, problems arise when islanders move into other societies where pleading *musu* is of no avail—societies in which people are responsible for meeting their obligations despite their feeling irritable and out of sorts. So when Tupuai neglects to hand in a homework assignment or misses a class, his attributing such behavior to *musu* is viewed as nonsense.

As a device for maintaining group cohesiveness and enabling all members of the family to succeed, Samoan culture places high value on cooperation within the family or village rather than emphasizing personal accomplishment and competition between individuals. Hence, among Samoan youths, helping one's peers succeed is more important than besting them. As a consequence, when Tupuai and his Samoan classmates turn in homework assignments that look much alike, their teachers admonish them for cheating rather than complimenting them for helping each other learn.

Child characteristics. The competencies that Tupuai will develop are affected not only by such environmental influences as his immediate and extended family, his neighborhood, his school, and his leisure-time settings. His accomplishments are obviously affected as well by his personal characteristics—his physical appearance, rate of development of intellectual and sexual functions, aspects of intelligence that depend on his genetic inheritance, his health condition, his interests, and his temperament (optimism versus pessimism, resiliency versus depression, pliability versus intransigence, quick-temper versus slow-to-anger, and more).

Physically, Tupuai is taller and huskier than most of his classmates. He is quick to take offense when he thinks he's been insulted, but he promptly recovers and doesn't usually hold a grudge. He becomes distressed if a teacher openly criticizes him in front of others. His interests in school are in football and basketball—both of which he plays well—and in art, mathematics, and history.

Family. In addition to the family characteristics already mentioned, two other aspects of family that affect Tupuai's competencies include his parents' values and their level of satisfaction with their status in the community.

In the parents' values hierarchy, social solidarity and emotional attachment among members of the extended family are given top priority. As a result, whenever family interests conflict with school or work interests, family concerns take precedence. This means that when such events as weddings and funerals occur in Samoa, the Lolotais take time off work assignments and schooling to return to the islands for a week or two. Likewise, when members of the extended family visit the Lolotais in Southern California, the Lolotai children are kept out of school to spend time with their relatives. Such absences have a negative effect on the children's school progress and on the attitudes of their teachers, who expect parents to keep children in school unless the children are ill.

In California, the Lolotais continue to be dedicated churchgoers who try to apply Christian ethics in their everyday lives. As in Samoa, after the Sunday church service the Lolotais join other members of the congregation for a midday meal and fellowship.

Although the Lolotai family income in Southern California is higher in terms of dollars than it was in Samoa, the cost of living is also higher in California. Consequently, the family's standard of living in California in terms of material goods is lower than it was in Samoa. Furthermore, the social status of the parents' jobs was higher in Samoa than it is in California. As a result, some parents of the Lolotai children's school mates view the Lolotais as a socially unsuitable family. Consequently, such parents discourage their own children from establishing friendships with the Lolotais.

Developmental competencies. Finally, we arrive at the cognitive, social, emotional, and linguistic competencies that Tupuai has acquired by dint of the foregoing influences on development.

An impression of the patterning of Tupuai's cognitive skills is suggested by the marks he received in school during the past semester:

physical education = A	art (drawing and painting) = B+
history = B	current events = B
algebra = C	biology = C+
English = C-	

In terms of social skills, Tupuai respects adults, particularly those in positions of authority. He has a ready smile and is not afraid to initiate conversation with peers as well as younger and older people. He sometimes embarrasses newly met companions by mentioning matters considered too intimate to bring up except after long acquaintance, such matters as sexual relations, personal finance, and intimate relationships among members of a family. He is never subjected to taunting and challenges from high school classmates, perhaps because of his size and strength, which have contributed to his reputation as a fierce competitor on the high school football team.

Emotionally, Tupuai is known to be generally "easy going." Though quick to take offense at what he considers unfair treatment and insults, he is equally quick to regain his composure. He is strongly dedicated to his family and their welfare and is protective of his three younger siblings.

Linguistically, Tupuai is able to communicate well in both Samoan and English. However, his English displays occasional errors, ones he is trying to correct. His reading comprehension in Samoan is quite good, but he has trouble understanding the more complex passages he encounters in English-language science, mathematics, and literature classes. His handwriting is rather difficult to read.

Such, then, is one way to apply Garcia Coll's model in explaining why people from a given ethnic background have acquired the sorts of competencies they exhibit.

RACIAL IDENTITY

In 1990, Janet E. Helms edited a book entitled *Black and White Racial Identity* in which she introduced a theory of the process by which Blacks and Whites come to conceive who they are in terms of their racial self.[*] The 1990 form of Helms's model was later expanded to embrace other nonwhites—members of prominent ethnic groups in North America referred to by such expressions as "people of color" (Helms, 1995). The observations on which Helms founded her

---

[*] The racial designators *Black* and *White* are capitalized in this section in keeping with Helms's usage.

model were carried out predominantly in the United States, so the extent to which her scheme applies in other societies is yet to be assessed.

Helms differentiates between *race* and *ethnicity* by adopting definitions that base *race* on genetically determined physical characteristics which distinguish one subgroup of humankind from another and that base *ethnicity* on a group's members sharing a common social and cultural heritage that includes such things as customs, language, and religious practices. Thus, *racial identity* refers to

> a Black or White person's identifying or not identifying with the racial group with which he or she is generally assumed to share *racial* heritage. In other words, racial identity partially refers to the person of black African ancestry's acknowledgment of shared racial-group membership with others of similar race as [genetically] defined or the person of white European ancestry's acknow-ledgment of shared racial-group membership with others of similar race as [genetically] defined. (Helms, 1990, p. 5)

Two key features of Helms's proposal are (a) her multiple, race-specific forms of identity development and (b) her arranging the types of identity for each race in a hierarchical sequence of desirability.

The expression *multiple, race-specific forms* refers to Helms's positing different racial-identity development stages or statuses for Blacks than for Whites. The nature of her stages is critically influenced by the dominant power and privilege relationships between races within the society, which in this instance is late-20th-century United States society. Whereas most stage theories of development envision a single hierarchy of stages for all humans, Helms proposes a different set for each race or for each cluster of races that occupy a similar, historically derived status within the society (Figure 10-2).

The expression *hierarchical sequence* refers to Helms's (a) recognizing several types of identity within each racial group—four types for Blacks and six types for Whites—and then (b) proposing that all types are not equally valued, as indicated by her organizing them in a sequence of desirability, a sequence representing stages that extend from the least acceptable to the most approved. Thus, her version of stages for each racial group is not a description of how identity inevitably or "normally" *does* evolve. Rather, each version is her prescription of how identity *should* evolve in order to carry people to the final stage that she regards as the most constructive and best for both the society and the individual.

We first consider Helms's Black identity stages (statuses), then turn to her White stages (statuses), to her expansion of Black-White theory that encompasses other prominent racial groups in American society, and finally to her racial-identity-interaction model that is used for analyzing the nature of same-race and cross-race encounters between individuals. For convenience of presentation, I describe the stages in a manner which implies that people advance from one distinct level to another, exhibiting all of the characteristics of their present stage and no characteristics of any other. However, Helms (1995) suggests that in real life people at any point in their development are likely to display an identity profile, one

Figure 10-2

Helms's Racial-Identity Hierarchies

Black Identity Stages   **White Identity Stages**

Black Identity Stages	White Identity Stages
5. Integrative Awareness 4. Internalization 3. Immersion/Emersion 2. Encounter 1. Preencounter	6. Autonomy 5. Immersion/Emersion 4. Pseudo-Independent 3. Reintegration 2. Disintegration 1. Contact

that includes features of more than one stage. The characteristics of one of the stages will usually be more prominent than the features of others, thereby qualifying that dominant stage as the principal indicator of racial identity at the present juncture of the person's life course.

Black Racial Identity Development

Helms's scheme is a modified version of a model introduced by Cross (1971, 1978). The model consists of five stages, each representing a different worldview, with the term *worldview* meaning "cognitive templates that people use to organize (especially racial) information about themselves, other people, and institutions" (Helms, 1990, p. 19). Each stage or worldview is the result of the interaction between an individual's cognitive-maturation level and forces in the social environment. The stages in their 1990 form bore the labels *preencounter, encounter, immersion/emersion,* and *internalization.* Later Helms offered another beyond internalization that she called *integrative awareness* (Helms, 1995, p. 186).

Preencounter stage

The preencounter level, which Helms considered the least desirable variety of Black identity, is characterized by Black persons (a) dismissing the proposition that people's positions in society are strongly affected by the racial identity assigned to them and (b) rejecting the notion that the opportunities and rewards individuals enjoy are influenced by traditional relations between races. Instead, they assume that their own status, as well as that of other Blacks and of Whites, is the result of personal effort and ability, unaffected by customs and attitudes.

Helms distinguished two subtypes of preencounter Blacks, the active and the passive. The reference group for both actives and passives is White-European culture. The actives idealize Whiteness and subscribe to the unrealistic belief that adopting characteristics of White-European culture (speech, modes of social intercourse, education, religion, customs, ideals) earns them an ascribed White identity in the dominant White-European society. In support of her contention that Blacks in this active phase damage themselves with their imagined identity, Helms alluded to empirical evidence suggesting that, compared with the other stages of her model, life for the actives

> is associated with poor self-concept, low self-esteem, high anxiety, and depression. These findings seem to indicate at least some interrelationship between personal identity and racial identity and suggest that psychosocial adjustment may be least healthy when one is in the earlier [active] phase of preencounter. (Helms, 1990, p. 22)

Preencounter passive Blacks typically denigrate Blackness and tend to believe that they themselves have no ascribed racial identity. Instead, they believe that they have only the personal identity they have earned through skill and effort.

Helms proposed that individuals in both the active and passive phases of the preencounter stage invest much energy rationalizing away the "racial affronts and indignities" that they constantly encounter in a racist society dominated by Whites.

Encounter stage

Unlike preencounter Blacks, those at the encounter stage clearly recognize that they are burdened with a socially ascribed status of inferiority to Whites. Even if they seldom have any direct contact with Whites, encounter-level Blacks are assailed by negative images of Blackness in the mass-communication media—including history textbooks—and in society's customary and institutionalized preferential treatment of Whites.

> For many people, at some point in their lives, it becomes impossible to deny the reality that they cannot become an accepted part of "the White world." Usually this awareness seems to be aroused by an event in the environment that touches the person's inner core and makes salient the contradiction that no matter how well he or she personally or other Black individuals conform to White standards, most Whites will always perceive him or her as Black and therefore inferior. (Helms, 1990, p. 25)

The encounter stage consists of two phases—early and late. During the early phase, the individual shuttles between the newly abandoned preencounter identity and a dimly envisioned potential Black identity. Such individuals often feel hurt, distressed, bitter, and angry about their plight. The reference group allied to their bitterness is White-European culture. Some people continue in this phase for a long time, perhaps never working their way out of it.

In the later phase of encountering the reality of their social status, individuals recognize the possibility of a positive Black racial identity and enter a state of optimism and euphoria as they emotionally adopt Black society as their reference group.

Immersion/emersion stage

During the immersion phase of this stage, the Black person withdraws psychologically—and often physically—into Blackness and a Black world, behaving and thinking in ways that "authentic Blacks" supposedly act and think. Such individuals judge themselves and other Blacks in terms of how well they fit this idealized racial portrait. And because much of this notion of Blackness has been defined by White society, persons in the immersion phase often act Black in stereotypical ways, thereby sacrificing their own personal identity—the kind of identity that makes each of them an individual.

The immersion phase typically includes a high level of hostility and anger toward Whites along with idealizing Blackness and African heritage and denigrating everything thought to be White and of Western heritage.

> Euphoria, rage, inordinate amounts of artistic and/or political energy, perturbation, effrontery, high risk taking, a destructive mood in constant tension with dreams of revitalization and an intense sense of intimacy toward Black life also characterize behavior in this stage. (Cross, 1978, p. 85)

Although some persons remain fixated in the immersion phase, others enter a transitional emersion phase during which their retreat into the Black community enables them to express their confusion and distress within a supportive environment.

> During emersion, one often finds individuals engaging in "rap" sessions, political action groups, exploration of Black and African culture, discussions of racial issues with Black elders whose experiences were formerly ignored, "hanging out" with other Blacks in a spirit of kinship, and so forth. (Helms, 1990, p. 28)

The hope during the emersion period is that individuals will adopt a non-stereotypical Afro-American worldview that permits their anger to subside and their modes of thought to become more flexible. It is no longer necessary for them to accept a single concept of Blackness as defined by others in order to consider themselves worthy individuals. They can begin to distinguish between the strengths and weaknesses of Black culture and gain greater control over their lives and move on to the next stage.

Internalization stage

Internalization involves integrating one's unique sense of self (personal identity) with one's acceptance of how Blackness influences one's life (ascribed racial identity). Individuals in this stage no longer reject all Whites. Instead, they continue to oppose racism and oppression, but they "reestablish relationships with individual White associates who merit such relationships, and analyze White culture for its strengths and weaknesses (Helms, 1990, p. 29).

Therefore, Helms's fourth stage of racial identity consists of Black persons transcending race, displaying a positive personal identity, and conducting their lives in a self-controlled, calm, secure fashion. Whereas they recognize their own Black ascribed identity, their reference group consists of the best of both Black and White cultures and individuals.

Some people at the internalization stage are not politically engaged. That is, they do not take social action aimed at reducing racial prejudice and exploitation. Others, however, include such action as part of their mission in life and thereby join both Black and White compatriots in promoting equality and respect among people of different racial identities.

Integrative awareness stage

According to Helms, a person who arrives at this fifth level of Black identity formation has the "capacity to value one's own collective identities as well as empathize and collaborate with members of other oppressed groups. Life decisions may be motivated by globally humanistic self-expression" with the individual's dominant information-processing strategies featuring "flexibility and complexity" (Helms, 1995, p. 186). At this "most sophisticated" level, a person is able "to express a positive racial self and to recognize and resist the multiplicity of practices that exist in one's environment to discourage positive racial self-conceptions and group expression" (Helms, 1995, p. 190).

White Racial Identity Development

In Helms's six-level White model, acquiring racial identity is

a linear process of attitudinal development in which the White person potentially progresses through a series of stages differing in the extent to which they involve acknowledgment of racism and consciousness of Whiteness. . . . The highest stage involves an awareness of personal responsibility for racism, consistent acknowledgment of one's Whiteness, and abandonment of racism in any of its forms as a defining aspect of one's personality. (Helms, 1990, p. 53)

The stages are labeled *contact, disintegration, reintegration, pseudo-independence, immersion/emersion,* and *autonomy.* These six are divided into two phases. The first three stages comprise the initial phase of abandonment of racism. The last three stages form the latter phase of adopting a nonracist White identity.

Contact stage

The lowest, earliest stage is entered when a White person first encounters the idea of Black people, either through direct experience or through such a medium as a parent speaking about Blacks or a storybook or television program that includes Black characters. The White person's feelings at this time may include naive curiosity, uneasiness, or fear of Blacks. The individual at this point has only a vague conception of what it means to be White.

If the contact with Blacks is entirely vicarious, then the society's traditional negative images of Blackness will become the identity the White person ascribes to Blacks. However, if the contact is direct, so that the White person interacts with a variety of Blacks, then the White person will gradually recognize that there are all sorts of Blacks so that the usual stereotypes fail to fit many Blacks. When enough of these personal encounters have accumulated, the White person begins judging Blacks as individuals and not as symbols of a racial stereotype. That person has thereby advanced beyond the contact stage.

Disintegration stage

The disintegration stage is characterized by people's conscious awareness of their Whiteness, and awareness accompanied by a disturbing recognition of moral dilemmas, such as those described by Dennis (1981, p. 78) as

- The desire to be a religious or moral person versus the recognition .that to be accepted by Whites one must treat Blacks immorally;
- The belief in freedom and democracy versus the belief in racial inequality;
- The desire to show love and compassion versus the desire to keep Blacks in their place at all costs;
- The belief in treating others with dignity and respect versus the belief that Blacks are not worthy of dignity or respect;
- The belief that each person should be treated according to his or her individual merits versus the belief that Blacks should be evaluated as a group without regard to individual merits and talents.

Reintegration stage

One way Whites can reduce the distress caused by such dilemmas, and at the same time be accepted by the White community, is to adopt the White community's widespread belief in White racial superiority and Black inferiority—the belief that Blacks' unfavorable status in the society results from their inadequate mental, moral, and social qualities. The Whites' lingering feelings of guilt and anxiety from the previous disintegration period are now recast as fear and anger toward Black people. The attempt by Whites to reintegrate their racial beliefs may be expressed passively by avoiding contact with Blacks and by seriously discussing race relations only with people who also hold Blacks in low regard. Many Whites remain fixated at this stage unless some personal experience with Blacks or some dramatic social event—such as the civil rights movement of the 1960s or the Vietnam War—jars them loose from their convictions. As soon as Whites begin to question their idealized definition of Whiteness and the justness of racism in any of its forms, they are ready for the next stage.

Pseudo-independent or liberal stage

Whites at this point begin (a) to doubt that Blacks are innately inferior to Whites, (b) to admit that they themselves have been contributing to racism by their attitude of White superiority, and (c) to redefine their own racial identity. Although they are likely to seek more interaction with Blacks, that interaction usually involves

> helping Blacks change themselves so they function more like Whites on White criteria for success and acceptability rather than recognizing that such criteria might be inappropriate and/or too narrowly defined. (Helms, 1990, p. 61)

A White person's efforts to have more friendly contact with Blacks can be viewed with suspicion by both Whites and Blacks. Whereas Whites can consider such behavior a violation of White racial norms, Blacks can question the motives of Whites who spend so much energy helping Blacks instead of trying to change Whites' racial perceptions.

Whites who gain sufficient satisfaction and a reduction of guilt during this stage are prepared to rise to the immersion/emersion level.

Immersion/emersion stage

In their search for a new racial identity, Whites often immerse themselves in accounts of other Whites who have progressed from a White-superiority racial identity to a belief system that judges people's social status and worth on individuals' personal qualities rather than on their racial category. "Changing Black people is no longer the focus of [the Whites'] activities, but rather the goal of changing White people becomes salient" (Helms, 1990, p. 92).

Autonomy stage

Whites have reached the pinnacle of Helms's racial-identity hierarchy when they no longer feel compelled to exploit, idealize, or disparage other people on the basis of their race, national origin, gender, religion, or social class, because such cultural differences are no longer seen as a threat to Whites' welfare. Individuals in the autonomy stage are open to new information about, and ways to perceive, racial and cultural matters. The autonomous White wishes to learn from other cultural groups, seeks out instances of racial and other types of oppression, and takes action to combat prejudice and exploitation.

Racial-Identity Development of Other Nonwhites

By 1995, Helms had updated her theory by extending it to include "people of color."

> In the United States, the term *people of color* refers to those persons whose ostensible ancestry is at least in part African, Asian, Indigenous, and/or combinations of these groups and/or White or European ancestry. Even a cursory overview of the history of race (rather than ethnic) relations in the United States

. . . reveals that peoples of the so designated groups have been subjected to similar (but not necessarily identical) deplorable political and economic conditions because they were not perceived to be "pure" White. (Helms, 1995, p. 189)

In effect, Helms has generalized her five-level model of Black-identity development to encompass a diversity of other non-White-European cultural groups. But critics have questioned whether such an extension of her Black-identity theory is warranted. Is the pattern of identity-formation the same for Americans of all such ancestral origins as African, Chinese, Fijian, Egyptian, Quechuan, Hopi, Filipino, Pakistani, and Mongolian? And is the pattern of identity development unaffected by time and place? That is, is the identity experience of a Japanese-American youth in 1950 the same as in 2000 or the same in San Francisco as in Kansas City, New Orleans, Washington, Miami, or Fargo? Consequently, convincing empirical data appear needed to clarify the suitability of expanding the Black-identity hierarchy to embrace the experience of all sorts of "people of color."

Helms's Interaction Model

From a counseling-psychology perspective, Helms proposed a model for analyzing the quality of personal relationships between a counselor and a client in terms of their stages of racial-identity development (Helms, 1984). The model is founded on the presumption that "when matters of race enter into the [counseling] discourse, either directly or indirectly, the quality of the interaction (i.e., relationship type) will be influenced by the prevailing racial identity status of each person within the dyad" (Thompson & Carter, 1997, pp. 26-27).

Three kinds of interaction that may occur in such encounters are labeled *regressive, parallel,* and *progressive.*

A *regressive* relationship produces an unsatisfactory counseling outcome because the counselor and client are at different levels of Helms's identity structure and fail to understand each other's point of view. For instance, a Black college counselor who interprets life primarily from a preencounter vantage point (idealizing White culture and believing that success depends on hard work and ability) may fail to understand the feelings and experiences of a Black graduate student whose perceptions are filtered through a Black-emersion identity. When the student comes for help in coping with incidents of what he feels is prejudicial treatment by White professors, his interpretation of his experiences may conflict with the counselor's perceptions, leaving the student unconvinced by such counseling advice as "Most college professors are mature and reasonable, so don't imagine they are going to treat you unfairly because you're Black; just work hard and everything will turn out all right."

A *parallel* condition exists when a person in a superordinate authority position is at the same racial-identity stage as the person in the subordinate position. Such can be the case in a counselor-client, teacher-student, coach-player, or employer-employee relationship. If both individuals are at the same racial-identity level, they will simply reinforce each other's present convictions and fail to foster the subordinate's rise to a higher stage.

In a *progressive* relationship

the person in the superordinate position operates primarily at an advanced status level while the person in the subordinate position operates primarily at a less advanced level. The promotion of racial identity development is likely because the influential person at the advanced status is able to perceive the limitations of the other person as it pertains to matters of race. The ideal relationship is when the person in the position of influence is operating primarily at the internalization (Blacks), integrative awareness status (People of Color), or the autonomy status (Whites). (Thompson & Carter, 1997, p. 28)

In summary, as illustrated in the foregoing counseling examples, implications of Helms's models of Black and White identity formation have been drawn for improving childraising practices and counseling methods among both Blacks and Whites in American society.

REMAINING CHALLENGES

Several questions raised by the Garcia Coll theory and the Helms model warrant the attention of investigators in the years ahead. For example, as Garcia Coll and her associates contemplated broader uses for their proposal, they identified two challenges posed by their model.

The first is to identify the alternative competencies in children of color that are not measured by traditional assessment tools, not only in the realms of established developmental competencies but in areas of bicultural adaptation and coping with racism. The second is to analyze the implications for social policy and interventions. (Garcia Coll et al., 1996, p. 1908)

There is also the question of how well the Garcia Coll scheme guides the analysis of development among members of ethnic groups in societies other than that of the United States. In other words, is the Garcia Coll model the most effective one for analyzing the sources of children's competencies in such varied cultures as those of Sikh villages in India, pastoral tribes in Northern Sudan, Quechua communities in the Peruvian Andes, Palestinian Moslems in Israel, Vietnamese refugees in Hong Kong, and Turks in Germany?

As already noted, questions about Helms's theory also call for further investigation to determine whether she has been justified in generalizing her Black-identity theory to include all other "people of color" in all places at all times. And to what extent does the sociopolitical climate of a given time and place influence the form of stages or statuses in White identity formation?

11

Feminist Perspectives

Throughout history there apparently have always been feminists of some kind—women who have sought rights, opportunities, and identities they believed they deserved. The most recent effort, sometimes referred to as "The Feminist Movement," began attracting widespread support after the middle of the 20th century, then gained momentum over the following years. According to Bonnie Watkins and Nina Rothchild,

> The modern American women's movement seemed to emerge spontaneously in the 1960s. It began at kitchen tables and in company cafeterias, at PTA meetings and in legislative hearing rooms. It happened in the lives of individual women who responded to the messages of the early days: the personal is political, sisterhood is powerful. (Watkins & Rothchild, 1996, xv)

The dual purpose of this chapter is (a) to furnish a brief overview of diverse forms of feminist theory that were contending for attention over the final two decades of the century and (b) to illustrate how those perspectives pictured the process of human development—or, more precisely, the process of female development.

RECENT THEORIES OF FEMINIST THOUGHT

Feminist activism has not been all of a piece but, rather, has evolved along diverse routes. To render the resulting panoply of feminist perspectives comprehensible, Rosemarie Putnam Tong (1998) located them under 11 headings: *liberal, radical, Marxist, multicultural, ecological, socialist, global, psychoanalytic, gender, postmodern,* and *existentialist.* Tong defended the use of these "old labels" on the grounds that

> They signal to the broader public that feminism is not a monolithic ideology, that all feminists do not think alike, and that, like all other time-honored modes of thinking, feminist thought has a past as well as a present and a future. . . .

Feminist thought's old labels . . . help mark the range of different approaches, perspectives, and frameworks a variety of feminists have used to shape their explanations for women's oppression and their proposed solutions for its elimination. (Tong, 1998, pp. 1-2)

Tong's categories provide a convenient structure within which to sketch an overview of the varied types. All of the specific perspectives under each general type are founded on the conviction that females[*] over the centuries have suffered unwarranted ill treatment within male-dominated societies and that such ill treatment must be corrected. Each of these multiple perspectives can be interpreted as comprising a pair of theories of female development. One member of the pair is a descriptive/explanatory theory portraying the traditional, flawed way females have been obliged to develop. The other member is a prescriptive theory, envisioning how females should develop if they are to attain their rightful place in society and to achieve their true identities and deserved satisfactions. The criterion that feminist writers adopt for evaluating the desirability of their postulated descriptive and prescriptive theories is a conception of what an exemplary female will be like at various stages of growth, especially what the ideal female will be like as an adult woman.

Whereas all versions of feminist thought agree that females have been victims of male oppression, the versions differ from each other in terms of

- The personal traits and lifestyles that constitute desirable female development. In effect, different theorists propose different images of the "ideal female within the optimal social environment."
- What has been wrong with traditional female development.
- Who is responsible for traditional conditions—who deserves the blame.
- What should be done to straighten matters out.

In the following pages, I locate Tong's varieties within two sets. The first set presents five types—*liberal, radical, multicultural, Marxist,* and *ecological*—in some detail. The cursory descriptions in the second set merely note the main thrust of each of Tong's additional types: *socialist, global, psychoanalytic, gender, postmodern,* and *existentialist.*

At the outset I should explain that under each type, in order to conserve space, I describe only one of several perspectives that fall within the type. Other viewpoints within the type would vary somewhat in their details from the option I depict.

FIVE THEORIES IN SOME DETAIL

The following section shows how five prominent feminist theories portray (a) the inadequacies of traditional female development, (b) proposed causes of the unsatisfactory tradition, (c) the image of the ideal female who grows up in an op-

---

[*] I use the word *female* rather than *woman* to indicate that the concern of the feminist movement is not restricted to adults, but includes juveniles as well.

timal social environment, and (d) steps that will be necessary to rectify the causes. Each theorist's descriptive/explanatory theory is reflected in phases (a) and (b) of this sequence, whereas the prescriptive theory is found in phases (c) and (d).

Liberal Feminism

Today's liberal feminism traces its roots back two centuries to Mary Wollstonecraft's 1792 *Vindication of the Rights of Woman* (1975) and to the 19th century women's suffrage movement. The chief complaint of liberal feminists, then and now, has been that females' opportunities to assume significant roles in society and to gain personal satisfaction have been severely restricted by laws, regulations, and unwritten customs that males have devised to subjugate females for males' benefit. Consequently, liberal feminists demand the removal of the legal and customary barriers that limit females' freedom to participate fully in the society.

According to the descriptive/explanatory human development theory that liberal feminists use in accounting for how the young have traditionally been raised, both girls and boys are taught from birth that

- Some of life's roles and rights are appropriate for both sexes, yet other roles and rights are appropriate for one sex but not for the other.
- Conforming to the customs regarding the gender division of roles and rights leads to social—and especially parental—approval and reward, whereas violating the customs leads to censure and punishment.
- The division of roles and rights is *natural* and *just*, because the division has been determined by the two sexes' innate characteristics. Males, compared to females, by nature are more aggressive and outspoken, are blessed with greater physical strength and stamina, display greater initiative, have higher intelligence, are more logical and objective in their judgments, and are more resolute in their decisions. In contrast, females by nature are more retiring and emotional, lack physical strength and stamina, are followers rather than leaders, are intellectually inferior, arrive at decisions through intuition rather than logical reasoning, and often change their minds. Consequently,

  > women are treated as if they are governed by their bodies and men as if they are ruled by their minds. . . . Where men think, women feel. The man is the head of the family, the woman the heart. (Jamieson, 1994, p. 53)

Proponents of liberal feminism contend that few, if any, such claims about differences between the sexes—except perhaps the one regarding physical strength—are supported by fact. So any observed differences between the genders in intelligence, logical reasoning, initiative, resoluteness, and leadership are the result of (a) the legal and customary restrictions placed on females' rights and opportunities and (b) the society's practice of convincing children that such a division of roles and rights is reasonable and fair.

According to liberal feminists, men and women are both responsible for the descriptive theory's distorted conception of human development. Men are to blame for establishing and perpetuating such a misconception, which is designed to enhance the fortunes and pleasures of males at the expense of exploited females. Women are to blame for tolerating their grievous condition.

To remedy the oppressed state of females that results from accepting the traditional conception of human development, liberal feminists offer an implied prescriptive theory, whose key features have been reflected in the National Organization for Women's (NOW) 1967 Bill of Rights for Women. NOW's proposal not only demanded that women enjoy the same legal and customary rights as men, but that females be accorded certain special protections as well. Therefore, not only would females receive the same consideration as males in educational and employment opportunities, but they would be furnished paid maternity leave from their jobs, tax deductions for working parents' child-care expenses, and the right to "control their own reproductive lives by removing from the penal code laws limiting access to contraceptive information and devices, and by repealing penal laws governing abortion" (Morgan, 1970, p. 514).

Consequently, according to the liberals' prescriptive theory, proper female development would be fostered by the members of society honoring, in word and deed, the equality of females and males in legal and customary rights, in intelligence, in leadership qualities, in emotional stability, and the like. This prescriptive theory would be conveyed to the young by example (by the young observing the actions of respected others through witnessing those actions directly or via mass-communication media) and by tutelage (through routine child-rearing practices and formal instruction in schools, clubs, and churches).

The prescriptive theory, when universally accepted as valid throughout the populace, would provide a new *socially constructed reality* that empowers females to realize their potentials. Under such optimal societal conditions, the ideal female would be one who has full opportunity to assume her freely chosen roles in society and to satisfy her personal desires.

Radical Feminism

Some feminists accept the liberals' agenda but contend that it doesn't go far enough. In particular, it fails to address matters of gender identity and sexual behavior. For instance, within the complex species that Tong calls *radical-libertarian feminism,* devotees of one line of belief propose that traits traditionally identified as masculine or as feminine should no longer be associated with a particular sex but should be shared by both sexes, thereby producing a single androgynous personality.

> Men should be permitted to explore their feminine dimensions and women their masculine ones. No human being should be forbidden the sense of wholeness that comes from combining his or her masculine and feminine dimensions. (Tong, 1998, p. 3)

Members of this particular radical-libertarian camp also assert that no single type of sexual behavior should be prescribed for liberated women. Instead, each woman "should be encouraged to experiment sexually with herself, other women, and men" in order to discover which sort of erotic experience is most satisfying (Tong, 1998, p. 3; Vance, 1984).

Consequently, in the descriptive version of the traditional development theory that they condemn, radical-libertarians not only object to the same legal and customary features that liberal feminists denounce but they protest additional aspects of the conventional model, aspects relating to masculinity versus femininity and to appropriate female sexual behavior.

Like the liberals, radical-libertarians blame both men and women for perpetuating the traditional theory—men for embedding the theory in the culture and women for accepting the theory without protest. To remedy tradition's harmful myth of proper female development, radical-libertarians urge drastic changes in the social institutions that most actively support the tradition—family, work site, church, education system, and mass-communication media.

In effect, the prescriptive theory implied in this strain of radical-libertarian feminism adds both the androgyny and sexual-free-choice provisions to the liberals' version of proper development. A society in which radical-libertarian development becomes the norm is one whose members behave in ways that reflect their endorsement of the theory. The process of socialization within such a culture involves convincing the growing child and youth that the prescriptive theory is just and well-founded.

Multicultural Feminism

The expression *multicultural feminists* identifies a cluster of women who see the nature of their oppressed condition as (a) strongly influenced by their particular ethnic origin, social class, or religion and (b) different from the condition of women of other ethnic, social-class, and religious backgrounds. Such feminists insist that the nature of oppression suffered by Hopi women on an Indian reservation in Arizona is radically different from that of wives in an Amish community in Pennsylvania or of women plying their trade in a bordello on the outskirts of Las Vegas. Consequently, multicultural feminists object to a single portrait of "*the* American woman" that results from having each woman's social status lumped together with that of women whose life circumstances are markedly different. They also object to women from one cultural origin assigning themselves to speak for those from other cultural backgrounds, such as upper-middle-class white liberal activists alleging that they accurately express the perceptions of lower-class black women.

In the United States, the arrival of this multicultural category of feminists on the social scene reflects a historical change in the conception of what the word *American* connotes within the general population. Prior to World War II, immigrants to the United States were expected to become *Americanized*, shedding their original language in favor of American English, pledging allegiance to the United States government, and substituting American customs for those from "the old country." Schools, political leaders, and the mass-communication media endorsed such a homogenizing Americanization effort. However, as noted in my introduction to Part II, after World War II most colonized regions around the world asserted their political and economic independence and sought to reinvigorate their societies with indigenous customs that the colonialists had tried to suppress. At the same time, disadvantaged groups within American society gained increased political acumen and power. Thereafter, ethnic, social-class, and religious groups increasingly celebrated ways that they were culturally different from, rather than similar to, other groups (Schlesinger, 1991). Multicultural feminism was both a cause and an effect of this movement.

From a multicultural viewpoint, the ideal woman is one who (a) independently chooses the goals and lifestyle she considers appropriate for herself, (b) speaks only for herself or perhaps for other women of her same social condition, and (c) grows up under conditions that eliminate the specific barriers to self-realization that her particular cultural circumstances have erected. Because different cultural environments pose somewhat different problems for women's pursuit of their aims, the task of eliminating females' oppression will not be the same in one cultural context as in another. Each case—or at least each cultural context—must be analyzed separately to determine the particular elements of oppression it involves (Spelman, 1988).

The blame for multicultural feminists' unsatisfactory social condition is placed on three sorts of people: (a) males who deny females their rights and who restrict their opportunities, (b) females who accept their oppressed status either as justified or as something they can do nothing to correct, and (c) females who fail to recognize important differences among cultural groups and, therefore, speak of *"the essential" oppressed woman*—a supposedly single universal type.

The descriptive/explanatory theory of human development implied in multicultural advocates' charges is much like that of liberal feminists, plus an *overgeneralization* feature—the assumption that the restrictions under which females grow up are pretty much the same from one female to another.

The prescriptive theory inferred from multiculturalist discourse envisions social conditions that (a) accord females rights, opportunities, and status equal to those enjoyed by males and (b) recognize that, historically, conditions restricting those rights and opportunities have varied somewhat from one cultural environment to another, so special attention should be given to identifying and combating the harmful tendencies that different cultural traditions have engendered. Thus, furnishing females equitable opportunities can require different changes in traditional social attitudes in the conventional Confucian Chinese family than in the typical Mexican Indian, Irish Catholic, or Syrian Islamic family.

Steps to alleviate the persecution of females include (a) establishing legal provisions that require rights and opportunities for females equal to those for males in all aspects of life, with substantial punitive sanctions applied to individuals and organizations that violate those provisions, (b) altering social customs by disseminating through the schools and mass-communication media rhetoric aimed at convincing the populace of the desirability of according females equal rights and deserved respect, and (c) directing special appeals to cultural groups to alter those groups' particular oppressive attitudes and practices that have been traditionally suffered by females growing up in such cultures.

Marxist Feminism

As already described in earlier chapters, in the middle of the 19th century Karl Marx and his comrade Friedrich Engels espoused a theory of social organization and human development that was intended (a) to account for the social evils of their day and (b) to show what needed to be done to eliminate those evils in order (c) to produce an equitable, just, and prosperous society. The target of the Marx-Engels attack was society's current capitalistic political/economic system (Marx, 1977a). The pair charged that capitalism was an unjust system because it placed the ownership of the production and distribution of goods and services in the hands of an elite few who exploited the masses of laborers by (a) paying workers low wages, (b) selling products at high prices, and (c) keeping the "surplus value" (the difference between production costs and selling prices) for themselves without having contributed enough of their own labor to warrant their receiving those unearned profits. The remedy for this unfair arrangement would be to change the system so that all production and distribution facilities, including nature's resources, would be owned in common by all members of the populace. Individual, personal ownership would be eliminated. Everyone would work for the public good and share equally in the fruits of their labor. The act of changing the production/consumption system from capitalism to state socialism might well require revolutionary action by the masses—proletariat workers forcibly wresting the control of the society from bourgeois owners.

Today's proponents of typical Marxist feminism attribute women's oppressed condition to the patriarchal, male-dominated capitalistic social order. In 19th-century capitalistic Europe, a coterie of men not only conspired to control political and economic affairs but exerted similar control over females' lives, allowing women few of the rights accorded to men. Present-day feminists of a Marxist persuasion continue to believe that

> women's oppression is not the result of individuals' intentional actions but is the product of the political, social, and economic structures within which people live. . . . Marxism promises to make people free, a promise women would like to see someone keep. There is, after all, something very liberating about the idea of women and men constructing together the social structures and social rules

that will permit both genders to realize their full human potential. (Tong, 1998, pp. 94, 101)

As explained in Chapter 1, Marxist developmental psychology proposes that how people think and what they conceive themselves to be—their images of *self*—are determined by their behavior. Rather than thought and belief leading to action, action generates thought, so that people's personalities are formed by what they do. Embedded in a traditional capitalistic system is a division of labor between males and females. Some kinds of work are men's work. Other kinds are women's work. Men perform leadership roles. Women should be followers, engaging primarily in work that serves the needs of men, such as householding and child care. Furthermore, men and women in a capitalistic society are compensated differently for the work they do. Men receive wages for their jobs outside the home, whereas women are expected to labor in the home for no pay. Likewise, if women do have jobs outside the home that yield wages, they are not freed from home responsibilities but still must perform their household duties, burdening them with two jobs but providing them pay for only one. In addition, for their labor outside the home, women typically have been paid lower wages than men who do the same kind of work.

The traditional theory of development to which Marxist feminists object teaches the young that the foregoing division of roles and of uneven compensation accords with nature's plan, that is, with the way gender relationships are meant to be. Consequently, the established social order is portrayed as fair, with both formal sanctions (laws, regulations) and customary sanctions (parent, school, church, and community disciplinary practices) serving to endorse and enforce the theory.

The way to remedy this unfair double standard is to rear females in a manner that affords them all the rights and opportunities available to males. Thus, the process of development should begin with engaging girls during their growing years in the same range of activities that boys pursue in the home, school, and community. Later, in adulthood, women must be free to engage in whatever sort of work they choose, enjoying the same chances for training and the same consideration and compensation as men across the entire range of occupations. Women who opt to invest their energy in traditional homemaking should be paid wages for such work—paid either by their spouses or by the state.

Implementing such a prescriptive theory of female development requires not only revised goals and methods of childrearing but also a major restructuring of society along Marxist lines. At present, Marxists' efforts to effect a restructuring of Western capitalistic societies' production/consumption systems and their childraising practices consist of messages aimed at convincing the public of the rectitude of their case. The more drastic option—that of forcing social-structure changes by means of the violence that brought communism to the Soviet Union, China, and other nations in the early and middle decades of the 20th century—seems unfeasible in prosperous Western societies, particularly after the spectacle of communism's demise in the Soviet Union and its allied Eastern European nations. However, the goal of altering childraising practices and providing females job opportunities equal to those available to men seems attainable, as evidenced by marked progress toward that end in Western societies during recent decades.

Ecological Feminism

Another array of theories described by Tong qualify as versions of *ecological feminism* or *ecofeminism*. Although there are some notable differences among the variants of ecofeminism, virtually all are founded on the six-part conviction that:

- All humans are related to each other and to everything in the nonhuman universe—whether animal, vegetal, or inert.
- Every person bears responsibility for the welfare of every other person and for the welfare of all nonhuman phenomena—animals, plants, the land, the air, bodies of water, and such.
- People daily destroy themselves and their fellow occupants of the universe "by laying waste to the earth from which we originate and to which we will return" (Tong, 1998, p. 277).
- Females are more intimately related to nature than are males and thereby have a clearer understanding of nature's ways than do males.
- Particularly in Western culture, people's beliefs and values have been shaped by "an oppressive patriarchal conceptual framework, the purpose of which is to explain, justify, and maintain relationships of domination and subordination [of nature's objects] in general and men's domination of women in particular" (Warren's allegation [1996, p. 20] as paraphrased in Tong [1998, p. 246]).
- In order to rescue both females and the natural world from further oppression and exploitation, people's belief systems must be revised to harmonize with an ecofeminist conception of reality.

Women must see that there can be no liberation for them and no solution to the ecological aims within a society whose fundamental model of relationships continues to be one of domination. They must unite the demands of the women's movement with those of the ecological movement to envision a radical reshaping of the basic socioeconomic relations and the underlying values of this [modern industrial] society. (Reuther, 1975, p. 204)

Consequently, the dual mission of ecofeminists is that of (a) ensuring females all the rights, privileges, and access to power available to males and (b) preventing the exploitation of humans' animate and inanimate surround. Because men are the conspirators behind both the oppression of females and the plundering of nature, the ecofeminist agenda calls for advancing women to positions of authority from which they can guarantee females their deserved rights and can halt further degradation of the natural world (Ferry, 1992, p. 118; Salleh, 1984, p. 339).

The descriptive, explanatory theory of human development that ecofeminists find offensive is one that contends, at least by implication, that

- Life is a constant, intense competition among individuals and groups for resources—physical (food, shelter, material goods), social (status, power), and psychological (self-esteem, emotional satisfaction).
- In this competition, humans are better qualified than other species to alter nature's resources in order to get what they desire. Furthermore, it is not only people's right, but indeed their obligation, to change nature in whatever ways seem necessary to satisfy people's self-identified needs so as to promote their survival and prosperity. In brief, nature is there to be used for people's benefit.
- Males naturally differ from females in their talents, personalities, and emotions. Males are better suited to leadership and decision-making roles than are females, whose proper functions are ones that support the ventures that males initiate for the common good.

Ecofeminists also object to the belief that children, throughout their growing years, should be raised in a manner that endorses the ostensible "natural differences" between the genders and that prepares the two genders for their "appropriate" adult roles. Rearing children in such a manner includes teaching them, through example and instruction, that the foregoing conception of gender relations and of the treatment of the environment is proper.

In contrast, a typical ecofeminist prescriptive theory of development embodies the six tenets listed at the beginning of this discussion of ecological feminism. According to ecofeminists, that conception should be taught to children and youths as the correct view of gender relations and of the environment.

In assigning blame for present conditions, ecofeminism holds men principally responsible for dominating women and destroying the natural environment. But those women who tolerate the existing exploitation of women and nature—or worse yet, who endorse it—are also held partially at fault for the current sad state of affairs.

Ecological feminists' efforts to win widespread support for their theory include (a) offering a line of logic via mass-communication media (books, periodicals, television, radio, the Internet) that convinces people of the reasonableness and moral virtue of their cause, (b) urging textbook publishers and schools' curriculum developers to present ecofeminist concerns in a light favorable to the ecofeminist agenda, (c) engaging in mass action (public demonstrations, boycotts) to promote women's rights and to stop individuals, corporations, and governments from harming nature, and (d) electing public officials—preferably women—who will promote ecofeminist programs.

SIX THEORIES IN BRIEF

Six additional modes of feminist thought that Tong identified are so similar in general pattern to the five described above that a brief sketch focusing solely on each of the six theories' most distinctive features should suffice to suggest the place that each occupies in the feminist movement. The six bear the labels *socialist, global, psychoanalytic, gender, postmodern,* and *existentialist.*

In Tong's typology, socialist feminism is a version of Marxist feminism that targets men's domination of women as much as—or even more than—the social-class conflict between owners and workers that Marxists claim results from capitalistic political-economic practices. Socialist feminists note that in the Soviet Union and other Marxist societies, women continued to be exploited sexually (prostitution, marriages of convenience), were burdened with dual jobs (as both worker and homemaker), and failed to enjoy positions of authority and power equal to those of men. Thus, socialist feminists, while agreeing that the general political-economic structure of society should be changed, would accord high priority to females' winning their independence from male domination.

Global feminists are much like multicultural feminists in charging that females' self-concepts are insecure and fragmented as a result of cultural and ethnic traditions that restrict females' freedom to develop in keeping with each one's potential individuality. However, multicultural feminists tend to focus on culturally based differences between women in the same society, such as differences found between childrearing practices in a U.S. white upper-middle-class, professional-occupation culture and childrearing practices in an American-Hispanic immigrant, agricultural-labor culture. Global feminists extend their concerns to women throughout the world, often accepting as their own the responsibility for helping relieve the exploitation of females in all cultures (Bunch, 1993, p. 250). Some global feminists stress the importance of cultural and socioeconomic differences between societies—differences that render the condition of women in the United States different from that of women in Hindu India, metropolitan France, the Papua New Guinea highlands, poverty-stricken Chad, and war-ravaged Kosovo. And some reject the premise that there is one essential type of oppression suffered by women throughout the world or one solution for oppression. There are also global feminists who contend that women of one society are not qualified to speak for women of another society; each society's women must speak and act for themselves. Hence, prescriptions for female development in one cultural setting may not identical with prescriptions for development in another setting.

Psychoanalytic and gender feminists share the conviction that the causes of females' plight are found in the depths of women's personalities rather than in the social customs that liberal and radical feminists blame or in the structures of societies that Marxist and socialist feminists hold at fault. However, psychoanalytic and gender feminists disagree with each other about the sources of females' deep-set personality characteristics.

Proponents of a psychoanalytic explanation accept Freud's proposal that female and male traits derive from early childhood experiences, particularly during (a) the pre-Oedipal stage's "family romance" and (b) the subsequent resolution of the Oedipus conflict (Chodorow, 1978; Dinnerstein, 1977). As noted in Chapter 1, the Oedipus conflict consists of the young child, age 3 through 5 or more, viewing her or his opposite-sex parent as a desired sexual love object. This conflict is resolved by children identifying themselves with their same-sex parent—daughters imitating their mothers and sons copying their fathers—and thereby adopting their particular society's established concepts of sexual-appropriate appearance and action. But what distresses psychoanalytic feminists is the traditional image of female and male perpetuated in so many cultures, with (a) sharp distinctions drawn between acceptable female and acceptable male personality traits and behavior, (b) masculinity portrayed a superior to femininity, and (c) the widespread adoption of childrearing practices that foster the development of sex-typed traits and behavior. The remedy for this offensive state of affairs is to alter existing cultural standards so as to produce a more androgynous society in which traits and behaviors formerly regarded as distinctly female or male become acceptable in both sexes. This new theory of sex-appropriate characteristics would be the one on which child-development practices should be based.

Gender feminists usually assume that age-old feminine and masculine characteristics are not merely cultural creations people adopt as personality attributes. Rather, those attributes are assumed to be grounded in females' and males' biological inheritance. Gender feminists also consider traditional feminine traits (gentleness, modesty, humility, sacrifice, supportiveness, empathy, compassion, tenderness, nurturance, intuitiveness, sensitivity, unselfishness) morally superior to the traditional masculine traits of courage, strong will, ambition, independence, assertiveness, initiative, rationality, and emotional control. However, gender feminists do not recommend that females and males both develop similar androgynous personalities that incorporate traditional feminine and masculine traits in equal measure. Rather, they urge females to retain their feminine selves intact and urge males to abandon excessive forms of traditional masculinity. Finally, in social relations a feminine ethics of *care* should replace the masculine ethics of *even-handed justice* (Tong, 1998, p. 131; Gilligan, 1982; Gilligan, Ward, & Taylor, 1988). The treatment of both girls and boys should henceforth conform to this feminized conception of proper development.

Women who might be categorized as postmodern feminists are a mixed lot who differ with each other in many of their beliefs, but they tend to be alike in subscribing to such typical postmodern convictions as

- In all cultures, marked distinctions have been drawn between females and males, with most cultures holding females in lower regard than males. The male has been the center of interest, with the female relegated to the marginal status of "the other."

- The invidious distinctions between female and male have been built into the language children acquire as they grow up. Language is the essence of culture, and people are taught to believe that a culture's utterances reflect or reveal *reality* or *truth*. However, according to such postmodern philosophers as Jacques Derrida (1976), that assumption is ill founded because there is no essential, objective *reality* or *truth*. Different people have their own realities and truths, with no one's version superior to anyone else's.
- In view of the fact that one person's vision of reality is as valid as any other's, it behooves everyone to be open to multiple lifestyles and to value diversities among people's beliefs and behaviors.

One theory of development that derives from such beliefs proposes that (a) children should be raised to learn about the many ways of life that people can pursue and (b) individual females should be free to choose which of those many ways they wish to adopt. No single mode life should be prescribed as *the* proper one (Tong, 1998, p. 193).

Somewhat similar to postmodern feminism is Tong's final variant of the women's movement—existentialist feminism. An existentialist worldview rejects the limited life imposed on females by a male-dominated society and by woman's own childbearing biological nature. Existential feminists propose that each women free herself from her gender's traditional shackles in order to fashion a self-satisfying, life pattern that is uniquely her own. Such a proposal implies that childraising practices should teach the growing girl an existentialist perspective and provide her opportunities for a wide range of experiences that acquaint her with a diversity of potential life-styles.

REMAINING CHALLENGES

As this chapter has shown, the feminist movement in the closing years of the 20th century brought to the fore a host of proposals about (a) how girls and women have traditionally been obliged to develop and (b) how they should be able to develop in a socially equitable world. Tong's analysis of feminist perspectives yielded 11 recognizable types, several of which could be divided into subtypes.

Frequently, challenges to feminist theorists have come from within the feminist movement itself. For instance, socialist feminists have claimed that Marxists assign too much blame to capitalism for women's exploited condition and assign too little blame to male domination. Radical feminists charge that gender feminists got it wrong in according such high regard to females' ostensibly inbred compassion that requires women to care for others rather than adopt self-identities that accord themselves rights and privileges equal to those held by males. Critics have portrayed postmodern feminists as a cadre of self-appointed intellectuals who have retreated from reality into a world of such opaque writing that no one outside their clique can understand what they are talking about

(Duchen, 1986, p. 102). Radical-cultural feminists have been censured for (a) categorizing women and men as two distinctly and irretrievably different kinds of humans—men corrupt and women innocent—thereby (b) denying the individuality observed when the lives of specific men and women are analyzed (Elshtain, 1981). These sorts of criticisms, and far more, from within the ranks of feminist thought continue to provide a lively arena of debate that has kept theorizing in a continuing state of agitation, a state that invites new and revised prescriptive models of development.

12

Sexual Orientations

The term *sexual orientations* is used in this chapter to mean people's preferences for the partners with whom they engage in sexual intercourse, or at least those whom they sense as sexually arousing. It seems likely that the concern societies have held about sex-partner preferences extends well back into prehistoric times. That concern has been reflected in customs and formal laws which accord greater approval to some kinds of sex partners and sexual acts than to other kinds.

Over the centuries, the diversity of sex partners has included (a) persons of the opposite sex (heterosexuality), (b) persons of one's same sex (homosexuality), (c) persons of both sexes (bisexuality), (d) one's own self (masturbation), (e) various kinds of inanimate objects (assisted masturbation), and (f) animals of different sorts (bestiality). Which of these types have been acceptable, and the degree of each type's acceptability, has differed from one culture to another and from one era to another within the same culture. An example of culturally based moral strictures against certain types of sexual partners is found in the Torah—Judaism's basic set of holy books that also form the early section of the Christian Old Testament. Such beliefs are also honored in Islamic tradition. The Torah condemns engaging in sexual intercourse with a person of one's own sex, with animals, or with a menstruating woman (Maimonides, 1967, in Thomas, 1997, p. 181).

Societies have also distinguished between acceptable and unacceptable sexual partners on the basis of the individuals' social relationship or status. For example, each of the following conditions has been approved in some societies and condemned in others: (a) formally married partners having sexual relations outside their marriage (extramarital sex), (b) sexual relations between a common-law husband and wife, (c) sexual relations prior to marriage (premarital sex), (d) one partner paying the other for sexual services (prostitution), (e) one partner forcing the other to engage in intercourse (rape), (f) one partner being an adult and the other a child (pedophilia), and (g) one partner lawfully having a diversity of other permanent partners within the bonds of marriage (polygamy) or outside of marriage (polyamory). For instance, the Torah denounces a man's copulating with another man's wife (adultery), his own mother (incest), his father's wife, his son's daughter, his father's sister, any other kinswoman, or a woman and her daughter (Maimonides in Thomas, 1997, p. 181).

Cultures have also differed in the acceptability of different sorts of sexual acts, parts of the body involved, and equipment used. In some societies, civil or religious laws have proscribed such practices as fellatio, cunnilingus, and sodomy as "unnatural acts," whereas other societies have accepted any acts considered satisfying by participants who are "consenting adults."

In summary, there are multiple viewpoints toward people's sexual orientations in different cultures. Controversies about such issues have resulted in a continuing flow of theories about the development of people's sexual preferences and about people's attitudes about their own and others' sexual predilections.

RECENT THEORIES

Recent theories of sexual orientation have rarely focused on heterosexual preferences and behavior. Instead, most have been designed to explain homosexuality and bisexuality, while the attention given to heterosexual development has usually been only incidental, granted no more than passing mention in discussions that contrast heterosexual to homosexual and bisexual practices. Hence, the four models described in this chapter are limited to homosexuality and bisexuality.

Two main types of homosexual/bisexual theories appeared over the final years of the 20th century—those intended to explain how such sexual orientations develop and those tracing the ways people of homosexual and bisexual tendencies come to terms with their sexual identities. This chapter offers two examples of each type. Explanations of cause are illustrated by (a) Hamer's theory of genetic involvement and (b) Friedman's "contemporary psychoanalytic perspective" on the development of male homosexuality. Proposals about the stages through which individuals advance in creating their sexual identities are illustrated with (a) Cass's version of lesbian sexual-identity development and (b) Weinberg, Williams, and Pryor's model of "becoming bisexual."

Before inspecting Hamer's and Friedman's notions about causes of homosexuality, we may profit from recognizing something of the diversity of theories that have been devised over the years to account for why individuals develop their sexual orientations. Theories that attempt to explain the roots of homosexuality are typically divided into three types: biological, sociopsychological, and interactionist.

Biological theories assume that a person's homosexual traits are the result of some characteristic of the physical organism, such as the person's ratio of male hormone (androgen) to female hormone (estrogen). A typical supposition is that the greater the proportion of androgen in a female's system the more likely she will become homosexual. Likewise, the greater the proportion of estrogen in the male, the greater will be his homosexuality. Such theories may include a belief in the genetic basis for the hormonal ratios, with the balance or imbalance of hormones due to gene patterns inherited from parents. However, a biological theory need not presume that genes are the underlying cause. Instead, a theorist can place responsibility for the hormonal ratio on physiological changes in the individual's composition before or after birth, changes perhaps influenced by such things as climate, diet, illness, or injury.

In contrast to biological theories are sociopsychological explanations which propose that it is not biological factors but, rather, the quality of an individual's relationships with other people during childhood and adolescence that determines whether a person becomes homosexual, heterosexual, bisexual, or even asexual (not interested at all in physical lovemaking). So, from a sociopsychological perspective, homosexuality is a learned or acquired characteristic. The determining social influence can be within the family (principally parents' childraising practices), among peers (the sexual proclivities of influential companions), or an older adult, such as a girl's governess or a boy's uncle who introduces the child to sexual acts.

Interactionist theories draw on both biological and sociopsychological factors in the belief that some combination of body chemistry and environmental influences accounts for the development of one's sexual orientation. In one common version of interactionism, differences between people in body chemistry or genetic inheritance will make some people more prone than others to homosexual practices. But whether such practices are actually adopted depends on sociopsychological factors, such as the models of behavior that parents provide; the influence of peers; standards of conduct taught by the church, school, Boy Scouts, or other social institutions; and the opportunities available at the moment to engage in heterosexual rather than homosexual acts. Supposedly, people who have a great biological predisposition to homosexuality will adopt such behavior even under social conditions that strongly discourage it. At the opposite extreme, people with little or no biological inclination to homosexuality will resist homosexual behavior even under environmental circumstances that foster it. In effect, a typical interactionist theory views the sexual orientation of different individuals as the result of different mixtures of causal factors. Thus, one person becomes homosexual for a different pattern of reasons than does another person.

In the waning years of the 20th century, rarely would any serious, well-informed theorist attribute homosexuality solely to biological, psychological, or social-environment factors. Virtually everyone would agree that all three such sources of influence can be involved. Hence, as suggested by Hamer and Copeland (1994, p. 177),

It's easy to say that nature and nurture work together and play important roles in human sexual development, but the tricky part is determining what the biological and psychological factors are, how they interact, and how much each contributes to the individual variations in human sexuality.

A GAY GENE?

In recent decades, the possibility that homosexuality is the result of biological inheritance has sent investigators on the hunt for genetic elements that could be responsible for sexual orientation. Such a possibility motivated "the search for the gay gene" that was conducted by Dean Hamer (chief of the Section on Gene Structure at the U.S. National Cancer Institute in Bethesda, Maryland) and his associates.

The method Hamer's team of scientists adopted consisted of:

- Interviewing a sample of 114 male homosexuals and many of their relatives.
- Reducing their sample to 40 families, each of which included a pair of homosexual brothers.
- Obtaining samples of biological cells from the study's participants in order to conduct a sophisticated analysis of their genetic structures.
- Estimating whether genetic structures in any way contributed to the brothers' gay sexual orientation.

To explain precisely what the research team was searching for and what they eventually found, we can usefully review a few basic elements of human genetics. The gene is the key component of all biological inheritance passed from parents to children. In most cases, each gene creates one protein that produces one biochemical reaction. Genes are transported on long, thread-like molecules called chromosomes located in the nucleus of each cell of the human body (except the red blood cells). A typical chromosome carries around 4,000 genes. At the time of conception, the about-to-be-created human receives 46 chromosomes, 23 from the mother and 23 from the father, with the total of 46 organized as 23 pairs. Twenty-two of the pairs are nearly identical in appearance. But the last pair, referred to as the sex chromosomes, can be quite different. A mother can contribute only one variety of sex chromosome, which Hamer has described as a rather small, dumpy sort labeled X. But the father can contribute either an X or a large, long one labeled Y. If the newly conceived human receives an X chromosome from each parent—giving the neonate an XX sex pair—then the resulting child will be female. But if the X from the mother is joined by a Y from the father, making the pair XY, then the child will be male.

The scientists employed two approaches. They used the latest gene-analysis technology to scrutinize the sex chromosomes of the homosexual brothers to learn whether their gene structures might differ from those of heterosexual males. At the same time, they interviewed relatives of their gay subjects to discover if there were other homosexuals in their extended families.

The search of the chromosomes consisted of finding DNA (deoxyribonucleic acid) markers that might indicate where along a chromosome a gay gene might reside. The hunt led them to the Xq28 region along the X (female contributed) chromosome as the area in which there could be a gene influencing a person's sexual orientation. "We concluded that 67% of the brothers were 'linked to' the Xq28 region" (Hamer & Copeland, 1994, p. 138). Furthermore, the group's data on the sexual oreintations among the gay men's relatives showed significantly more homosexual males on the mother's side of the family than on the father's.

These results enabled Hamer to conclude that the cause of sexual orientation in at least some cases of homosexuality involves a gene inherited through the mother and located in a limited neighborhood on the X chromosome. Although this discovery could be considered one step toward answering the question of whether genetic endowment can contribute to a person's sexual orientation, it left much yet to be explained.

> Proving that a gene exists is one thing. Isolating or finding the gene, measuring its incidence and effect on people, and understanding how it works is another, and those goals may take many years to achieve. (Hamer & Copeland, 1994, p. 144)

Hamer recognized that the notion of a genetic component in the development of people's sexual orientation was not universally welcomed.

> Many people are disturbed by the idea that genes influence behavior . . . [because they believe theorists are claiming that] "Genes are destiny." This common misconception is most avidly professed by people who don't understand how genes work. They visualize genes as "master puppeteers" rather than as what they really are—chemical structures that code for protein production or regulate the activity of other genes. . . . [The truth is that] genes influence behavior through indirect and complex paths that require inputs from physiology, the environment, society, and culture. (Hamer & Copeland, 1994, pp. 203-204).

In conclusion, this example of a gay-gene hunt illustrates the way theories are often tested and either confirmed or disconfirmed. However, empirical testing—although it may refine a portion of a theory—may still fail to clarify in detail how the phenomenon in question operates overall. Far more empirical investigation and theory revision are needed.

UPDATED PSYCHOANALYSIS

A model of male homosexuality development as formulated by Richard C. Friedman of Columbia University is intended to modernize Sigmund Freud's proposal about why people adopt homosexual behavior.

Sigmund Freud, at various times in his career, offered different explanations of how a person's sexual orientation develops. The best known of these theories—and apparently Freud's favorite—proposes that homosexuality is a personality disorder resulting from a failure of a prepuberal boy or girl to resolve psychoanalytic theory's "family romance." According to Freud, during the infantile-genital stage of the psychoanalytic model (around ages 3-5), the boy's penis and the girl's clitoris become the key objects of erotic pleasure. In the first phase of that stage—the *phallic period*—the child discovers that fondling the genitals gives erotic pleasure. The child then associates this experience with a love object with whom he or she wishes to have some sort of sexual relations. For the boy, Freud wrote:

> The object that has been found turns out to be almost identical with the first object of the oral pleasure-instinct, which was reached by attachment (to the nutritional instinct). Though it is not actually the mother's breast, at least it is the mother. We call the mother the first *love*-object. (1917, p. 329)

While the boy is viewing his mother as the desired object, he is at the same time recognizing that he cannot have her all to himself, since his father is the successful competitor for her affections. Freud applied the label *Oedipus complex* or *Oedipus conflict* to the resulting psychological discord of wanting to possess his mother but being prevented by the powerful father. The girl is in the opposite fix, wanting her father as her love partner but being defeated in this contest by her mother—a problem that Freud dubbed the *Electra conflict*.

During this period the child experiences strong ambivalent feelings, seeking the parent of the opposite sex as a lover, but at the same time both fearing and loving the parent of the same sex. An adequate resolution of the Oedipus problem results when the child rejects the sexual feelings toward the forbidden object—the opposite-sex parent—and simultaneously identifies with the parent of the same sex. By identifying with the same-sex parent, the child both assuages feelings of fear of reprisal and incorporates into his or her own personality the traits of the same-sex parent—those traits that made the parent win the mate's love. Thus, the boy identifies with his father and seeks to adopt his father's characteristics, while the girl does the same with her mother. This is the way Freud accounted for the development of masculine and feminine characteristics that fit the traditional culture into which the child is socialized.

If the Oedipus conflict is not adequately resolved through identification with the like-sex parent, remnants of the conflict remain in the unconscious to distort the personality of the adolescent and adult. Thus, in psychoanalytic tradition homosexuality is typically explained as the child's identifying with the opposite-sex parent, thereby modeling his or her subsequent living habits and sexual tastes after the opposite-sex parent rather than the same-sex one. Various family conditions contribute to such an outcome. For the boy, no father or other influential male may be present as a model of masculinity, or else the father in the home may be emotionally detached from, or antagonistic toward, his son. In addition, the boy may over-identify with the feminine role if his mother or other adult females in the home have unduly protected and indulged him and have taught him to prefer feminine ways. Therefore, homosexuality, according to the dominant psychoanalytic tradition, results from distorted childrearing settings and practices. The family environment, and particularly the parents, are the cause.

Whereas Friedman (himself a psychoanalyst) subscribed partially to Freud's classical explanation of homosexuality, he also suggested a revision on the basis of research findings over the past several decades.

> The major limitations of Freud's views about homosexuality resulted from insufficient appreciation of prenatal psychoendocrine influences, insufficient distinction between gender-related behavior [a society's traditional notions of individuals' masculine versus feminine or active versus passive appearance] and sexual behavior [heterosexual versus homosexual acts], and lack of knowledge about the timing of development of sex differences in behavior. In these three areas a great expansion of knowledge occurred after Freud's death [in 1939]. (Friedman, 1988, pp. 51-52)

The following brief summary of Friedman's views is presented in two parts. The first part outlines principal components that Friedman believed contribute to the development of male homosexuality. The second identifies a series of events at different age levels that can affect boys' adopting feminine characteristics and homosexual preferences.

Components of Homosexual Development

Friedman's extensive review of the biological, sociological, and psychological literature on homosexuality led him to conclude that, from the perspective of causal factors, homosexual males can be divided into subgroups that represent different combinations of biological, social, and psychological influences. Biological factors, such as genetic endowment and hormone levels, would be credited with exerting a major influence in one subgroup, whereas childrearing methods would be dominant causes in another subgroup. Important also is the time in an individual's life that different influences assume a key role in sexual orientation. Thus, high testosterone levels during the prenatal period could have a different effect than high levels during adolescence. Furthermore, the sexual nature of peer relationships in early childhood could produce a different outcome than such relationships produced at the time of puberty.

Therefore, Friedman postulated that biological, social, and psychological factors combine to determine sexual preferences, but the power of each of those factors in determining the sort of homosexuality an individual exhibits can differ from one person or subgroup to another. Hence, there are multiple kinds of homosexuals, with each kind the result of a different mixture of causal conditions.

Age-Period Correlates of Sexual Orientation

In Friedman's model, age-related indicators that can appear in homosexual development include (a) childhood effeminacy, (b) juvenile unmasculinity, and (c) sexually stimulating fantasies.

Childhood effeminacy

The word *effeminacy* refers to a male's physical appearance and preference for activities associated with female behavior in a particular culture. *Effeminacy* is contrasted to *masculinity*, which means physical appearance and activity preferences regarded as culturally appropriate for males.

According to Friedman, both severe childhood effeminacy and less extreme varieties usually result in adult homosexuality. Effeminacy in early childhood occurs in boys who

> have a disturbance in core gender identity, since they feel they possess the qualities of the opposite sex. . . . Thus, gender-disturbed boys wish to be girls, prefer feminine interests and activities, and express a dislike of their male anatomy. (Coates & Zuker in Friedman, 1988, p. 192)

Evidence of childhood effeminacy typically appears around ages 2 through 4 or so.

> The combined results of numerous investigations lead to the conclusion that childhood gender-identity/gender-role disturbances [as in a boy's identifying with females] are associated with predominant or exclusive homosexuality in adulthood. . . . This does not mean that homosexuality invariably results from such disturbances or that homosexuality invariably begins with them. . . . But an association as powerful from the statistical and scientific point of view as that between childhood gender identity disturbance and adult homosexuality must command the attention of clinicians and theoreticians alike. (Friedman, 1988, pp. 47-48)

To what extent the sort of gay gene that Hamer searched for contributes to childhood effeminacy is unclear, since genetic endowment is so entwined with environmental influences that the relationship is difficult to untangle. For example, the families of markedly effeminate boys often display characteristics of the families of homosexual males described in the professional literature—father is absent or detached from the child, mother holds negative attitude toward men and especially toward male aggressivity, and mother is overly involved in her son's life and discourages him from becoming independent. Such a picture of family dynamics fits Freud's view of faulty childrearing practices that contribute to homosexuality.

Juvenile unmasculinity

During the juvenile years (Freud's latency period), which range from around age 4 to age 10 or so, some boys fit neither an effeminacy profile nor the typical profile of masculinity. They display poor skill in rough-and-tumble play activities, avoid contact sports, fear bodily injury, dislike aggressive interactions with other boys, are relegated to low status in peer groups, lack positive interpersonal relationships with male peers, and have no compensatory positive relationships with older males. They may or may not have positive relationships with females; therefore, while some turn to females for companionship, others remain loners.   Juvenile unmasculinity may predispose boys to become homosexual adults.

Sexual fantasies

In Friedman's model, the age at which a boy first experiences sexual fantasies involving male images can signal the onset of individuals' consciously recognized homosexual tendencies.   The age at which such erotic fantasies begin—and are associated with erections—varies greatly across subjects, with the range in one study extending from age 4 to age 13, with a mean of 9.5 years.   In the same study, heterosexual boys' erotic fantasies in which the objects were female first appeared within the age range 5-13, with a mean of 9.9 years (Friedman, 1988, p. 195).

> Once sexual fantasies appear in a consolidated [continuing] way and as a significant motivating force, they result in further developmental differences between homosexual and heterosexual males.   Often boys experience consolidated homosexual fantasies as shameful, . . . [fantasies] not communicated to family or friends and disavowed as part of the self system.   The juvenile-age boy often does not interpret the presence of homosexual fantasies and the absence of heterosexual fantasies as evidence that he is gay.   This is consistent with the fact that many of the psychological processes involved in identity formation normally occur years later, during adolescence and young adulthood.   (Friedman, 1988, p. 195)

Conclusion

To summarize, Friedman devised a model of male homosexual development which included certain traditional psychoanalytic assumptions about the effect of childrearing practices on sexual orientation but which deviated from Freudian tradition by directing more attention to the role of genetic and other biological factors in the development of homosexuality.   Friedman's model also goes beyond Freud in describing age-stage influences of effeminacy, nonmasculinity, and sexual fantasies in homosexuals' life course.

HOMOSEXUAL IDENTITY FORMATION

In North America and other parts of the world, the change in social attitudes that accompanied the putative "cultural revolution" of the 1960s motivated a growing number of homosexuals to admit to themselves and to the world that their sexual preferences were not of the heterosexual variety generally endorsed by society.   This phenomenon of formerly covert gays and lesbians "coming out of the closet" spawned a number of theories about how such individuals can come to terms with their sexual predilections.   Among those theories, the one offered by Vivenne Cass (1979, 1984) is perhaps the best known and best supported with published evidence.   Her theory addresses the question of how individuals who are sensually attracted to members of their own sex come to accept homosexuality as an appropriate, publicly admitted lifestyle.   In Cass's scheme, people who tend toward homosexual rather than heterosexual feelings and practices advance through six stages of establishing a positive homosexual identity (Figure 12-1).

Stage 1: Identity confusion. At first, covert gay and lesbian individuals are confused about their sexual inclination, wondering whether they truly are attracted to people of their own sex and whether this is a socially admissible, mentally healthy propensity. Their initial confusion can be resolved in any of three ways. The first consists of deciding that a homosexual propensity and homosexual behavior are, indeed, suitable and personally acceptable; the individual then automatically advances to the second stage. A second kind of response is that of recognizing one's homosexual inclination but feeling ashamed of it and thus seeking to avoid information about homosexuality, believing that such information is not personally relevant. Such a response results in "identity foreclosure," with the individual unwilling to view herself or himself as a potential homosexual. The third choice is the one adopted by those who consider homosexual emotions and behavior both incorrect and unacceptable, so they redefine themselves as nonhomosexual and thereby shut off the process of identity formation (Falco, 1991, p. 86).

Stage 2: Identity comparison. Individuals who have sensed their homosexual orientation and have begun to accept it can next be expected to contrast their own feelings with those of people whose orientation is heterosexual. Such persons tell themselves that "I may very well be homosexual," and they sense an increasing alienation from others—family, friends, schoolmates, work associates—who have heretofore considered them heterosexual. Previous ideals, plans, and expectations that were built on viewing themselves as heterosexual are no longer relevant, but those attitudes have not been replaced with homosexual perspectives. The conflicts at this stage can be dealt with in any of four ways. First, the person may accept a homosexual orientation as a good thing, but still have to struggle with fitting into society by feigning heterosexual behaviors. Second, the individual may consider a homosexual identity as undesirable, yet continue homosexual behavior by rationalizing that it's not really indicative of homosexuality. Third, the person can recognize his or her actions as those of homosexuals but tries to change in order to be "normal." The fourth reaction is to despise both homosexual behavior and identity; this results in identity repudiation, "and the individual can be left with an extreme sense of self-hatred" (Falco, 1991, p. 87).

Stage 3: Identity tolerance. As a further step, the self-accepted gay or lesbian recognizes that it's all right for people to follow their own nature, whether homosexual or heterosexual. Such persons are increasingly convinced that they probably are homosexual, and they begin to associate with selected gays and lesbians for the purpose of companionship. The quality of their reception by homosexuals exerts an important influence on the identity they develop. A positive, friendly reception casts homosexuality in an attractive light and makes

Figure 12-1

Cass's Stages of Homosexual Identity Formation

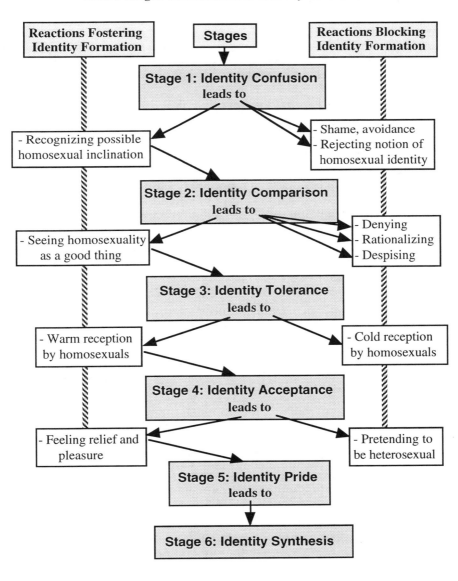

gays and lesbians desirable models to emulate. A negative, harsh reception tends to discourage continued contact with homosexuals and can retard progress toward a secure sexual self-image.

Stage 4: Identity acceptance. Homosexuality is now fully embraced as one's own proper orientation. Individuals prefer homosexual social contacts, but may still attempt to appear heterosexual—to "pass as straight"—to most of their social world.

> The individual may also continue to cope with identity by minimizing contacts with heterosexuals who threaten to increase incongruency, such as families, and by selectively disclosing a homosexual identity to significant heterosexual others. (Falco, 1991, p. 87)

Stage 5: Identity pride. The person derives pleasure from being homosexual and is not only willing to announce it publicly but is inclined to boast about its propriety and satisfactions. By viewing homosexuality as of greater worth and virtue than heterosexuality, individuals at this stage are ready to risk alienating heterosexuals by openly disclosing their homosexual orientation. Thus, openly expressing pride in their gay/lesbian preference becomes a tactic for actively coping with criticism directed at homosexuals by heterosexuals.

Stage 6: Identity synthesis. The process of identity formation becomes complete for gays and lesbians who finally integrate homosexuality into their overall worldview and mode of life. No longer does the person divide the world into two conflicting groups—homosexuals and heterosexuals. At this stage, such individuals recognize that they are accepted and respected by certain heterosexuals and that those people can be valued as friends. Thus, sexual identity becomes integrated with the other facets of the person's overall self-identity, that is, integrated with such facets of the personality as the artistic, the intellectual, the physical, the vocational, the recreational, and more.

Other popular conceptions of sexual-identity formation (Coleman, 1982; Lewis, 1984; Ponse, 1978; Troiden, 1988) are similar to Cass's model in their sequence of stages. Cass and the others admit that a person may enter the sequence at any stage, may move through the stages in a slightly different sequence than the one described as typical, and may become fixated at any point along the way.

CONSTRUCTING A BISEXUAL IDENTITY

As noted earlier, bisexuals are people whose choice of sexual companions includes both males and females. But as a designator of sexual preferences and practices, *bisexual* is an imprecise label, for it encompasses a very mixed bag of sexual preferences and behaviors. A man who continually engages in intercourse with his wife at his own home and with a male companion at the companion's home is bisexual. So is a woman who frequently sleeps with a female friend, but during a business convention in another city becomes involved sexually over a period of 3 days with a man she met at the convention. The label *bisexual* can also be applied to a male soldier who was continually involved sexually with another male soldier during their six-month assignment on a remote Aleutian island, but he then avoided any future homosexual encounters once he returned to his longtime girlfriend in the United States. Likewise, two teenage girls could qualify as bisexual after they experimented briefly with reciprocal masturbation, but soon abandoned that relationship in favor of sexual activities exclusively with male partners.

Just as the task of developing a secure homosexual identity is a worrisome challenge in a predominately heterosexual culture, so also is the task of developing a satisfactory bisexual identity. Martin S. Weinberg and Colin J. Williams (Indiana University) and Douglas W. Pryor (Wake Forest University) have sought to delineate the process of establishing such a bisexual self-image by postulating a four-stage sequence (Figure 12-2). The model is based chiefly on the authors' study of a sample of bisexuals. The model also includes certain features of the homosexual-identity theories offered by Cass, Coleman, Lewis, Ponse, and Troiden. In the Weinberg, Williams, and Pryor proposal, the experience of evolving a bisexual identity shows

> some overlap with the basic process involved in becoming homosexual. But there are differences which require modifications of that model. For example, the label *bisexual* is not widely recognized and is not readily available to most people as an identity. Also, the absence of a bisexual subculture in most locales means a lack both of information and of support for sustaining a commitment to the identity. Thus, with our subjects, there seem to be four distinct stages: problems with finding the label, understanding what the label means, dealing with social disapproval from two directions, and continuing to use the label once it is adopted. (Weinberg, Williams, & Pryor, 1998, pp. 169-170)

Stage 1: Identity confusion. Bisexuals interviewed by the authors reported experiencing one or more of four types of identity confusion resulting from being sexually aroused by members of both sexes. The first type consisted of feeling disoriented and sometimes frightened by such apparently uncontrollable emotion. The second type involved distress they felt in recognizing that their newly discovered bisexual propensity threatened the stability of their already established heterosexual identity. As one woman explained,

> When I first had sexual feelings for females, I had the sense I should give up my feelings for men. I think it would have been easier to give up men. (Weinberg, Williams, & Pryor, 1998, p. 170)

The third type of reaction was a feeling of loss of any sort of clear identity in the person's attempt to clarify who he or she really was.

> Being unaware of the term *bisexual,* some [respondents] tried to formulate and organize their sexuality through recourse to readily available labels of *heterosexual,* or *homosexual*—but these did not seem to fit. Thus, there was a period of time in which no sense of sexual identity jelled. It was an aspect of themselves that remained unclassifiable. (Weinberg, Williams, & Pryor, 1998, p. 171)

Figure 12-2

A Four-Stage Model of Bisexual Identity Formation

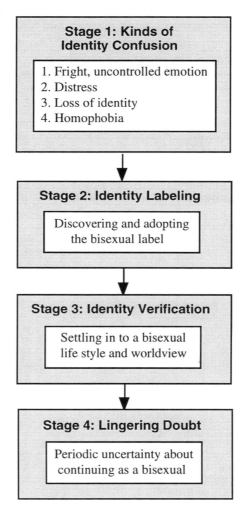

A fourth kind of response, expressed most often by males, was that of *homophobia*—fear and revulsion at the notion of being sexually stimulated by one's own sex.

Stage 2: Identity labeling. After spending time in the first stage of confusion—sometimes as long as several years—individuals found and adopted the label *bisexual* as a device for stipulating and accepting their sexual inclination. This stage could assume various forms. For some people, simply discovering the term *bisexual* was enough to settle their confusion. For others, the confusion was dispelled by their concluding that their pleasure from encounters with both sexes was so strong that there was no need to choose between males and females but simply to accept the bisexual condition as proper. For still others, the resolution of their perplexed state was fostered by the support of other bisexuals or of such organizations as the San Francisco-based Bisexual Center and San Francisco Sex Information.

Stage 3: Identity verification. The third stage of settling securely into a bisexual self-image usually came several years after first identifying oneself as bisexual. Fully achieving third-stage status typically resulted from the person's gaining increased self acceptance and being less concerned about others criticizing one's bisexual preference. When asked whether some day they might adopt an exclusive homosexual or heterosexual lifestyle, 82% of the study's participants said that might be possible, but most of them added that they would still maintain a bisexual self-image (Weinberg, Williams, & Pryor, 1998, p. 171).

Stage 4: Lingering identity doubt. When asked whether they ever felt confused about their sexual identity since the time they originally identified themselves as bisexual, 84% of the males and 59% of the females interviewed by the authors answered "Yes." In effect, for a substantial portion of the bisexuals studied, uncertainty about their sexual identity still cropped up from time to time. Thus, in the authors' progression of stages, the final stage for a noteworthy proportion of self-styled bisexuals did not represent a complete integration of their sexual identity into their overall lifestyle, though for others it apparently had become an established feature of their worldview.

REMAINING CHALLENGES

I believe the field of sexual orientations could profit from a more refined system for classifying people's sexual preferences and behavior. The predominant scheme used in the past has consisted of the three categories—heterosexual, homosexual, and bisexual. However, such a system is far too crude to reveal significant differences among people who are assigned to the same category. Furthermore, it is often difficult to determine the proper class in which to place individuals whose sexual interests and behavior do not fit neatly into one of the categories. For example, which is the proper designation for a 28-year-old woman if her present sexual behavior is entirely heterosexual but she previously had several homosexual experiences? Into which class should a man be placed if he finds himself sexually aroused by certain women as well as certain men, but he limits himself to engaging in sex acts only with women?

A more adequate sexual-orientation typology would be one that provides for the classification of individuals along a series of dimensions, thereby yielding a more individualized profile of each person's sexual attributes. One person's pattern could then be compared with another's to show in greater detail how the two are alike and different. Appropriate dimensions might include ones focusing on (a) sources of sexual arousal, (b) the variety of sexual partners, (c) types of sexual acts, and (d) a person's sexual identity. Information about each dimension could be reported in terms of frequencies within different periods of the lifespan. By compiling information by time periods (providing comparisons among adolescence, early adulthood, middle age, and old age), investigators could trace changes over time in the contents of each dimension and could estimate reasons for such changes.

Further items for theorists' future agenda derive from Dean Hamer's hunt for a gay gene. Guide questions for continuing the search include: Exactly which gene, or combination of genes, determines—at least partially—an individual's sexual preferences? Is sexual orientation the result of a single gene, or do different genes combine in patterns conducive to (a) a gay or lesbian orientation, (b) a heterosexual rather than bisexual orientation, and (c) other combinations of preference? How does a gay or lesbian genetic pattern interact with environmental influences to determine a person's sexual identity and sexual behavior? What is the relationship between a posited gay gene and a young boy's exhibiting childhood effeminacy, juvenile unmasculinity, and sexual fantasies? What is the relationship between a postulated lesbian gene and a girl's displaying childhood masculinity, juvenile unfemininity, and sexual fantasies?

In the realm of sexual identity, theorists face a variety of questions yet to be answered. To what extent are the stages of homosexual identity formation that Cass posited the same in all cultures? In other words, how are the stages of homosexual identity formation influenced by the general attitudes toward homosexuality held in different societies? Is the four-stage bisexual identity-formation process abstracted from interviews with San Francisco bisexuals an accurate reflection of bisexual identity formation in North American society in general? How well does the four-level Weinberg, Williams, and Pryor model represent bisexual-identity development in other cultures, such as those of Iran, the Netherlands, China, and Papua New Guinea? What is the relationship between individuals' hormone patterns at different periods of life and those individuals' sexual preferences and identity within each period?

Part III

Final Observations

The single chapter in Part III offers both a backward glance at the preceding 11 chapters and a forward glance toward what might be expected of human development in the near future.

13

Retrospect and Prospect

The purpose of this book has been to offer brief descriptions of a variety of human-development theories that appeared in print during the final two decades of the 20th century. The models chosen for inclusion have represented only a limited selection of the many dozens of proposals published over the 1980-2000 period. Furthermore, the examples that have been included are chiefly from North American authors, supplemented by a few proposals from Western Europe. Consequently, no claim can be made that the contents of Chapters 2 through 12 form a complete or evenly balanced depiction of theories created throughout the world in the closing years of the century. The most that can be claimed is that 40-or-so versions described throughout this book reflect some main lines of theorizing in recent times and illustrate some of the diverse ways scholars have portrayed development.

As the title *Retrospect and Prospect* implies, this chapter is presented in two parts. Part 1 looks back at the previous 12 chapters, summarizing their contents from a variety of perspectives. Part 2 looks forward, estimating what might be expected of theory construction in the early decades of the 21st century.

LOOKING BACK

The theories described in Chapters 2 through 12 can be grouped in various clusters, with the members of each cluster determined by the particular vantage point from which the theories are viewed. The following paragraphs demonstrate how such an approach equips us to summarize the book's recent theories from six perspectives that bear the labels (a) segments of the lifespan, (b) aspects of persons, (c) aspects of environments, (d) phylogeny and ontogeny, (e) description and prescription, and (f) combining multiple viewpoints.

Throughout the presentation, the identification of a theory is followed by a number in brackets that designates the chapter—2 through 12—in which that theory was described.

Segments of the Lifespan

One obvious way to group theories is by the principal age periods that each encompasses, as illustrated in the following list.

Preschool years, ages 2-5. Children's theories of mind [5].

Early childhood, ages 0-7. Psychoanalytic interpretation of homosexuality [12].

Childhood and adolescence, ages 0-20. Mind/brain development [3], revised Piagetian stages of intelligence [5], disadvantaged ethnic groups [10], and friendship functions of play [8].

Early and middle adulthood, ages 20-50. Matching personality types with occupations [4].

Entire lifespan, ages 0-80+. The effect of activity on spatial cognition [4], making sense of environments [4], the societal milieu's interaction with an individual's stages of development [4], socially constructed emotions [5], holistic versus analytical perception [6], racial identity [10], and feminist perspectives [11].

Aspects of Persons

Another method of grouping theories is by person characteristics that serve as the central focus of a model.

Cognition. Activity's influence on spatial cognition [4], making sense of environments [4], stages in the development of intelligence [5], children's theories of mind [5], and holistic versus analytical perception [6].

Brain/mind relations. Correlating mental experiences with brain functions [3].

Emotions. Genetically rooted emotions [2], socially constructed emotions [5], and events' influence on emotions [7].

Occupational satisfaction. Matching personality types and occupations [4].

Personality in general. The effect of societal events on a person's current stage of development [4] and life-span personality development [8].

Sexual preferences. Revised psychoanalysis [12], homosexual identity formation [12], and bisexual identity formation [12].

Aspects of Environments

The primary concern of some theories is with one or more parts of the environment that influence human development. The following are among the more common aspects of environments featured in development models.

Environmental opportunities. Valsiner's zones of free movement and of promoted action [6] and disadvantaged ethnic groups [10].

Events. Wicker's behavior settings [4] and ways of generating event knowledge [8].

Family. Family systems [7], absent fathers' financial support [9], and revised psychoanalysis [12].

Macro environments. Bronfenbrenner's macrosystem [4], Wicker's social-physical world [4], Elder's life-course model [4], and societal/cultural selectivity [7].

Peers, companions. Developing friendships [8], collaboration and expertise [7], and physical play [8].

Social class. Growing up poor [9] and disadvantaged ethnic groups [10].

Phylogeny and Ontogeny

Some theories are designed to explain the development of the human species (phylogeny), whereas others are concerned only with the development of the individual person (ontogeny).

Phylogenetic focus. The models that most obviously concern phylogeny are the ones in Chapter 2—Sulloway's birth-order proposal, Weisfeld's analysis of pride and shame, Bjorklund and Harnishfeger's interpretation of the roots of inhibition, and Lumsden and Wilson's gene-culture coevolution theory.

Ontogenetic focus. Nearly all of the theories in Chapters 3 through 12 have been designed to explain individuals' development during their lifetime.

Description and Prescription

Some theories are intended to describe how development *does occur*. Others prescribe how development *should occur* if an individual is to fulfill his or her optimal potential.

With rare exception, the models depicted in Part I are meant to be solely descriptive—purporting to show how development takes place, without suggesting that such development is good or bad, proper or improper. Examples of descriptive models include: dynamic systems [3], connectionism [3], how activity affects spatial knowledge [4], how people make sense of their environments [4], societal events linked to stages of individuals' development [4], a revision of Piaget's cognitive-development stages [5], Valsiner's zones of free movement, promoted action, and proximal development [6], and numerous others.

The theories offered in Part II are a mixture of descriptive and prescriptive models. The distinction between description and prescription is most obvious in the collection of feminist theories [11], each of which contrasts the way the development of males and females has typically taken place (description) and the way it should take place in order to produce the outcomes the theorists favor (prescription). In Part II, Hamer's search for a gay gene [12] is descriptive, as is Smeeding's plan for studying poverty children's development [9]. Helms's series of stages in racial-identity development for blacks and whites is offered as a descriptive model [10]. However, observers might claim that Helms's proposal is actually a prescriptive scheme reflecting her social values, since she arranged the stages in a sequence that progresses toward an ultimate status that she considered the most desirable for both the individual and the society.

Combining Multiple Viewpoints

An enriched understanding of an aspect of development is often achieved by inspecting that aspect from the perspectives of more than one theory.

For instance, a more complete understanding of the effect of family life on a child's development can result from analyzing child-family interactions from the combined viewpoints of Kreppner's family systems scheme [7], L'Abate's personality-development model [8], Sulloway's interpretation of the influence of birth order [2], and Garfinkel and McLanahan's financial-support proposal [9].

Likewise, understanding peer relationships is more complete when social interaction is viewed in terms of Granott's analysis of partners' cooperation and expertise [7], Lazarus's proposal about the emotional outcomes of social encounters [7], and Parker and Gottman's friendship functions of children's play [8].

In conclusion, as the above examples have suggested, the recent theories described in Chapters 2 through 12 can be organized into various patterns, with each pattern casting human development in a different light.

LOOKING AHEAD

On the assumption that recent trends are useful guides to what can be expected in the future, in this final section I speculate about the likely character of theorizing during the opening decades of the 21st century. This estimate of things to come views the future from four vantage points, those of (a) macrotheories and microtheories, (b) positivism and postmodernism, (c) technological progress, and (d) intercultural exchange versus culturalcentrism.

Macrotheories and Microtheories

The concepts *macrotheory* and *microtheory* (or *minitheory*) can be portrayed as the opposite ends of a scale on which different theories can be located to show what fraction of overall human development each is intended to explain. A theory at the extreme macro end of the scale would be one designed to encompass a person's entire development. A theory at the extreme micro end would focus on no more than a minuscule aspect of development.

As an example of a macrotheory, consider the general growth principles posited by Kurt Lewin (1936), who suggested that children's development is marked by a common set of changes in all of their physical and psychological attributes. In Lewin's view, with the passing years children's structures and functions become more differentiated and specialized, the boundaries separating one function from another grow more pronounced and rigid, the organization of functions increases in complexity, and behavior becomes more realistic. Macrotheories that are broadly inclusive, but not as extreme as Lewin's, include Skinner's behaviorism, Bandura's social-cognition model, and Piaget's conception of intellectual development. Each of those theories is expected to explain a wide range of beliefs and actions.

Two models near the micro extremity of the scale are (a) the Cohens' (Chapter 4) view of how people's activity within an environment contributes to their spatial cognition and (b) Wellman's (Chapter 5) proposal about the age at which young children display a theory of mind.

A growing number of critics have charged that the explanatory and predictive power of macrotheories is frequently weak and off-target when applied to specific people's lives. Such ostensible shortcomings of macrotheories have led to greater emphasis in recent times on the creation of microtheories that are obliged to explain only a restricted aspect of human thought, appearance, or behavior. The advantage of macromodels is that they embrace many facets of development, but their very abstractness causes them to neglect the multitude of variables that can differentiate one aspect from another. For instance, however true Lewin's principles of differentiation, complexity, and rigidity may be, they are of little or no help to someone who wishes to understand precisely the beliefs, emotions, values, or overt behavior of individual children as they extract knowledge from the events in which they participate, as they profit developmentally from physical play, as they fashion their conception of masculinity and femininity, or as they adjust to their family's configuration.

I expect that the recent trend toward emphasizing minitheories will continue in the future. Most theorizing will focus on rather specific facets of human development. At the same time, there will still be scholars seeking to identify components and interactions that can explain many kinds of thinking, emotion, and action.

Positivism and Postmodernism

I imagine that the coming years will find more theorists abandoning the strict variety of positivism that dominated developmental psychology in the early and middle 1900s. They will adopt, instead, some variety of postpositivism. In other words, more developmentalists will admit to the subjectivity underlying their work, while they will still subscribe to many of the tenets of traditional scientific inquiry, including such beliefs as: (a) there's a "real world" to be investigated beyond the theorist's minds, and that world is perceived somewhat the same (though not identically) by various observers, (b) it's worthwhile to create theories that postulate causal factors and their interactions and to test those theories empirically, (c) generalizations drawn from studying the development of one group of people can usefully be applied to understanding other groups that appear to be similar in terms of factors that are thought to affect development, and (d) the observations and measurements made by one investigator should be compared with those made by others to determine how closely they agree.

I think that versions of postmodernism will continue to influence the theorizing of a minor proportion of the scholars who study human development. But I presume that few researchers will adopt such radical postmodern beliefs as (a) denying the existence of a "real world" beyond one's own mind, (b) disputing the usefulness of drawing generalizations that can apply to more than one individual's development, and (c) assuming that anyone's explanation of development is as good as anyone else's.

Technological Progress

As mentioned in Chapter 1, the rapid advance of computer and television technologies during the final years of the 20th century enabled more people in more nations to obtain more information more promptly from more sites around the world than anyone had imagined a few years earlier. Thanks to the World Wide Web, an anthropology student at her home computer in Amsterdam can discover which books about theories of play are available in hundreds of libraries around the globe. A professor at his laptop computer in Yokohama can learn which journal articles in Australia, Britain, France, Sweden, and the United States concern moral development; and he can print out the contents of many of those articles without having to obtain the journals themselves. A social-psychology student in South Africa can send an e-mail inquiry to the German author of a monograph on determinism and receive an immediate reply. At her office computer in a Moscow university, a cognitive-development theorist can take part in a chat group that includes participants in Nashville, Buenos Aires, Edinburgh, Auckland, Singapore, Bombay, Dakar, and Helsinki. By means of satellite communication facilities, a documentary television program on brain physiology and connectionism, broadcast from London, can be seen simultaneously by viewers in universities throughout the world. Through an interactive, live-video television hookup, psychology students in their classroom in Beijing not only can view a demonstration of brain-scanning by a professor in his laboratory in Los Angeles, but they can also engage in a dialogue with the professor.

Such technological innovations were invented at a rapid rate in the latter years of the 20th century. During the 21st century more new technologies are bound to appear at an even faster pace, thereby speeding the work of theorists and strengthening the empirical foundations of their models. Not only will the task of locating information be performed far more efficiently than in the past, but the job of testing theories will become more efficient as researchers are able to create increasingly complex computer simulations of the interactions among the factors that are assumed to influence human development.

Intercultural Exchange Versus Culturalcentism

The expression *intercultural exchange* refers to the transfer of beliefs, technologies, or practices from one cultural group to another. In the case of human-development theories, it means that a cultural group adopts notions about development from another group. The term *culturalcentrism* refers to people resisting the intrusion of beliefs and practices from other cultures. Culturalcentrism is a way of protecting established traditions and of depending solely on members of one's own culture for innovative ideas about development. These two processes—intercultural exchange and culturalcentrism—can be seen as forces in opposition to each other.

Intercultural exchange

It's my impression that the greater the amount and strength of cultural exchange, (a) the more diverse the conceptions of development that will be found in a society and (b) the more likely theories indigenous to the society will be weakened, revised, and/or replaced. In other words, the more open a society is to information from other cultures, the greater the variety of conceptions of development that will appear, and the more likely that society's traditional views of development will be altered.

Furthermore, the strength of influence of one culture can be greater than the strength of others, because some cultures enjoy greater opportunities than others to wield influence over other people's beliefs. For instance, the extent to which a society will be open to cultural importations can depend on the society's sociopolitical conditions. One of the more obvious conditions has been that of colonialism, in which one society is obliged to tolerate the domination of another. Colonizers often impose their beliefs and institutions on the conquered peoples. Among the more influential institutions are schools. From the 17th century through the first half of the 20th century, European colonial powers propagated their beliefs about human development via religious and scientific instruction in widespread regions of Africa, Asia, the Americas, and the Pacific Islands. Furthermore, the sons and daughters of politically important native families of colonized territories have been enrolled in schools and universities in the colonizers' homelands, such as Belgium, Britain, France, Germany, Japan, the Netherlands, Portugal, Spain, and the United States. Then, influenced by their foreign education, the native youths have returned home to disseminate the culture they acquired abroad.

Some cultures also exert greater influence than others by dint of their greater command of mass-communication media—books, newspapers, and magazines and, more recently, radio, television, and the Internet.

Cultural traditions and the socioeconomic strength of different societies also affect their power to exert influence. For example, traditions of research and scholarship in European and North American nations, along with those countries' economic strength, has enabled them to support scholars whose energies are devoted to creating, publicizing, and evaluating theories of development. As a consequence, the largest body of theorizing and empirical research about such matters has come from Europe and North America, with somewhat lesser amounts from Southwest Oceania (Australia, New Zealand), Japan, China, India, and a limited number of South American nations. This dominance in academic productivity is reflected in the numbers of publications from different countries found in lists of scholarly works—books, journals, conference proceedings, and Internet sites. Those societies have exerted greater influence over other cultures' belief systems than have most African, Asian, Middle East, South American, Central American, and Pacific Island societies.

Despite the dominant influence of Europe and North America, cultural exchange has not been a one-way street. Beliefs from such Asian religions as Buddhism, Hinduism, and Taoism have been included in American and European humanistic models (Muzika, 1990; Tart, 1990). And a growing collection of theories deriving from African sources (such as Voodoo theory in Haiti) is receiving more attention from scholars (Verhoef & Michel, 1997).

In summary, because of the rapid increase in the media for effecting cultural exchange, and because of the more favorable conditions for theory creation and testing in certain countries (European and North American, as well as such nations as Australia, Israel, and Japan), theories of development from those societies are likely to dominate cultural exchanges during the early decades of the 21st century, at least in the academic community if not among the populace at large.

Culturalcentrism

The practice of adopting "scientific" theories of development has not gone unchallenged. In a variety of societies, efforts to resist imported theories and to revitalize indigenous traditions have gained momentum in recent years.

In North America, a resurgence of Native American conceptions of human development surfaced in the closing decades of the 20th century, energized by "the new pan-Indian movements [such as that of the Great Plains Indians], which so facilitate intertribal exchange, provide example and stimulus to tribal groups of distant areas" (Brown, 1989, p. 12). As a result, an increase in the return to traditional beliefs and a heightened participation in age-old rites has been observed among members of the expanding Native American population.

The final draft of Australia's national science curriculum, issued in 1993, obligated science teachers to produce "students with an understanding of and respect for our cultural heritage, including the particular cultural background of Aboriginal and ethnic groups, and for other cultures" (Maratos, 1995, p. 358). The concept *scientific,* as intended by positivists and postpositivists, was thus expanded to accord all interpretations of phenomena the same validity, thereby giving Aborigines' and other ethnic groups' traditional worldviews the same "truth value" in explaining human development. As John Maratos of Flinders University of South Australia explained, school officials generally questioned the soundness of the curriculum committee's recommendation, despite the strong endorsement of the committee's proposal by teachers' unions.

At present [1995], all Australian States and Territories have withheld endorsement of [the committee's] *Statement. . . .* Ministers of Education will only trial the [plan] in selected public schools for an agreed period of time. A crucial condition for the States and Territories agreeing to trials, was that schools should be free to modify and revise the *Statement*. (Maratos, 1995, p. 367)

Consequently, the curriculum plan launched a debate between Australia's cultural relativists and traditional scientists over the propriety of considering all interpretations of phenomena—including human development—of equal worth.

Throughout the 1990s, Christian fundamentalists in various regions of the United States sought to prevent the teaching of Darwinism in the schools or, at least, to require that a biblical version of human origins be given equal time to Darwinian theory in school curricula. In 1999, the issue of who determines science curricula in U.S. schools pitted creationists against evolutionists when the Kansas state board of education prohibited any mention of Darwin's theory of evolution on state achievement tests, thereby effectively eliminating the theory from the curriculum. Critics of the decision charged that the board's move was an attempt on the part of religious fundamentalists to circumvent court rulings which, over the past four years, had overturned legislation in New Hampshire, Ohio, Tennessee, Texas, and Washington that had been designed to reduce or eliminate the teaching of Darwinism in public schools (Marcus, 1999, p. 32).

What is sometimes called "the Islamic educational crisis" is the struggle of defenders of Islam to maintain a traditional Muslim worldview in educational institutions against the intrusion of Western scientific and philosophical beliefs, including the theories of human development popular in Western societies. According to Chandra Muzaffar, this Moslem resistance movement was founded on the conviction that

the Quran and Sunnah, [Islam's most fundamental holy books], lay out a complete way of life whose sanctity and purity should not be tarnished by new interpretations influenced by time and circumstances. . . . Indeed, the initiators and participants in the dominant trend of the movement have been vehement critics of Western civilization. They argue that the secularization of life, the subversion of eternal values, the pervasive growth of materialism are all indications that Western civilization, which has long been in a state of crisis, is on the verge of collapse. . . . The dethronement of the West as a civilization worthy of emulation and the importance of returning to the Quran and Sunnah are ideas which have gained tremendous popularity among Muslim youths, particularly in the last decade or so. (Muzaffar, 1986, pp. 10-11)

As a result, throughout the Muslim world, religious fundamentalists continued to mount a strong attack on theories of development whose content differed from the version embedded in Islamic doctrine. However, the efforts to reject ideologies from outside Islamic societies met with mixed results. Consider, for example, Aziz Talbani's assessment of the attempts of religious leaders (*ulama*) and the military to impose an exclusively Islamic curriculum in Pakistan's schools.

The impact of Islamization on the Pakistani educational system has been devastating. The emphasis on ideological education has intensified cultural and religious differences, resulting in communal conflicts and resentment of other cultures and other areas of knowledge. However, there is public resistance to this control. For example, in spite of warnings by Muslim clergy that Western model schools are anti-Islamic and promoters of immorality, people in Pakistan have flocked to such schools. . . . Such popular resistance continues to be an important part of public discourse in Pakistan. (Talbani, 1996, p. 82)

In summary, in many parts of the world, long-held customary interpretations of human development continue to vie with more recent theories for acceptance within both the academic community and the general populace. Such conflicts can be expected to continue in the future, with traditional belief systems probably losing adherents as a result of the spread of literacy and the inevitable increase in international communication and intercultural exchange during the coming years.

References

Adler, A. (1927a). *The practice and theory of individual psychology.* New York: Harcourt, Brace, and World.

Adler, A. (1927b). *Understanding human nature.* New York: Greenberg.

Adler, A. (1928). Characteristics of the first, second, and third child. *Children 3,* 14-52.

Adler, A. (1958). *What life should mean to you.* New York: G. P. Putnam's Sons.

Aldous, J. (1978). *Family careers.* New York: Wiley.

Altman, I, & Rogoff, B. (1987). World views in psychology: Trait, interactional, organismic, and transactional perspectives. In D. Stokols & I. Altman (Eds.), *Handbook of environmental psychology* (Vol. 1, pp. 7-40). New York: Wiley.

Ambert, A. M. (1995). Toward a theory of peer abuse. *Sociological Studies of Children, 7,* 177-205.

Angell, J. R. (1903). *The relations of structural and functional psychology to philosophy.* Chicago: University of Chicago Press.

Angell, J. R. (1904). *Psychology: An introductory study of the structure and function of human consciousness.* New York: Holt.

Arbib, M. A., Érdi, P., & Szentágothai, J. (1998). *Neural organization: Structure, function, and dynamics.* Cambridge, MA: MIT Press.

Ashcraft, M. H. (1994). *Human memory and cognition* (2nd ed.). New York: HarperCollins.

Baer, M. F., Connors, B. W., & Paradiso, M. A. (1996). *Neuroscience: Exploring the brain.* Baltimore: Williams & Wilkens.

Baev, K. V. (1998). *Biological neural networks: Hierarchical concept of brain function.* Boston: Birkhäuser.

Baldwin, J. M. (1894). *Mental development in the child and race.* New York: Macmillan.

Baldwin, J. M. (1897). *Social and ethical interpretations in mental development.* New York: Macmillan.

Bandura, A. (1969). *Principles of behavior modification.* New York: Holt, Rinehart & Winston.

Bandura, A. (1986). *Social foundations of thought and action, a social cognitive theory.* Englewood Cliffs, NJ: Prentice Hall.

Barker, R. (1968). *Ecological psychology.* Stanford, CA: Stanford University Press.

Barker, R. (1978). *Habitats, environments, and human behavior.* San Francisco: Jossey-Bass.

Baron-Cohen, S. (1995). *Mindblindness.* Cambridge, MA: MIT Press.

Baudrillard, J. (1996). *Cool memories II: 1987-1990.* Durham, NC: Duke University Press.

Baudrillard, J. (1998). *The consumer society: Myths and structures.* Thousand Oaks, CA: Sage.

Beltrami, E. (1987). *Mathematics for dynamical modeling.* Boston: Academic.

Benvenuto, B., & Kennedy, R. (1986). *The works of Jacques Lacan.* New York: St. Martin's.

Berlin, B., & Kay, P. (1969). *Basic color terms: Their universality and evolution.* Berkeley: University of California Press.

Bjorklund, D. F., & Harnishfeger, K. K. (1995). The evolution of inhibition mechanisms and their role in human cognition and behavior. In F. Dempster & C. J. Brainard, *Interference and inhibition in cognition* (pp. 141-173). San Diego, CA: Academic Press.

Bowlby, J. (1969). *Attachment and loss. Vol. 1. Attachment.* London: Hogarth.

Bricmont, J. (1998). Exposing the emperor's new clothes: Why we won't leave postmodernism alone. *Free Inquiry, 18* (4), 23-26.

Bronfenbrenner, U. (1979). *The ecology of human development.* Cambridge, MA: Harvard University Press.

Bronfenbrenner, U. (1993). The ecology of cognitive development: Research models and fugitive findings. In R. H. Wozniak & K. W. Fisher (Eds.), *Development in context: Activity and thinking in specific environments* (pp. 3-24). Hillsdale, NJ: Erlbaum.

Broughton, J. M. (Ed.). (1987). *Critical theories of psychological development.* New York: Plenum.

Brown, J. E. (1989). *The spiritual legacy of the American Indian.* New York: Crossroad.

Bunch, C. (1993). Prospects for global feminism. In A. M. Jagger & P. S. Rothenberg (Eds.), *Feminist frameworks* (3rd ed.). New York: McGraw-Hill.

Bütz, M. R. (1997). *Chaos and complexity.* Washington, DC: Taylor & Francis.

Campbell, D. T. (1996). Can we overcome worldview incommensurability? In R. Jessor, A. Colby, & R. A. Shweder (Eds.), *Ethnography and human development* (pp. 153-171). Chicago: University of Chicago Press.

Case, R. (1985). *Intellectual development: Birth to adulthood.* Orlando, FL: Academic.

Case, R. (1992a). *The mind's staircase.* Hillsdale, NJ: Erlbaum.

Case, R. (1992b). Neo-Piagetian theories of intellectual development. In H. Beilin & P. Pufall (Eds.), *Piaget's theory: Prospects and possibilities* (pp. 61-104). Hillsdale, NJ: Erlbaum.

Case, R. (1998). The development of conceptual systems. In W. Damon (General Ed.) & R. M. Lerner (Vol. Ed.), *Handbook of child development: Perception, cognition, and language* (5th ed., pp. 745-800). New York: Wiley.

Case, R., & Okamoto, Y. (1996). The role of central conceptual structures in the development of children's thought. *Monographs of the Society for the Study of Child Development, 61* (1-2). Chicago: Society for the Study of Child Development.

Cass, V. (1979). Homosexual identity formation: A theoretical model. *Journal of Homosexuality, 4,* 219-235.

Cass, V. (1984). Homosexual identity formation: Testing a theoretical model. *Journal of Sexual Research, 20,* 143-167.

Chase-Lansdale, P. L., & Brooks-Gunn, J. (1995). Introduction. In P. L. Chase-Lansdale & J. Brooks-Gunn, *Escape from poverty: What makes a difference for children* (pp. 1-8). New York: Cambridge University Press.

Cherry, M. (1998). Truth and consequences: Introduction. *Free Inquiry, 18* (4), 20.

Chodorow, N. (1978). *The reproduction of mothering: Psychoanalysis and the sociology of gender.* Berkeley: University of California Press.

Clark, A. (1993). Minimal rationalization. *Mind, 102* (408), 587-610.

Clark, T. W. (1994). Reply to Haughness. *The Humanist, 53* (4), 22.

Cohen, R. (1985). What's so special about spatial cognition? In R. Cohen (Ed.). *The development of spatial cognition* (pp. 1-12). Hillsdale, NJ: Erlbaum.

Cohen, S. L., & Cohen, R. (1985). The role of activity in spatial cognition. In R. Cohen, (Ed.). *The development of spatial cognition* (pp. 199-223). Hillsdale, NJ: Erlbaum.

Coleman, E. (1982). Developmental stages of the coming out process. In J. C. Gonsiorek (Ed.), *Homosexuality and psychotherapy* (pp. 31-43). New York: Haworth.

Cross, W. E., Jr. (1971). The Negro-to-Black conversion experience: Toward a psychology of Black liberation. *Black World, 20* (9), 13-27.

Cross, W. E., Jr. (1978). Models of psychological nigrescence: A literature review. *Journal of Black Psychology, 5* (1), 13-31.

Dahlstrom, W. G., Welsh, G. S., & Dahlstrom, L. E. (1972). *An MMPI handbook.* Minneapolis: University of Minnesota Press.

Darwin, C. (1859). *On the origin of species by means of natural selection.* London: John Murray.

Davidov, V. V. (1985). Soviet theories of human development. In T. Husén & T. N. Postlethwaite (Eds.), *International encyclopedia of education* (Vol. 8, pp. 4721-4727). Oxford: Pergamon.

Dennis, R. M. (1981). Socialization and racism: The White experience. In. B. P. Bowser & R. G. Hung (Eds.), *Impacts of racism on White Americans* (pp. 71-85). Beverly Hills, CA: Sage.

Denzin, N. K. (1997). *Interpretive ethnography.* Thousand Oaks, CA: Sage.

Derrida, J. (1976). *Of grammatology* (G. C. Spivak, Trans.). Baltimore,: Johns Hopkins University Press.

Dewey, J. (1891). *Psychology* (3rd ed.). New York: Harper.

Dewey, J., & Bentley, A. F. (1949). *Knowing and the known.* Boston: Beacon.

DeWinne, R. F., Overton, T. D., & Schneider, L. J. (1978). Types produce types: Especially fathers. *Journal of Vocational Behavior, 12*, 140-144.

Dewsbury, D. A. (1991). Psychobiology. *American Psychologist, 46* (3), 198-205.

Dinnerstein, D. (1977). *The mermaid and the minotaur: Sexual arrangements and human malaise.* New York: Harper Colophon Books.

Duchen, C. (1986). *Feminism in France: From May '68 to Mitterrand.* London: Routledge & Kegan Paul.

Dupont, H. (1994). *Emotional development, theory and applications.* Westport, CT: Praeger.

Duvall, E. (1977). *Marriage and family development.* New York: Lippincott.

Ehrenreich, B. (1999). Farewell to a fad (postmodernism). *Progressive, 63* (3), 17.

Eiser, J. R. (1994). *Attitudes, chaos, and the connectionist mind.* Cambridge, MA: Blackwell.

Elder, G. H., Jr. (1996). Human lives in changing societies: Life course and developmental insights. In R. B. Cairns, G. H. Elder, Jr., & E J. Costello (Eds.), *Developmental science* (pp, 31-62). Cambridge, UK: Cambridge University Press.

Elder, G. H., Jr., Modell, J., & Parke, R. D. (1993). Studying children in a changing world. In G. H. Elder, Jr., J. Modell, & R. D. Parke (Eds.), *Children in time and place* (pp. 3-21). Cambridge, UK: Cambridge University Press.

Elshtain, J. B. (1981). *Public man, private woman.* Princeton, NJ: Princeton University Press.

Erikson, E. H. (1959). Identity and the life cycle [Monograph]. *Psychological Issues, 1*(1). New York: International Universities Press.

Erikson, E. H. (1963). *Childhood and society* (2nd ed.). New York: W. W. Norton.

Erikson, E. H. (1964). *Insight and responsibility.* New York: W. W. Norton.

Erikson, E. H. (1968). *Identity, youth, and crisis.* New York: W. W. Norton.

Ernst, C., & Angst, J. (1983). *Birth order: Its influence on personality.* New York: Springer-Verlag.

Erulkar, D. E. (1994). Form and function of nervous systems. In *Encyclopaedia Britannica* (Vol. 24, pp. 785-798). Chicago: Encyclopaedia Britannica.

Falco, K. L. (1991). *Psychotherapy with lesbian clients.* New York: Brunner/Mazel.

Feldman, C. F. (1992). The new theory of theory of mind. *Human Development, 35,* 107-117.

Ferry, L. (1992). *The new ecological order* (C. Volk, trans.). Chicago: University of Chicago Press.

Flavell, J. H. (1971). Stage-related properties of cognitive development. *Cognitive Psychology, 2,* 421-453.

Flavell, J. H. (1988). The development of children's knowledge about the mind: From cognitive connections to mental representations. In J. Astington, P. Harris, & D. Olson (Eds.), *Developing theories of mind* (pp. 244-267). New York: Cambridge University Press.

Fodor, J. A. (1987). *Psychosemantics: The problem of meaning in the philosophy of mind.* Cambridge, MA: MIT Press.

Fogel, A. (1993). *Developing through relationships.* Chicago: University of Chicago Press.

Ford, D. H., & Lerner, R. M. (1992). *Developmental systems theory.* Newbury Park, CA: Sage.

Forguson, L., & Gopnik, A. (1988). The ontogeny of commonsense. In J. Astington, P. Harris, & D. Olson (Eds.), *Developing theories of mind* (pp. 226-243). New York: Cambridge University Press.

Foucault, M. (1982). *The archeology of knowledge: The discourse on language.* New York: Pantheon.

Foucault, M. (1988). *The history of sexuality.* New York: Vintage.

Foucault, M. (1998). *Aesthetics, method, and epistemology.* New York: New Press.

Freud, S. (1957). Introductory lectures on psychoanalysis, part III. In J. Strachey (Ed.), *The standard edition of the complete psychological works of Sigmund Freud* (Vol. 16, pp. 243-482). London: Hogarth. (Original work published 1917)

Freud, S. (1973). *An outline of psychoanalysis.* London: Hogarth. (Original work published 1938.)

Friedman, R. C. (1988). *Male homosexuality.* New Haven, CT: Yale University Press.

Fromm, E. (1994). *The Erich Fromm reader.* Atlantic Highlands, NJ: Humanities Press.

Garcia Coll, C., Lamberty, G., Jenkins, R., McAdoo, H. P., Crnic, K., Wasik, B. H., & Garcia, H. V. (1996). An integrative model for the study of developmental competencies in minority children. *Child Development, 67,* 1891-1914.

Gardner, H. (1983). *Frames of mind.* New York: Basic Books.

Garfinkel, I., & McLanahan, S. (1995). The effects of child support reform on child well-being. In P. L. Chase-Lansdale & J. Brooks-Gunn, *Escape from poverty: What makes a difference for children* (pp. 211-238). New York: Cambridge University Press.

Gerber, E. R. (1985). Rage and obligation: Samoan emotion in conflict. In G. M. White & J. Kirkpatrick (Eds.), *Person, self, and experience: Exploring Pacific ethnopsychologies* (pp. 121-167). Berkeley: University of California Press.

Gilligan, C. (1982). *In a different voice.* Cambridge, MA: Harvard University Press.

Gilligan, C., Ward, J. V., & Taylor, J. M. (Eds.). (1988). *Mapping the moral domain.* Cambridge, MA: Harvard University Press.

Giroux, H. A. (1992). *Border crossings: Cultural workers and the politics of education.* New York: Routledge.

Grandy, T. G., & Stahmann, R. F. (1974). Types produce types: An examination of personality development using Holland's theory. *Journal of Vocational Behavior, 5,* 231-239.

Granott, N. (1993). Patterns of interaction in the co-construction of knowledge: Separate minds, joint effort, and weird creatures. In R. H. Wozniak & K. W. Fischer (Eds.), *Development in context: Acting and thinking in specific environments* (pp. 183-207). Hillsdale, NJ: Erlbaum.

Grotevant, H. D., Scarr, S., & Weinberg, R. A. (1977). Patterns of interest similarity in adoptive and biological families. *Journal of Personality and Social Psychology, 35,* 667-676.

Group for a Radical Human Science. (1981). An oral history of the group. In *PsychCritique Newsletter, 1,* 2-3.

Grusec, J. E. (1994). Social learning theory and developmental psychology: The legacies of Robert R. Sears and Albert Bandura. In R. D. Parke, P. A. Ornstein, J. J. Rieser, & C. Zahn-Waxler (Eds.), *A century of developmental psychology* (pp. 473-497). Washington, DC: American Psychological Association.

Gulerce, A. (1997). Change in the process of change: Coping with indeterminism. In A. Fogel, M. C. D. P. Lyra, & J. Valsiner (Eds.), *Dynamics and indeterminism in developmental and social processes* (pp. 39-63). Mahwah, NJ: Erlbaum.

Hales, D., & Hales, R. E. (1999, November 21). The brain's power to heal. *Parade Magazine,* 10-12.

Hamer, D., & Copeland, P. (1994). *The science of desire: The search for the gay gene and the biology of behavior.* New York: Simon & Schuster.

Hammersley, M. (1992). *What's wrong with ethnography?* London: Routledge.

Havighurst, R. J. (1953). *Human development and education.* New York: Longmans, Green.

Heckhausen, J., & Schulz, R. (1999). Selectivity in life-span development. In J. Brandstädter & R. M. Lerner (Eds.), *Action and self-development* (pp. 67-103). Thousand Oaks, CA: Sage.

Heider, F. (1958). *The psychology of interpersonal relations.* New York: Wiley.

Helms, J. E. (1984). Toward a theoretical explanation of the effects of race on counseling: A black and white model. *The Counseling Psychologist, 12,* 153-165.

Helms, J. E. (1990). *Black and white racial identity: Theory, research, and practice.* Westport, CT: Greenwood.

Helms, J. E. (1995). An update on Helms's white and people of color racial identity modes. In J. Ponterotto, J. M. Casas, L. A. Suzuki, & C. M. Alexander (Eds.), *Handbook of multicultural counseling* (pp. 181-198). Thousand Oaks, CA: Sage.

Hilgard, E. R., & Bower, G. H. (1975). *Theories of learning* (4th ed.). Englewood Cliffs, NJ: Prentice Hall.

Hofstede, G. (1980). *Culture's consequences: International differences in work-related values.* Beverly Hills, CA: Sage.

Holland, J. L. (1961). Creative and academic performance among talented adolescents. *Journal of Educational Psychology, 52,* 126-147.

Holland, J. L. (1962). Some explorations of a theory of vocational choice: I. One and two year longitudinal studies. *Psychological Monographs, 76* (26), 1-49.

Holland, J. L. (1985a). *Making vocational choices: A theory of vocational personalities and work environments* (2nd ed.). Englewood Cliffs, NJ: Prentice Hall.

Holland, J. L. (1985b). *Manual for the Vocational Preferences Inventory.* Odessa, FL: Psychological Assessment Resources.

Holland, J. L., & Rayman, J. R. (1986). The self-directed search. In W. B. Walsh & S. H. Osipow (Eds.), *Advances in vocational psychology: I, The assessment of interests* (pp. 55-82). Hillsdale, NJ: Erlbaum.

Holt, S. A., Fogel, A., & Wood, R. M. (1998). Innovation in social games. In M. C. P. Lyra & J. Valsiner (Eds.), *Construction of psychological processes in interpersonal communication* (pp. 35-51). Stamford, CT: Ablex.

Horgan, T., & Tienson, J. (1996). *Connectionism and the philosophy of psychology.* Cambridge, MA: MIT Press.

Horney, K. (1937). *The collected works of Karen Horney.* New York: Norton.

James, W. (1890). *The principles of psychology.* New York: Holt.

Jamieson, K. H. (1994). *Beyond the double bind.* New York: Oxford University Press.

Jessor, R. (1996). Ethnographic methods in contemporary perspective. In R. Jessor, A. Colby, & R. A. Shweder (Eds.), *Ethnography and human development* (pp. 3-14). Chicago: University of Chicago Press.

Jung, C. G. (1959). *The basic writings of C. G. Jung.* New York: Modern Library.

Kelso, J. A. S. (1995). *Dynamic patterns: The self-organization of brain and behavior.* Cambridge, MA: MIT Press.

Kemler, D. G. (1983). Holistic and analytic modes in perceptual and cognitive development. In T. J. Tighe & B. F. Shepp (Eds.), *Perception, cognition, and development* (pp. 77-102). Hillsdale, NJ: Erlbaum.

Kendler, H. H. (1987). *Historical foundations of modern psychology.* Philadelphia: Temple University Press.

Koffka, K. (1935). *Principles of Gestalt psychology.* New York: Harcourt Brace.

Köhler, W. (1929). *Gestalt psychology.* New York: Liveright.

Kolb, B., & Whishaw, I. Q. (1990). *Fundamentals of human neuropsychology* (3rd ed.). New York: Freeman.

Kreppner, K. (1989). Linking infant development-in-context research to the investigation of life-span family development. In K. Kreppner & R. M. Lerner (Eds.), *Family systems and life-span development* (pp. 33-64). Hillsdale, NJ: Erlbaum.

Kristeva, J. (1986). *The Kristeva reader.* New York: Columbia University Press.

Kuhn, T. S. (1970). *The structure of scientific revolutions* (2nd ed.). Chicago: University of Chicago Press.

L'Abate, L. (1994). *A theory of personality development.* New York: Wiley.

Lazarus, R. S. (1991). *Emotion and adaptation.* New York: Oxford University Press.

Leahey, T. H. (1987). *A history of psychology.* Englewood Cliffs, NJ: Prentice Hall.

Lerner, D. (1965). Introduction. In D. Lerner (Ed.), *Cause and effect.* New York: Free Press.

Levy, R. I. (1996). Essential contrasts: Differences in parental ideas about learners and teaching in Tahiti and Nepal. In S. Harkness & C. M. Super (Eds.), *Parents' cultural belief systems* (pp. 123-142). New York: Guilford.

Lewin, K. (1936). *Principles of topological psychology.* New York: McGraw-Hill.

Lewis, L. A. (1984, Sept-Oct). The coming out process for lesbians: Integrating a stable identity. *Social Work,* 464-469.

Lloyd, D. (1994). Connectionist hysteria: Reducing a Freudian case study. *Philosophy, Psychiatry, and Psychology, 1* (2), 69-88.

Lumsden, C. J., & Wilson, E. O. (1981). *Genes, mind, and culture—The coevolutionary process.* Cambridge, MA: Harvard University Press.

Maimonides, M. (1967). *Sefer Ha-Mitzvoth of Maimonides* (Vols. 1 & 2). London: Soncino Press.

Main, M., Kaplan, N., & Cassidy, J. (1985). Security in infancy, childhood, and adulthood: A move to the level of representation. In I. Bretherton & E. Waters (Eds.), *Growing points of attachment theory and research. Monographs of the Society for Research in Child Development, 50*: 66-194.

Mandler, J. M. (1979). Categorical and schematic organization in memory. In C. R. Puff (Ed.), *Memory organization and structure* (pp. 259-299). New York: Academic.

Maratos, J. (1995). Ideology in science education: The Australian example. *International Review of Education, 41*, (5), 357-369.

Marcus, D. L. (1999, August 30). Darwin gets thrown out of school. *U.S. News & World Report.*

Marek, J. C. (1988). A Buddhist theory of human development. In R. M. Thomas (Ed.), *Oriental theories of human development* (pp. 75-115). New York: Peter Lang.

Marx, K. (1977a). *Kapital: A critique of political economy* (English translation of *Das kapital*). New York: Vintage Books.

Marx, K. (1977b). Preface to "A critique of political economy." In D. McLellan (Ed.), *Karl Marx, selected writings* (pp. 388-392). Oxford: Oxford University Press. (Original work published 1859)

McClelland, J. L., & Rumelhart, D. E. (1986). *Parallel distributed processing: Explorations in the microstructure of cognition: Vol. 2. Psychological and biological models.* Cambridge, MA: Bradford.

McLoyd, V. C., & Wilson, L. (1991). The strain of living poor: Parenting, social support, and child mental health. In A. C. Huston (Ed.), *Children in poverty: Child development and public policy* (pp. 105-135). New York: Cambridge University Press.

Menninger, K. A. (1960). *Love against hate.* New York: Harcourt Brace.

Miller, P. (1963). *The New England mind: The seventeenth century.* Cambridge, MA: Harvard University Press.

Moore, J. (1995). Some historical and conceptual relations among logical positivism, behaviorism, and cognitive psychology. In J. T. Todd & E. K. Morris (Eds.), *Modern perspectives on B. F. Skinner and contemporary behaviorism* (pp. 51-74). Westport, CT: Greenwood.

Morgan, R. (Ed.). (1970). *Sisterhood is powerful.* New York: Random House.

Murray. H. A. (1938). *Explorations in personality.* New York: Oxford University Press.

Muzaffar, C. (1986). Islamic resurgence: A global view. In T. Abdullah & S. Siddique (Eds.), *Islam and society in Southeast Asia* (pp. 10-15). Singapore: Institute of Southeast Asian Studies.

Muzika, E. G. (1990). Evolution, emptiness, and the fantasy self. *Journal of Humanistic Psychology, 30* (2), 89-108.

Nagel, E. (1965). Types of causal explanation in science. In D. Lerner (Ed.), *Cause and effect* (pp. 11-32). New York: Free Press.

Nelson, K. (1986a). Event knowledge and cognitive development. In K. Nelson (Ed.), *Event knowledge: Structure and function in development* (pp. 1-19, 231-247). Hillsdale, NJ: Erlbaum.

Nelson, K. (Ed.). (1986b). *Event knowledge: Structure and function in development.* Hillsdale, NJ: Erlbaum.

Noback, C. R. (1994). Anatomy of the nervous system. In *Encyclopaedia Britannica* (Vol. 24, pp. 803-804). Chicago, IL: Encyclopaedia Britannica.

Parke, R. D., Cassidy, J., Burks, A., Carson, J., & Boyum, L. (1992). Familial contributions to peer competence among young children: The role of interactive and affective processes. In R. D. Parke & G. W. Ladd (Eds.), *Family-peer relationships* (pp. 107-134). Hillsdale, NJ: Erlbaum.

Parker, J. G., & Gottman, J. M. (1989). Social and emotional development in a relational context. In T. H. Berndt & G. W. Ladd (Eds.), *Peer relationships in child development* (pp. 95-131). New York: Wiley.

Pellegrini, A. D., & Smith, P. K. (1998). Physical activity play: The nature and function of a neglected aspect of play. *Child Development, 69* (3), 577-598.

Pepper, S. C. (1942). *World hypotheses: A study in evidence.* Berkeley: University of California Press.

Pepper, S. C. (1967). *Concept and quality: A world hypothesis.* La Salle, IL: Open Court.

Perner, J. (1988). Developing semantics for theories of mind: From propositional attitudes to mental representations. In J. Astington, P. Harris, & D. Olson (Eds.), *Developing theories of mind* (pp. 141-172). New York: Cambridge University Press.

Perner, J. (1991). *Understanding the representational mind.* Cambridge, MA: MIT Press.

Piaget, J. (1929). *The child's conception of the world.* London: Routledge & Kegan Paul.

Piaget, J. (1967). *Six psychological studies.* New York: Random House.

Piaget, J. (1973). *The child and reality.* New York: Viking.

Piaget, J. (1981). *Intelligence and affectivity: Their relationship during child development.* Palo Alto, CA: Annual Reviews.

Piaget, J., & Inhelder, B. (1969). *The psychology of the child.* New York: Basic Books.

Ponse, B. (1978). *Identities in the lesbian world: The social construction of self.* Westport, CT: Greenwood.

Premack, D., & Woodruff, G. (1978). Does the chimpanzee have a theory of mind? *Behavioral and Brain Sciences, 1* (4), 515-526.

Rabinow, P. (Ed.). (1984). *The Foucault reader.* New York: Pantheon.

Reuther, R. R. (1975). *New woman/new earth: Sexist ideologies and human liberation.* New York: Seabury.

Roberton, M. A. (1993). New ways to think about old questions. In L. B. Smith & E. Thelen (Eds.), *A dynamic systems approach to development* (pp. 95-117). Cambridge, MA: MIT Press.

Robertson, S. S., Cohen, A. H., & Mayer-Kress, G. (1993). Behavioral chaos: Beyond the metaphor. In L. B. Smith & E. Thelen (Eds.), *A dynamic systems approach to development* (pp. 119-150). Cambridge, MA: MIT Press.

Rodgers, R. (1973). *Family interaction and transaction: The developmental approach.* Englewood Cliffs, NJ: Prentice Hall.

Rumelhart, D. E., & McClelland, J. L. (1986). *Parallel distributed processing: Explorations in the microstructure of cognition: Vol. 1. Foundations.* Cambridge, MA: Bradford.

Salleh, A. K. (1984). Deeper than deep ecology: The ecofeminist connection. *Environmental Ethics, 6* (1), 339.

Saussure, F. de. (1966). *Course in general linguistics.* New York: McGraw-Hill.

Schlesinger, A. M., Jr. (1991). *The disuniting of America.* Knoxville, TN: Whittle.

Shweder, R. A. (1996). True ethnography: The lore, the law, and the lure. In R. Jessor, A. Colby, & R. A. Shweder (Eds.), *Ethnography and human development* (pp. 15-52). Chicago: University of Chicago Press.

Siegler, R. S. (1996). *Emerging minds: The process of change in children's thinking.* New York: Oxford University Press.

Sigel, I., Stinson, E. T., & Flaugher, J. (1991). Socialization of representational competence in the family: The distancing paradigm. In L. Okagaki & R. J. Sternberg (Eds.), *Directors of development: Influences on the development of children's thinking* (pp. 121-144). Hillsdale, NJ: Erlbaum.

Skinner, B. F. (1974). *About behaviorism.* New York: Knopf.

Smeeding, T. M. (1995). An interdisciplinary model and data requirements for studying poor children. In P. L. Chase-Lansdale & J. Brooks-Gunn, *Escape from poverty: What makes a difference for children* (pp. 291-298). New York: Cambridge University Press.

Smith, L. B., & Thelen, E. (Eds.). (1993). *A dynamic systems approach to development.* Cambridge, MA: MIT Press.

Spelman, E. V. (1988*). Inessential woman: Problems of exclusion in feminist thought.* Boston: Beacon.

Sroufe, L. A., & Fleeson, J. (1986). Attachment and the construction of relationships. In W. Harup & Z. Rubin (Eds.), *Relationships and development* (pp. 51-71). Hillsdale, NJ: Erlbaum.

Stich, S. P. (1994). The virtues, challenges, and implications of connectionism. *British Journal of the Philosophy of Science, 45* (4), 1047-1058.

Stokols, D., & Altman, I. (1987). Introduction. In D. Stokols & I. Altman (Eds.), *Handbook of environmental psychology* (Vol. 1, pp. 1-6). New York: Wiley.

Stolz, L. M. (1968). *Father relations of war-born children.* Westport, CT: Greenwood.

Sullivan, H. S. (1965). *The collected works of Harry Stack Sullivan.* New York: Norton.

Sulloway, F. J. (1996). *Born to rebel: Birth order, family dynamics, and creative lives.* New York: Pantheon.

Talbani, A. (1996). Pedagogy, power, and discourse: Transformation of Islamic education. *Comparative Education Review, 40* (1), 66-82.

Tarrow, N. B. (Ed.). (1985). *Human rights and education.* Oxford: Pergamon.

Tart, C. T. (1990). Extending mindfulness to everyday life. *Journal of Humanistic Psychology, 30* (1), 81-106.

Thelen, E., & Smith, L. B. (1994). *A dynamic systems approach to the development of cognition and action.* Cambridge, MA: MIT Press.

Thomas, R. M. (1975). *Social strata in Indonesia: A study of West Java villagers.* Jakarta: Antarkarya.

Thomas, R. M. (1979). *Comparing theories of child development* (1st ed.). Belmont, CA: Wadsworth.

Thomas, R. M. (1988). A Hindu theory of human development. In R. M. Thomas (Ed.), *Oriental theories of human development* (pp. 29-72). New York: Peter Lang.

Thomas, R. M. (1997). *Theories of moral development: Secular and religious.* Westport, CT: Greenwood.

Thomas, R. M. (1998). Education. In D. R. Calhoun, (Ed.). *Britannica book of the year* (pp. 201-204). Chicago: Encyclopaedia Britannica.

Thomas, R. M. (2000). *Comparing theories of child development* (5th ed.). Belmont, CA: Wadsworth.

Thompson, C. E., & Carter, R. T. (1997). *Racial identity theory.* Mahwah, NJ: Erlbaum.

Tong, R. P. (1998). *Feminist thought* (2nd ed.). Boulder, CO: Westview.

Toulmin, S. E. (1994). Philosophy of science. In *Encyclopaedia Britannica* (Vol. 25, pp. 652-669). Chicago: Encyclopaedia Britannica.

Troiden, R. R. (1988). *Gay and lesbian identity: A sociological analysis.* New York: General Hall.

Tryon, C., & Lilienthal, J. (1950). Developmental tasks: I. The concept and its importance. In *Fostering mental health in our schools* (pp. 77-89). Washington, DC: Association for Supervision and Curriculum Development.

Valsiner, J. (1987, 1997). *Culture and the development of children's action.* New York: Wiley.

Valsiner, J. (1988). *Developmental psychology in the Soviet Union.* Bloomington: Indiana University Press.

Vance, C. S. (1984). Pleasure and danger: Toward a politics of sexuality. In C. S. Vance (Ed.), *Pleasure and danger: Exploring female sexuality* (pp. 1-27). Boston: Routledge & Kegan Paul.

van Geert, P. (1993). A dynamic systems model of cognitive growth: Competition and support under limited resource conditions. In L. B. Smith & E. Thelen (Eds.), *A dynamic systems approach to development* (pp. 265-331). Cambridge, MA: MIT Press.

van Geert, P. (1997). Que serà, serà: Determinism and nonlinear dynamic model building in development. In A. Fogel, M. C. D. P. Lyra, & J. Valsiner (Eds.), *Dynamics and indeterminism in developmental and social processes* (pp. 34-38). Mahwah, NJ: Erlbaum.

van Gelder, T. (1995). Modeling, connectionist and otherwise. In L. D. Niklasson & M. B. Bode (Eds.), *Current trends in connectionism: Proceedings of the Swedish conference on connectionism* (pp. 217-235). Hillsdale, NJ: Erlbaum.

Verhoef, H., & Michel, C. (1997). Studying morality within the African context: A model of moral analysis and construction. *Journal of Moral Education, 26* (4), 389-407.

Vygotsky, L. S. (1962). *Thought and language.* Cambridge, MA: MIT Press.

Vygotsky, L. S. (1978). The development of higher mental processes. In M. Cole, V. John-Steiner, S. Scribner, & E. Souberman (Eds.), *Mind in society*. Cambridge, MA: Harvard University Press.

Walsh, W. B., Craik, K. H., & Price, R. H. (1992). Person-environment psychology: A summary and commentary. In W. B. Walsh, K. H. Craik, & R. H. Price, (Eds.). *Person-environment psychology: Models and perspectives* (pp. 243-269). Hillsdale, NJ: Erlbaum.

Walsh, W. B., & Holland, J. L. (1992). A theory of personality types and work environments. In W. B. Walsh, K. H. Craik, & R. H. Price, (Eds.). *Person-environment psychology: Models and perspectives* (pp. 35-69). Hillsdale, NJ: Erlbaum.

Warren, K. J. (1996). The power and promise of ecological feminism. In K. J. Warren (Ed.), *Ecological feminist philosophies*. Bloomington: Indiana University Press.

Watkins, B., & Rothchild, N. (1996). *In the company of women: Voices from the women's movement*. St. Paul: Minnesota Historical Society Press.

Watson, J. B. (1913). Psychology as a behaviorist views it. *Psychological Review, 20* (2), 159-177.

Watson, J. B., & McDougall, W. (1929). *The battle of behaviorism*. New York: Norton.

Weinberg, M. S., Williams, C. J., & Pryor, D. W. (1998). Becoming and being "bisexual." In E. J. Haeberle & R. Gindorf (Eds.), *Bisexualities* (pp. 169-181). New York: Continuum.

Weisfeld, G. E. (1997). Discrete emotions theory with specific reference to pride and shame. In N. L. Segal, G. E. Weisfeld, & C. C. Weisfeld (Eds.), *Uniting psychology and biology* (pp. 419-443). Washington, DC: American Psychological Association.

Wellman, H. M. (1990). *The child's theory of mind*. Cambridge, MA: MIT Press.

Werner, H. (1961). *Comparative psychology of mental development*. New York: Science Editions.

White, B. L. (1979). *The origins of human competence: The final report of the Harvard preschool project*. Lexington, MA: Heath.

White, L. A. (1994). The concept of culture. In *Encyclopaedia Britannica* (Vol. 16, pp. 874-881). Chicago: Encyclopaedia Britannica.

Wicker, A. W. (1987). Behavior settings reconsidered: Temporal stages, resources, internal dynamics, context. In D. Stokols & I. Altman (Eds.), *Handbook of environmental psychology* (Vol. 1, pp. 613-653). New York: Wiley.

Wicker, A. W. (1992). Making sense of environments. In W. B. Walsh, K. H. Craik, & R. H. Price (Eds.). *Person-environment psychology: Models and perspectives* (pp. 157-192). Hillsdale, NJ: Erlbaum.

Wilson, E. O. (1975). *Sociobiology: The new synthesis.* Cambridge, MA: Harvard University Press.

Wilson, E. O. (1978). *On human nature.* Cambridge, MA: Harvard University Press.

Wollstonecraft, M. (1975). *A vindication of the rights of woman* (C. H. Poston, Ed.). New York: Norton.

Name Index

Adam, 5
Adler, A., 9, 45
Aldous, J., 137
Alger, H., Jr., 207
Altman, I., 27-28, 31, 34-38, 83-84, 90, 137
Ambert, A. M., 31-32, 35
Angell, J. R., 12-13
Aquinas, T., 4
Arbib, M. A., 67
Ashcraft, M. H., 74

Baer, M. F., 62, 78-79
Baev, K. V., 80
Baldwin, J. M., 12, 121
Bandura, A., 20, 30, 130, 159, 273
Barker, R., 84, 91
Baudrillard, J., 202
Beltrami, E., 69
Bentley, A. F., 27
Benvenuto, B., 202
Berlin, B., 55
Binet, A., 23
Bjorklund, D. F., 47-49, 59, 271
Bolívar, S., 196
Bower, G. H., 20
Bowlby, J., 138
Boyum, L., 192
Breuer, J., 77
Bronfenbrenner, U., 83, 94-96, 271
Brooks-Gunn, J., 208
Broughton, J. M., 202
Brown, J. E., 276

Buddha, 3, 169-170
Bunch, C., 247
Burks, A., 192
Bütz, M. R., 70, 171
Campbell, D. T., 199
Carson, J., 192
Carter, R. T., 234-235
Case, R., 105-110, 118
Cass, V., 252, 259, 263
Cassidy, J., 138, 192
Chase-Lansdale, P. L., 208
Cherry, M., 204
Chodorow, N., 248
Clark, A., 77
Clark, T. W., 202
Cohen, A. H., 80, 273
Cohen, R., 83-90, 102, 273
Cohen, S. L., 84-90, 102
Coleman, E., 262-263
Confucius (Kung Fu-tzu), 3
Connors, B. W., 62, 78-79
Copeland, P., 252-253, 255
Craik, K. H., 33
Crnic, K., 222
Cross, W. E., Jr., 228, 230
Czar Nicholas, 23

Dahlstrom, L. E., 33
Dalhstrom, W. G., 33
Darwin, C., 11-12, 40, 43-44
Davidov, V. V., 19
Dennis, R. M., 232
Denzin, N. K., 200, 203-204

Subject Index

About the Author

R. Murray Thomas (PhD, Stanford University) is an emeritus professor at the University of California, Santa Barbara, where for three decades he taught educational psychology and directed the program in international education. He began his 50-year career in education as a high school teacher at Kamehameha Schools and Mid-Pacific Institute in Honolulu, then continued at the college level at San Francisco State University, the State University of New York (Brockport), and Pajajaran University in Indonesia before moving to Santa Barbara.

His professional publications exceed 300, including 44 books for which he served as author, coauthor, or editor. His earlier books that relate to the contents of *Recent Theories of Human Development* include:

Oriental Theories of Human Development (editor, 1988)
The Encyclopedia of Human Development and Education (editor, 1990)
Moral Development Theories—Secular and Religious (1997)
An Integrated Theory of Moral Development (1997)
Human Development Theories: Windows on Culture (1999)
Comparing Theories of Child Development (5th ed., 2000)
Multicultural Counseling and Human Development Theories (2000)